Garth Jones
Dan Toll
Kerrie Meyler

System Center Configuration Manager Reporting

UNLEASHED

SAMS | 800 East 96th Street, Indianapolis, Indiana 46240 USA

System Center Configuration Manager Reporting Unleashed

ISBN-13: 978-0-672-33778-9

ISBN-10: 0-672-33778-9

Library of Congress Control Number: 2016901207

Printed in the United States of America

First Printing May 2016

Trademarks

All terms mentioned in this book that are known to be trademarks or service marks have been appropriately capitalized. Sams Publishing cannot attest to the accuracy of this information. Use of a term in this book should not be regarded as affecting the validity of any trademark or service mark.

Warning and Disclaimer

Every effort has been made to make this book as complete and as accurate as possible, but no warranty or fitness is implied. The information provided is on an "as is" basis. The authors and the publisher shall have neither liability nor responsibility to any person or entity with respect to any loss or damages arising from the information contained in this book.

Special Sales

For information about buying this title in bulk quantities, or for special sales opportunities (which may include electronic versions; custom cover designs; and content particular to your business, training goals, marketing focus, or branding interests), please contact our corporate sales department at corpsales@pearsoned.com or (800) 382-3419.

For government sales inquiries, please contact governmentsales@pearsoned.com.

For questions about sales outside the U.S., please contact intlcs@pearson.com.

Editor-in-Chief
Greg Wiegand

Acquisitions Editor
Joan Murray

Development Editor
Mark Renfrow

Managing Editor
Kristy Hart

Senior Project Editor
Lori Lyons

Copy Editor
Kitty Wilson

Indexer
Tim Wright

Proofreader
Paula Lowell

Technical Editor
Steve Rachui

Editorial Assistant
Cindy Teeters

Cover Designer
Mark Shirar

Compositor
codeMantra

Contents at a Glance

Note: Download all examples and scripts presented in this book as they become available from informit.com/title/9780672337789

Table of Contents

Note: Download all examples and scripts presented in this book as they become available from informit.com/title/9780672337789

About the Authors

Garth Jones, System Center Enterprise Client Manager MVP, is chief architect at Enhansoft, an Ottawa-based company that develops products and services to extend the value of System Center Configuration Manager. Garth started working with the product in 1996, when it was known as SMS. He is the founder of the Ottawa Windows Server User Group and its associated study group. In addition to being an active participant in Microsoft's forums, Garth also participates on OWSUG.ca, SMSug.ca, FAQshop.com, and myITForum.com. He has presented at OWSUG, MMS, EnergizeIT, ITProTeach, and Techdays. Garth also creates webcasts for SMSUG.ca and myITForum.com.

Dan Toll, a System Center Configuration Manager administrator, has worked with different versions of the product starting with SMS 2003. Dan specializes in OS deployment for workstations and servers using Microsoft Deployment Toolkit (MDT) with ConfigMgr, as well as Configuration Manager reporting. In his current job, Dan is the SME for Configuration Manager as well as the client computing environment, which includes deployment, functionality, and maintenance of systems; their operating systems; applications; patching compliancy; and reporting.

Kerrie Meyler, System Center Cloud and Datacenter Management MVP, is the lead author of numerous System Center books in the *Unleashed* series, including *System Center 2012 Configuration Manager Unleashed* (2012), *System Center 2012 R2 Configuration Manager Unleashed Supplement* (2014), *System Center 2012 Service Manager Unleashed* (2014), *System Center 2012 Operations Manager Unleashed* (2013), and *System Center 2012 Orchestrator Unleashed* (2013). She is an independent consultant with more than 17 years of information technology experience. Kerrie was responsible for evangelizing SMS while a senior technology specialist at Microsoft and has presented on System Center technologies at TechEd and MMS.

Dedication

To our spouses for their patience, and to the team at Enhansoft for their assistance.

Acknowledgments

Writing a book is an all-encompassing and time-consuming project, and this book certainly meets that description. Configuration Manager is a massive topic, and this book benefited from the input of many individuals. The authors and contributors would like to offer their sincere appreciation to all those who helped with *System Center Configuration Manager Reporting Unleashed*, including Wally Mead and Steve Rachui.

We would also like to thank our spouses and significant others for their patience and understanding during the many hours spent on this book.

Thanks also to the staff at Pearson, in particular to Joan Murray and Cindy Teeters.

Foreword

Some people think that Configuration Manager is scary and complex—and it can be if you don't have a good, solid background in it before you attempt to tackle it for your enterprise. I think that training is essential to having a great background in Configuration Manager before you take on its challenges in a production environment. When you throw reporting into the picture, it is even scarier.

Reporting is a bit of a black box for most Configuration Manager admins: They don't deal with it much, other than running the default reports, and they certainly don't know how to create custom reports. Each of the various releases of Configuration Manager has had a great set of default reports (and that count is nearing 500 now) that cover all the various features and functions of the product. But what happens when management comes to you and says, "We need a report that shows x and y?" Now you get nervous and wonder how you are going to accomplish that. Hopefully you have a SQL guru who can help you out, but not everyone is that fortunate.

If you don't have a SQL guru handy to help out, you search the web for content that others have created in an attempt to find something that will work to satisfy management's request. Often, customizations are needed, such as adding charts, logos, colors, drillthrough actions, and so on. That's where it really gets complicated for most of us. And there have not been a lot of great resources out there to help us novices really learn how to quickly and efficiently create custom reports that will not only satisfy the desires of management but really empower the admin to no longer be afraid, and maybe even welcome, the opportunity to create reports.

Now along comes this book, a treasure chest of gold for admins who need to create reports in Configuration Manager, who may not have a SQL background, and who have shied away from these types of requests in the past. Knowing some of the authors of the book, I have great confidence that you will really enjoy the product they have produced to assist you on your path to learning how to create Configuration Manager reports. For those of you who are already familiar with the process, I'm sure that you will find some nuggets here to help take your reports to an even more impressive level than they already are. And, knowing the brilliant mind of the book's technical reviewer, I know how accurate and detailed the final result will be. Steve won't let anything slip through that is not 100% correct.

With all that, I really do hope that you enjoy the book, and expect that you will be creating great reports in no time at all.

All the best,

Wally Mead, (former) Senior Program Manager
Configuration Manager Product Group
Microsoft Corporation
Now Principal Program Manager, Cireson

We Want to Hear from You!

As the reader of this book, *you* are our most important critic and commentator. We value your opinion and want to know what we're doing right, what we could do better, what areas you'd like to see us publish in, and any other words of wisdom you're willing to pass our way.

We welcome your comments. You can email or write to let us know what you did or didn't like about this book—as well as what we can do to make our books better.

Please note that we cannot help you with technical problems related to the topic of this book.

When you write, please be sure to include this book's title and author as well as your name and email address. We will carefully review your comments and share them with the author and editors who worked on the book.

Email: feedback@samspublishing.com

Mail: Sams Publishing
ATTN: Reader Feedback
800 East 96th Street
Indianapolis, IN 46240 USA

Reader Services

Register your copy of *System Center Configuration Manager Reporting Unleashed* at informit. com for convenient access to downloads, updates, and corrections as they become available. To start the registration process, go to informit.com/register and log in or create an account*. Enter the product ISBN, 9780672337789, and click Submit. Once the process is complete, you will find any available bonus content under Registered Products.

Be sure to check the box that you would like to hear from us in order to receive exclusive discounts on future editions of this product.

Introduction

System Center Configuration Manager (ConfigMgr) stores a wealth of information about users, hardware, software inventory, software updates, applications, site status, and other Configuration Manager operations in a relational database. The trick is to know how to retrieve that data out of the SQL Server database and present it in meaningful, useful, and reusable reports.

Microsoft provides some out-of-the-box reports; however, these reports only scratch the surface of what is available for use by management, end users, and Configuration Manager administrators. This book is written based on the premise that ConfigMgr reporting is not very difficult if you use the concepts, tools, and techniques discussed throughout its chapters. It walks you through installing SQL Server Reporting Services (SSRS), understanding SQL views to find data in the Configuration Manager site database, writing SQL queries, designing and building basic reports, advanced reporting techniques, and using role-based administration to securely deliver reports to the individuals to whom they are intended. Here are the benefits *System Center Configuration Manager Reporting Unleashed* delivers:

▶ Enables an optimal installation of SSRS and Configuration Manager reporting

▶ Provides the tools to understand how to retrieve ConfigMgr data from its SQL Server database and to retrieve that data in the most efficient way

▶ Simplifies report design and creation

▶ Shows how to create reports that can be used with the role-based administration security feature of ConfigMgr and SSRS.

Part I: Installing and Configuring SSRS for Configuration Manager

System Center Configuration Manager Reporting Unleashed begins with a guide to installing and configuring SSRS and Configuration Manager reporting. Chapter 1, "Installing SQL Server Reporting Services," walks you through the steps in installing and configuring SSRS, including configuring email and enabling remote errors to assist with any troubleshooting that might be necessary. Chapter 2, "Installing and Configuring Configuration Manager Reporting," continues the installation discussion by showing you how to configure the reporting services point and use ConfigMgr security roles to control access to reports. It also provides information on how to change the report logo used in the reports to one specific to your own organization.

Part II: About Data and Retrieval

Before creating reports, you need to understand the data kept in the ConfigMgr site database, the tools Microsoft provides to access that data, and how to effectively and efficiently use Transact-SQL queries to retrieve that data. Chapter 3, "Understanding Configuration Manager Data," discusses where ConfigMgr stores its inventory data and how to find that information. It also introduces you to SQL Server Management Studio, the tool you use to write your queries. Chapter 4, "Transact-SQL Primer," provides a concise tutorial of the sections in a SQL query, the best ways to retrieve data, SQL functions, how to use different data types, and how to join data from multiple views.

Part III: Using SSRS for Configuration Manager Reporting

Part III of this book focuses on reporting, including report design, best practices for developing and designing reports, basic and more advanced reporting concepts, features of SSRS reporting, and implementing role-based administration in ConfigMgr reports. Chapter 5, "Basic Report Design," discusses considerations for report designs and the types of reports you can use in a report series. Chapter 6, "Building a Basic Report," introduces report projects, data sources and data sets, and elements you use in creating a report. The topic of building reports is continued in Chapter 7, "Intermediate Reporting Concepts," which discusses creating report templates, using report parameters to customize the content of your reports, and the different types of charts you can include in SSRS reports. Chapter 8, "SSRS Reporting Features," covers even more reporting concepts, including using drillthroughs, using custom color palettes, and adding reports into SSRS. Chapter 9, "Role-Based Administration and Reporting," wraps up the discussion by showing you how to integrate ConfigMgr role-based administration into your SQL queries to provide an additional level of security in terms of who can access your reports.

Part IV: Appendixes

By this time, you should have at your disposal all the tools necessary to become a Configuration Manager reporting expert. The last part of the book includes three appendixes:

▶ Appendix A, "Glossary," includes acronyms and terms useful to know when working with Configuration Manager and SQL Server Reporting Services.

▶ Appendix B, "Demonstration Outcomes," contains the expected outcome from all chapter demonstrations throughout this book.

▶ Appendix C, "Available Online," discusses value-added content available for download under the Downloads tab at Pearson's InformIT website, at www.informit.com/title/9780672337789.

This book provides in-depth reference and technical information about System Center Configuration Manager reporting as well as information about other products and technologies on which its features and components depend.

Disclaimers and Fine Print

The authors want to offer several disclaimers. While the authors of *System Center Configuration Manager Reporting Unleashed* have made every attempt to present information that is accurate and current as known at the time, they are not infallible. In addition, screenshots were taken with version 1511, and it is certainly possible that Microsoft could slightly tweak the user interface in later versions.

Any updates and corrections will be provided as errata on the InformIT website.

Thank you for purchasing *System Center Configuration Manager Reporting Unleashed*. The authors hope it is worth your while.

PART I

Installing and Configuring SSRS for Configuration Manager

IN THIS PART

Installing SQL Server Reporting Services

SQL Server Reporting Services (SSRS) is a server-based reporting platform that provides comprehensive reporting functionality. An optional feature of System Center Configuration Manager (ConfigMgr), it enables you to use an industry-standard reporting system to query the ConfigMgr database.

This chapter walks you through the steps needed to install the features required for SSRS and enable ConfigMgr to leverage SSRS for reporting. It describes how to install the SQL SSRS features, configure SSRS, enable SSRS remote errors, and install the client tools so that you can review the existing ConfigMgr reports and create your own custom reports.

Although technically an optional feature, SSRS facilitates pulling data from ConfigMgr so that you can better understand your client computing environment. SSRS reporting in ConfigMgr allows you to understand items such as the software updates that are deployed, the computers to which those software updates are deployed, and the software installed on each computer. SSRS provides virtually endless possibilities in terms of what you can report on.

SSRS helps expose the information hidden within ConfigMgr, allowing you and your management team to make informed decisions on all aspects of your ConfigMgr environment. This could be key performance indicators (KPIs) of software deployments to software updates, or it might be as simple as understanding your hardware inventory assets. By making informed decisions, you provide increased efficiency and compliance, which ultimately helps your company's bottom line.

Installing the SQL SSRS Component

Although an optional feature, SSRS is the only reporting mechanism available for ConfigMgr. If you don't install and configure SSRS, even the default reports provided with ConfigMgr do not work properly.

SSRS allows you to display information within a SQL database in a graphical and formatted manner. Instead of showing row upon row of static tabular information, it enables you to mix and match charts, table data, and images within reports that can be used on websites, with SharePoint, or even within printed publications. SSRS reports display the information such that anyone can quickly digest it and make informed decisions based on that information.

Before you can use SSRS successfully, it must be properly installed and configured. This section discusses installing SSRS for ConfigMgr. The authors recommend installing SSRS on a Windows Server system that already has SQL Server 2014 configured without SSRS installed, preferably using the same SQL Server machine as your ConfigMgr SQL database. This server is also known as your ConfigMgr site database server. Chapter 2, "Installing and Configuring Configuration Manager Reporting," discusses installing your ConfigMgr reporting services point.

> **TIP: BEFORE INSTALLING SSRS**
>
> Prior to installing SSRS, the authors recommend applying the latest software updates to both your Windows Server and SQL Server instance. In addition, confirm that you have full administrator permissions on both the Windows Server and SQL Server instance on which SSRS will be installed.

Using the default SQL instance on a Windows server, perform the following steps to install SSRS:

1. Launch SQL Server 2014 setup and select **Installation** from the left-hand menu (see Figure 1.1) and then select **New SQL Server stand-alone installation or add features to an existing installation**, as shown in Figure 1.2.

2. The Global Rules page (displayed in Figure 1.3) checks for rule errors. If you see this page, click **Next**. If the Global Rules Check does not generate any errors, the setup wizard automatically continues to the next step.

3. Click **Next** at the Microsoft Update page, shown in Figure 1.4.

4. On the Install Rules page shown in Figure 1.5, ignore the warning about the firewall if the firewall ports were previously opened. Click **Next** to continue.

> **TIP: USING MICROSOFT UPDATE**
>
> The **Use Microsoft Update to check for updates (recommended)** check box displayed in Figure 1.4 is not selected by default. The authors recommend selecting this option unless the server is already managed by ConfigMgr or an internal Windows Server Update Services (WSUS) server. Be aware that if the server does not have Internet access, selecting this check box may cause this step to fail and generate an error message.

If the server is managed by WSUS or ConfigMgr, any missing software updates are identified on the server's next scan cycle, and the information about missing software updates is returned to WSUS/ConfigMgr. At this point those software updates could be deployed to the server using normal software update deployment strategies.

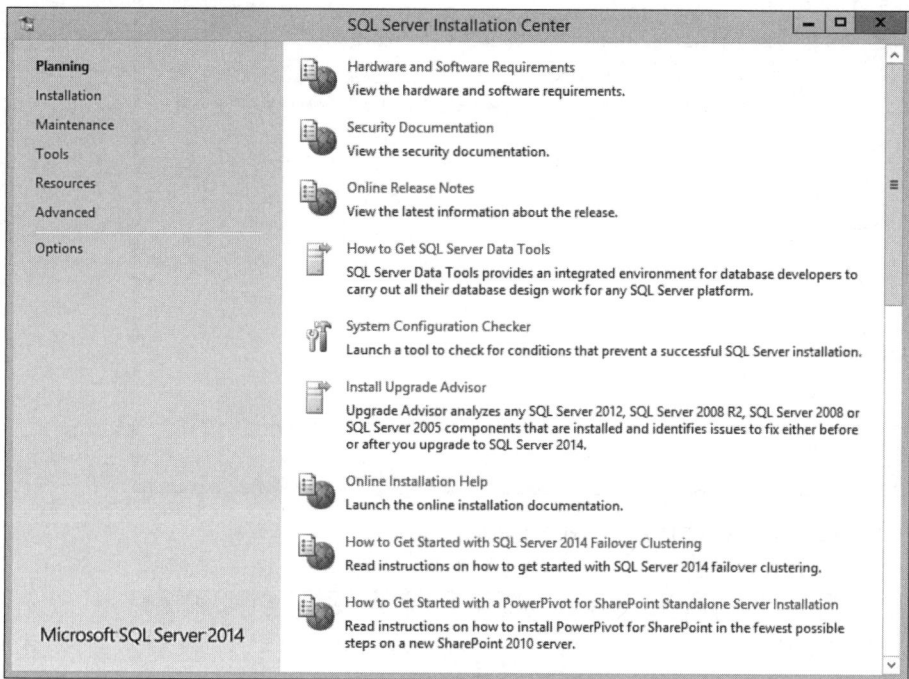

FIGURE 1.1   SQL Server Installation Center.

5. On the Installation Type page, select **Add feature to an existing instance of SQL 2014** (see Figure 1.6) and then click **Next**.

REAL WORLD: LOCATION FOR INSTALLING SQL SERVER AND CONFIGMGR

The authors recommend for performance reasons that you not install SQL Server or ConfigMgr on the C:\ drive.

6. As shown in Figure 1.7, on the Feature Selection page select the **Reporting Services - Native** check box. As the authors generally do not recommend installing SQL or any of its components on the C: drive for performance and security reasons, you should change the installation drive\folder to a more appropriate location. (For example, Figure 1.7 shows that SQL/SSRS was installed on E:\.) After selecting the installation location, click **Next** to continue.

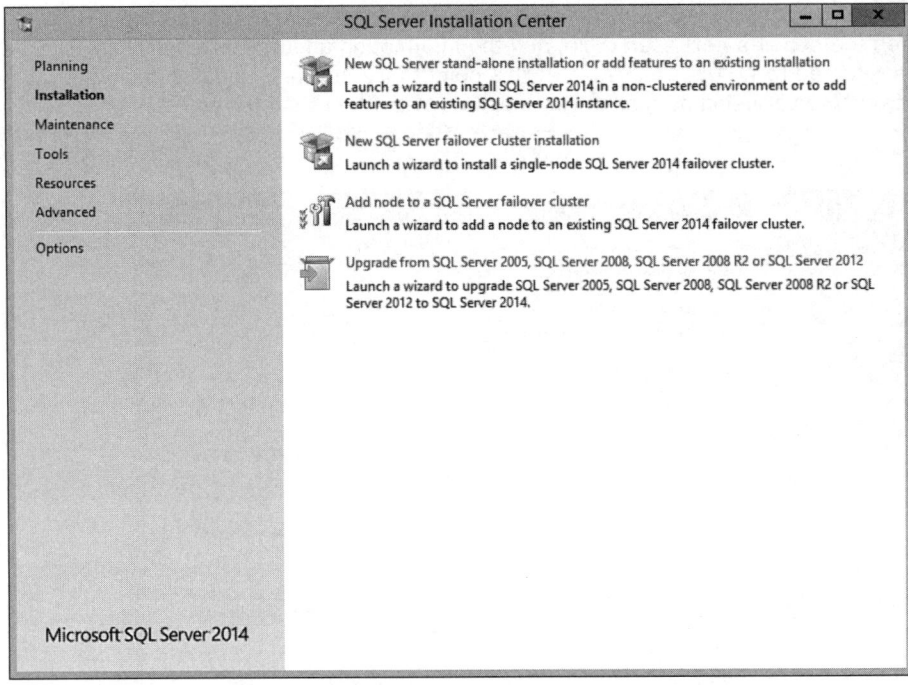

FIGURE 1.2   Selecting a new SQL Server installation.

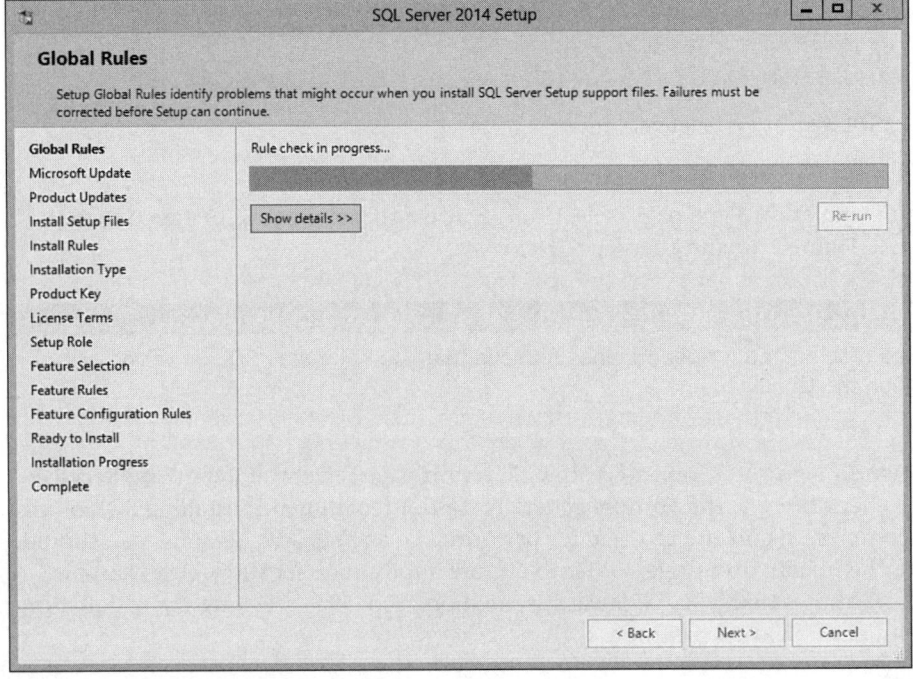

FIGURE 1.3   The Global Rules page.

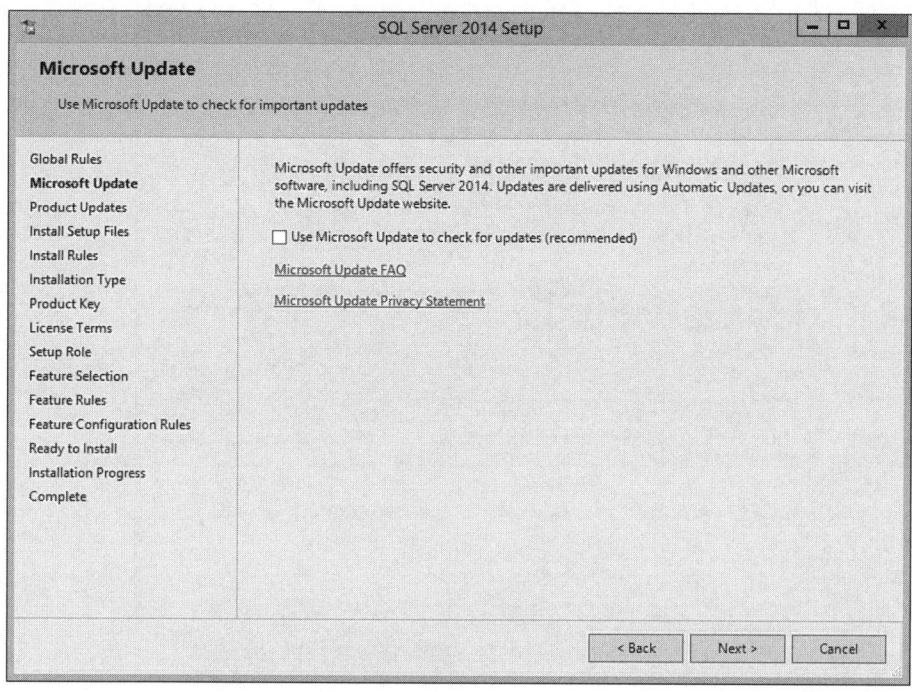

FIGURE 1.4   The Microsoft Update page.

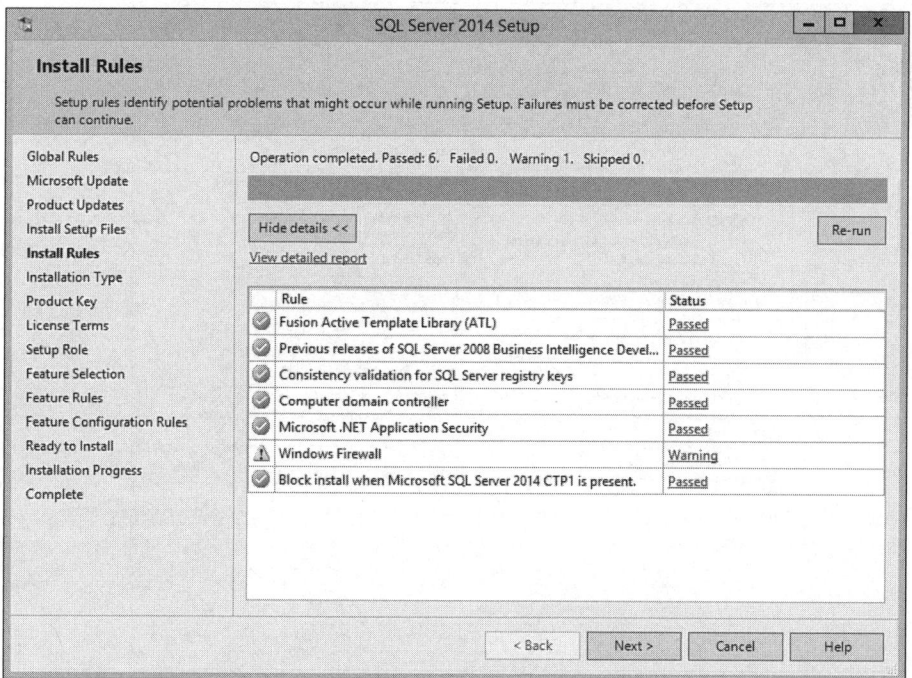

FIGURE 1.5   The Install Rules page.

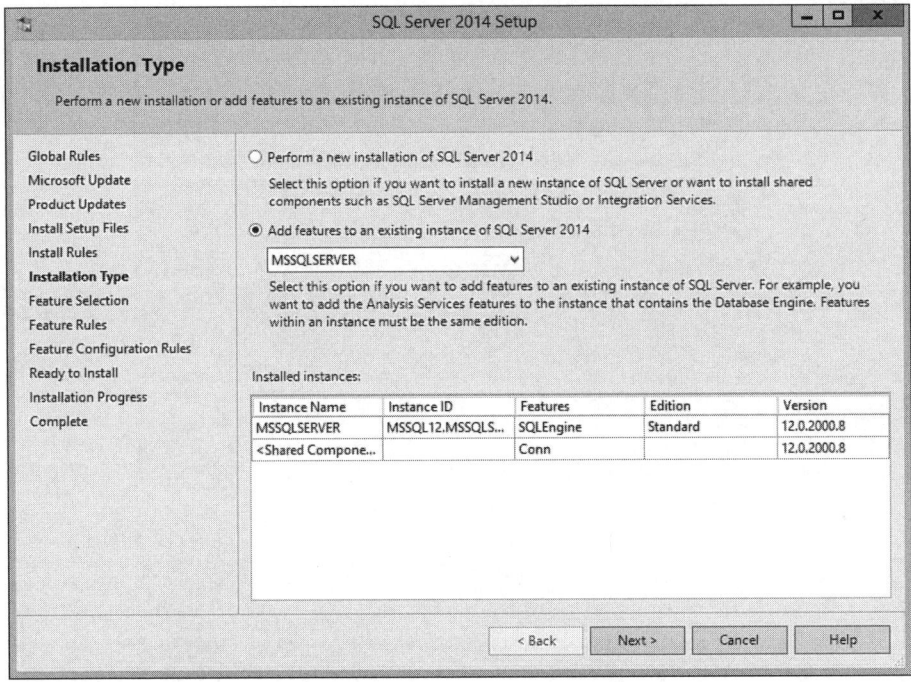

FIGURE 1.6   Selecting the feature to install.

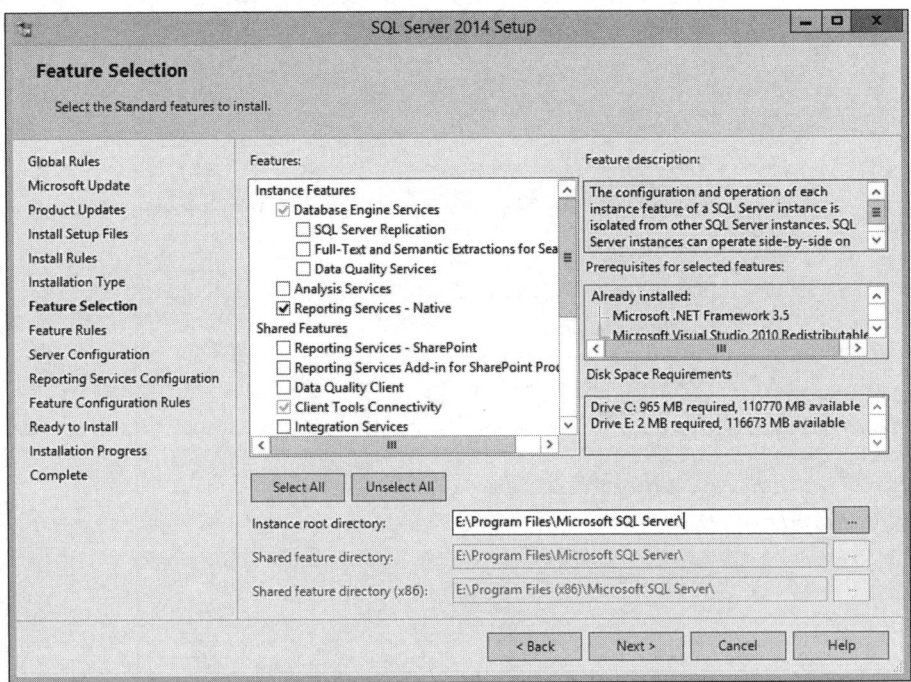

FIGURE 1.7   Selecting the Reporting Services feature and specifying the installation location.

7. On the Server Configuration page (see Figure 1.8), update SQL Server Reporting Services to use the **NT AUTHORITY\NETWORK SERVICES** account. Leave the default of Automatic as the Startup Type and click **Next**.

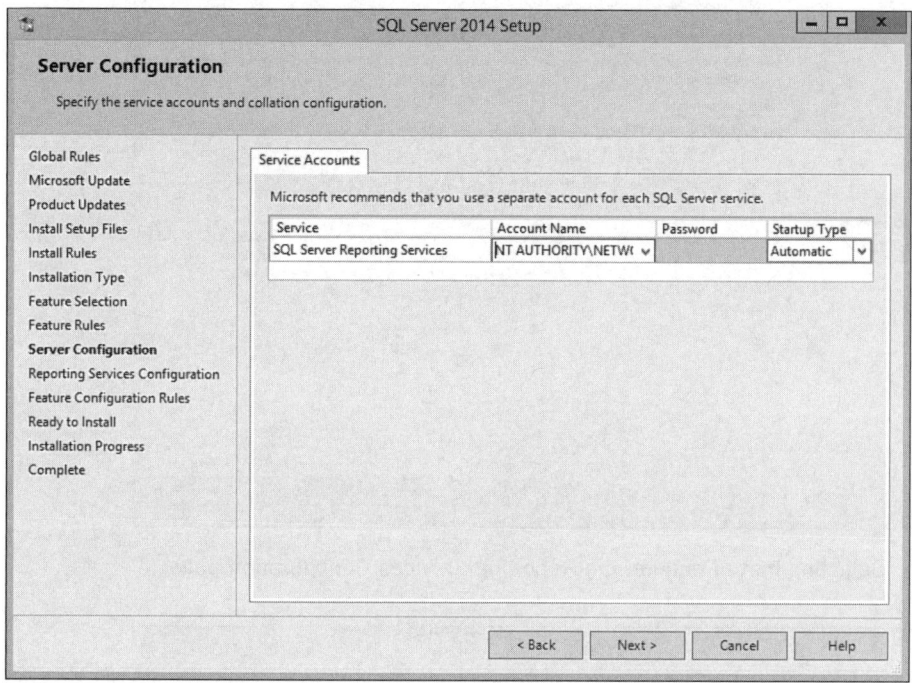

FIGURE 1.8   Specifying the service account on the Server Configuration page.

8. On the Reporting Services Configuration page shown in Figure 1.9, ensure that **Install only** is selected; you can later configure the optional email component discussed in the "Configuring Email" section of this chapter. Click **Next**.

9. On the Ready to Install page (see Figure 1.10), click **Install** to begin the installation process.

10. Wait until the SQL Server Reporting Services installation completes. Figure 1.11 shows an example of an installation in progress.

11. Click **Close** when the installation is complete. With a successful installation, you get the results shown in Figure 1.12.

This section has shown how to install SSRS. The next section discusses customizing your setup and enabling email subscriptions for SSRS.

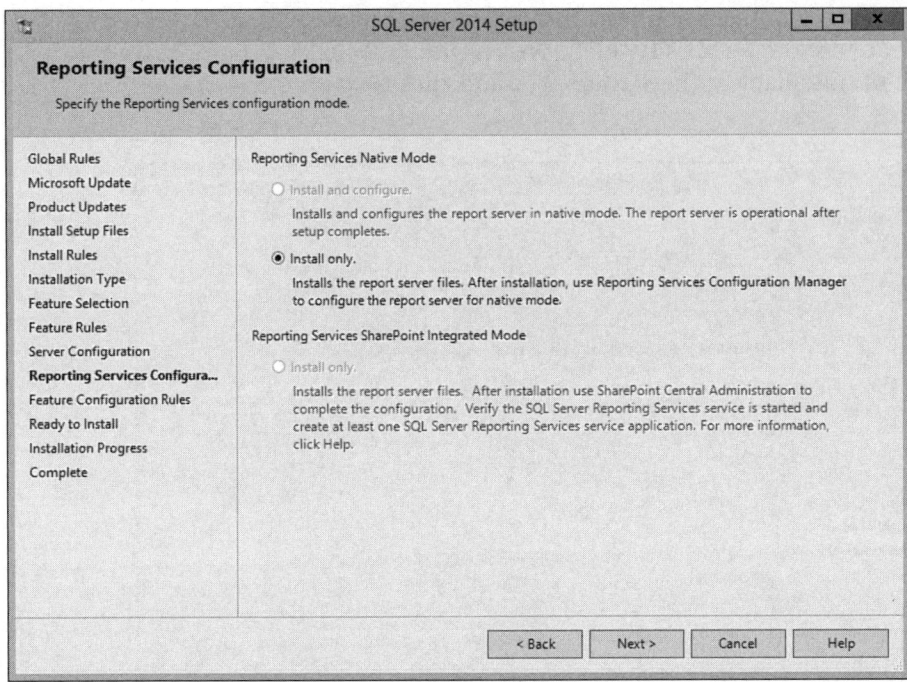

FIGURE 1.9   Selecting **Install only** on the Reporting Services Configuration page.

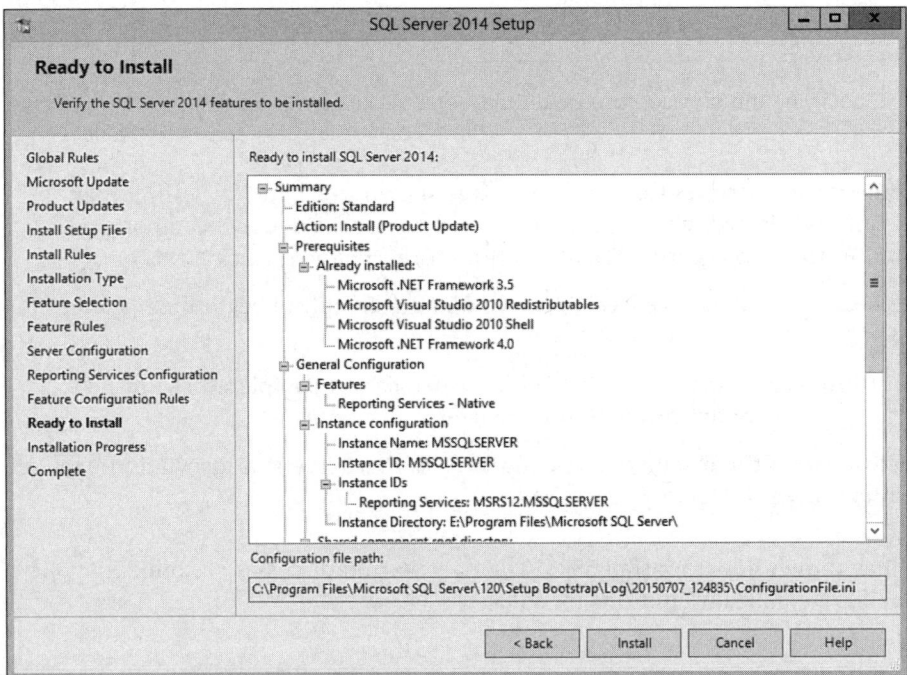

FIGURE 1.10   The Ready to Install page.

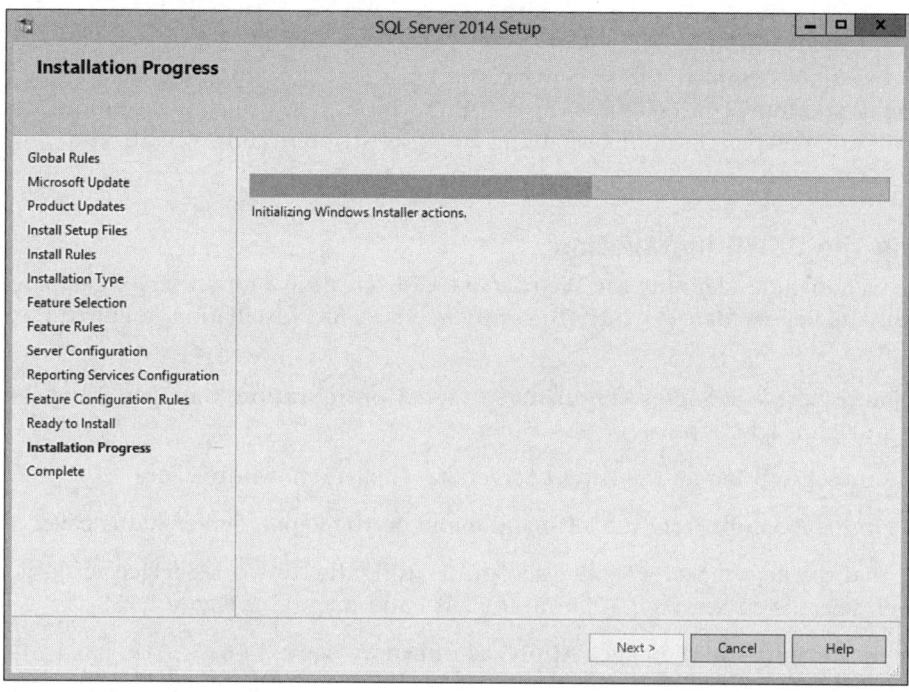

FIGURE 1.11   Installation in progress.

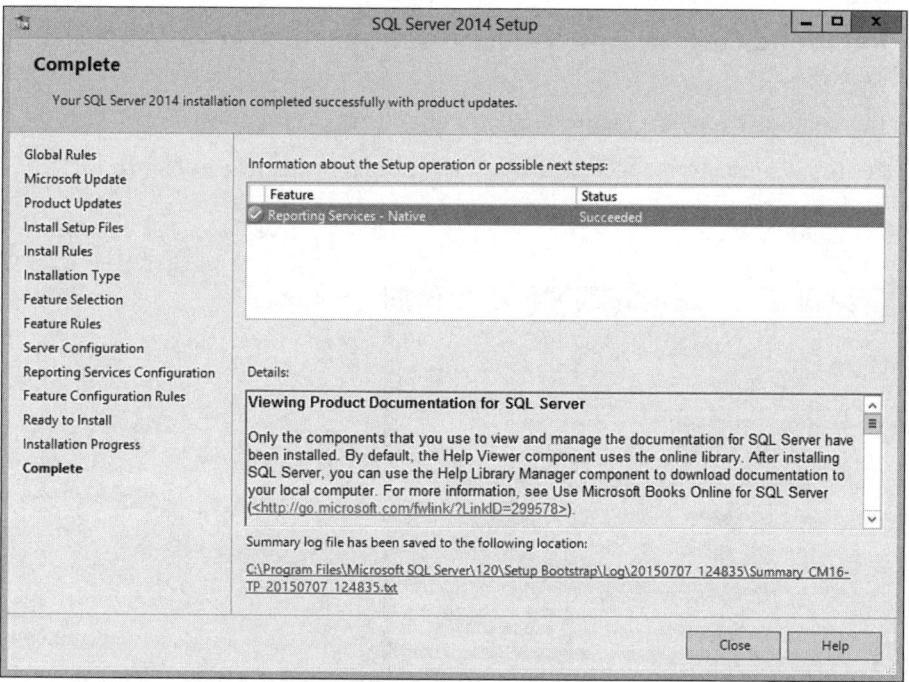

FIGURE 1.12   Successful installation of SQL Server Reporting Services.

Configuring SSRS

The following sections complete the SSRS installation process. After installing SSRS but prior to using it, you must configure SSRS by defining various items such as execution account details and database locations, enabling email subscription functionality and remote errors, and so on.

Configuring the SSRS Installation

Configuring SSRS includes defining the Web Service URL, creating a report server database, and specifying the Report Manager URL. To configure your SSRS installation, follow these steps:

1. From Start, select **SQL Server Reporting Services Configuration Manager**. The page shown in Figure 1.13 appears.

2. Click **Connect** to bring up the Report Server Status page, shown in Figure 1.14.

3. Select **Service Account** from the left-hand menu on the Report Server Status page.

4. Ensure that the Report Server Service account is using the **Network Service** account and then select **Web Service URL** from the left-hand menu (see Figure 1.15).

5. Accept the defaults and then click **Apply**, as shown in Figure 1.16.

6. In the Results pane shown in Figure 1.17, confirm that the configuration was successful and then select **Database** from the left-hand menu and **Change Database** on the right (see Figure 1.18).

7. Ensure that **Create a new report server database** is selected (see Figure 1.19) and then click **Next**.

8. Accept the defaults shown in Figure 1.20 and click **Test Connection**.

9. When the Test Connection Succeeded message appears (as shown in Figure 1.21), click **OK**.

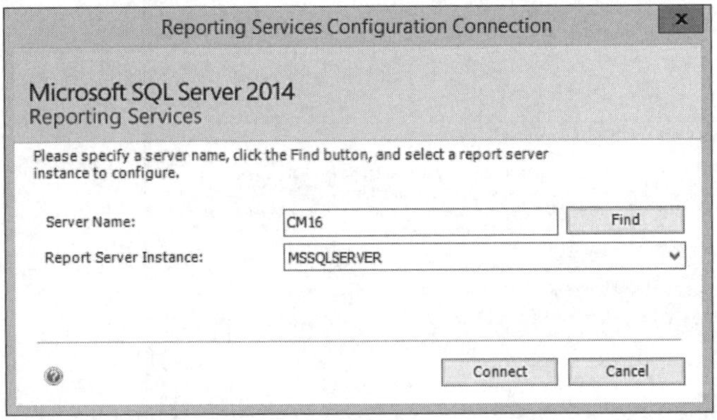

FIGURE 1.13   The Reporting Services Configuration Connection page.

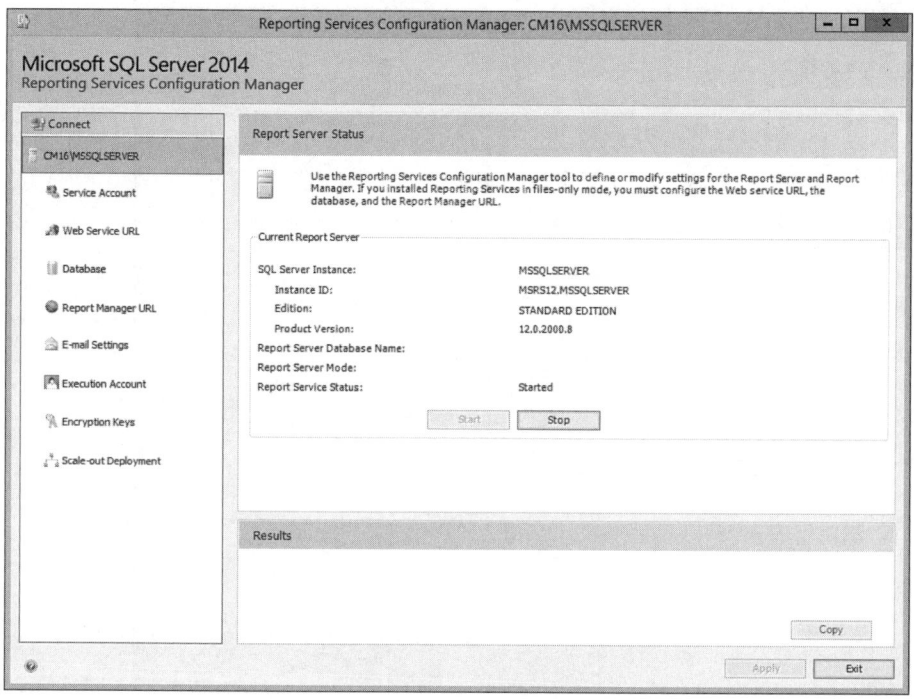

FIGURE 1.14   The Report Server Status page.

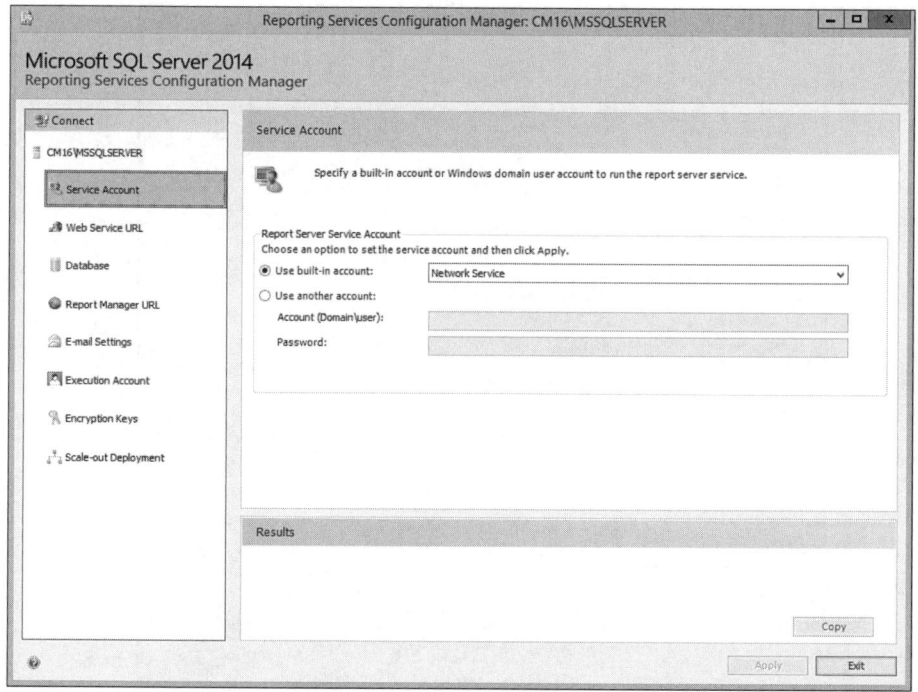

FIGURE 1.15   Specifying the Network Service built-in account.

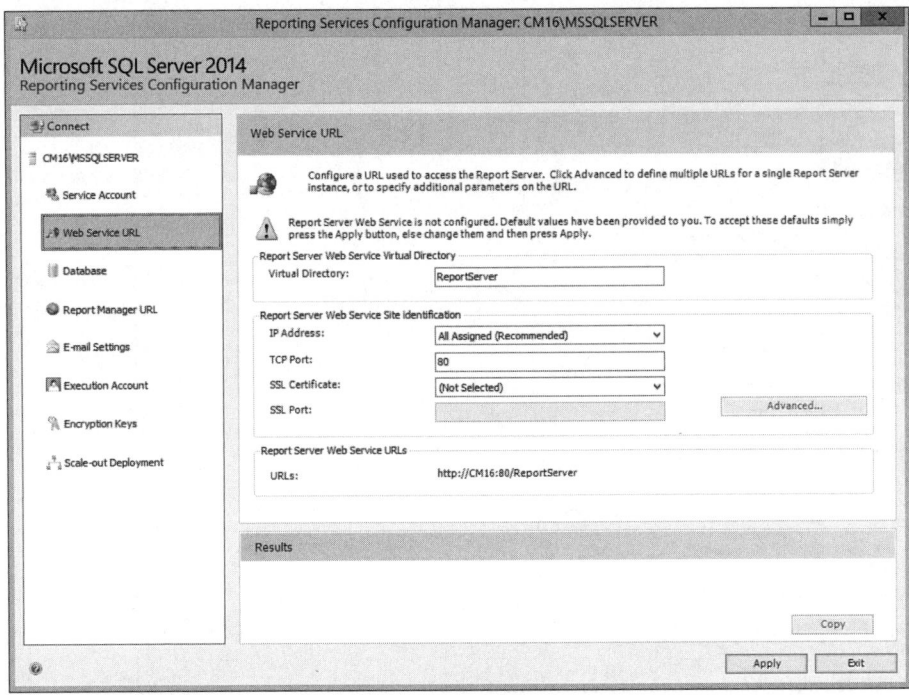

FIGURE 1.16   Configuring the Reporting Services virtual directory and Web Service URL.

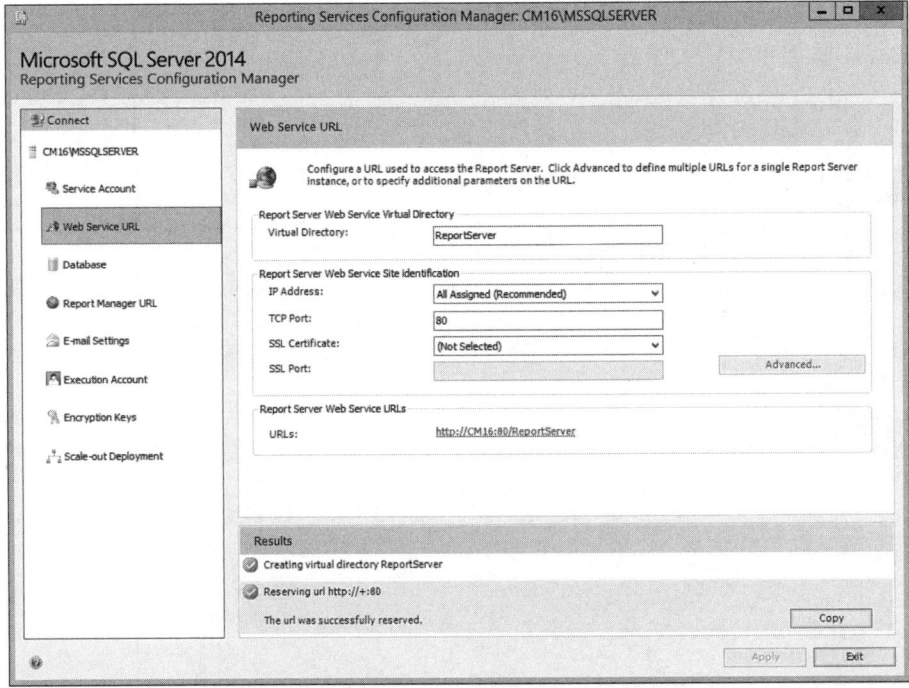

FIGURE 1.17   Successful configuration of the Web Service URL.

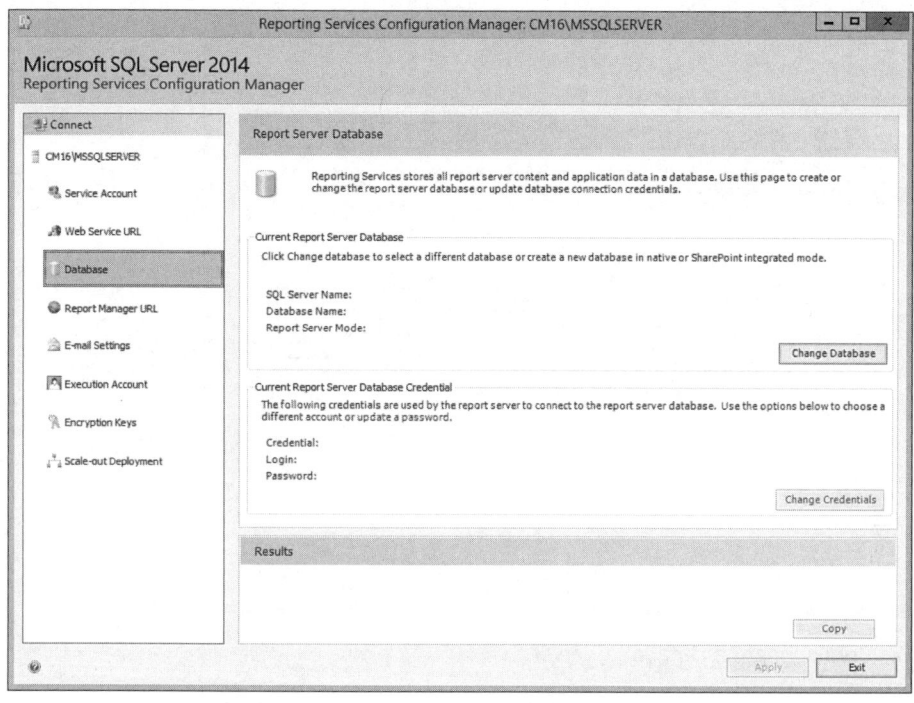

FIGURE 1.18   Selecting **Database** from the left-hand menu to define the report server database.

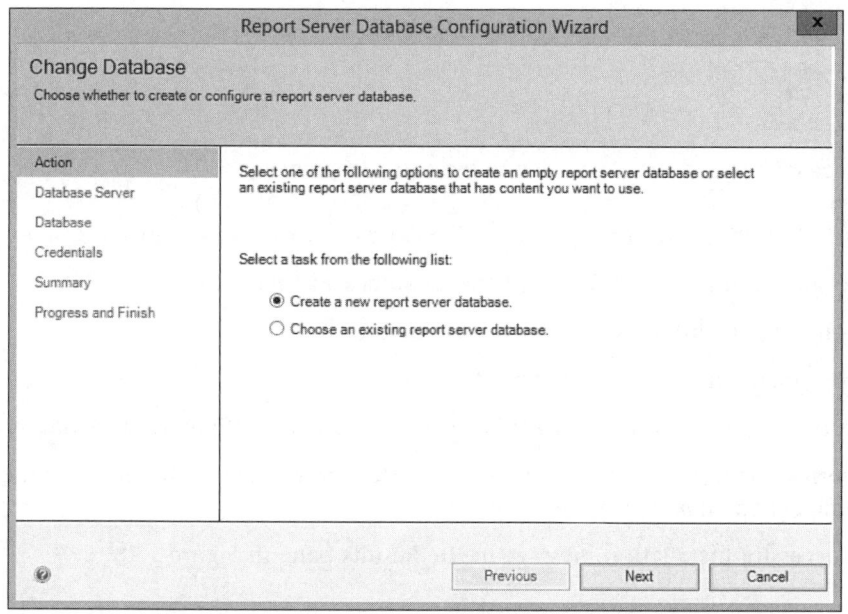

FIGURE 1.19   Selecting **Create a new report server database**.

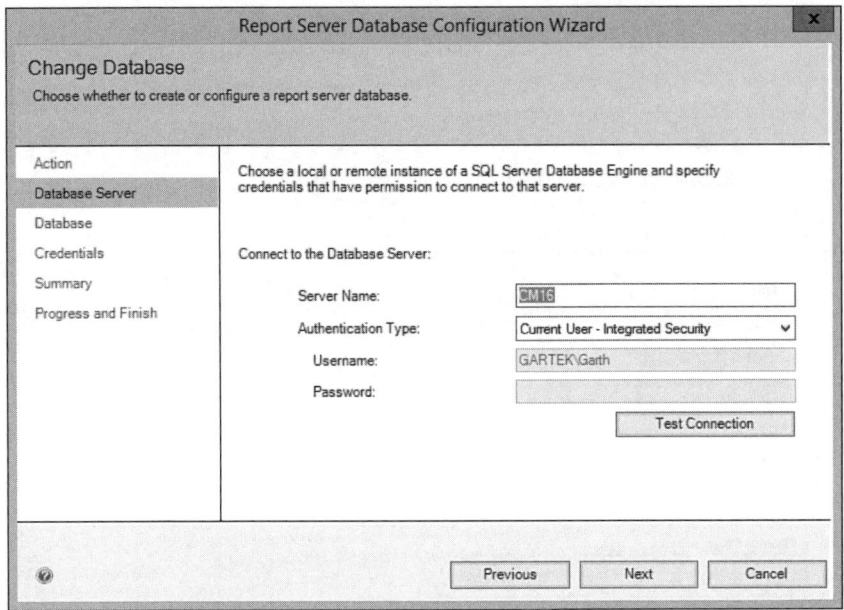

FIGURE 1.20   Configuring the database server.

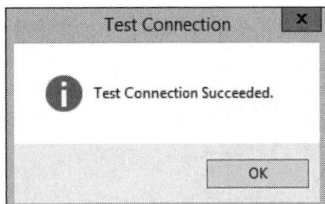

FIGURE 1.21   Successful test of the connection to the database server.

10. After successfully testing the connection, click **Next** to continue (see Figure 1.22).

11. On the page shown in Figure 1.23, accept the defaults and click **Next**.

12. Click **Next** on the Credentials page, shown in Figure 1.24.

13. Click **Next** on the Summary page, shown in Figure 1.25.

14. Click **Finish** (see Figure 1.26) to return to Reporting Services Configuration Manager.

15. After configuring the report server database, select **Report Manager URL** on the left-hand menu and then click **Apply** (see Figure 1.27).

16. Notice the successful installation message in the Results pane in Figure 1.28.

You have completed your initial configuration of SSRS.

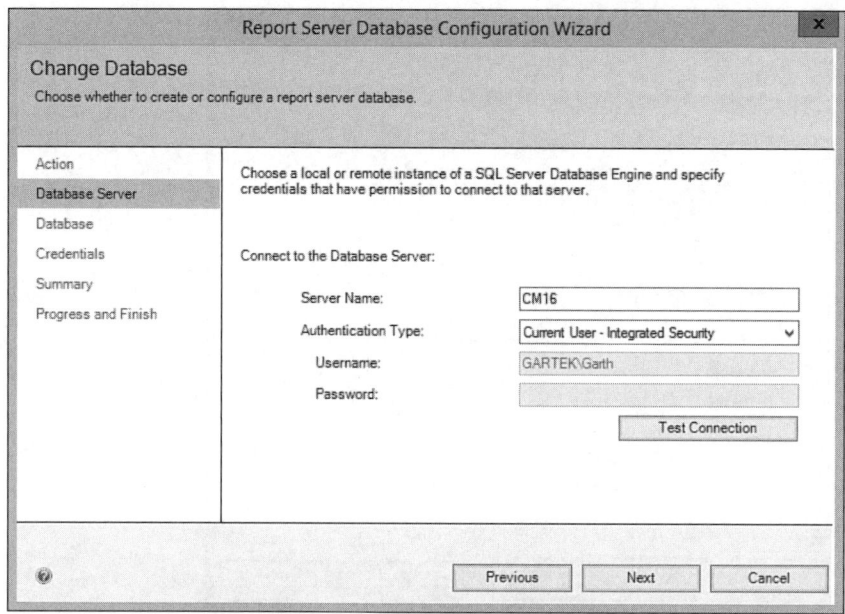

FIGURE 1.22   Clicking **Next** after successfully testing the connection.

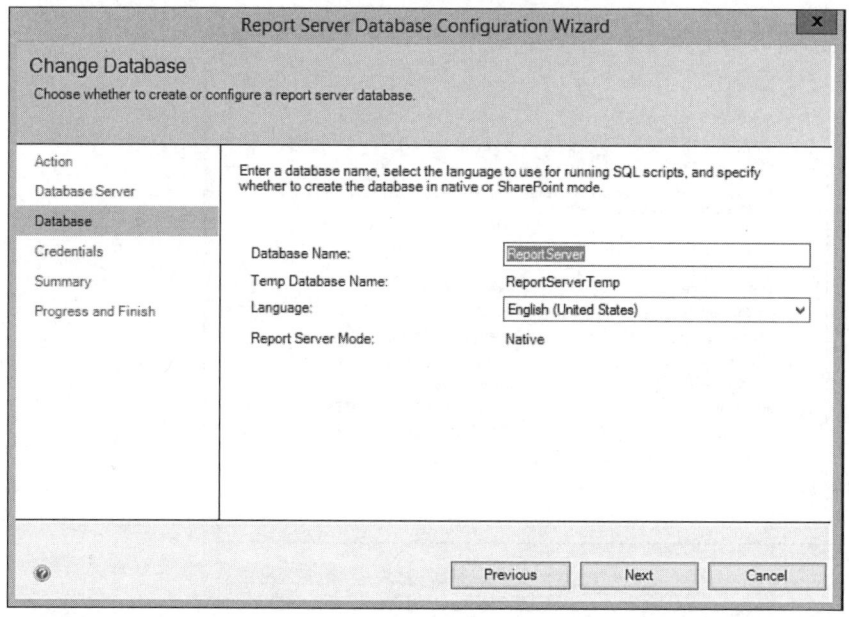

FIGURE 1.23   Clicking **Next** to accept the ReportServer database settings.

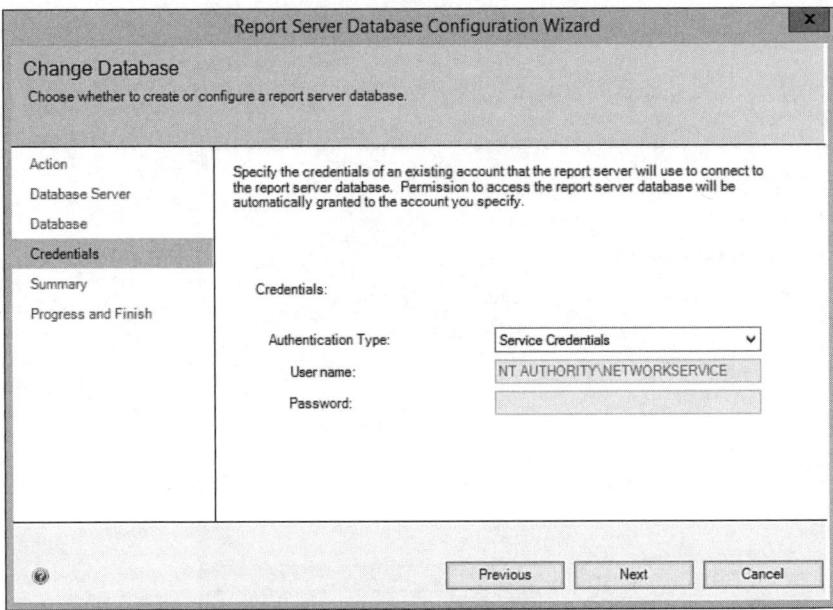

FIGURE 1.24   Accepting the security credentials.

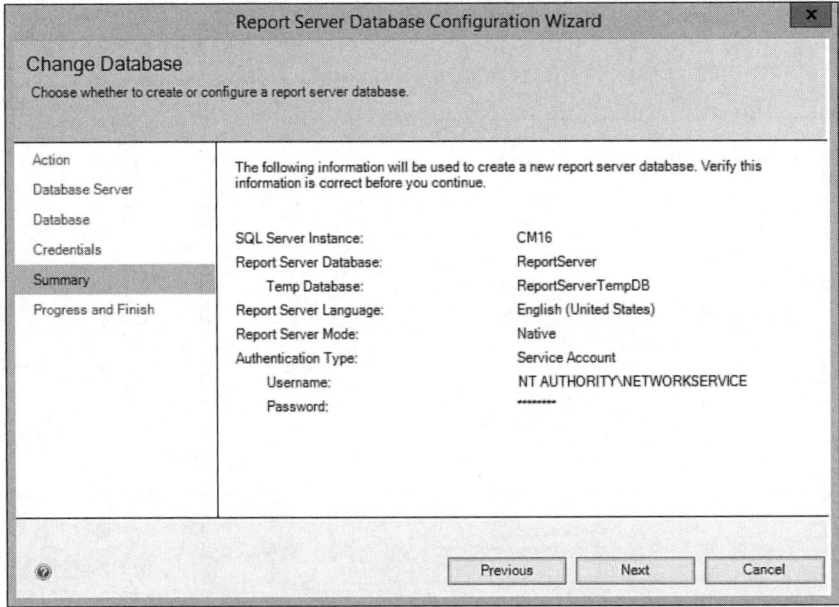

FIGURE 1.25   Selected options displayed on the Summary page.

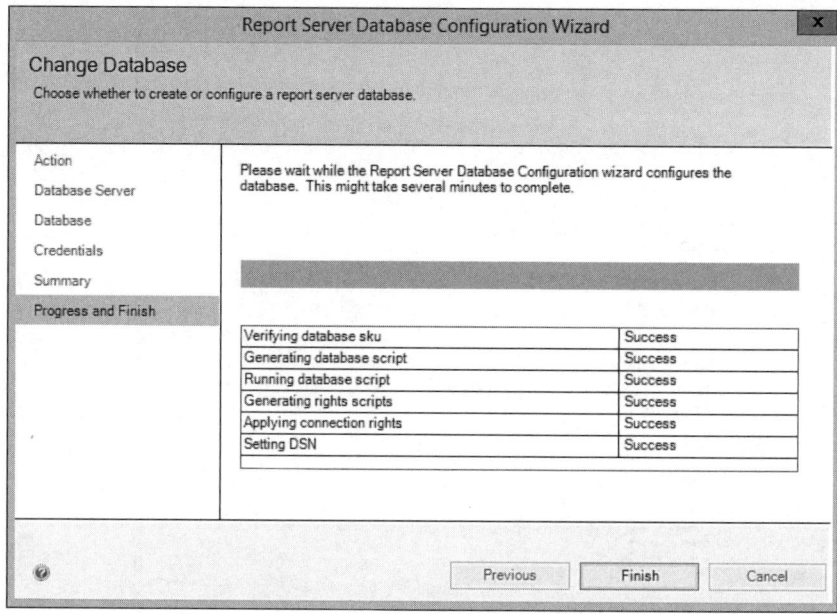

FIGURE 1.26   Clicking **Finish** after configuring the report server database.

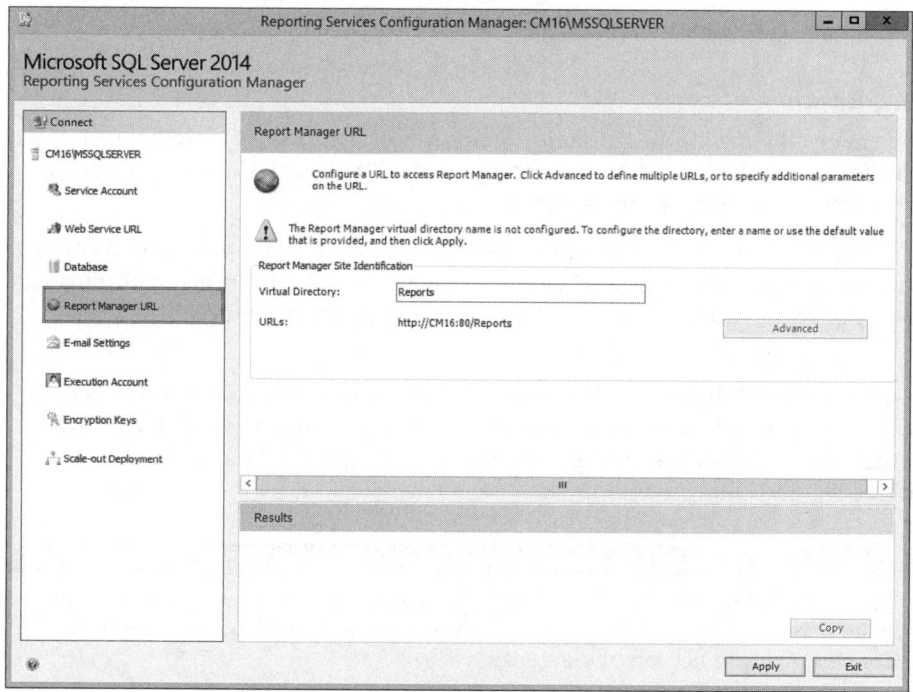

FIGURE 1.27   Selecting the **Report Manager URL**.

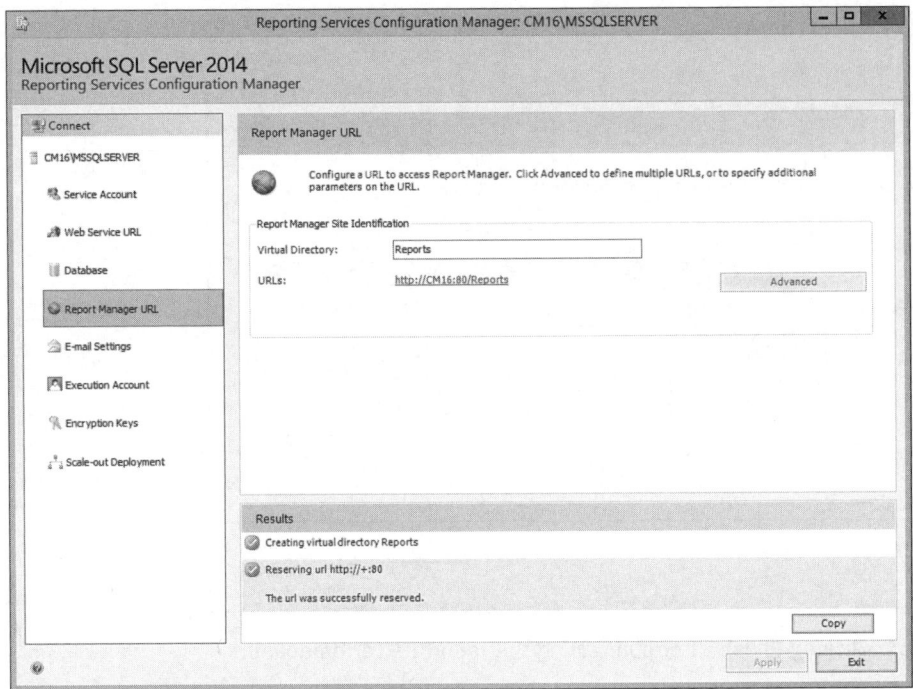

FIGURE 1.28   Successful installation message.

Configuring Email

Although the email subscription functionality is an optional feature, it is well worth enabling. This feature allows you to automatically send SSRS reports via email at a scheduled time to one or more email accounts.

If you're planning to enable the email feature, before starting this task you should contact your email administrator to obtain the email sender address and the simple mail transfer protocol (SMTP) address, which are required for this configuration. Then follow these steps:

1. (This step is optional; however, the authors recommend it due to the added benefit it provides.) Select **E-Mail Settings** from the left-hand menu shown in Figure 1.29. Fill in the appropriate details in the screen shown in Figure 1.29 and then click **Apply** (see Figure 1.30).

TIP: PROVIDING EMAIL SETTINGS LATER

If you don't have the details for the email settings available, you can return at a later time and enter them here by skipping over all other links and going directly to E-Mail Settings. Remember to click **Apply** to activate the settings.

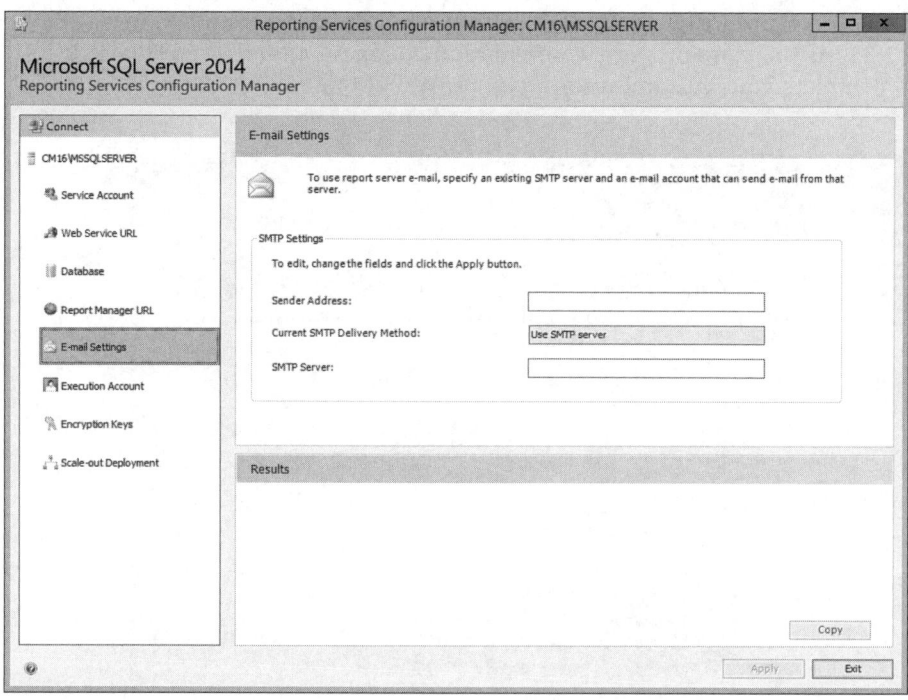

FIGURE 1.29   The E-mail Settings page.

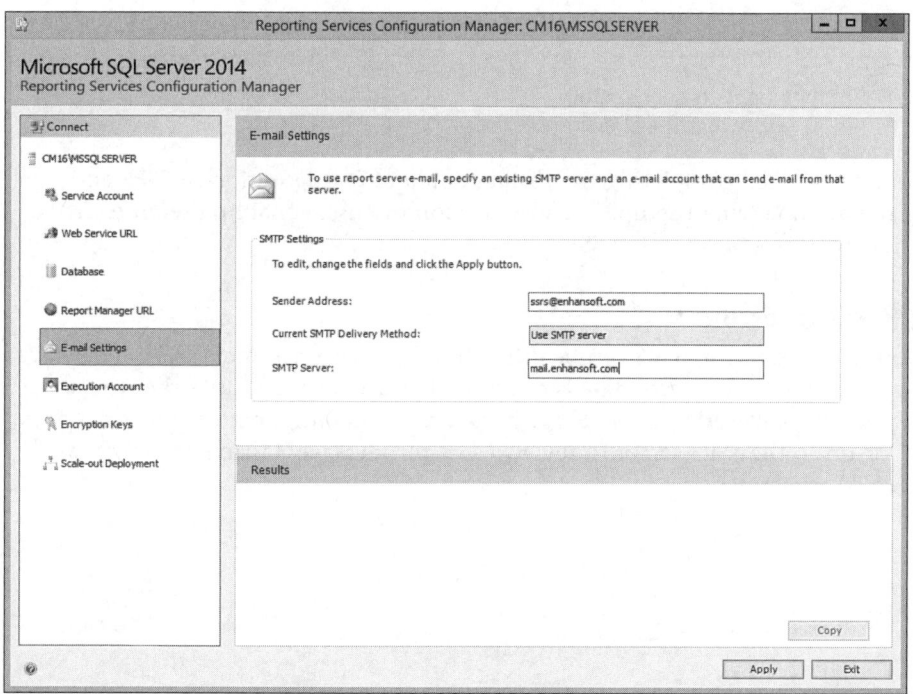

FIGURE 1.30   Clicking **Apply** to commit your changes.

2. Notice the successful installation message in the Results pane, as shown in Figure 1.31. As there are no more configuration changes required for SSRS, click **Exit** to complete your customization.

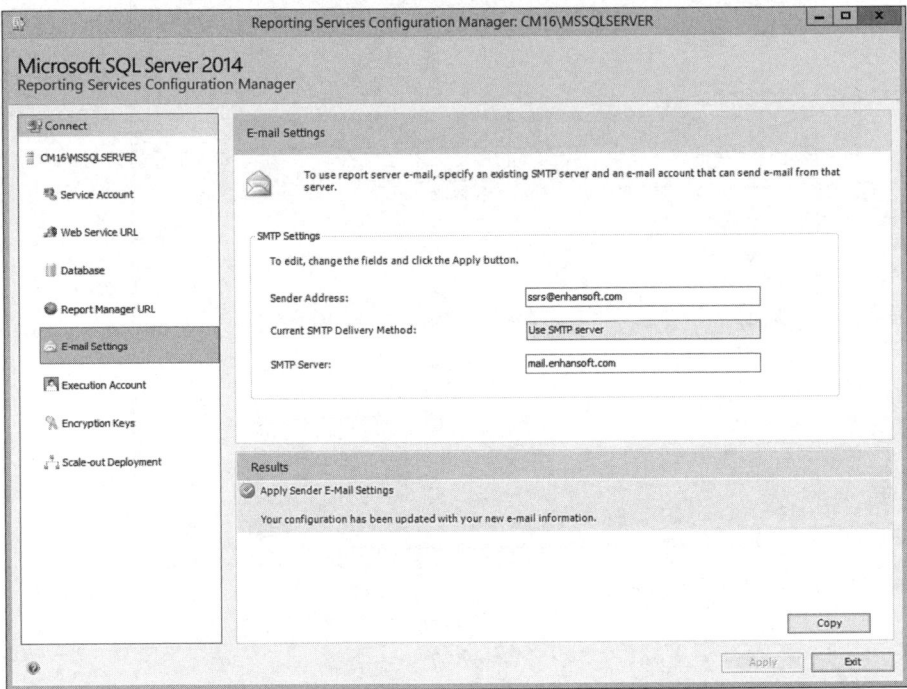

FIGURE 1.31   Settings applied successfully.

This section has discussed completing the installation and configuration of SSRS and configuring the optional email setup. The next section discusses enabling remote errors, which can help with troubleshooting SSRS.

Enabling Remote Errors

Troubleshooting errors within SSRS can be difficult, as generic error messages are displayed in most cases. To be able to receive details of errors that occur, you must either execute a report locally on the SSRS server or enable remote errors. Enabling remote errors removes the need to log on to the SSRS server to review the error message. Listing 1.1 shows an example of an error message.

LISTING 1.1   Error Message Example

```
An error has occurred during report processing. (rsProcessingAborted)
Query execution failed for dataset 'DataSet0'. (rsErrorExecutingCommand)
For more information about this error navigate to the report server on the local
server machine, or enable remote errors
```

To enable remote errors, follow these steps:

1. From Windows, launch **SQL Server 2014 Management Studio** with administrative rights, as shown in Figure 1.32.

2. Change the server type to **Reporting Services** (see Figure 1.33) and log in.

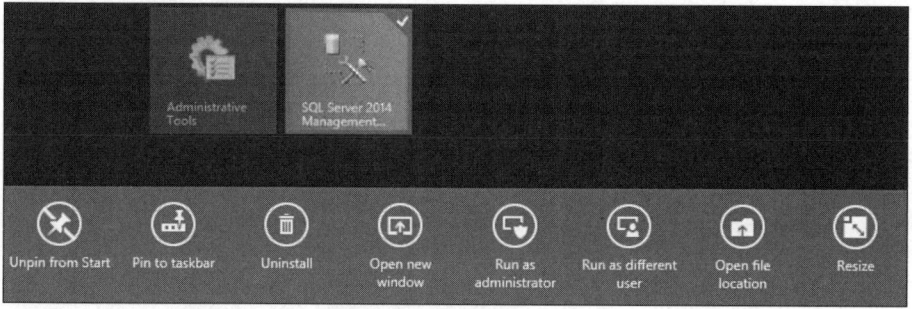

FIGURE 1.32   Launching SQL Server 2014 Management Studio with administrative rights.

FIGURE 1.33   Change the server type to **Reporting Services** and click **Connect** to log in.

3. Next, right-click the server name, as shown in Figure 1.34, and select **Properties**.

4. Click **Advanced** on the Server Properties page shown in Figure 1.35 to open the page shown in Figure 1.36.

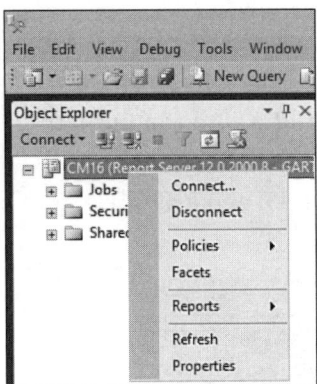

FIGURE 1.34   Right-clicking the report server and selecting **Properties**.

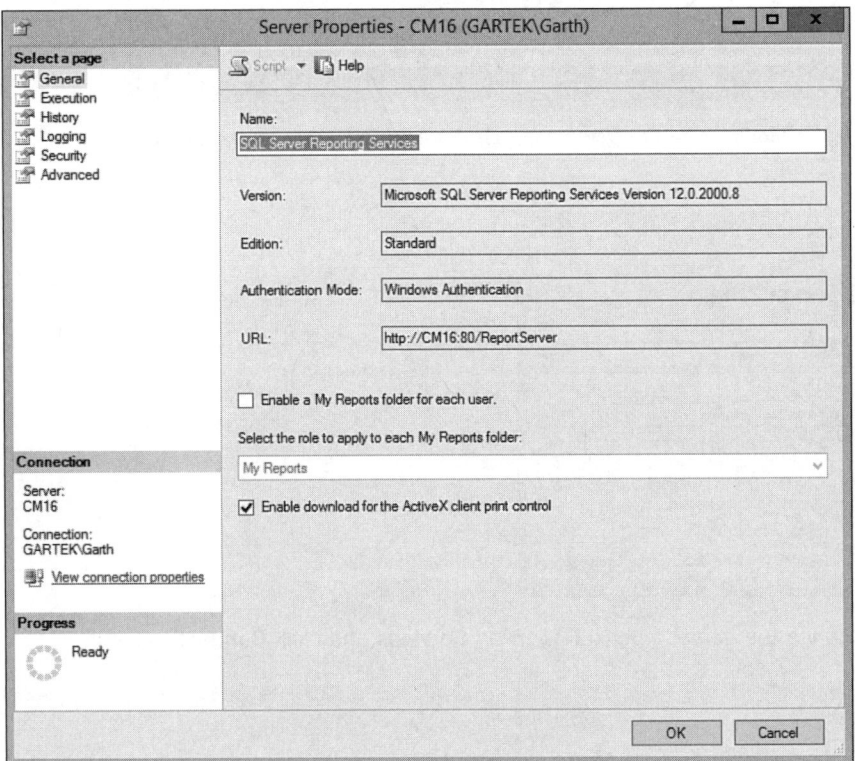

FIGURE 1.35   Selecting **Advanced** on the Server Properties page.

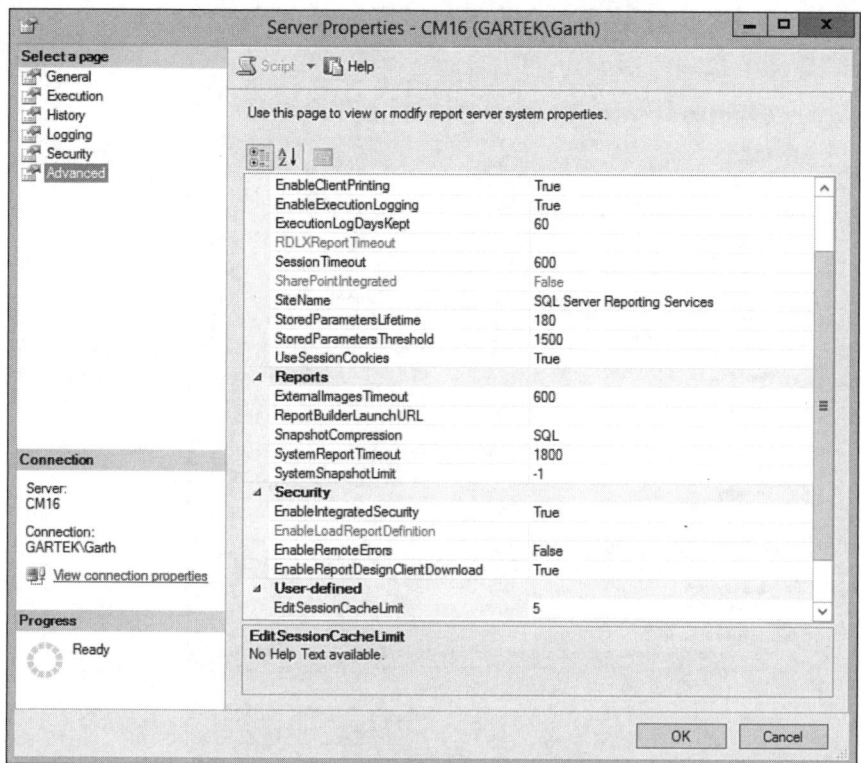

FIGURE 1.36   Advanced server properties page.

5. Change the value of **EnableRemoteErrors** to **True** and click **OK** (see Figure 1.37). When you've completed the steps, the Advanced page should look similar to Figure 1.38.

Once EnableRemoteErrors is enabled, you can re-execute the report to see the actual error that occurred and correct the issues. Using the previous example, shown in Listing 1.1, the true error is displayed in Listing 1.2.

LISTING 1.2   Complete Error Listing After Enabling Remote Errors

```
An error has occurred during report processing. (rsProcessingAborted)

Query execution failed for dataset 'DataSet0'. (rs ErrorExecutingCommand)

The multi-part identifier "PDisk.ResourceID" could not be bound. The multi-part
identifier "PDisk.Size0" could not be bound. The multi-part identifier "PDisk.Size0"
could not be bound. The multi-part identifier "PDisk.Size0" could not be bound. The
multi-part identifier "PDisk.Size0" could not be bound.
```

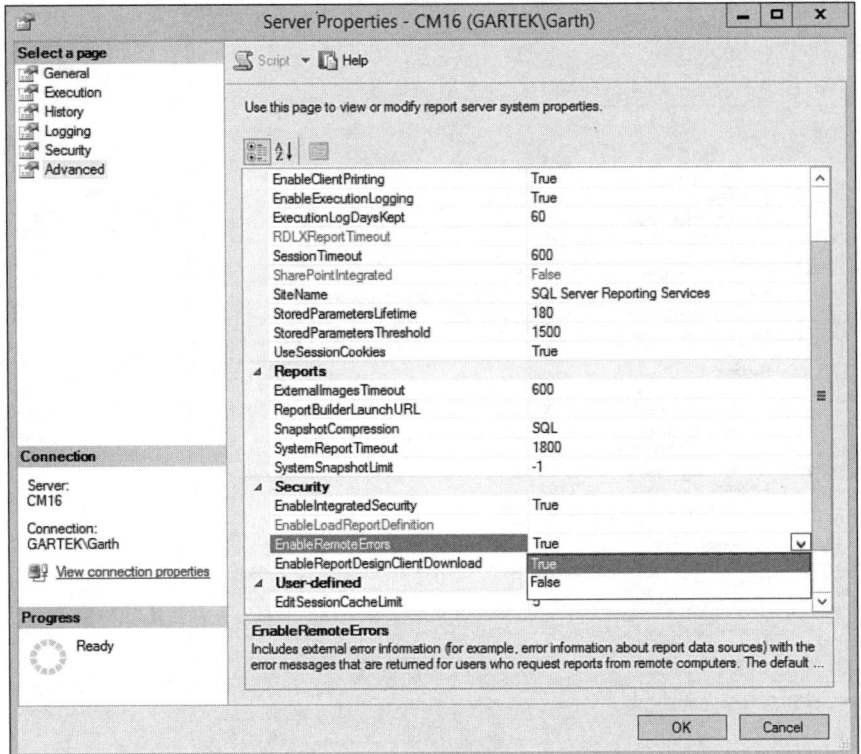

FIGURE 1.37   Changing the setting for **EnableRemoteErrors** to **True**.

This section has shown how to enable remote errors. Using remote errors allows you to troubleshoot reporting issues. The next section discusses installing client tools and following Microsoft best practices by not creating SSRS reports on your ConfigMgr site server.

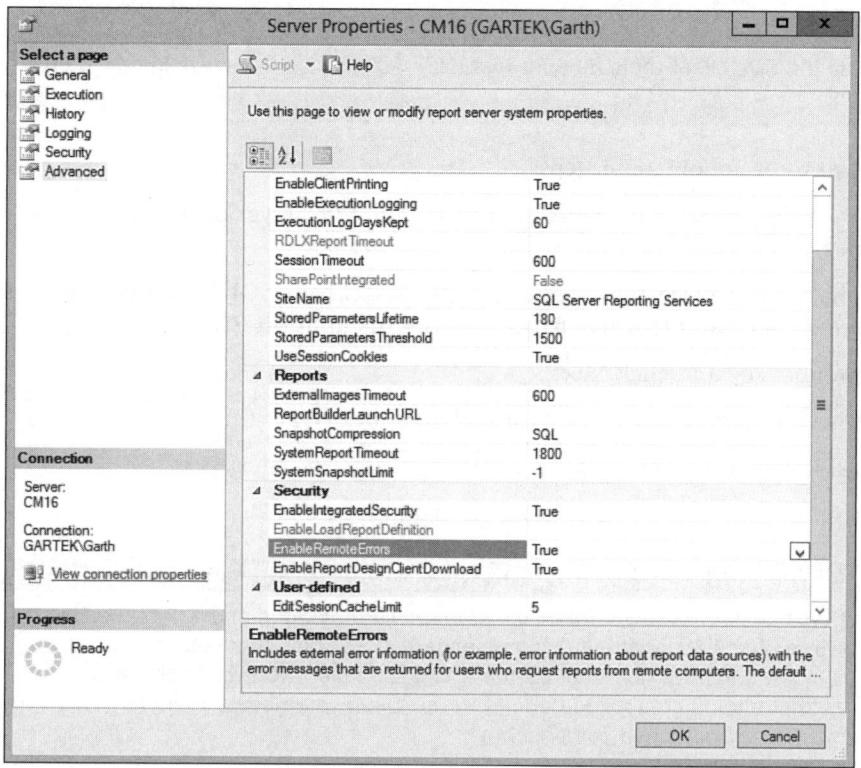

FIGURE 1.38   Advanced server properties page with changed applies.

Installing Client Tools for SSRS Reporting

As with any other enterprise application, for security and performance reasons, you should not perform query and report development/testing in a production environment. This is true with SSRS, as you could easily create a query or report that will affect the performance of your SQL Server. Whenever possible, create and test your queries and reports in a development environment. Even in a development environment, it is better to perform your work on a workstation than on the server itself.

The following sections show how to install the SQL Server client tools, which you use to create SQL queries, and the SQL Server Data Tools Business Intelligence tool. These tools enable you to create SSRS reports that can help increase the productivity of those who will use your custom reports.

Installing Client Tools

You typically would not develop or create reports on a SQL Server or on the ConfigMgr site server. Rather, you create reports on your own workstation and then update those reports to your report server. In order to develop SQL queries and reports, it is necessary to install several tools on your workstation. This section discusses what you need to install.

TIP: INSTALLING .NET 3.5

Prior to installing the SQL client tools, ensure that .NET 3.5 Service Pack 1 is installed on your workstation.

To install the client tools, follow these steps:

1. Launch SQL Server 2014 setup. Figure 1.39 shows the SQL Server Installation Center that appears.

2. Select Installation in the left-hand pane and then select **New SQL Server stand-alone installation or add features to an existing installation** (see Figure 1-40).

3. Enter the product key and click **Next**.

4. Accept the license terms shown in Figure 1.41 and click **Next**.

5. If the Global Rules page like the one in Figure 1.42 appears, click **Next**.

6. Click **Next** on the Microsoft Update page, shown in Figure 1.43.

TIP: ERRORS USING MICROSOFT UPDATE TO CHECK FOR UPDATES

If you are using ConfigMgr or WSUS to manage your software updates and select the **Use Microsoft Update to check for updates (recommended)** check box, this step may fail. Although such a failure will have no effect on the final installation, you will likely have software updates that should be applied during your next software update cycle for each computer on which you install these components.

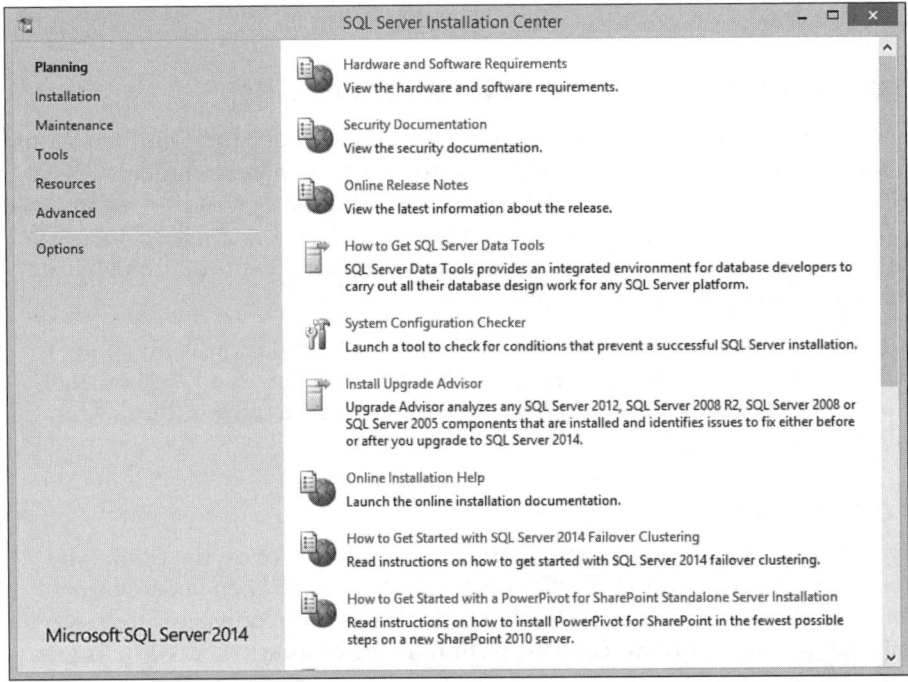

FIGURE 1.39   Opening SQL Server Installation Center and selecting **Installation**.

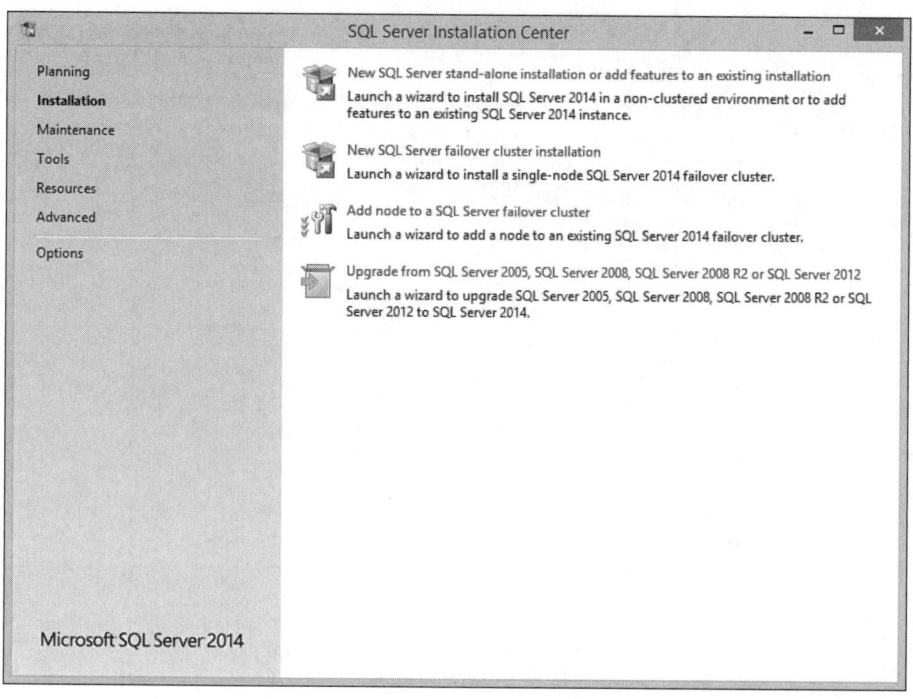

FIGURE 1.40   Selecting the first option on the Installation page.

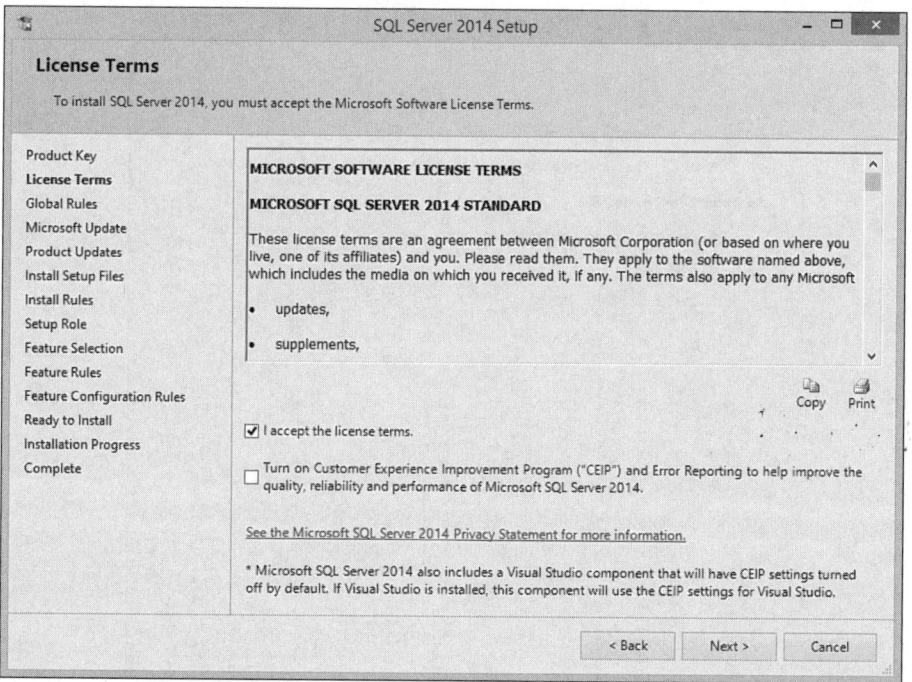

FIGURE 1.41   Accepting the Microsoft software license terms.

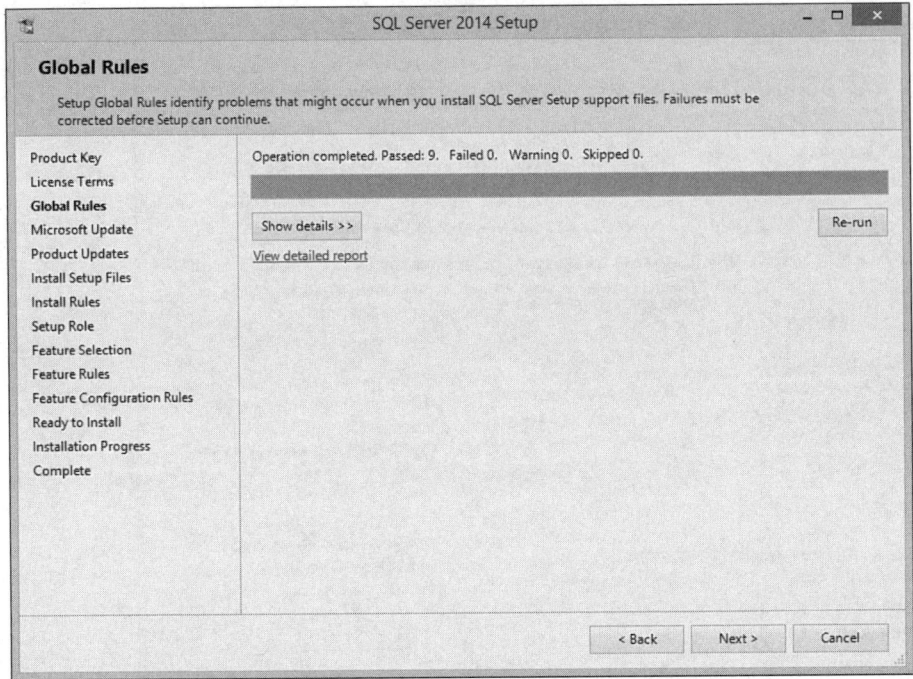

FIGURE 1.42   The Global Rules page.

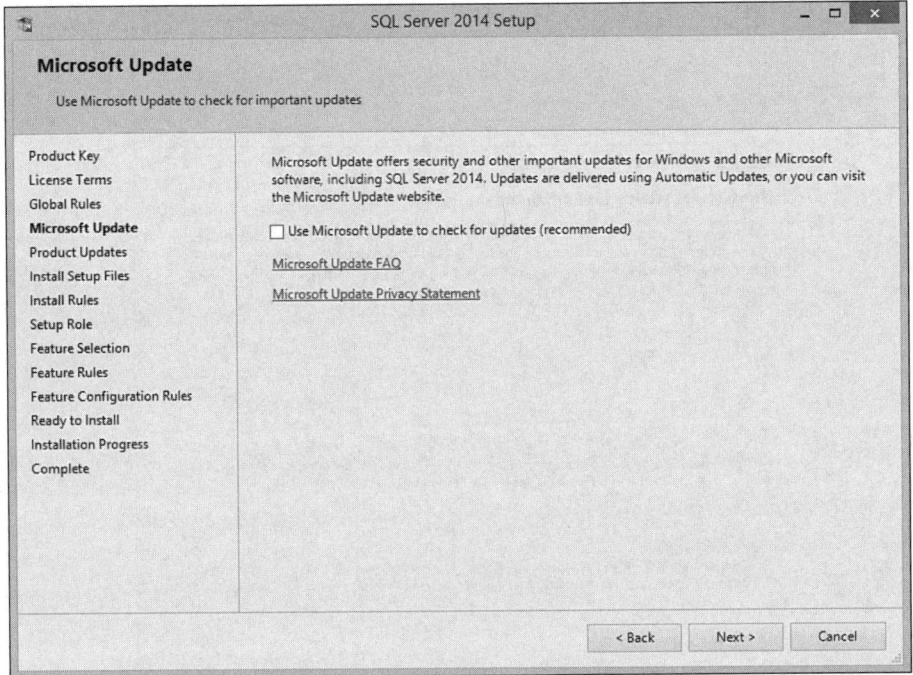

FIGURE 1.43   Microsoft Update for SQL Server components.

7. On the Install Rules page (see Figure 1.44), ignore the warning about the firewall and click **Next**.

8. On the Setup Role page, displayed in Figure 1.45, select **SQL Server Feature Installation** and click **Next**.

9. Select **Management Tools - Basic** and then **Management Tools - Complete**, as shown in Figure 1.46, and click **Next**.

10. Click **Next** on the Feature Configuration Rules page, if it appears. This page is shown in Figure 1.47.

11. Click **Install** on the Ready to Install page (see Figure 1.48) to proceed with the SQL client tools installation.

12. When the setup is complete and the features are successfully installed, as shown in Figure 1.49, click **Close**.

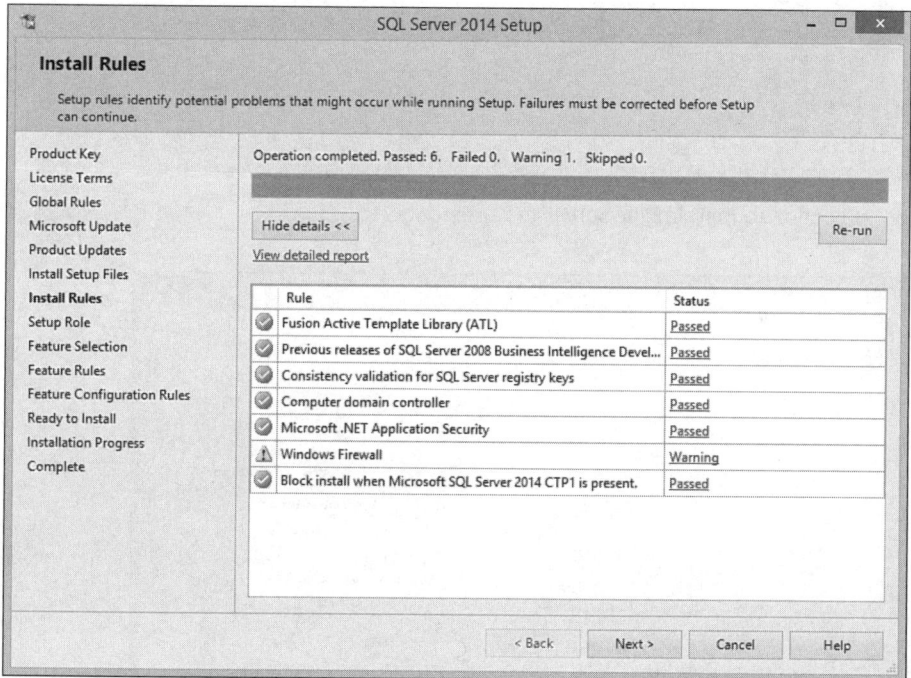

FIGURE 1.44   The Install Rules page.

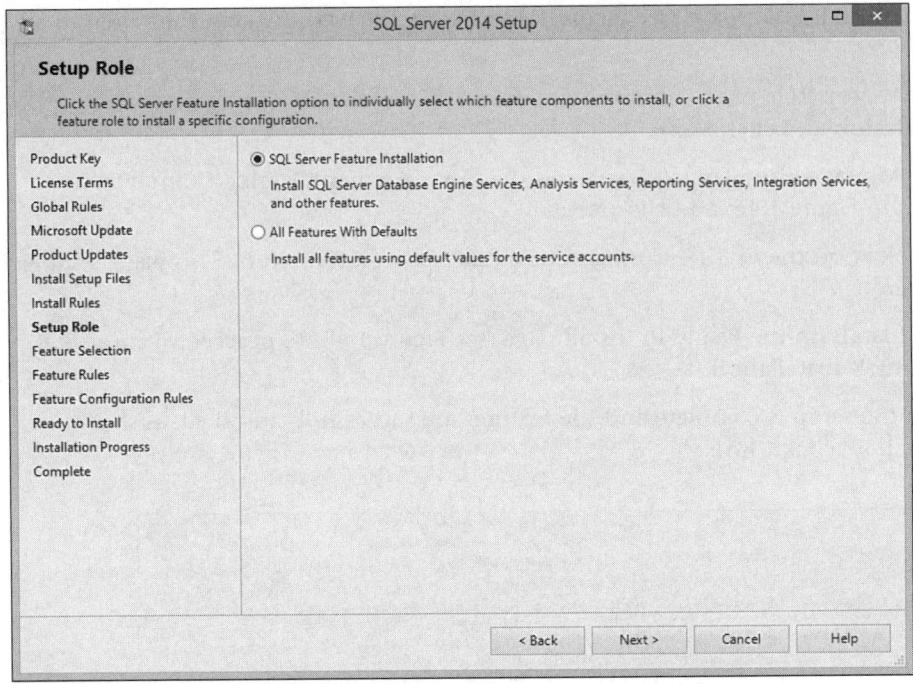

FIGURE 1.45   Selecting to install SQL Server features only.

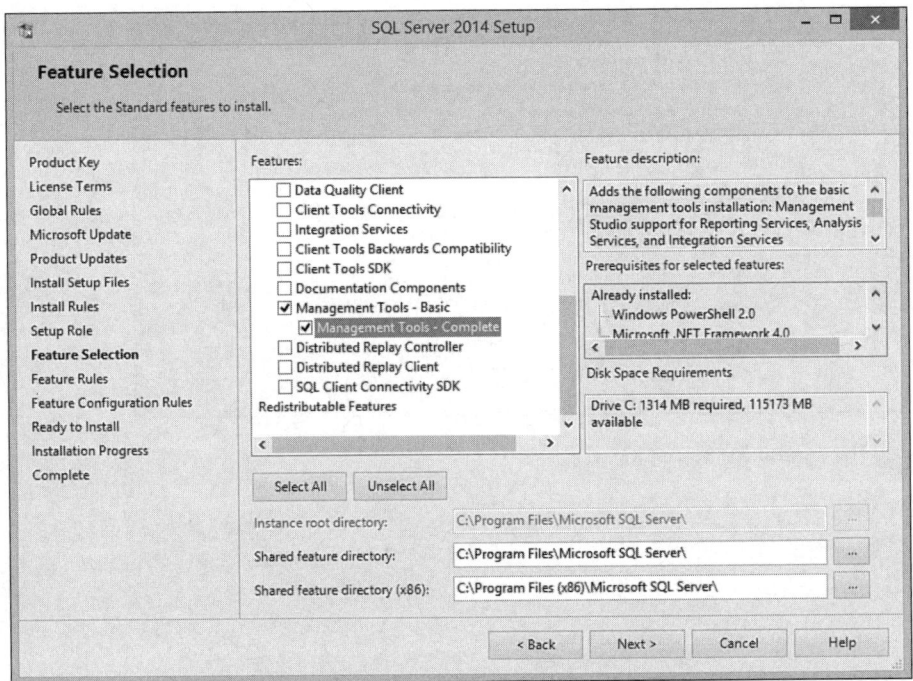

FIGURE 1.46   Selecting the Management Tools features to install.

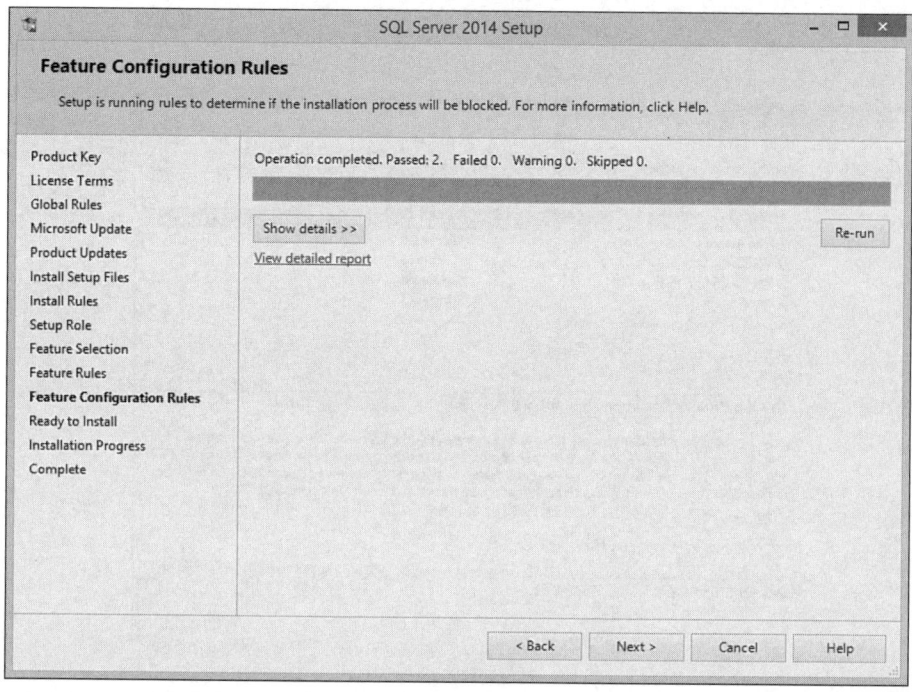

FIGURE 1.47   Feature Configuration Rules page.

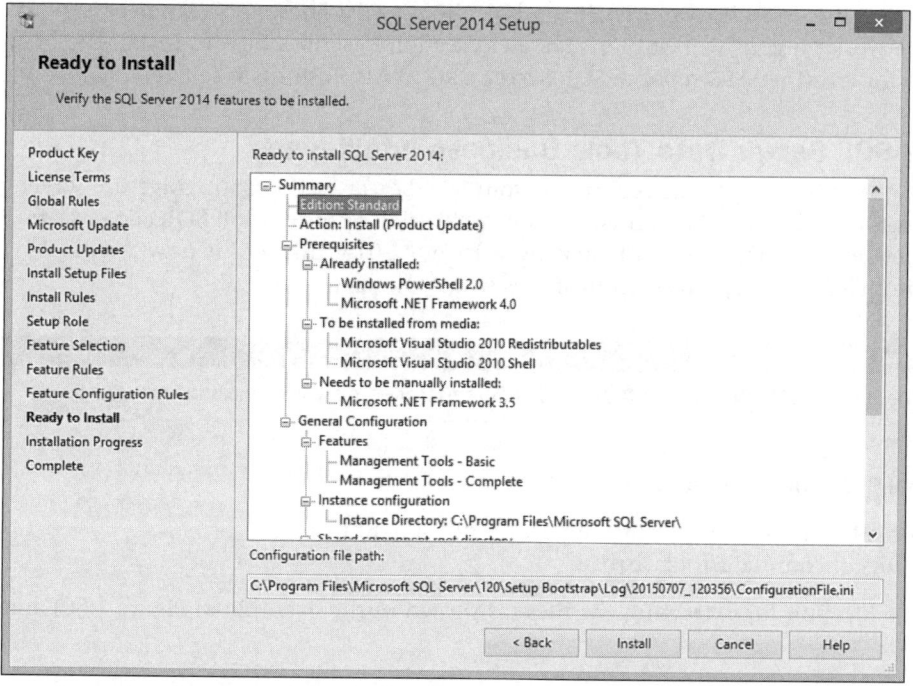

FIGURE 1.48   The Ready to Install page.

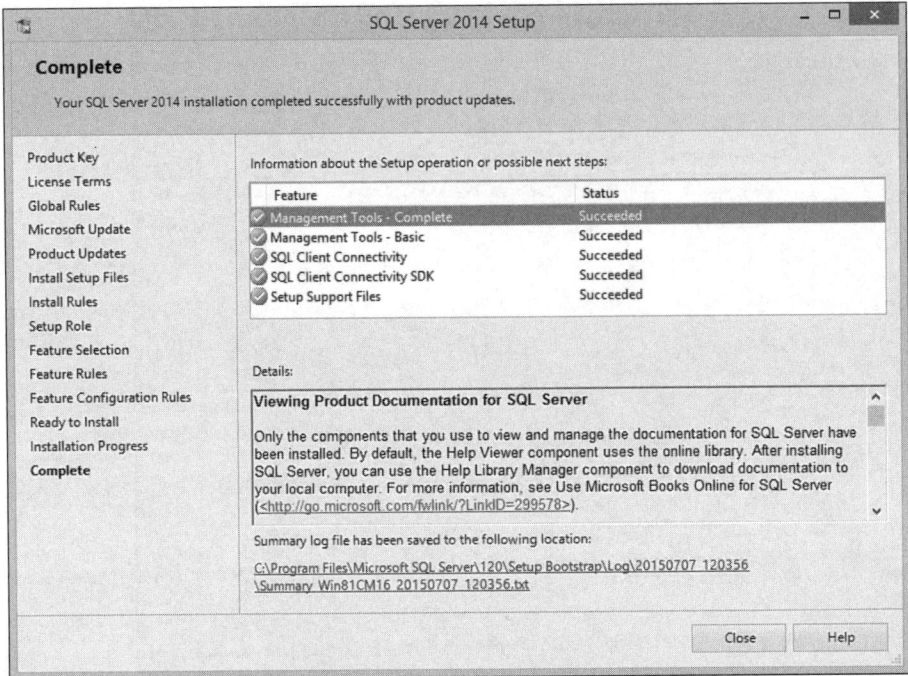

FIGURE 1.49   Successful client tools installation.

This section has discussed how to install the SQL client tools. These tools are necessary to perform SQL work on your workstation. The next section describes how to install the final tool needed for creating SSRS reports: SQL Server Data Tools Business Intelligence.

Installing SQL Server Data Tools Business Intelligence

You should not develop or create reports on your SQL Server or the ConfigMgr site server. Therefore, before creating SSRS reports, you need to install another tool: SQL Server Data Tools Business Intelligence (SSDT-BI). Starting with SQL 2014, this tool is now a separate download from SQL Server. This section shows what you need to install.

TIP: INSTALLING .NET 4.5

Prior to installing SSDT-BI, ensure that .NET 4.5 is installed on your workstation.

To install SSDT-BI, follow these steps:

1. Download and execute the current version of SSDT-BI from http://msdn.com/data/tools.aspx.

2. Select a location for extracting the files (as shown in the example in Figure 1.50) and click **OK**.

3. Accept the license terms and click **Next**.

4. Click **Next** on the Microsoft Update page, shown in Figure 1.51.

5. Click **Next** on the Feature Selection page, shown in Figure 1.52.

6. Click **Close** on the Complete page, shown in Figure 1.53, to exit the setup.

This section has discussed the steps involved in installing the SSDT-BI tool, which is required for creating SSRS reports.

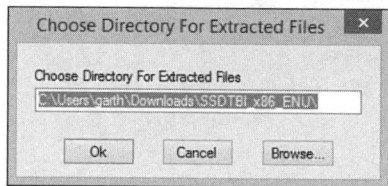

FIGURE 1.50   Choosing a directory (folder) for extracted files.

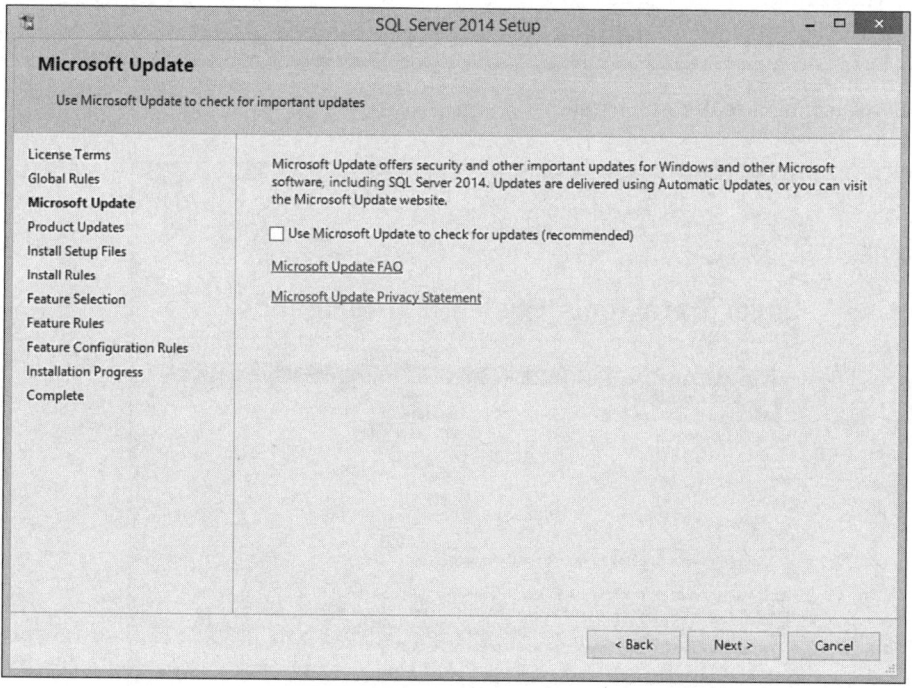

FIGURE 1.51   Selecting whether to use Microsoft Update.

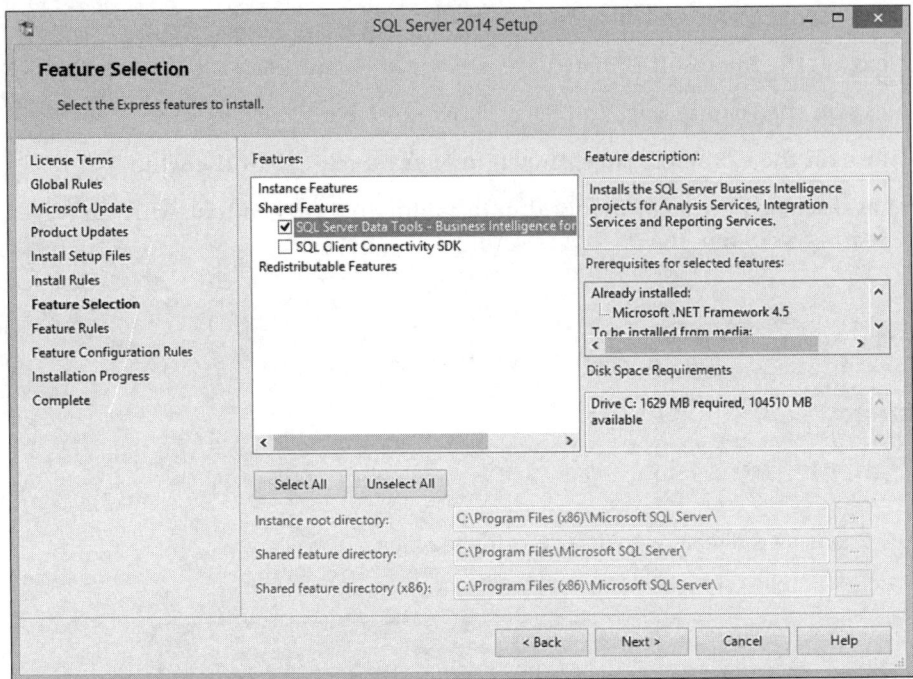

FIGURE 1.52   Selecting a feature to install.

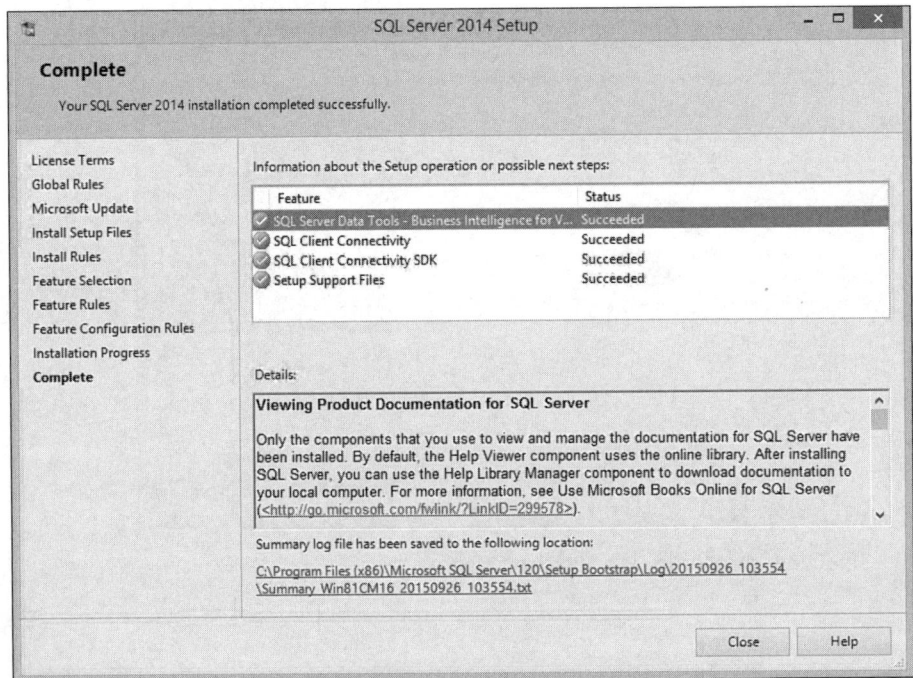

FIGURE 1.53   Installation complete.

Summary

This chapter has discussed the steps for installing SQL Server's SSRS component, which is required for the ConfigMgr reporting services to leverage SSRS for its reporting needs. This chapter has also discussed the post-installation tasks involved in configuring SSRS, including enabling email support for report subscriptions and enabling remote errors for troubleshooting.

You use several client tools to create custom SQL queries and SSRS reports. This chapter has discussed installing these tools. SQL Server Management Studio is installed using the SQL 2014 installation media on computers where you plan to create your SSRS reports. This tool allows you to create and test your SQL queries without having to log on or use Remote Desktop Protocol (RDP) to access your SQL Server directly. Ideally, you should test your SQL queries in a development environment and not in your production environment.

The chapter has also discussed installation of the SQL Server Data Tools Business Intelligence client tool, which is the primary tool used for creating custom SSRS reports and exposing the information hidden within ConfigMgr. Creating custom SSRS reports provides virtually endless possibilities in terms of reporting and customization of the appearance of your reports. With custom SSRS reports for ConfigMgr, you can make informed decisions using the information exposed from your ConfigMgr environment; this can help your company's bottom line.

The next chapter describes the steps for installing your ConfigMgr reporting services point and validating that it is working correctly. It also introduces an often-overlooked feature in ConfigMgr—role-based administration (RBA)—and how RBA and the principle of least privilege required can be used with ConfigMgr reporting. Chapter 2 also discusses how to customize Microsoft-provided ConfigMgr reports by adding your own company's logo. The chapter also contains several demonstrations that you can perform within your own environment.

CHAPTER 2

Installing and Configuring Configuration Manager Reporting

System Center Configuration Manager (ConfigMgr) uses a reporting services point to host its reports, apply permissions to access reports, and check the health of SQL Server Reporting Services (SSRS). While the reporting services point is technically an optional role for ConfigMgr, not adding this role to your environment would leave you unable to leverage ConfigMgr's reporting capabilities, which would seriously affect your ability to manage your ConfigMgr environment.

By leveraging the reporting services point and SSRS to utilize built-in and custom reports, you can get a better understanding of your environment and measure key performance indicators (KPIs). When you couple reporting with creating custom dashboards and using built-in SSRS features such as report subscriptions, your entire business organization can make informed decisions based on ConfigMgr information.

This chapter shows you how to install the reporting services point. It discusses using security roles to allow non-ConfigMgr administrators to access information within ConfigMgr without the need for the console; this is referred to as role-based administration (RBA). It also introduces a utility you can use to change the default report logo used by ConfigMgr.

Creating the Reporting Services Point

The reporting services point (RP) has several purposes:

▶ You use it to create the data source and upload the default ConfigMgr reports.

▶ It checks for new reports added directly to SSRS and applies the appropriate permissions on all folders and reports. This check occurs every 10 minutes, and this default cannot be modified.

Adding the reporting services point is similar to adding any other role in ConfigMgr. A key point to remember when installing the RP is that when SSRS is installed remotely to the ConfigMgr site server, you should install this role on your SSRS server and not your ConfigMgr server.

TIP: PREREQUSITIES FOR INSTALLING THE REPORTING SERVICES POINT

Prior to installing the RP, the authors recommend that you apply the latest software updates to your SQL Server instance. In addition, confirm that you and the ConfigMgr site server have full administrative privileges on both the Windows Server and the SQL Server instance where you will be installing SSRS.

As a general rule, you should install SSRS on the same server as your ConfigMgr database. This is for performance reasons: When you execute an SSRS report, the SSRS report needs to access the ConfigMgr database. If the SQL SSRS instance is remote to ConfigMgr, report execution time increases, as does network traffic to access the ConfigMgr database.

The exception to installing SSRS on the same server as your ConfigMgr database is when you are using SQL clustering for the ConfigMgr database. Because Microsoft does not support SSRS on a SQL cluster, SSRS needs to be installed on another server.

TIP: SYSTEM CENTER OPERATIONS MANAGER AND SSRS SECURITY

Microsoft does not support an installation with ConfigMgr and Operations Manager sharing the same SQL SSRS instance. This is due to the fact that Operations Manager changes the way security permissions are handled within an SSRS instance. You need to create a separate SSRS instance for each System Center component.

Before you begin the installation process, create an Active Directory (AD) security user account and give it a name such as CM16SSRS. This user account is a low-rights security account, requiring no special permissions within AD. The account will be used by ConfigMgr to access reports and the SQL Server database, and it will be used when SSRS subscriptions are executed. During the RP installation, this account is granted the appropriate permissions within both ConfigMgr and SSRS.

Follow these steps to create the reporting services point on the default SQL instance for SSRS on your Windows server:

1. Open the ConfigMgr console and navigate to **Administration -> Site Configuration**. Select **Servers and Site System Roles**, as shown in Figure 2.1.

2. Right-click the server name and then select **Add Site System Roles** (see Figure 2.2).

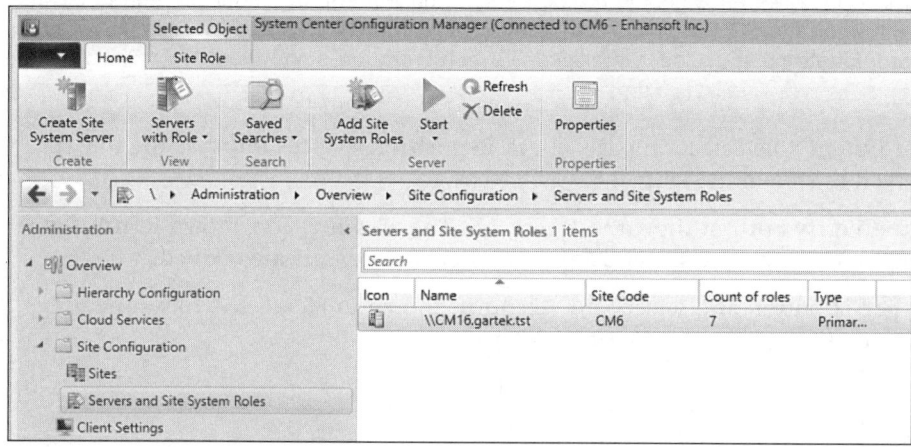

FIGURE 2.1   Selecting **Servers and Site System Roles** in the ConfigMgr console.

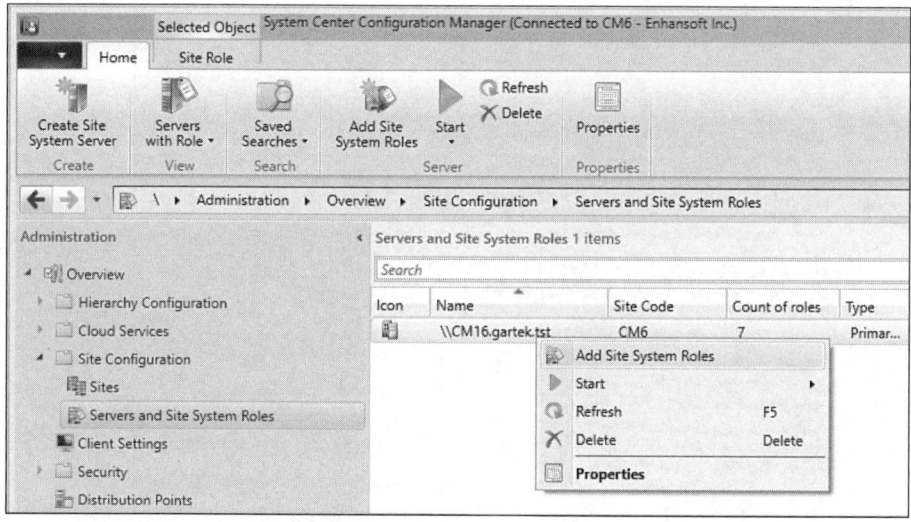

FIGURE 2.2   Selecting **Add Site System Roles**.

3. On the General page of the Add Site System Roles Wizard (see Figure 2.3), click **Next**.

4. On the Proxy page, accept the default proxy setting (displayed in Figure 2.4) by clicking **Next**.

REAL WORLD: ABOUT THE PROXY SETTINGS

In most cases, proxy settings should not be set. The only time proxy settings need to be configured is when the SQL Server is also hosting roles requiring Internet access, such as the software update point or asset intelligence synchronization point roles.

5. On the System Role Selection page, check **Reporting services point** as the role for this server, as shown in Figure 2.5. Click **Next**.

6. Click the **Verify** button, shown in Figure 2.6. The warning icon shown in this figure disappears when the site server database and database name are verified.

7. Click the **Set** button and select **New Account**, shown in Figure 2.7, to set the user account used to connect to the site database.

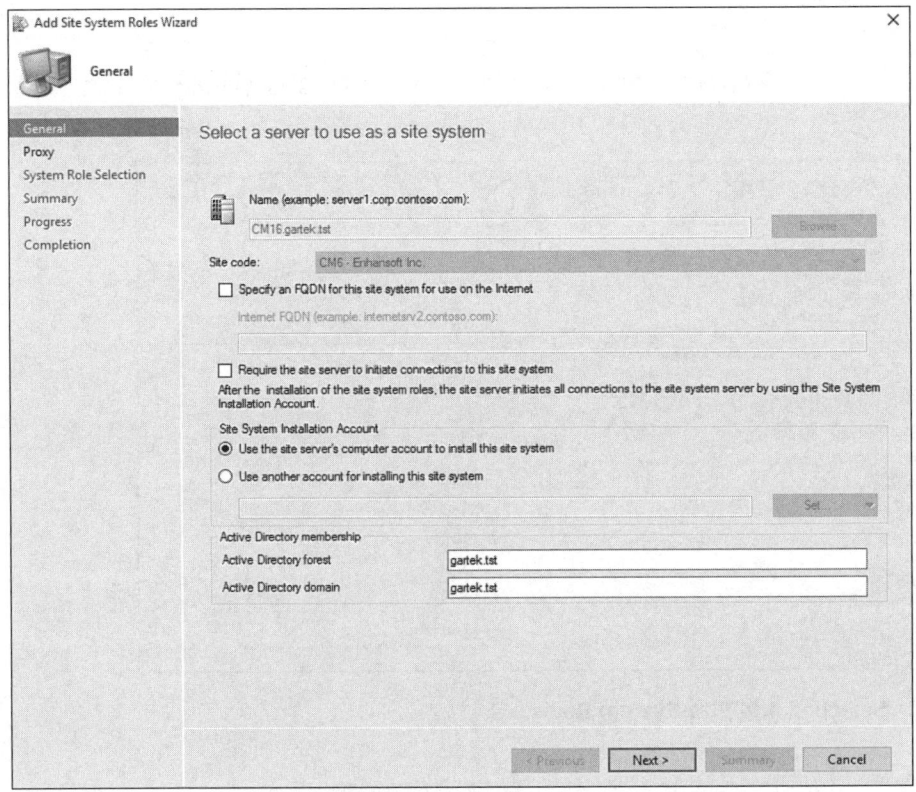

FIGURE 2.3   Specifying a server to use as a site system.

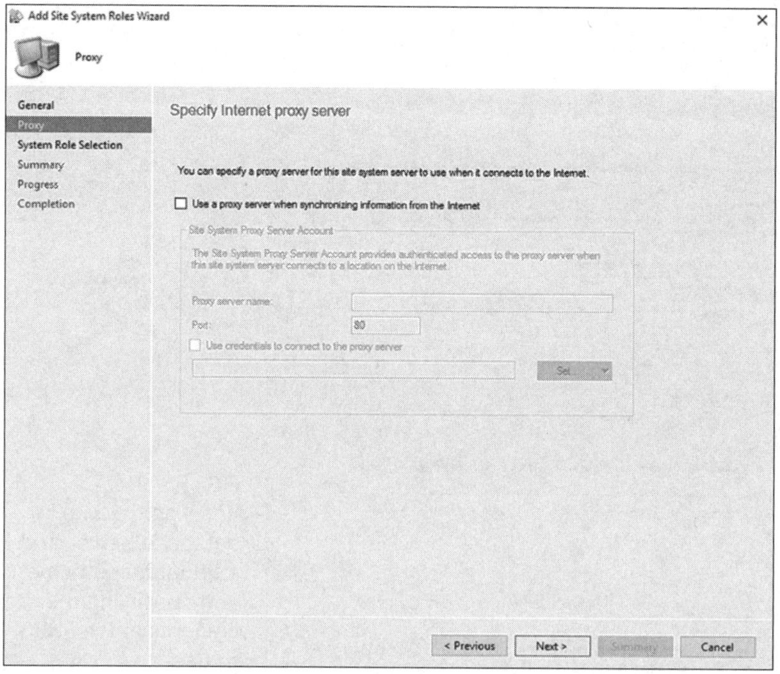

FIGURE 2.4   The Proxy page of the Add Site System Roles Wizard.

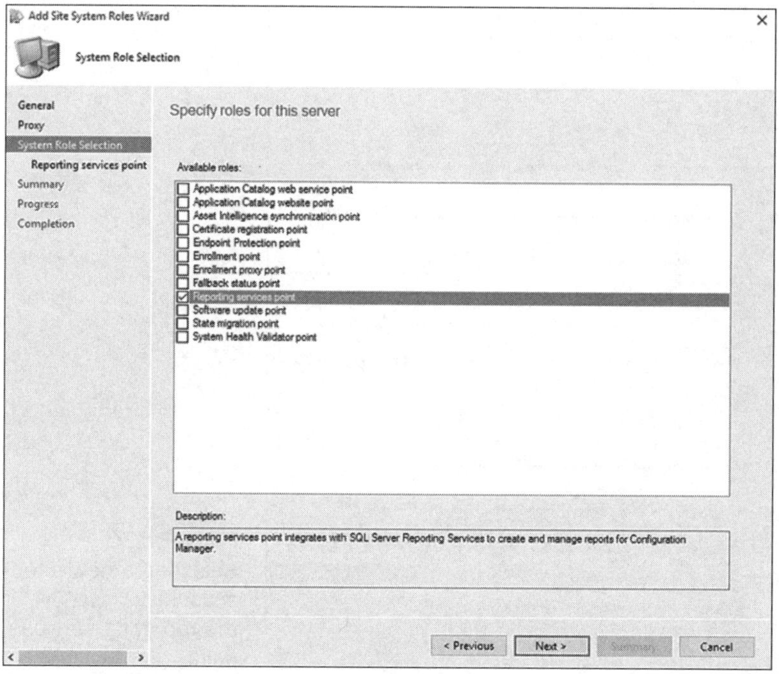

FIGURE 2.5 Selecting the **Reporting services point** role.

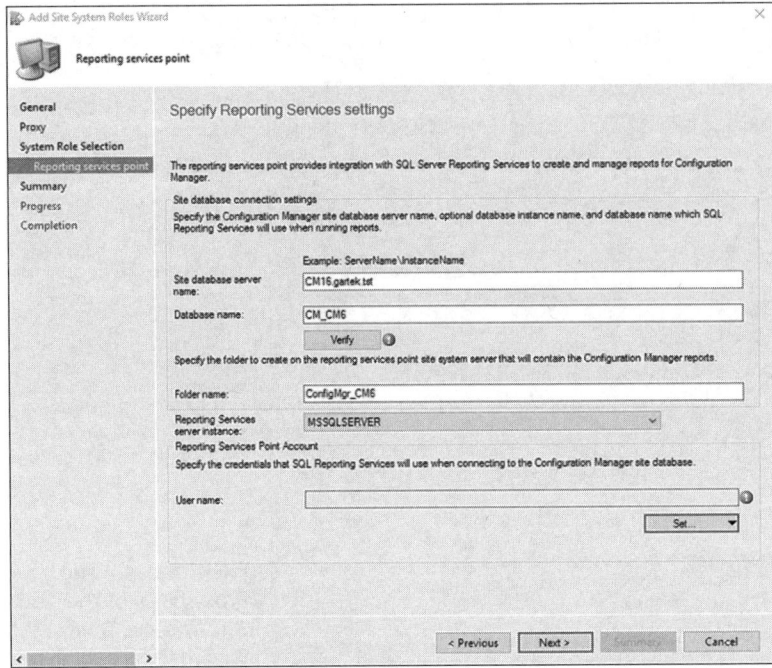

FIGURE 2.6
Verifying the site database server and site database name and specifying the credentials for SSRS to use.

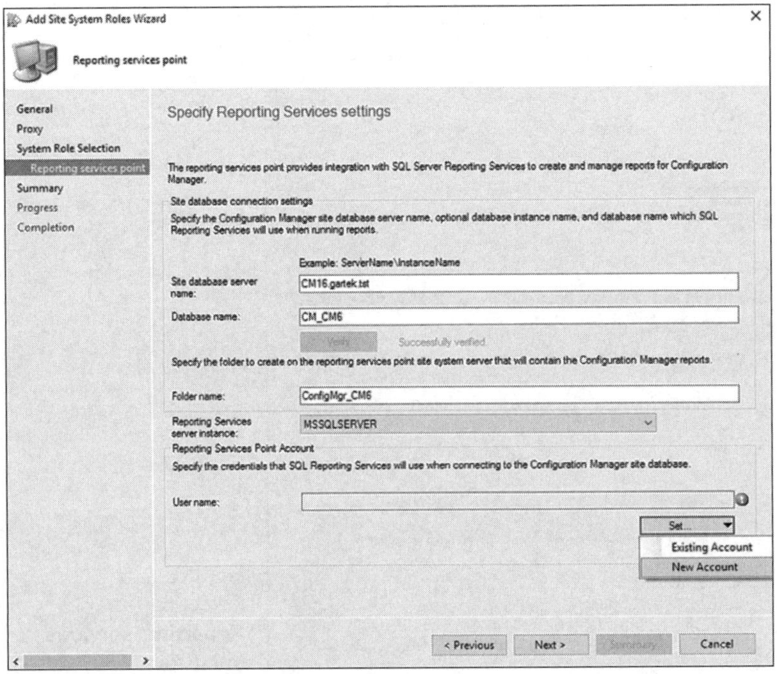

FIGURE 2.7
Selecting a new user account for use by the reporting services point.

8. In the Windows User Account window (see Figure 2.8), type in the user account name or browse to select it. Enter the associated password and click **OK**.

9. Back on the Reporting services point page of the wizard, notice that the User name field is now populated, as shown in Figure 2.9. Click **Next** to continue.

10. Verify the settings on the Summary page (displayed in Figure 2.10) and click **Next** to add the reporting services point role.

11. The Completion page, shown in Figure 2.11, appears after the site system role is successfully added. Click **Close** to exit the wizard.

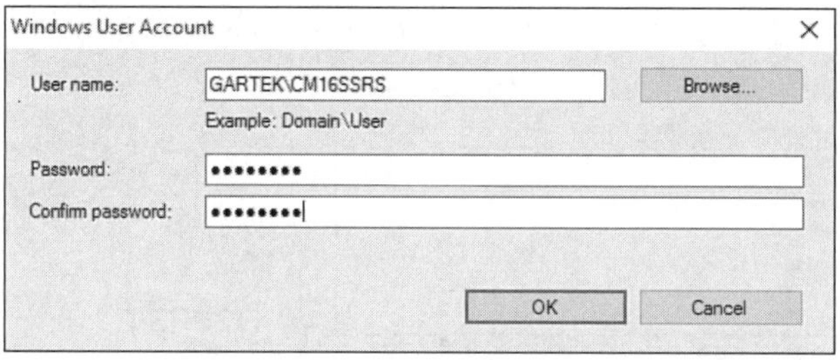

FIGURE 2.8   Specifying Windows user account credentials to use with the reporting services point.

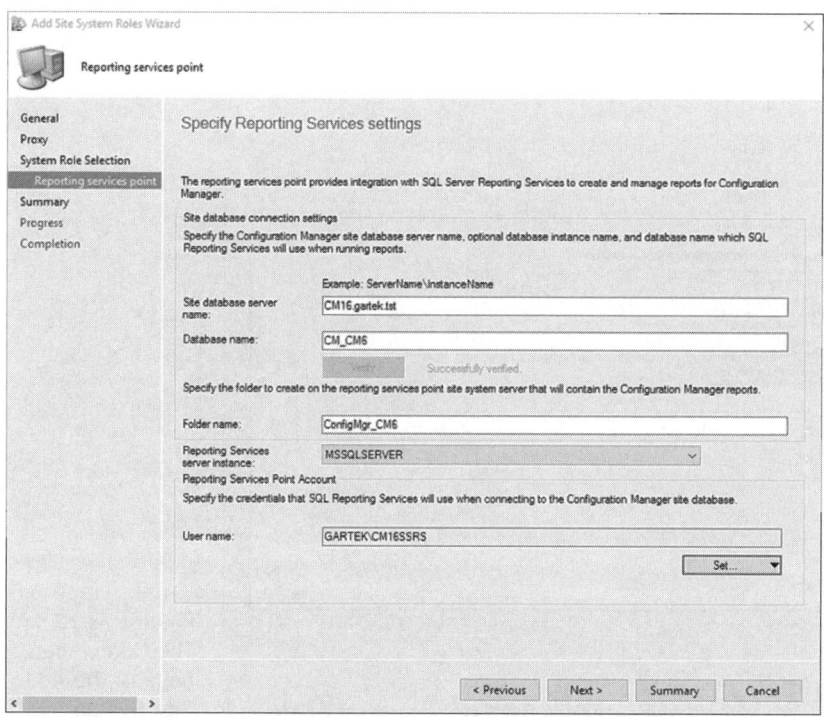

FIGURE 2.9   A completed Reporting services point page.

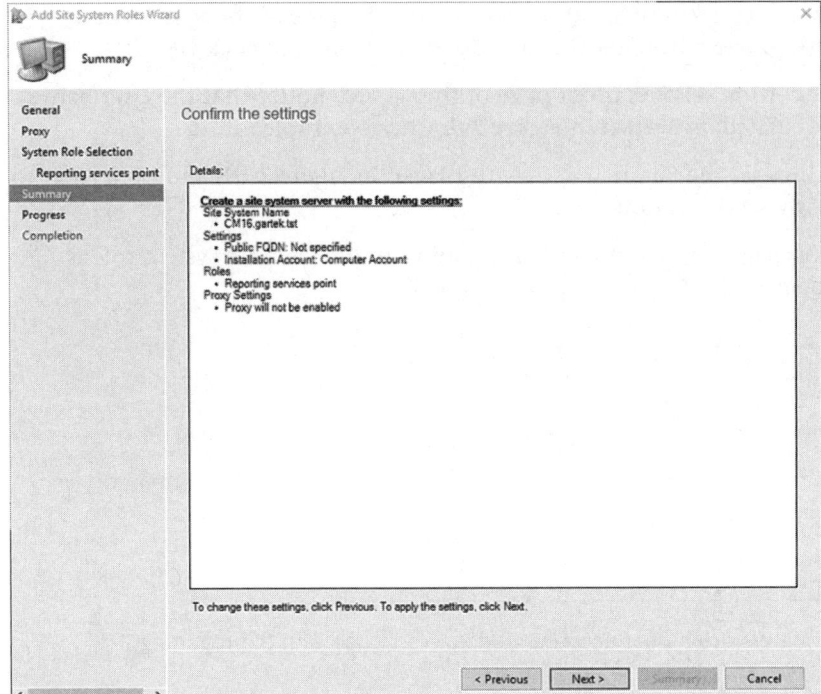

FIGURE 2.10
The Summary
page of the Add
Site System
Roles Wizard.

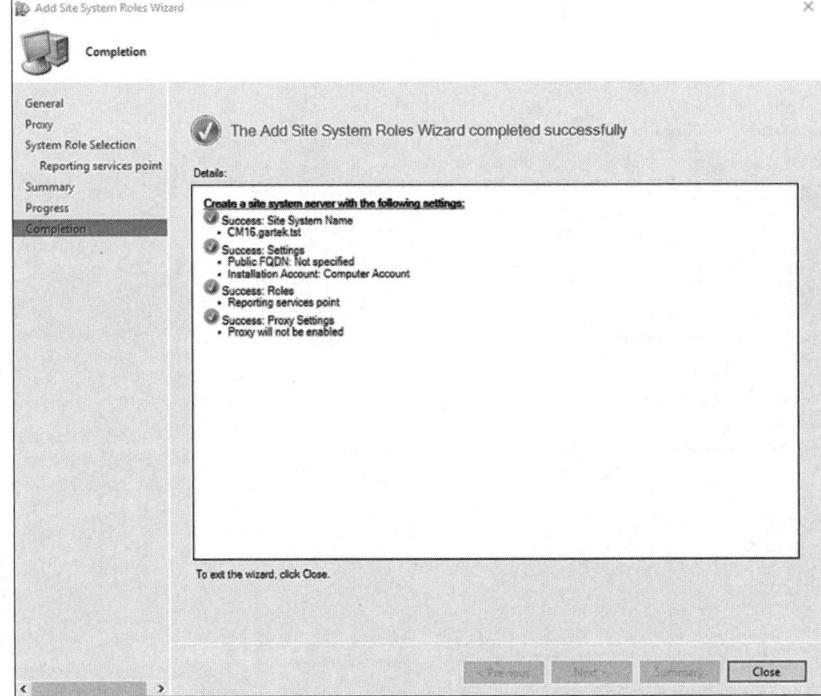

FIGURE 2.11
The Completion
page of the Add
Site System
Roles Wizard.

The simplest way to validate that the ConfigMgr reporting services point was installed correctly is to use Internet Explorer to browse to http://*<SSRS servername>*/reports. When the RP is successfully installed, you see a folder named ConfigMgr_*<SiteCode>*, as shown in Figure 2.12.

Drill down through the folder, and you should see a number of folders listed, as shown in Figure 2.13. Keep in mind that it will take several minutes for all the SSRS reports and folders to become populated.

You can review two sets of logs to check the health of your RP:

▶ The first set of log files (srsrpMSI.log and srsrpsetup.log) records the installation of the reporting services point.

▶ srsrp.log checks the ongoing status of the RP. Captured within this log file are permissions changes on the RP and when the RP sees new folders and reports. The reporting services point check occurs every 10 to 15 minutes.

This section has discussed how to add the reporting services point role to ConfigMgr. The next section discusses creating security roles to allow users to access the SSRS reports without accessing the ConfigMgr console.

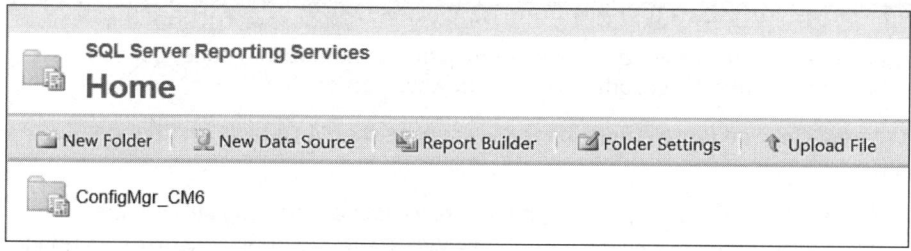

FIGURE 2.12   Validating a successful reporting services point installation.

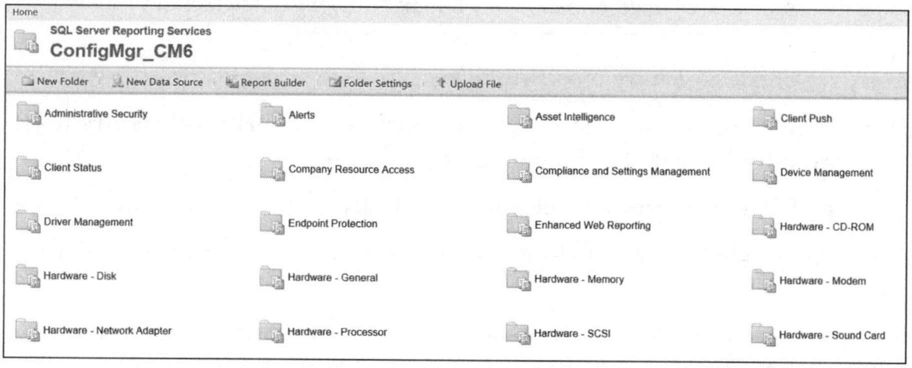

FIGURE 2.13   ConfigMgr SSRS report category folders.

Using ConfigMgr Security Reporting Roles

As soon as you have installed ConfigMgr, someone, typically a manager, will ask you for information stored by ConfigMgr. As with any other enterprise application, it is best to reduce the number of people who can access the console, but this creates a conundrum: How can you grant access to information such as software update status, and hardware inventory without giving users access to the console? Luckily, ConfigMgr with SSRS allows you to provide information to end users without the need for any console; only an Internet browser is required. Security reporting roles, which are discussed in the following sections, make this possible.

Creating a Security Reporting Role

It's important to follow the principle of least privileges needed when creating security reporting roles. This book uses ConfigMgr's RBA feature to enable users to view SSRS reports. You can view the security roles RBA uses at Administration -> Security -> Security Roles in the ConfigMgr console. This section walks through the steps involved in creating a security role that allows users to access reports without accessing the ConfigMgr console. Creating a new security role is most easily accomplished by copying an existing role and removing unnecessary permissions.

REAL WORLD: COPYING AN EXISTING SECURITY ROLE FOR REPORT ACCESS

When creating a new security role to access reports, the authors recommend that you copy from the read-only auditor security role. Here's why:

▶ Using the read-only auditor role requires fewer changes than if you use another role for your base.

▶ Using this role follows the best practice of least privileges as the read-only auditor security role cannot make any changes to ConfigMgr. Therefore, if any mistakes are made when using this role as your model, the worst that might occur is someone using the new security role could be able to view more information than was intended. However, that user would not be able to change or cause any damage to your ConfigMgr environment.

Follow these steps to create a security reporting role:

1. In the ConfigMgr console, navigate to **Administration -> Security -> Security Roles** to open the Security Roles node, as shown in Figure 2.14.

2. Right-click the **Read-only Analyst** role and select **Copy**, as shown in Figure 2.15.

3. In the Copy Security Role window displayed in Figure 2.16, enter **Report Reader** in the Name field.

4. Remove the unneeded permissions by expanding the various nodes within the Permissions section. Table 2.1 lists the desired nodes and permissions.

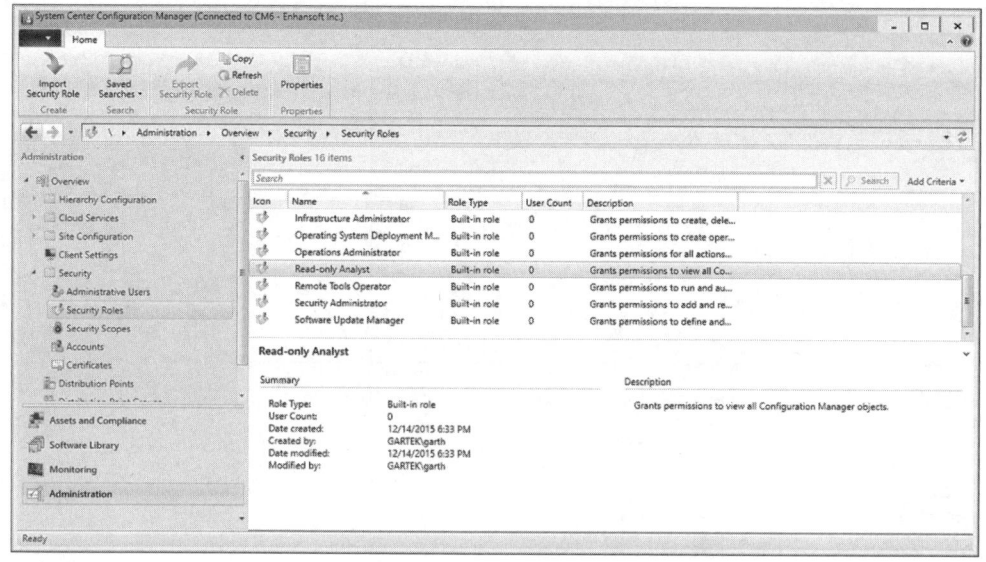

FIGURE 2.14   Security Roles node in the ConfigMgr console.

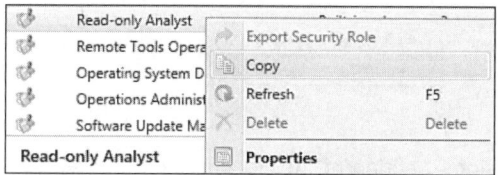

FIGURE 2.15   Copying a security role.

5. Starting with the Alert Subscription permission, expand Alert Subscription (displayed in Figure 2.17) and change the Read permission from Yes to **No**, as shown in Figure 2.18 and Figure 2.19. Repeat this process for each node until the results match Table 2.1.

TIP: IMPORT THE SECURITY ROLE

To reduce the work required to change the security role, the authors have provided the Report Reader.xml file, to which this security role has been exported. You can import this role as value-added content for this book. See Appendix C, "Available Online," for further information.

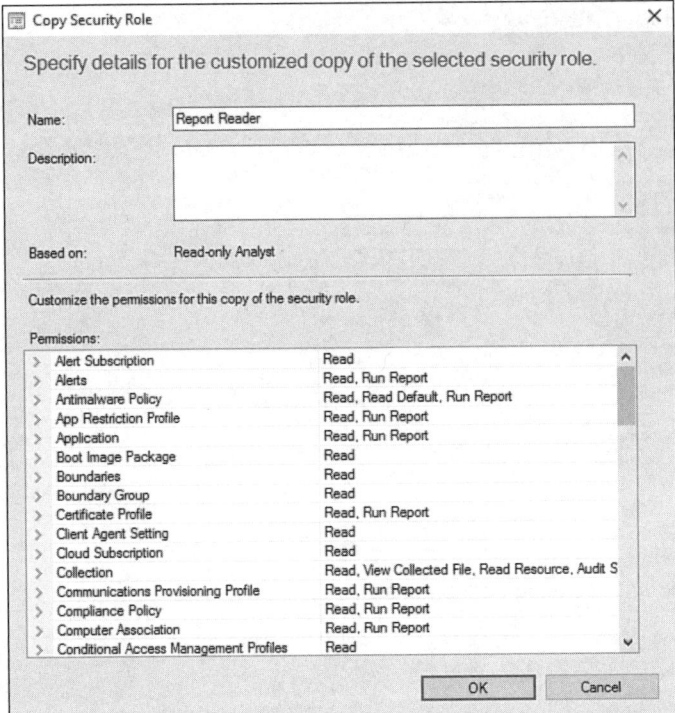

FIGURE 2.16   Copy Security Role window.

TABLE 2.1   Node and Permissions for the Permissions Section of the Security Role

Permission Title	Permissions
Alerts	Run Reports
Antimalware Policy	Run Reports
App Restriction Profile	Run Reports
Application	Run Reports
Certificate Profile	Run Reports
Collection	Read, Read Resources
Communication Provisioning Profile	Run Reports
Compliance Policy	Run Reports
Computer Association	Read, Run Reports
Configuring Item	Run Reports
Custom Configuration Settings	Run Reports
Device Drivers	Run Reports
Firewall Settings	Run Reports
Inventory Reports	Run Reports
Migration Job	Run Reports
Packages	Run Reports
PFX Certificate Profile	Run Reports

TABLE 2.1   *continued*

Permission Title	Permissions
Setting for remote Connection Profile	Read, Run Reports
Setting for user data and profile management	Read, Run Reports
Sideload Key	Run Reports
Site	Read, Run Reports
SMS_AllowOrDenyAppsSetting	Run Reports
SMS_UnManagedApps	Run Reports
Software Metering	Run Reports
Software Titles	View Asset Intelligence
Software Update Group	Read
Software Update Packages	Read
Software Updates	Read, Run Reports
Status Messages	Run Reports
Task Sequence Package	Run Reports
Trusted CA Certificate Profile	Run Reports
User Device Affinities	Read, Run Reports
User	Read, Run Reports
VPN Profile	Run Reports
Wi-Fi Profile	Run Reports
Windows CE Device Setting Item	Run Reports

FIGURE 2.17   Alert Subscription permissions.

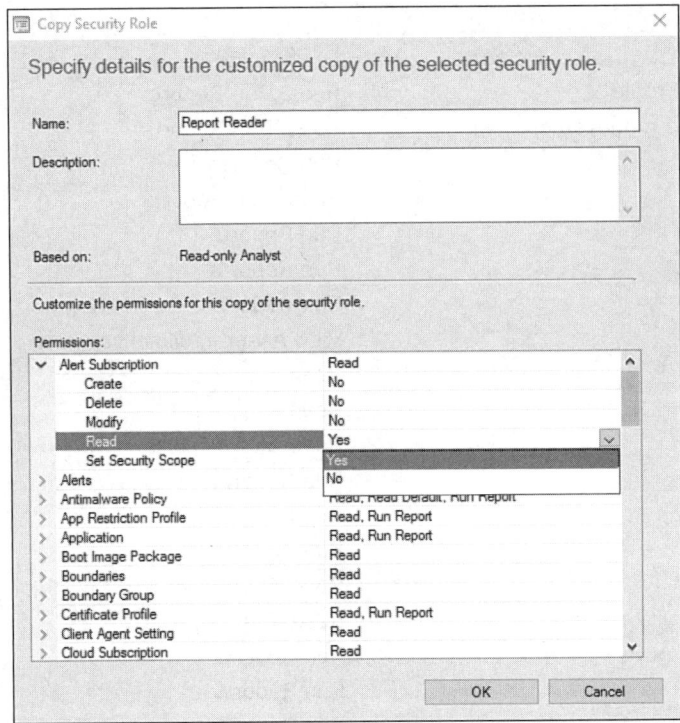

FIGURE 2.18   Changing the Read item within the Alert Subscription permissions.

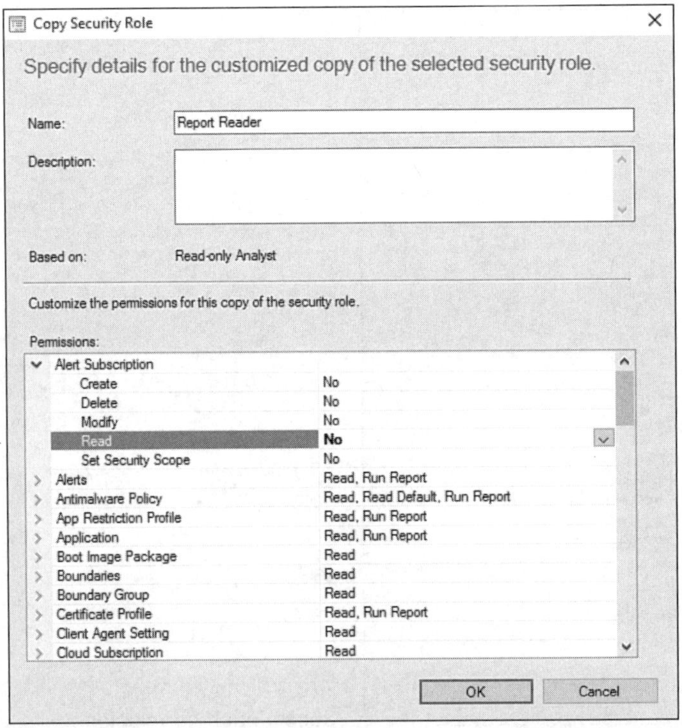

FIGURE 2.19   Read Item set to **No** within the Alert Subscription permissions.

Restricting Access to Reports

The previous section discussed creating a security role to grant all reports to a security group or user. Let's say you want to grant selected reports, such as the software update reports, to certain groups, such as your server and workstation security teams. Accomplishing this would require adjusting the permissions within the Report Reader security role to include only the items shown in Table 2.2 and Figure 2.20, which would limit access to just the software update reports.

After the security role is created, it is displayed within the ConfigMgr console as shown in Figure 2.21.

TABLE 2.2   Permissions for Software Update Reports

Permission Title	Permissions
Collection	Read, Read Resources
Site	Read,
Software Update Group	Read
Software Update Packages	Read
Software Updates	Read, Run Reports

TIP: IMPORT THE SECURITY ROLE

The Software Updates Report Reader.xml file contains an XML export for the Software Updates Report Reader security role. This file is provided as additional content for this book (see Appendix C).

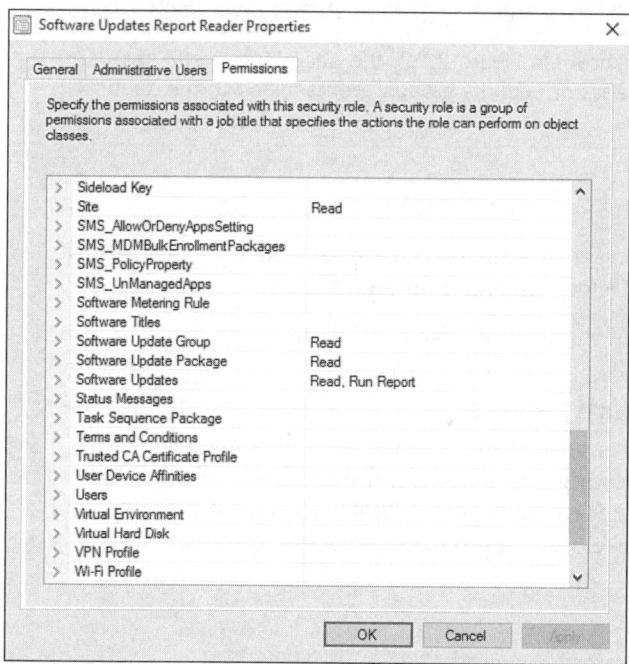

FIGURE 2.20   Software Updates Report Reader permissions.

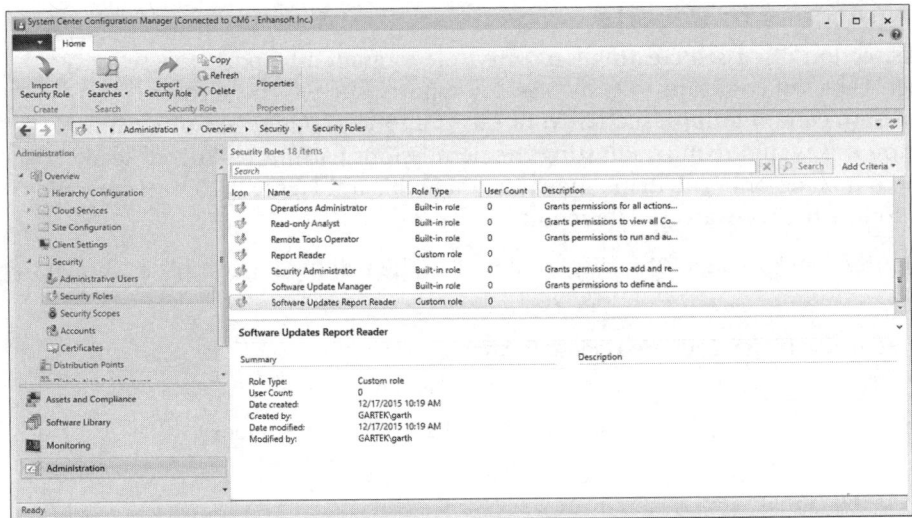

FIGURE 2.21   The Software Updates Report Reader security role listed in the ConfigMgr console.

Removing a Security Role

You cannot remove a security role that has members assigned to it. Be sure to first remove all AD users and security groups assigned to a security role before you try to remove it.

NOTE: WARNING WHEN TRYING TO DELETE A SECURITY ROLE

If you receive the warning message shown in Figure 2.22, the security role still has users associated with it. Ensure that no users or security groups are assigned to the security role before trying to remove it.

To remove a security role, perform the following steps:

1. In the ConfigMgr console, navigate to **Administration -> Security -> Security Roles**. Right-click the role and select **Delete**, as shown in Figure 2.23.

2. Click **Yes** to confirm deletion of the security role (see Figure 2.24).

Exporting and Importing Security Roles

Best practices call for a development environment maintained separately from your production environment. When following best practices, the security role previously created in the "Creating a ConfigMgr Security Reporting Role" section of this chapter would have been created within a development environment.

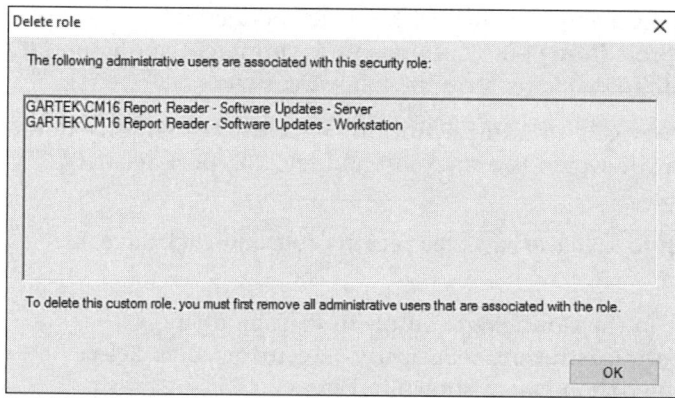

FIGURE 2.22   Warning message when trying to delete a role that has users associated with it.

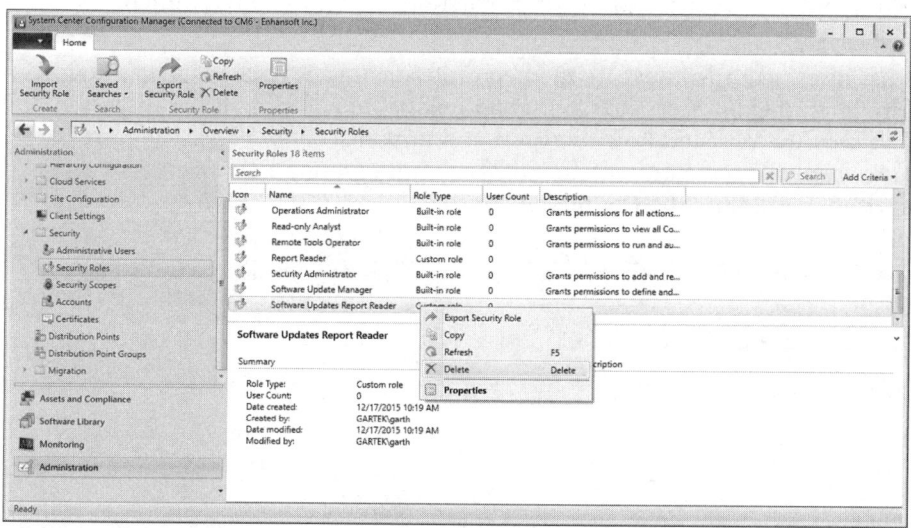

FIGURE 2.23   Selecting the option to delete a security role.

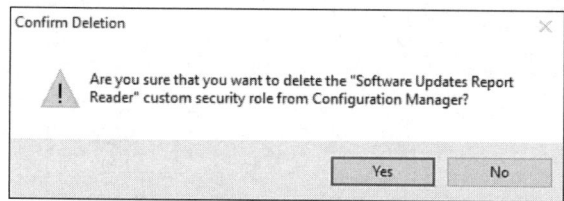

FIGURE 2.24   Warning message asking you to confirm deletion.

To ensure that exactly the same role is implemented within your production environment, export the security role from your development environment and import it into the production environment. To do so, perform the following steps:

1. In the ConfigMgr console, navigate to **Administration -> Security -> Security Roles**. Right-click the security role you would like to export and select **Export Security Role**, as shown in Figure 2.25.

2. Select the location to which to save the exported security role and click **Save**, as shown in Figure 2.26.

3. To import the security role, in the ConfigMgr console in your production environment, navigate to **Administration -> Security -> Security Roles**. Select **Import Security Role** on the ribbon bar, as shown in Figure 2.27.

4. Locate and select the security role XML file exported from your development environment to the file system and click **Open**, as shown in Figure 2.28. The security role is imported into your production ConfigMgr environment.

This section has discussed how to create the Report Reader and Software Updates Report Reader security roles to grant access to ConfigMgr reports. In addition, it has discussed how to remove security roles and how to export and import security roles. The next section discusses applying a security role to an AD security group to allow users to access SSRS reports without accessing the ConfigMgr console.

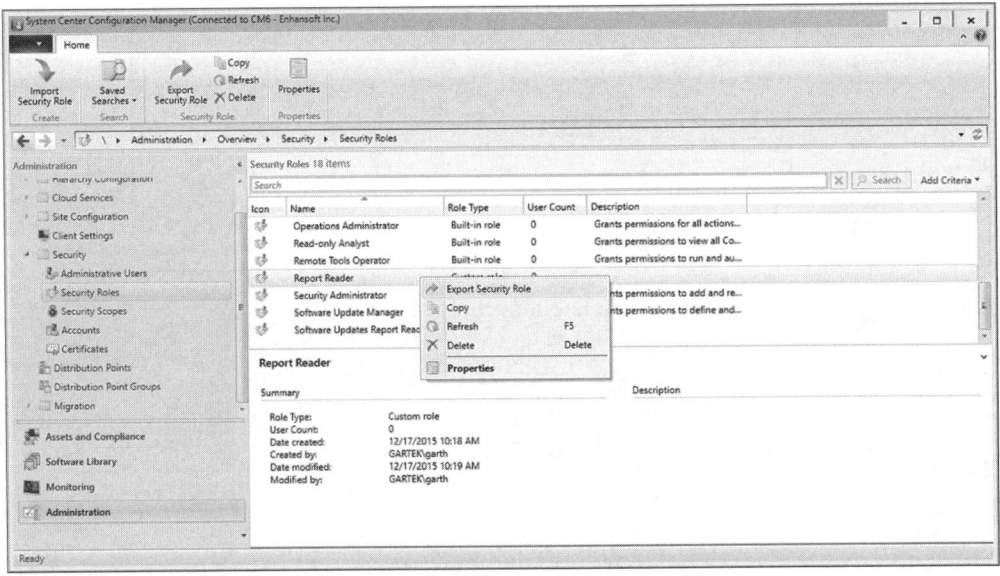

FIGURE 2.25   The Export Security Role option.

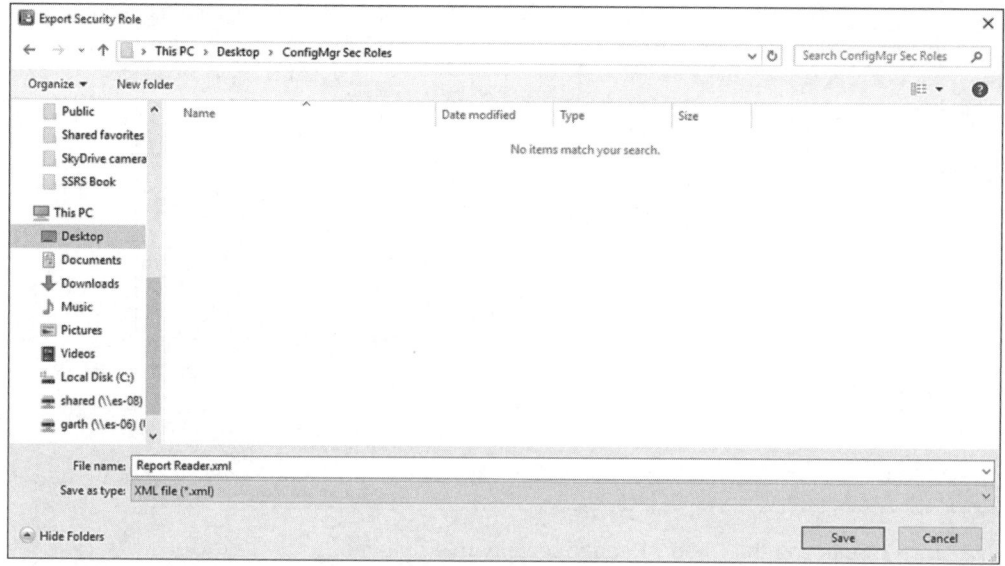

FIGURE 2.26   Saving the Report Reader security role.

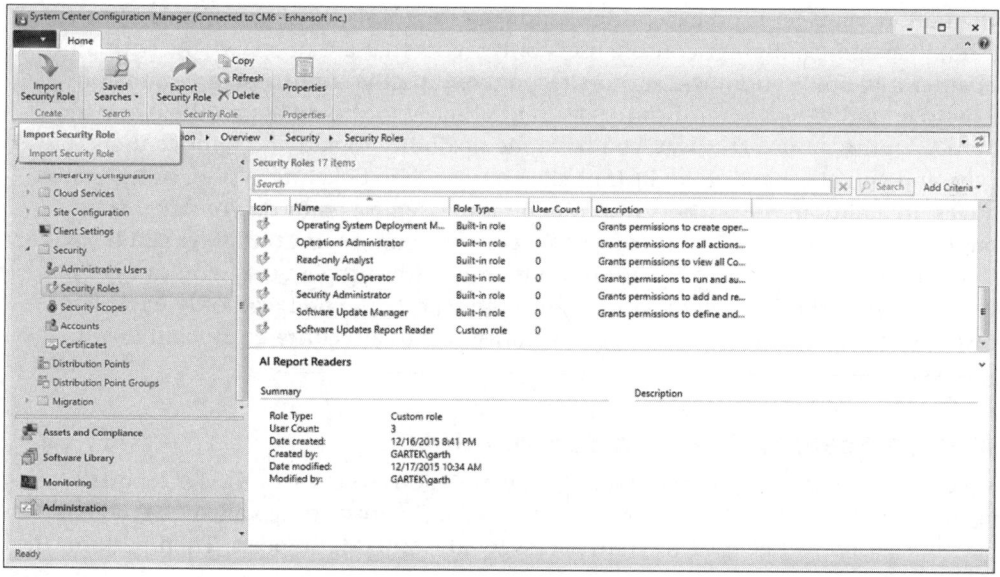

FIGURE 2.27   Importing a security role.

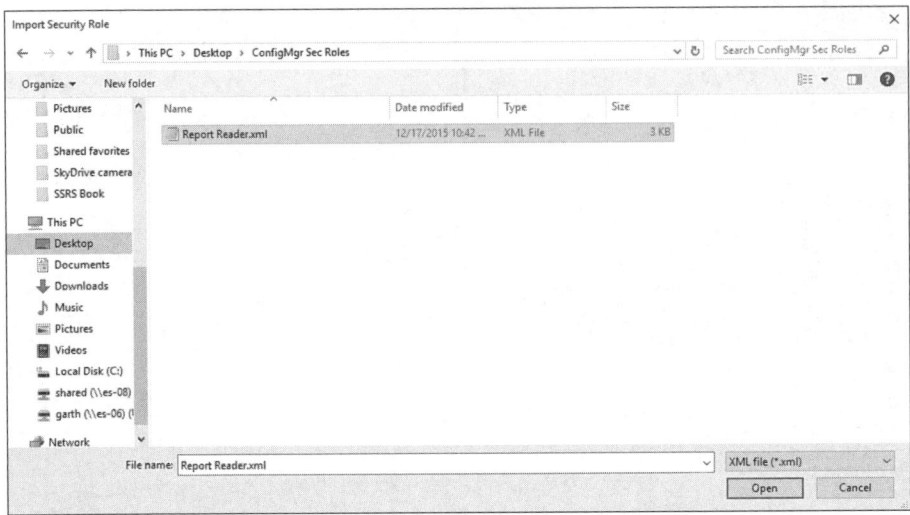

FIGURE 2.28   Selecting the Report Reader security role XML file.

Working with Security Roles

Security is an important part of any enterprise application, and System Center Configuration Manager is no exception. Following the principle of granting least privilege, you should assign ConfigMgr console users only rights that are necessary. As with any other enterprise application, the authors recommend that you not assign permissions directly to an individual administrator or user; rather, you should assign the permissions to an AD security group. This way you have the flexibility to add and remove users quickly, and you also have an audit trail via a service desk ticketing system or AD status messages. In addition, the authors recommend not assigning your day-to-day user accounts access to the ConfigMgr console where any changes to ConfigMgr can be made. If a user needs to access read-only information only within the reports, you can grant rights to access to the SSRS reports only, since the reports provide read-only data. The following sections discuss how to apply a security role to a security group and how to remove permissions.

Applying a Security Role to a Security Group

This section discusses the process of granting permissions to the ConfigMgr reports using an AD security group. Begin by creating an AD security group called CM16 Report Reader; this group will be used to grant access to all ConfigMgr reports. Then perform the following steps:

1. In the ConfigMgr console, navigate to **Administration -> Security -> Administrative Users**.

2. Click **Add User or Group** in the ribbon bar. When the Add User or Group window opens, click **Browse** (see Figure 2.29).

3. Select the **CM16 Report Reader** security group, as shown in Figure 2.30, and click **OK**.

4. In the Add User or Group window, click **Add** next to the Assigned security roles text box (see Figure 2.31).

5. Select the Report Reader check box in the Add Security Role window and click **OK** (see Figure 2.32).

6. In the Add User or Group window, shown in Figure 2.33, click **OK** to complete this task.

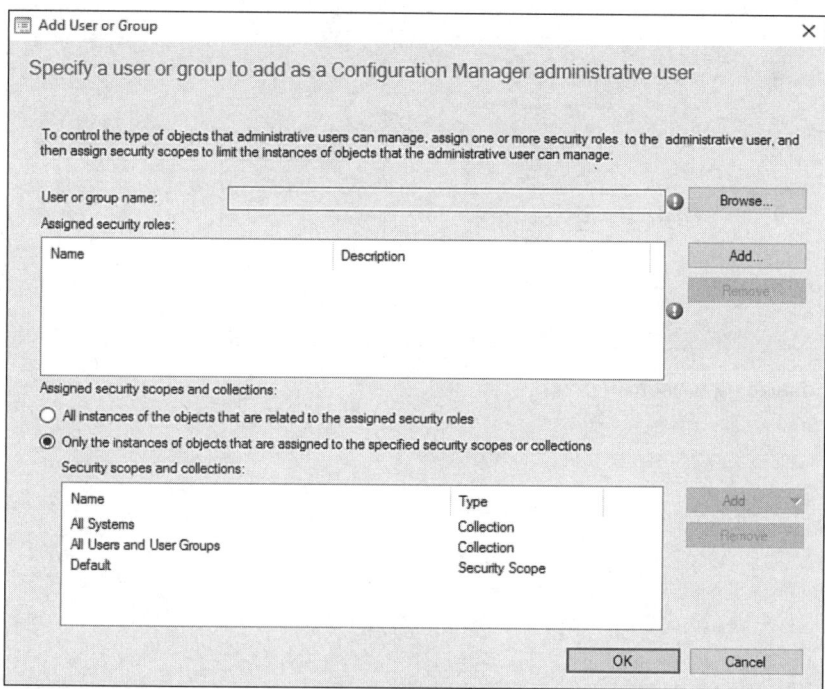

FIGURE 2.29   Add User or Group window.

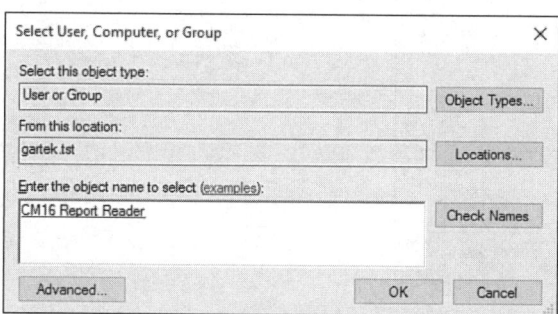

FIGURE 2.30   Selecting a user, computer, or group.

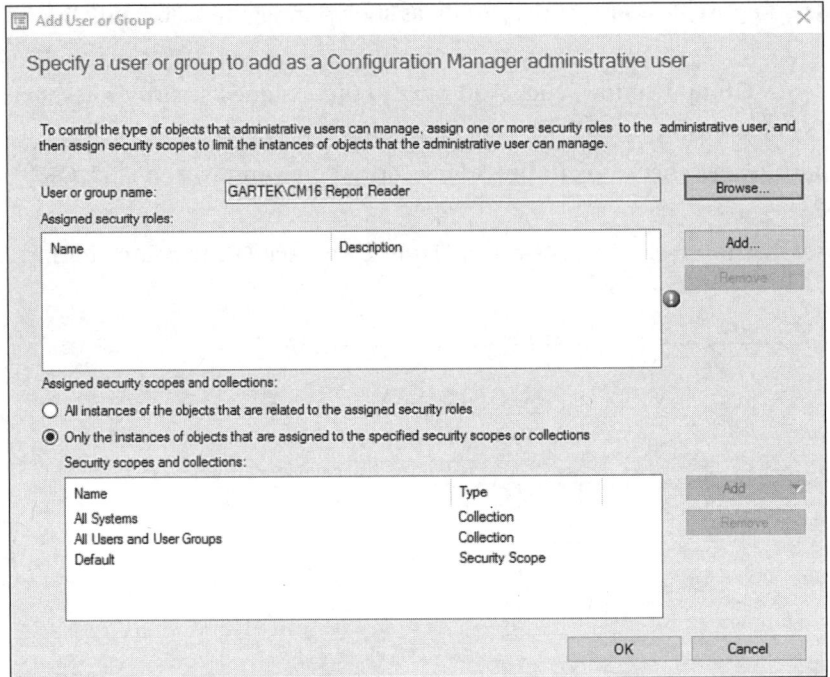

FIGURE 2.31   After assigning a user or group.

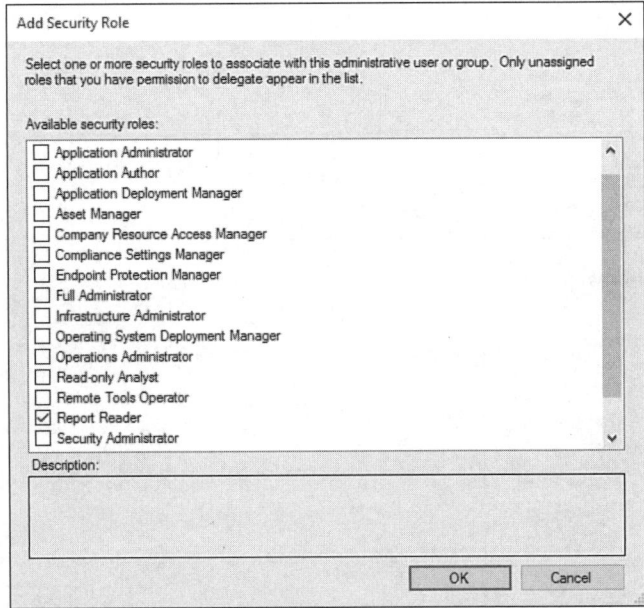

FIGURE 2.32   Adding a security role.

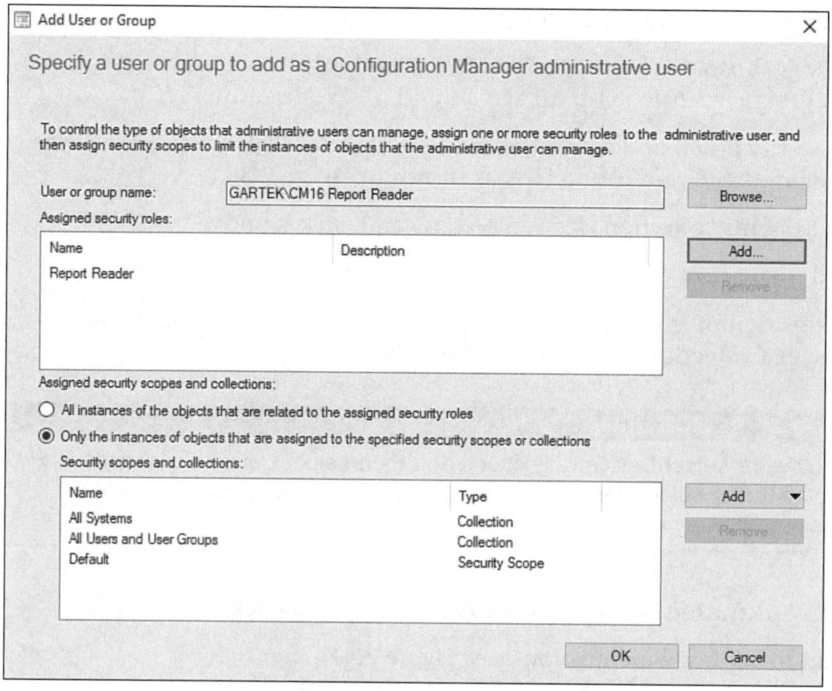

FIGURE 2.33 After assigning a security role to a user or group.

In the ConfigMgr console, navigate to **Administration** -> **Security** -> **Administrative Users** to view the permissions assigned to the CM16 Report Reader AD security group, as shown in Figure 2.34.

According to the principle of least privilege for providing access to software update reports to only the server and workstation security teams, you would create two AD security groups:

- CM16 Report Reader - Software Updates - Server
- CM16 Report Reader - Software Updates - Workstation

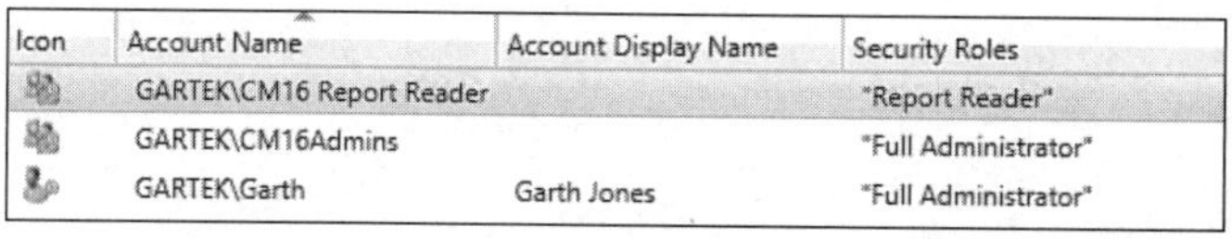

Icon	Account Name	Account Display Name	Security Roles
	GARTEK\CM16 Report Reader		"Report Reader"
	GARTEK\CM16Admins		"Full Administrator"
	GARTEK\Garth	Garth Jones	"Full Administrator"

FIGURE 2.34 Permissions assigned to the CM16 Report Reader AD Security Group.

Follow these steps to create these security groups:

1. In the ConfigMgr console, navigate to **Device Collections**. Figure 2.35 shows the two collections that currently exist: All Servers and All Workstations.

2. Add the AD security group and assign the Software Updates Report Reader security role. At this point, the wizard would look as shown in Figure 2.36.

3. Select the **All Systems** collection (see Figure 2.37) and click **Remove**.

4. Click **Add** and then select **Collection** from the dropdown (see Figure 2.38).

5. In the top-left section of the window, click the User Collections dropdown menu and select **Device Collections** as shown in Figure 2.39.

NOTE: NAVIGATING TO DEVICE COLLECTIONS

It would seem intuitive to select Device Collections and then select Device Collections again, but here you actually select the User Collections dropdown menu and then select Device Collections.

---

6. Select the **All Workstations** collection (see Figure 2.40) and click **OK**.

7. Click **OK** again to apply the permissions (see Figure 2.41).

8. Repeat the process to apply permissions to the CM16 Report Reader - Software Updates - Server AD users group, as shown in Figure 2.42.

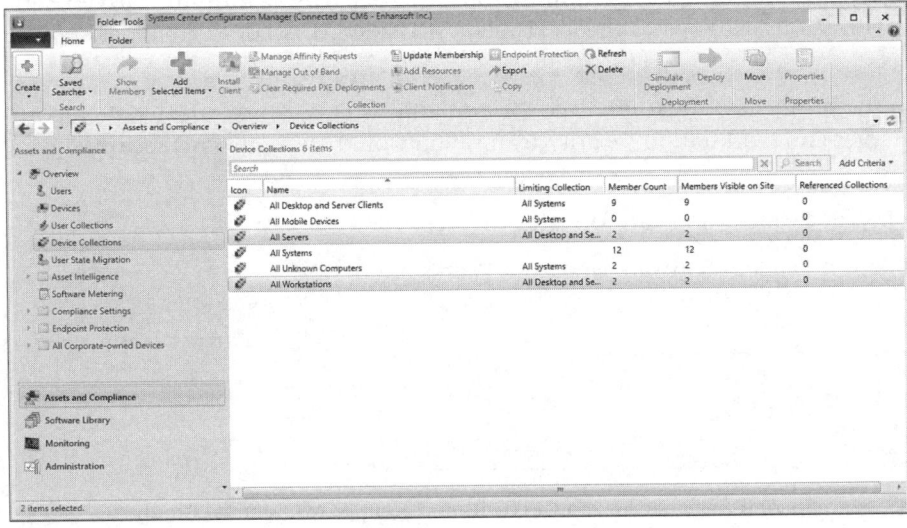

FIGURE 2.35   The All Servers and All Workstations collections.

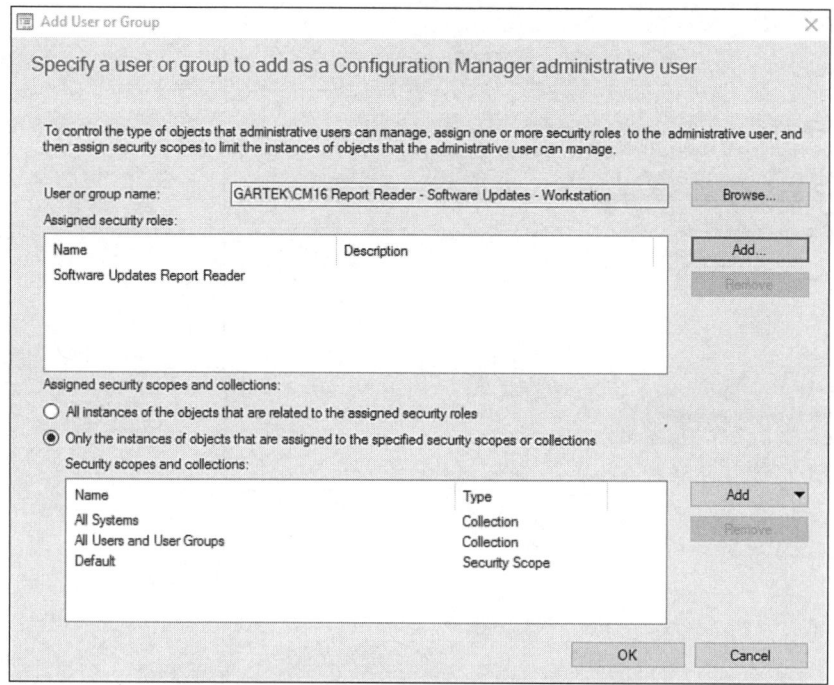

FIGURE 2.36 Assigning the Software Updates Report Reader security role to CM16 Report Reader - Software Updates - Workstation.

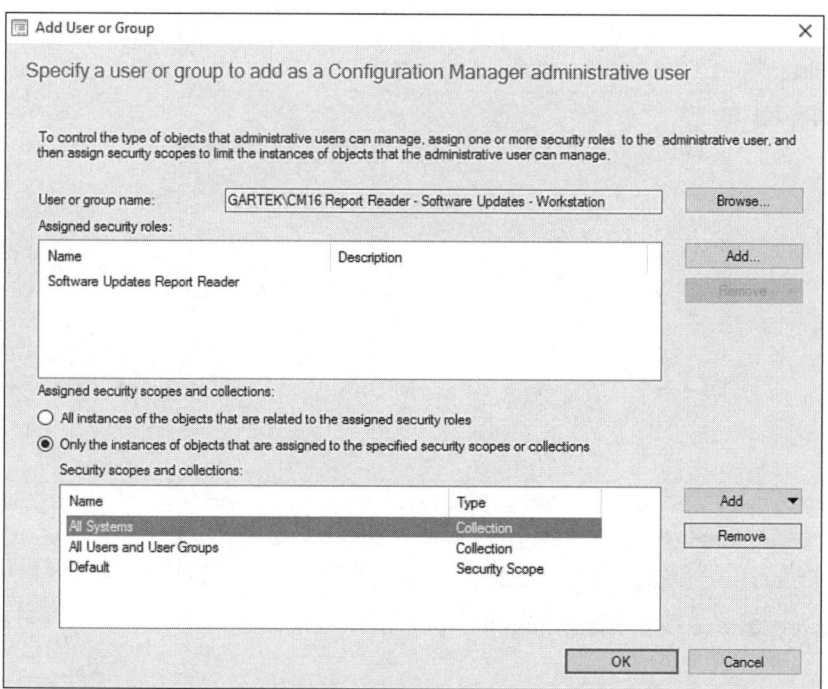

FIGURE 2.37 Removing the All Systems collection.

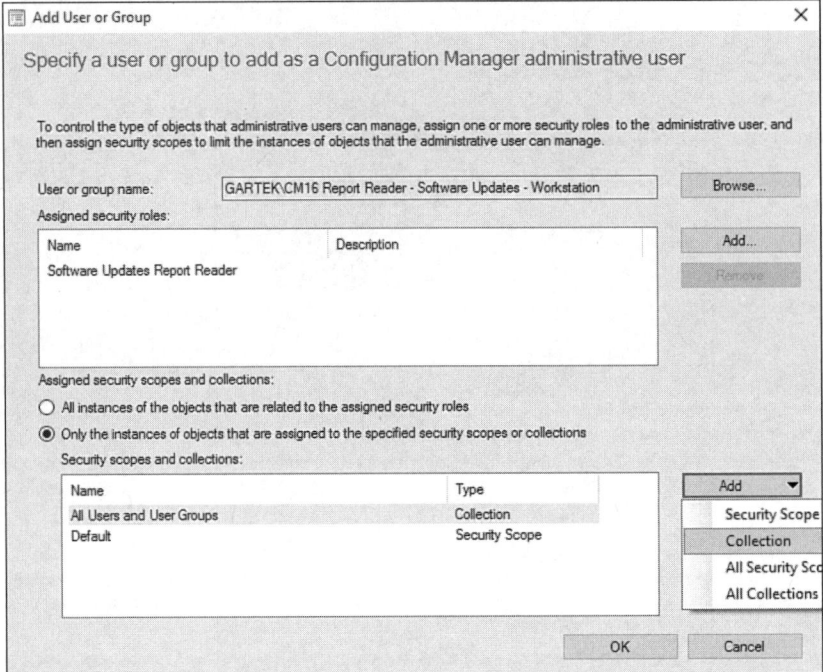

FIGURE 2.38   Adding a collection.

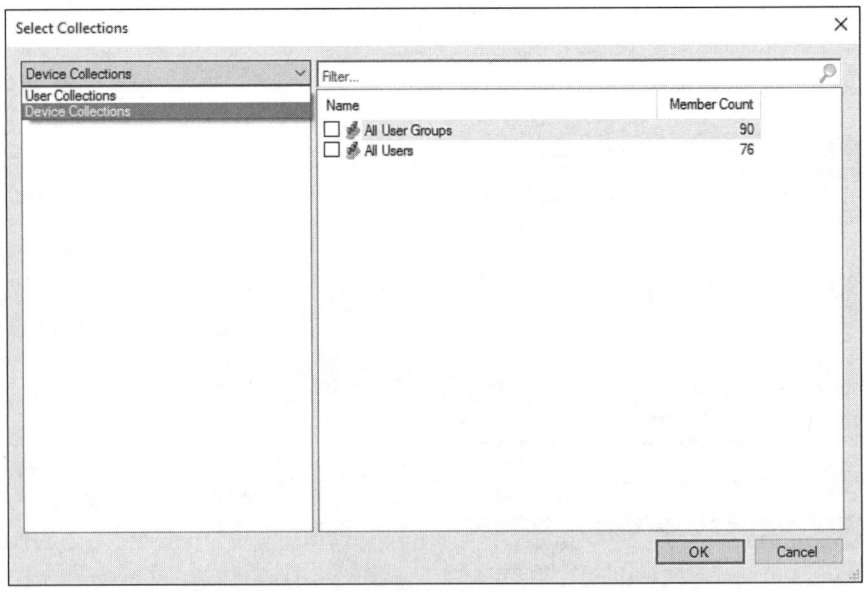

FIGURE 2.39   Selecting **Device Collections** from the dropdown menu.

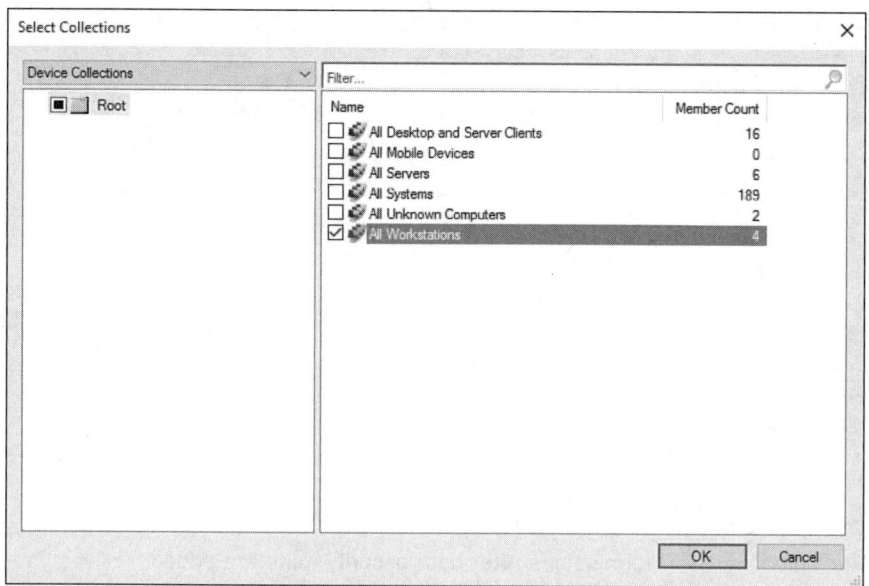

FIGURE 2.40   Selecting the **All Workstations** collection.

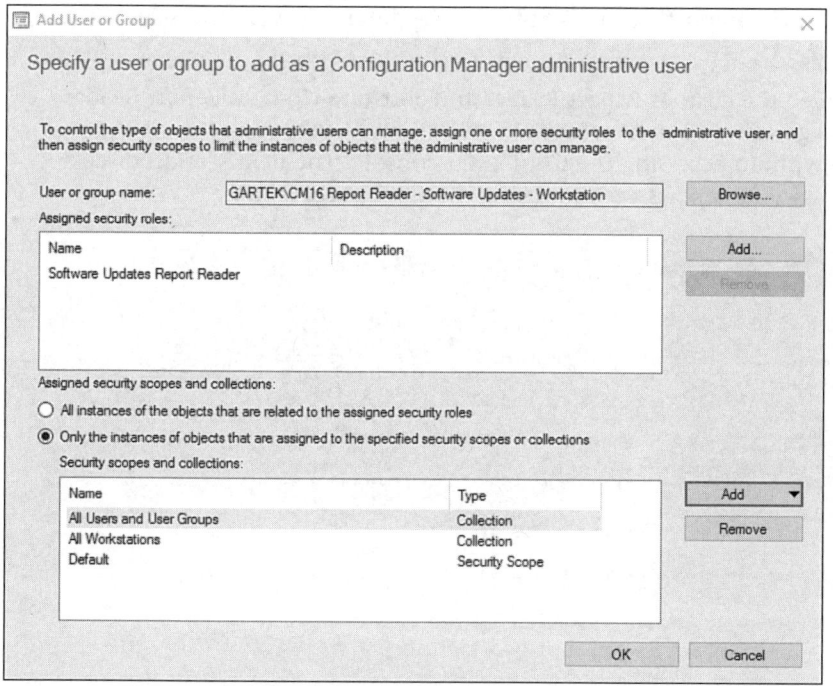

FIGURE 2.41   Adding a user or group to the All Workstations collection.

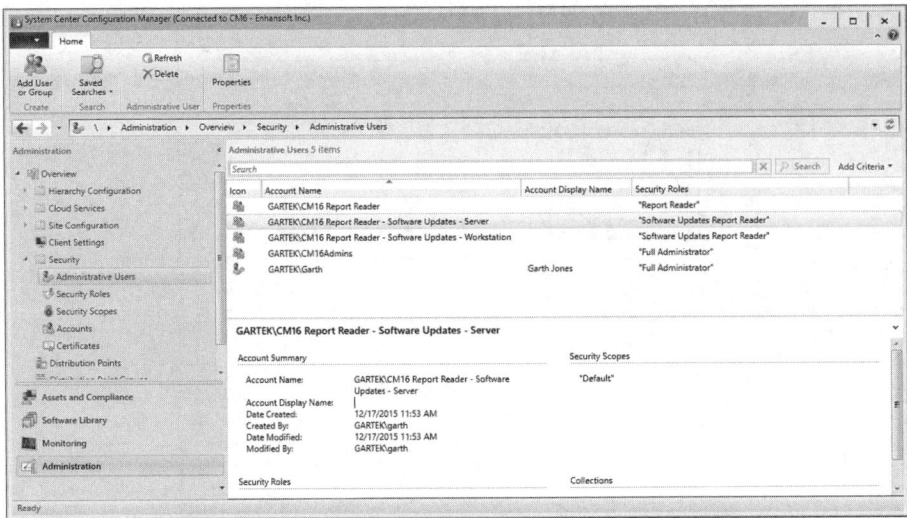

FIGURE 2.42   Administrative user permissions after both security roles are added.

Removing Permissions

To completely remove permissions from an AD security group or user, right-click the group (in this case **CM16 Report Reader - Software Updates - Server**) and select **Delete**, as shown in Figure 2.43.

You have now applied the custom Report Reader and Software Updates Report Reader security roles to AD groups and the appropriate collections. A user can now view ConfigMgr reports without accessing the ConfigMgr console. The next section discusses how a user can access SSRS reports without using the ConfigMgr console.

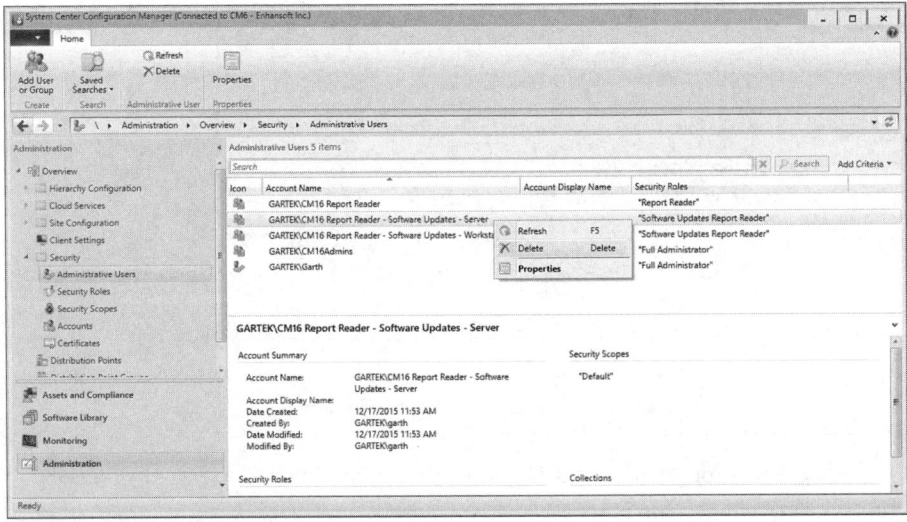

FIGURE 2.43   Deleting an AD security group from the ConfigMgr Administrative Users node.

Accessing ConfigMgr Reports

Providing users a simple way to access ConfigMgr reports is important to ensure that they can access the information in a timely and efficient manner.

To access ConfigMgr reports from a workstation, open Internet Explorer (IE) and enter the URL to your SSRS site, which is typically http://<*SSRS servername*>/reports (see Figure 2.44).

At the main SSRS site, click ConfigMgr_<*SiteCode*> to expose the ConfigMgr report categories. View the report titled Count physical disk configurations, found under the Hardware - Disk category and shown in Figure 2.45.

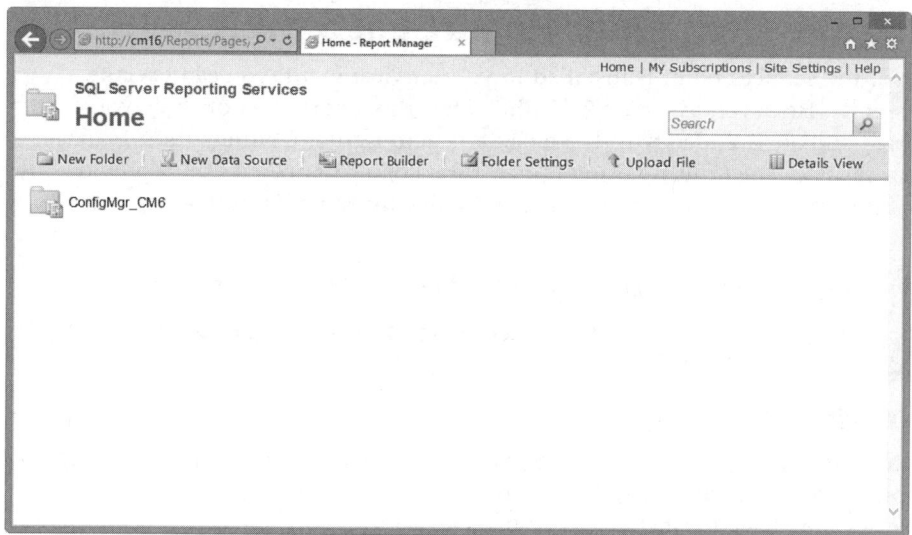

FIGURE 2.44   Viewing the ConfigMgr SSRS reporting website.

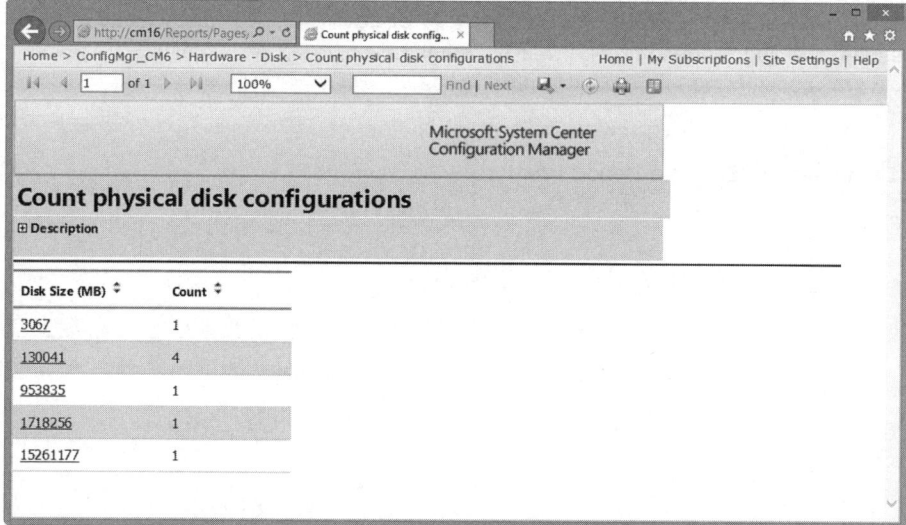

FIGURE 2.45   Results of the Count physical disk configurations report.

TIP: ACCESSING CONFIGMGR REPORTS FROM YOUR SITE SERVER

To avoid any User Account Control (UAC) issues, launch Internet Explorer in an elevated mode. This ensures that your account can access ConfigMgr reports. Note that this issue does not occur on remote computers.

This section has shown how to access the ConfigMgr reports from a remote computer through a browser, thereby allowing for easy and efficient access to the ConfigMgr data without the user needing to access the ConfigMgr console.

Changing the ConfigMgr Report Logo

Once the reporting services point is installed in your environment, you can execute the default reports. However, as Figure 2.45 illustrates, the reports do not show your company's logo and are branded with the default System Center Configuration Manager logo. You can easily change this by using Enhansoft's Logo Changer, a utility provided by the authors. This free tool allows you to change the default reports to use logos that you specify.

Before learning how to use the tool, you first need to understand these technical details:

▶ The report header is broken into three sections, as shown in Figure 2.46, with the default sizes listed in Table 2.3.

▶ All image files must be PNG files.

▶ Both the Left and Right image locations automatically adjust their sizes to match the image size. The Center image location does not adjust its size; it stretches or compresses the image to fit the 367×72-pixel space.

TIP: CONFIGMGR REPORTS DEFAULT IMAGE SIZES

For best results, the authors recommend that all images files be 72 pixels high. Otherwise, a gray background fills the extra pixel area.

TABLE 2.3   Default Image Size in a Report Header

Location	Size (pixels)
Left	20×72
Center	367×72
Right	225×72

Table 2.4 and Figure 2.46 demonstrate the three image file locations, the significance of image sizes, and how those locations adjust their sizes based on the file image size:

▶ Table 2.4 shows that the image files are solid blue, red, and green, with each image file having a size of 100×72 pixels.

▶ Notice in Figure 2.46 that the blue image extends the left image area by 80 pixels and that the center image expands to fill the 367×72-pixel area. The right image fills only 100 pixels of the 225-pixel area; the remaining area is filled with the default gray color.

TABLE 2.4   Demonstration Image Sizes

Image Color	Location	Size (pixels)
Blue	Left	100×72
Green	Right	100×72
Right	Center	100×72

Once the images are uploaded to your SSRS site, compare Figure 2.47 and Figure 2.48 and notice the following items:

▶ The blue image has expanded the left image area to become 100×72 pixels.

▶ The red image has stretched to fill the 367×72-pixel area.

▶ The green image uses only the 100×72-pixel area or the 225×72-pixel area. Gray color fills in the remaining area at the end of the header.

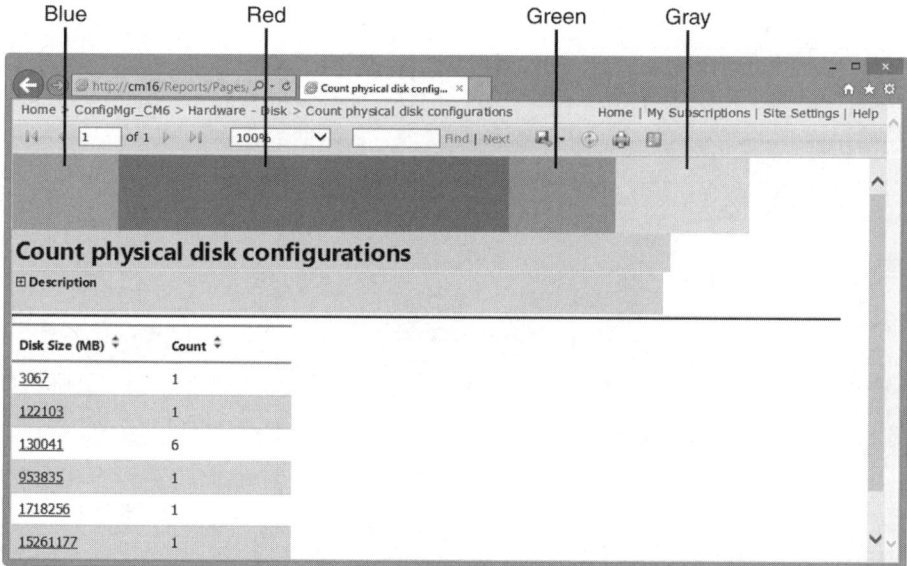

FIGURE 2.46   Blue, Red, Green, and Gray images replacing the default ConfigMgr logo header.

With the background information addressed, you can now quickly customize the default ConfigMgr reports to be more to your liking. To change the default logo in your ConfigMgr reports using Enhansoft's Logo Changer, follow these steps:

1. Log on to the Enhansoft site and download the Logo Changer from http://www.enhansoft.com/customer-area. If you don't have an account, you need to create one.

2. To avoid UAC issues, execute Logo Changer in elevated mode on your ConfigMgr site server.

3. Browse for your image (PNG) files for each location—left, center, and right—as shown in Figure 2.47. Click **Upload**.

> **TIP: SSRS SERVER DETAILS**
>
> When executed on your ConfigMgr site server, Enhansoft's Logo Changer automatically detects your SSRS Reporting Services String, ConfigMgr Report Folder, and SQL Port. If any of these details are incorrect, adjust them before clicking the Upload button.

4. Click **OK** to acknowledge that the image files have been uploaded to your SSRS site. The Logo Changer closes automatically.

5. Browse to your SSRS site and execute one of the default reports to confirm that the image files are uploaded correctly and look as expected. Figure 2.48 shows an example.

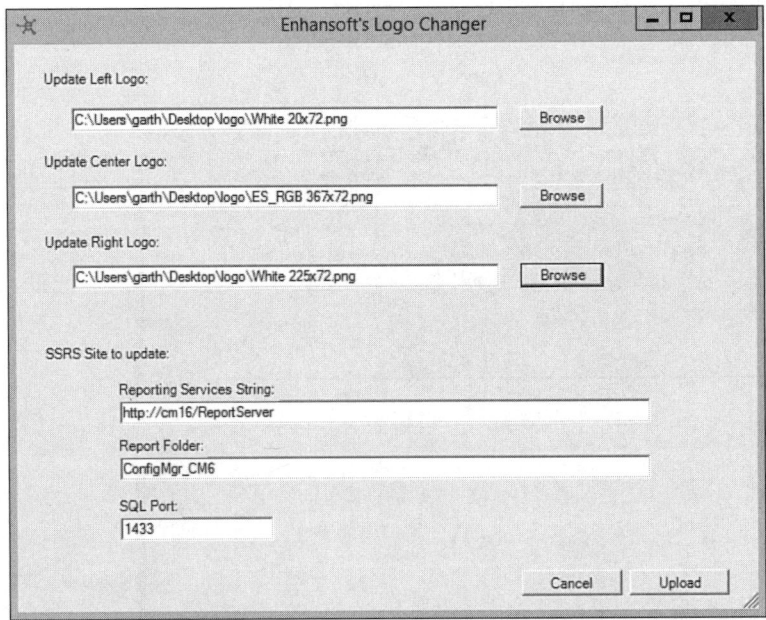

FIGURE 2.47   Browsing for image files with Enhansoft's Logo Changer.

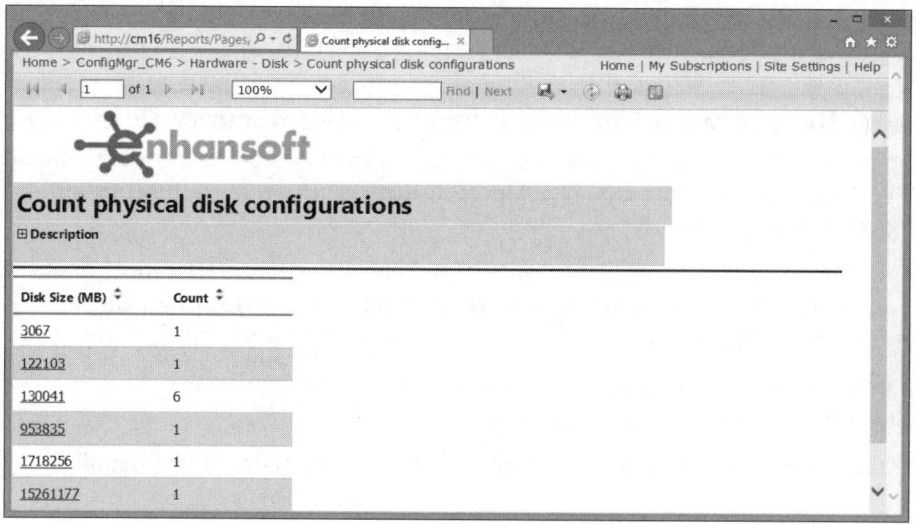

FIGURE 2.48   ConfigMgr's default report logo changed to a custom logo.

TIP: RESTORING DEFAULT IMAGES

If you need to restore the default Microsoft ConfigMgr image files, you can find those files stored on your SSRS site server, in the SMS_SRSRP\style folder.

Repeat the process of running the Enhansoft Logo Changer, this time selecting the original image files.

Demonstrating Creating and Assigning ConfigMgr Security Roles

The purpose of this part of the chapter is to help you become familiar with creating and assigning ConfigMgr security roles. In each of the following sections, you will create and assign an AD security group to the ConfigMgr security role. Use the information explained throughout this chapter to perform these tasks.

Working with the Report Reader Security Role

After creating the AD security group in step 1, access the ConfigMgr console to create and assign the ConfigMgr Report Reader security role. Follow these steps:

1. Create an AD security group called **ConfigMgr Report Reader** and assign a test user account to this group.

2. Copy the Read-only Analyst security role and name the new security role **Report Reader**.

3. Adjust the permissions for the role to match those in Table 2.1, earlier in this chapter.

4. Assign the AD security group called ConfigMgr Report Reader to the Report Reader ConfigMgr security role, with access to All Systems collection.

Working with the Software Updates Report Reader Security Role

After creating the two AD security groups in step 1, access the ConfigMgr console to create and assign the ConfigMgr Software Updates Report Reader security role to the appropriate AD security groups. Follow these steps:

1. Create two AD security groups called **ConfigMgr Report Reader - Software Updates - Server** and **ConfigMgr Report Reader - Software Updates - Workstation**. Create two different test user accounts and assign one to each of these new security groups.

2. Create two collections, one called **All Servers** for servers and one called **All Workstations**.

3. Import the Software Updates Report Reader.xml file. See Appendix C for details regarding this file.

4. Assign the ConfigMgr Report Reader - Software Updates - Server AD Security group to the Software Updates Report Reader ConfigMgr security role, with access to the All Servers collection.

5. Assign the ConfigMgr Report Reader - Software Updates - Workstation AD security group to the Software Updates Report Reader ConfigMgr security role, with access to the All Workstations collection.

Working with the Inventory Report Reader Security Role

Once the AD security group is created in step 1, access the ConfigMgr console to create and assign the ConfigMgr Inventory Report Reader security role to the AD security group. Follow these steps:

1. Create an AD security group called **ConfigMgr Inventory Report Reader** and assign a test user account to this AD security group.

2. Copy the Software Update Report Reader security role and call the new security role **Inventory Report Reader**.

3. Adjust the permissions for this ConfigMgr security role to match the permissions listed in Table 2.5.

4. Assign the ConfigMgr Inventory Report Reader AD security group to the Inventory Report Reader ConfigMgr security role with access to the All Systems collection.

TABLE 2.5   Permissions for Inventory Reports

Permission Title	Permissions
Collection	Read, Read Resources
Site	Read
Inventory Reports	Run Reports

Summary

This chapter has shown how to install the ConfigMgr reporting services point. It has discussed the importance of security and how to leverage ConfigMgr security roles and AD groups to adhere to the principle of least privilege required. You saw an example of this in the creation of the Software Updates Report Reader role to show only the computers in the All Workstation collection to the service desk team.

Keeping with the best practice of testing in a development environment, the chapter has discussed how you can leverage ConfigMgr's export and import feature. As discussed in this chapter, there is no need to deploy a ConfigMgr console to everyone who needs to view reports; instead, you can allow access to reports without the console. This chapter has also shown how you can replace the logo that comes with the default ConfigMgr reports with your own company's logo.

The next chapter reviews the most common and important data ConfigMgr classes as well as their corresponding SQL data views. It also discusses how to launch and connect to the ConfigMgr site database, as well as how to execute some sample queries using the SQL Server Management Studio tool.

2

PART II

About Data and Retrieval

IN THIS PART

Understanding Configuration Manager Data

Before discussing how to write reports, let's take a few steps back and consider where Configuration Manager (ConfigMgr) stores its inventory data and how to find that information.

As you may know, ConfigMgr collects a large amount of data out-of-the-box. Understanding how data is collected and stored within the site database can help you produce SQL Server Reporting Services (SSRS) reports that expose this raw data. This chapter discusses the major ConfigMgr data classes and how those classes are used, and it outlines some sample SQL views and queries. It also introduces you to the SQL Server Management Studio tool.

Using Data Classes and SQL Views

Many SQL database administrators (DBAs) prefer to use SQL tables rather than views. The question arises: *Is it better to use a SQL table or a SQL view for queries in ConfigMgr reporting?* The short answer is that Microsoft only supports using SQL views to access ConfigMgr data. Here's a longer answer:

▶ Microsoft does not support creating queries against SQL tables because of the risk of table locking issues. If you are running a query directly against a SQL table at the same time ConfigMgr is trying to update or write to that table, there is a possibility that the table will be locked by your query and the ConfigMgr update will fail.

▶ It is also best to use SQL views for reporting because Microsoft does not guarantee that SQL tables will remain the same after you install updates, service packs, or major version upgrades. If a table name is changed, removed, or modified, your reports might return errors or cease to run as intended. By referencing the ConfigMgr SQL views, all the reports, queries, and view names used throughout this book are accurate and work in all versions of ConfigMgr 2007, 2012, 2012 R2, and 1511 environments.

While this chapter provides examples of SQL views, it is impractical to cover all the SQL views. To obtain additional information on views used in ConfigMgr, you can reference Microsoft's ConfigMgr SQL schema via the following links:

▶ **ConfigMgr:** At this writing, ConfigMgr 1511 had recently been released, and as such, no official SQL schema had yet been released.

▶ **ConfigMgr 2012:** The ConfigMgr 2012 SQL schema can be referenced at http://technet.microsoft.com/en-us/library/dn581954.aspx.

▶ **ConfigMgr 2007:** Information on the ConfigMgr 2007 SQL schema is available at http://technet.microsoft.com/en-us/library/dd334611.aspx.

Using Discovery Classes

Discovery data generally comes from the following ConfigMgr discovery options:

▶ Active Directory System Discovery

▶ Active Directory User Discovery

▶ Heartbeat Discovery

▶ Network Discovery

You can enable and configure these discovery options for your environment in your ConfigMgr site. ConfigMgr discovery then begins gathering data based on your configurations—for example, gathering all systems from a specific Active Directory organization unit (OU) or domain. As a general rule, the SQL view for each of the discovery options starts with either v_R_* or v_RA_*. Table 3.1 lists the commonly used SQL views related to discovery classes.

TABLE 3.1   Discovery Data Views

SQL View	Description
v_R_System	Lists all systems discovered by ConfigMgr.
v_R_User	Lists all users discovered by ConfigMgr.
v_R_System_Valid	Lists all active clients within ConfigMgr. This is a subset of v_R_System.

> **TIP: CHANGING THE HEARTBEAT DISCOVERY CYCLE TO DAILY**
>
> To increase the reliability of the data captured by ConfigMgr, you can change the heartbeat discovery cycle from 7 days (default) to daily. This change generally has no adverse effect.

The query shown in Listing 3.1 lists all computers and their last discovery times for heartbeat discovery. Figure 3.1 shows the results of Listing 3.1.

> **NOTE: SQL SOURCE FILES FOR THE LISTINGS IN THIS CHAPTER**
>
> The SQL queries included in this chapter are available as online content. See Appendix C, "Available Online," for additional information.

LISTING 3.1   Discovery Data Sample Query

```
SELECT
  RV.Netbios_Name0 as 'Pc Name',
  RV.User_Name0 as 'User Name',
  AGD.Agenttime as 'Discovery Time'
FROM
  dbo.v_R_System_Valid RV
  INNER JOIN dbo.v_AgentDiscoveries AGD ON RV.ResourceID = AGD.ResourceId
WHERE
  AGD.AgentName = 'Heartbeat Discovery'
ORDER BY
  RV.Netbios_Name0
```

	Pc Name	User Name	Discovery Time
1	ACERASPIRE	JYedid	2015-12-09 16:03:34.000
2	AZUREAD	jyedid	2015-11-14 14:18:41.000
3	CM12R2-CM6	NULL	2015-12-09 20:38:03.000
4	DELLE6430	jyedid	2015-12-09 16:38:26.000
5	ELLEN-PC	ellen	2015-12-08 23:03:07.000
6	ES-06	garth	2015-12-09 20:37:53.000
7	ES-08	Garth	2015-12-09 20:35:11.000
8	ES-10	NULL	2015-12-09 20:09:34.000
9	ES-20	Garth	2015-12-09 20:36:45.000
10	FRAME	frame	2015-08-31 21:35:36.000
11	GARTEK-DC10	NULL	2015-12-09 20:16:51.000
12	GARTEK-DC21	NULL	2015-12-09 20:19:56.000
13	GARTEK-DC5	jyedid	2015-12-09 20:22:47.000
14	GARTEK-DC9	NULL	2015-12-09 19:44:34.000
15	garth_Android_7/29/2015_6:16 PM	NULL	2015-09-01 14:00:44.000
16	Garth's iPhone	NULL	2015-12-09 02:33:51.000
17	GJ5	jyedid	2015-10-23 12:00:03.000
18	M6	garth	2015-12-09 20:14:51.000
19	M8	garth	2015-09-18 12:32:41.000

Query executed successfully.

FIGURE 3.1   Discovery data sample results.

3

Using Hardware Inventory Classes

As the title of this section implies, data within the hardware inventory classes is obtained from hardware inventory. However, hardware inventory covers additional data, including all the data collected from Windows Management Instrumentation (WMI), the Windows Registry, and the actual hardware details for each ConfigMgr client. These inventory classes will be the main source of data for most of your reports. While it may seem counterintuitive, almost every query uses data from hardware classes.

These inventory classes also maintain history data that you can use in your reports. None of the other inventory classes maintain history data. As a general rule, there are two SQL view name identifiers for these items:

▶ The SQL view names that start with v_GS_* identify the latest and current hardware inventory data.

▶ The v_HS_* views identify history data for the hardware inventory.

Table 3.2 and Table 3.3 list hardware inventory data views.

TABLE 3.2   Current Hardware Inventory Data Views

SQL View	Description
v_GS_COMPUTER_SYSTEM	Lists basic details about a computer, such as manufacturer, model, and user name.
v_GS_DISK	Provides details about hard drives attached to a computer.
v_GS_ADD_REMOVE_PROGRAMS	Provides details about 32-bit Add/Remove Programs data for computers.
v_GS_ADD_REMOVE_PROGRAMS_64	Provides details about 64-bit Add/Remove Programs data for computers.

TABLE 3.3   History Hardware Inventory Data Views

SQL View	Description
v_HS_COMPUTER_SYSTEM	Provides history data for the basic details of a computer.
v_HS_DISK	Provides history data for the hard drives attached to a computer.
v_HS_ADD_REMOVE_PROGRAMS	Provides history data for the 32-bit Add/Remove Programs data for computers.
v_HS_ADD_REMOVE_PROGRAMS_64	Provides history data for the 64-bit Add/Remove Programs data for computers.

There is one very important exception to the SQL views listed in Table 3.2 and Table 3.3 that doesn't start with v_GS_ or v_HS_—this is the v_Add_Remove_Programs view. This view provides exactly the same column information as v_GS_ADD_REMOVE_PROGRAMS and v_GS_ADD_REMOVE_PROGRAMS_64, with the data of both views combined. This view is extremely helpful for viewing both 32-bit and 64-bit Add/Remove Programs entries.

TIP: CHANGING HARDWARE INVENTORY CYCLE

To increase the reliability of the data captured by ConfigMgr, the authors recommend changing the hardware inventory cycle from 7 days (default) to daily. This change generally has no adverse effect on ConfigMgr server or client performance.

Although there are no hard-and-fast rules about setting the hardware inventory schedules, most ConfigMgr MVPs and senior consultants make the same recommendation for setting hardware inventory to daily. The authors estimate that there is 10% increase in database size and a minimal increase in CPU usage and disk input/output (I/O) when this change is made.

However, the value to an organization of having the most up-to-date inventory in most cases outweighs these minimal increases to database size, CPU usage, and disk I/O. As with any other changes to ConfigMgr, the authors recommend that you evaluate the value and impact to your company before making this change.

The query in Listing 3.2 lists all computers that have the software product Warranty Information Reporting v3 installed. To find a different software title, replace `Warranty Information Reporting v3` with the software title for which you are looking. Figure 3.2 shows the results of Listing 3.2.

LISTING 3.2   Hardware Inventory Sample Query

```
SELECT
    RV.Netbios_Name0 as 'Pc Name',
    RV.User_Name0 as 'User Name',
    ARP.DisplayName0 as 'Application Name',
    ARP.Version0 as 'Version',
    ARP.InstallDate0 as 'Install Date'
FROM
    dbo.v_R_System_Valid RV
    INNER JOIN dbo.v_Add_Remove_Programs ARP ON RV.ResourceID = ARP.ResourceID
WHERE
    ARP.DisplayName0 = 'Warranty Information Reporting v3'
ORDER BY
    RV.Netbios_Name0
```

	Pc Name	User Name	Application Name	Version	Install Date
1	ACERASPIRE	JYedid	Warranty Information Reporting v3	3.20	20150507
2	CM12R2-CM6	NULL	Warranty Information Reporting v3	3.22	20150708
3	CM12R2-CM6	NULL	Warranty Information Reporting v3	3.27	20151022
4	ES-20	Garth	Warranty Information Reporting v3	3.5.0.1	20150908
5	M8	garth	Warranty Information Reporting v3	3.11	20140813

FIGURE 3.2   Hardware inventory sample results.

Listing 3.3 shows a query that lists all computers where the hard drive size has changed from a previous inventory cycle. This query is a good example of how you can use the history SQL views and current hardware inventory views together in a single query. Figure 3.3 shows the results of Listing 3.3.

LISTING 3.3   Hardware Inventory History Sample Query

```
SELECT DISTINCT
  RV.Netbios_Name0 as 'Pc Name',
  RV.User_Domain0 as 'User Name',
  GD.DeviceID0 as 'Device ID',
  GD.Size0 as 'Current HD Size',
  HD.Size0 as 'Historic  HD Size'
FROM
  dbo.v_R_System_Valid RV
  INNER JOIN v_GS_DISK GD ON RV.ResourceID = GD.ResourceID
  INNER JOIN v_HS_DISK HD ON RV.ResourceID = HD.ResourceID
WHERE
  GD.Size0 <> HD.Size0 and GD.DeviceID0 = HD.DeviceID0
```

	Pc Name	User Name	Device ID	Current HD Size	Historic HD Size
1	SM12-DW	GARTEK	\\\\PHYSICALDRIVE0	204797	130041
2	WIN2K8	NT AUTHORITY	\\\\PHYSICALDRIVE1	262138	130041
3	win81-cm4	GARTEK	\\\\PHYSICALDRIVE0	262138	130041
4	win81-cm4	GARTEK	\\\\PHYSICALDRIVE1	51199	7161

FIGURE 3.3   Hardware inventory history sample results.

Using Software Inventory Classes

Data from software inventory classes comes from the software inventory action run by the ConfigMgr client on computers, which runs every seven days by default. This inventory gathers details from individual files. In the ConfigMgr software inventory settings, you define which file types will be inventoried (for example, *.exe from all hard drives). ConfigMgr stores details from the files inventoried, such as file name, version, size, path to the file, modified date, and so on. Table 3.4 lists the software inventory data views.

> **NOTE: IMPACT OF USING THE SOFTWARE INVENTORY DATA VIEWS**
>
> Try to avoid using the software inventory classes. You might think that based on their name, these would be the most popular set of SQL views, but this is not the case. There are many reasons, in the authors' opinion, why these views are not popular, but the most important is that the process of gathering the data to populate these SQL views is extremely slow, and clients will notice their hard drive being accessed for extended periods of time during the data-gathering process. Unlike the hardware inventory classes or the heartbeat discovery class, which take less than four minutes to run without clients even noticing that the inventory process is running on their computer, the software inventory classes can run for hours and hours.

TABLE 3.4   Current Software Inventory Data Views

SQL View	Description
v_GS_LastSoftwareScan	Provides status details about the last software scan cycle.
v_GS_SoftwareFile	Provides details about all inventory files.

The query in Listing 3.4 provides a count of Internet Explorer versions. Figure 3.4 shows the results of Listing 3.4.

LISTING 3.4 Software Inventory Sample Query

```
SELECT
  SF.FileName,
  replace(left(SF.FileVersion,2), '.','') as 'IE Version',
  Count (Distinct SF.ResourceID) as 'Total Installs'
FROM
  dbo.v_GS_SoftwareFile SF
  INNER JOIN dbo.v_FullCollectionMembership fcm ON SF.ResourceID=FCM.ResourceID
WHERE
  SF.FileName = 'iexplore.exe'
  and SF.FilePath like '%Internet Explorer%'
GROUP BY
  SF.FileName,
  replace(left(SF.FileVersion,2), '.','')
ORDER BY
   'IE Version'
```

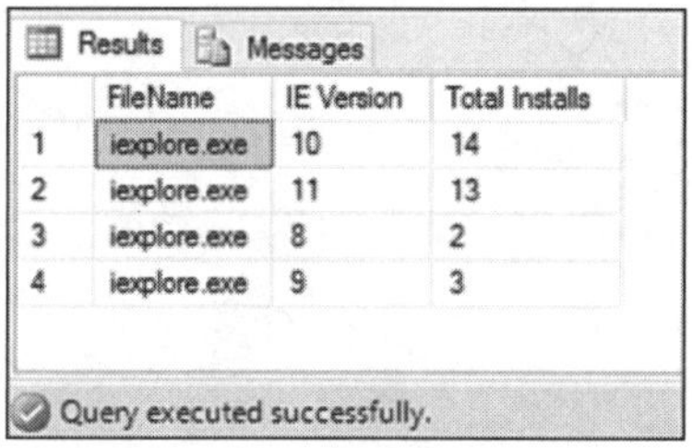

	FileName	IE Version	Total Installs
1	iexplore.exe	10	14
2	iexplore.exe	11	13
3	iexplore.exe	8	2
4	iexplore.exe	9	3

Query executed successfully.

FIGURE 3.4 Software inventory sample results.

TIP: CHANGING THE SOFTWARE INVENTORY CYCLE

The authors recommend turning off the software inventory cycle due to its overhead. However, if you keep it on, change it from 7 days (default) to run every 14 to 21 days in order to improve performance.

Using Software Update Inventory Classes

Software update reports are among the hardest reports to write. Writing a single software update SSRS report could take from four hours to multiple weeks. The complexity of using these views is due to the way the data is stored in ConfigMgr. The data spans multiple views that are required to be joined before the information is useful to the report reader. The primary views for software updates are listed in Table 3.5.

TABLE 3.5   Software Update Data Views

SQL View	Description
v_UpdateComplianceStatus	Provides compliance status details for each PC's software update.
v_CategoryInfo	Provides details about software update categories.

Listing 3.5 shows a query that provides a count of all missing software updates for each computer in the All Systems collection in ConfigMgr. Figure 3.5 shows the results of this query.

LISTING 3.5   Software Update Sample Query

```
SELECT DISTINCT
 CS.Name0,
 CS.UserName0,
 CASE
  when (sum(case when UCS.status=2 then 1 else 0 end))>0
   then ('Needs '+(cast(sum(case when UCS.status=2 then 1 else 0 end)
   as varchar(10))+ ' Patches'))
  else 'Good Client'
 end as 'Status',
 WS.lasthwscan as 'Last HW scan'
FROM
 dbo.v_UpdateComplianceStatus as UCS
 LEFT OUTER JOIN dbo.v_GS_COMPUTER_SYSTEM as CS
  on CS.ResourceID = UCS.ResourceID
 INNER JOIN v_CICategories_All as catall2
  on catall2.CI_ID = UCS.CI_ID
 INNER JOIN v_CategoryInfo as catinfo2
  on catall2.CategoryInstance_UniqueID = catinfo2.CategoryInstance_UniqueID
  and catinfo2.CategoryTypeName = 'UpdateClassification'
 LEFT OUTER JOIN v_GS_WORKSTATION_STATUS as WS
  on ws.resourceid = CS.ResourceID
 LEFT OUTER JOIN dbo.v_FullCollectionMembership as FCM
  on FCM.ResourceID = CS.ResourceID
WHERE
 UCS.Status = '2'
 and FCM.CollectionID = 'SMS00001'
GROUP BY
 CS.Name0,
 CS.UserName0,
 WS.lasthwscan,
 FCM.CollectionID
ORDER BY
 CS.Name0,
 CS.UserName0
```

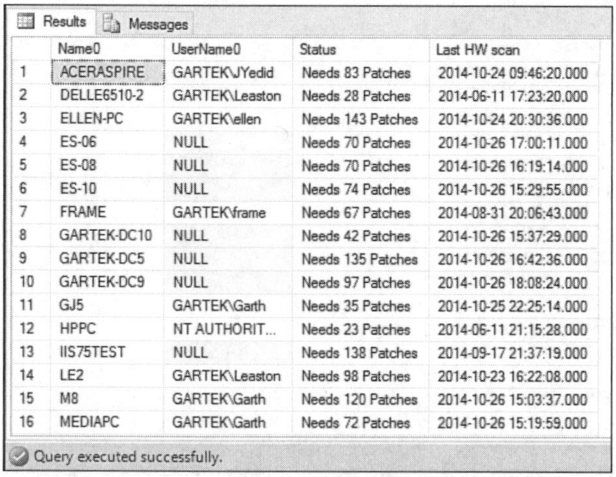
Results | Messages

	Name0	UserName0	Status	Last HW scan
1	ACERASPIRE	GARTEK\JYedid	Needs 83 Patches	2014-10-24 09:46:20.000
2	DELLE6510-2	GARTEK\Leaston	Needs 28 Patches	2014-06-11 17:23:20.000
3	ELLEN-PC	GARTEK\ellen	Needs 143 Patches	2014-10-24 20:30:36.000
4	ES-06	NULL	Needs 70 Patches	2014-10-26 17:00:11.000
5	ES-08	NULL	Needs 70 Patches	2014-10-26 16:19:14.000
6	ES-10	NULL	Needs 74 Patches	2014-10-26 15:29:55.000
7	FRAME	GARTEK\frame	Needs 67 Patches	2014-08-31 20:06:43.000
8	GARTEK-DC10	NULL	Needs 42 Patches	2014-10-26 15:37:29.000
9	GARTEK-DC5	NULL	Needs 135 Patches	2014-10-26 16:42:36.000
10	GARTEK-DC9	NULL	Needs 97 Patches	2014-10-26 18:08:24.000
11	GJ5	GARTEK\Garth	Needs 35 Patches	2014-10-25 22:25:14.000
12	HPPC	NT AUTHORIT...	Needs 23 Patches	2014-06-11 21:15:28.000
13	IIS75TEST	NULL	Needs 138 Patches	2014-09-17 21:37:19.000
14	LE2	GARTEK\Leaston	Needs 98 Patches	2014-10-23 16:22:08.000
15	M8	GARTEK\Garth	Needs 120 Patches	2014-10-26 15:03:37.000
16	MEDIAPC	GARTEK\Garth	Needs 72 Patches	2014-10-26 15:19:59.000

Query executed successfully.

FIGURE 3.5 Software update sample results.

Using Software Metering Inventory Classes

Data collected during the software metering inventory cycle is based on the software metering rules you create in ConfigMgr. As such, until at least one rule is created, no data appears within these SQL views. Table 3.6 lists the software metering data views.

TABLE 3.6 Software Metering Data Views

SQL View	Description
`v_MeterData`	Lists all gathered software metering data.
`v_MeteredProductRule`	Lists all software metering rules.

The query shown in Listing 3.6 displays the start and stop times for all software metering data beginning with a specific date, in this case February 16, 2013. Figure 3.6 displays an example of the results from executing this query.

LISTING 3.6 Software Metering Sample Query

```
SELECT
  RV.Netbios_Name0,
  MRIB.ProductName,
  MD.StartTime,
  MD.EndTime
FROM
  dbo.v_R_System_Valid RV
  INNER JOIN dbo.v_MeterData MD ON RV.ResourceID = MD.ResourceID
  INNER JOIN dbo.v_MeterRuleInstallBase MRIB ON MD.FileID = MRIB.MeteredFileID
WHERE
    MD.starttime > '2013-02-16'
```

Results | Messages

	Netbios_Name0	ProductName	StartTime	EndTime
1	DELLE6510	Internet Explorer	2013-09-05 19:40:39.847	2013-09-12 19:32:14.623
2	DELLE6510	Internet Explorer	2013-09-05 19:40:39.847	2013-09-12 19:32:14.623
3	DELLE6510	Internet Explorer	2014-01-09 15:25:51.000	2014-01-09 15:27:38.157
4	DELLE6510	Internet Explorer	2014-03-13 20:47:23.520	2014-03-20 20:47:23.707
5	GJ5	Internet Explorer	2014-10-20 01:11:09.000	2014-10-20 01:47:03.287
6	ACERASPIRE	Internet Explorer	2014-10-20 14:50:46.000	2014-10-20 19:42:57.127
7	ACERASPIRE	Internet Explorer	2014-10-20 14:50:46.000	2014-10-20 19:42:57.127
8	ACERASPIRE	Internet Explorer	2014-10-20 14:50:46.000	2014-10-20 19:42:57.127
9	ACERASPIRE	Internet Explorer	2014-10-20 14:50:46.000	2014-10-20 19:42:57.127
10	ACERASPIRE	Internet Explorer	2014-10-20 13:28:14.000	2014-10-20 14:42:28.277
11	ACERASPIRE	Internet Explorer	2014-10-20 13:28:14.000	2014-10-20 14:42:28.277

Query executed successfully.

FIGURE 3.6 Software metering sample results.

TIP: CREATING SOFTWARE METERING RULES

The authors recommend creating software metering rules for any software that has a significant cost and is not installed in the base image of your computers. It is best to create these rules as early as possible, as it takes approximately 75 days to get useful data from software metering reports.

It is not necessary or ideal to create software metering rules for products installed on every computer in your environment, such as Microsoft Word, due to the amount of overhead and data collected by the software metering Inventory.

Using Status Message Classes

Although status messages are not gathered from inventory classes, they contain the details and results of ConfigMgr client actions. For example, when a deployment is sent to a ConfigMgr client, it sends a status message back the ConfigMgr server, saying that it has received the deployment notice. When the ConfigMgr client starts to download an application, the client sends a status message indicating that the download has started. Table 3.7 lists the status message data views.

TABLE 3.7 Status Message Data Views

SQL View	Description
`v_StatusMessage`	Provides status messages. This view is generally used in conjunction with `v_StatMsgAttributes` and `v_StatMsgInsStrings` to get the complete status message information.
`v_StatMsgAttributes`	Lists the attributes for a status message.
`v_StatMsgInsStrings`	Lists status messages.

The query shown in Listing 3.7 returns the last ConfigMgr backup for each site server. Notice that the `stat.MessageID` is `5035`. Figure 3.7 shows the results of this query.

LISTING 3.7   Status Message Sample Query

```
SELECT
  stat.MachineName as 'Server',
  max(Time) as Time
FROM
  dbo.v_StatusMessage as stat
WHERE
  stat.Component = 'SMS_SITE_BACKUP'
  AND stat.MessageID = 5035
GROUP BY
    stat.MachineName
```

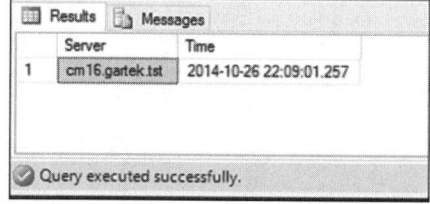

FIGURE 3.7   Status message sample results.

Using State Messages

Specific components of ConfigMgr clients use state messages to report details of a specific event, such as software updates, client health, and configuration items. State messages are broken into topic types, which identify the client component, and the StateID, which identifies a specific status for the component. Each topic type contains multiple state IDs. The v_StateName SQL view maps topic types and their respective state IDs to a descriptive state name. Popular views that use state messages are identified in Table 3.8.

TABLE 3.8   State Message Views

SQL View	Description
v_StateName	Maps topic types and their state IDs to descriptive names.
v_ClientHealthState	Provides the last client health state reported by ConfigMgr clients.
V_CIAssignmentStatus	Provides the evaluation state messages for assigned configuration items (CIs).
V_UpdateComplianceStatus	Provides the compliance state for software updates scanned by ConfigMgr clients.

The query shown in Listing 3.8 returns the last enforcement message for software updates scanned by the system named GJ5. Sample results from this query are shown in Figure 3.8.

LISTING 3.8   Software Update State Message Sample Query

```
SELECT
  sys.Name0,
  UI.ArticleID,
  UI.BulletinID,
  UI.Title,
  sn.StateName as Status
FROM
  v_UpdateComplianceStatus UCS
  JOIN v_UpdateInfo UI ON UCS.CI_ID = UI.CI_ID
  JOIN v_R_System sys ON UCS.ResourceID=sys.ResourceID
  JOIN v_StateNames sn ON UCS.LastEnforcementMessageID=sn.StateID
WHERE
  sys.Netbios_Name0 LIKE 'GJ5'
  AND sn.TopicType = '402'
ORDER BY
  ui.ArticleID,
  sn.StateName
```

	Name0	ArticleID	BulletinID	Title	Status
1	GJ5	2251481	MS11-049	Security Update for Microsoft Visual Studio 2005 Ser...	Successfully installed update
2	GJ5	2538242	MS11-025	Security Update for Microsoft Visual C++ 2005 Servi...	Successfully installed update
3	GJ5	2538243	MS11-025	Security Update for Microsoft Visual C++ 2008 Servi...	Successfully installed update
4	GJ5	2543854		Update for Microsoft Office 2003 (KB2543854)	Successfully installed update
5	GJ5	2635973		Update for Microsoft Visual Studio 2010 Service Pac...	Successfully installed update
6	GJ5	2645410	MS12-021	Security Update for Microsoft Visual Studio 2010 Ser...	Successfully installed update
7	GJ5	2850036		Service Pack 1 for Microsoft Office 2013 (KB285003...	Successfully installed update
8	GJ5	2917500		Security Update for Windows 8, 8.1 and Windows S...	Successfully installed update
9	GJ5	2931358	MS14-026	Security Update for Microsoft .NET Framework 3.5 o...	Successfully installed update
10	GJ5	923618		Office 2003 Service Pack 3 (SP3)	Successfully installed update
11	GJ5	932232		Visual Studio 2005 Service Pack 1 Update for Wind...	Successfully installed update
12	GJ5	976002		Microsoft Browser Choice Screen Update for EEA U...	Successfully installed update

Query executed successfully.

FIGURE 3.8   Software update state message sample results.

TIP: STATE MESSAGES

Refer to https://technet.microsoft.com/en-us/library/bb932203.aspx for a list of topic types and their state messages reported by ConfigMgr clients. Note that although the link is for ConfigMgr 2007, the information also applies to later versions of ConfigMgr.

Using Collection Data Classes

There are several SQL views for collection classes—one for each collection within your environment. From an administrator's perspective, however, there are only two SQL views you need to use, as shown in Table 3.9.

TABLE 3.9   Collection Data Views

SQL View	Description
v_Collection	Lists all collections and the CollectionID of each.
v_FullCollectionMembership	Lists the membership of each collection (user account, computer, and security group).

Running the query in Listing 3.9 provides a list of all computer names within the All Systems collection. Sample results are shown in Figure 3.9.

LISTING 3.9   Collection Data Sample Query

```
SELECT
  RV.Netbios_Name0,
  RV.User_Name0
FROM
  dbo.v_R_System_Valid RV
  INNER JOIN dbo.v_FullCollectionMembership FCM ON RV.ResourceID = FCM.ResourceID
  INNER JOIN dbo.v_Collection Coll ON FCM.CollectionID = Coll.CollectionID
WHERE
  Coll.Name = 'All Systems'
```

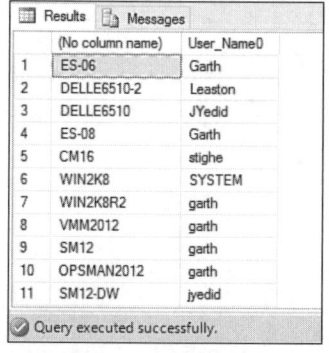

FIGURE 3.9   Collection data sample results.

Using Tools for Creating Reports

This section of the chapter explores the SQL Server Management Studio tool. This is the first of three major tools you can use to create reports for ConfigMgr. Chapter 1, "Installing SQL Server Reporting Services," detailed the steps for installing SQL Server Management Studio 2014.

Chapter 6, "Building a Basic Report," explains the two remaining tools:

▶ SQL Server Data Tools Business Intelligence (SSDT-BI) for Visual Studio 2013

▶ Report Builder

These tools are used to design SSRS reports for ConfigMgr as well as other System Center products, such as Operation Manager and Service Manager.

Introducing SQL Server Management Studio

Using the SQL Server Management Studio tool is the recommended way to create the queries required to build and design ConfigMgr reports. SQL Server Management Studio allows you to access, configure, manage, administer, and develop SQL Server components. It combines the features of Enterprise Manager, Query Analyzer, and Analysis Manager with script editors to provide access to SQL Server to administrators and developers of all skill levels. SQL Server Management Studio allows you to easily find SQL views and their columns in the ConfigMgr database. Using this tool, you can also write and execute queries as well as confirm results before creating a custom ConfigMgr report. Chapter 4, "Transact-SQL Primer," can help you become familiar with this core tool as well as how to write proper SQL queries.

Connecting to the ConfigMgr Database Server

Once the SQL Server Management Studio tool is installed on your workstation, launch it and follow these steps:

1. Connect to the database server used for ConfigMgr by entering the server name and clicking **Connect** (see Figure 3.10).

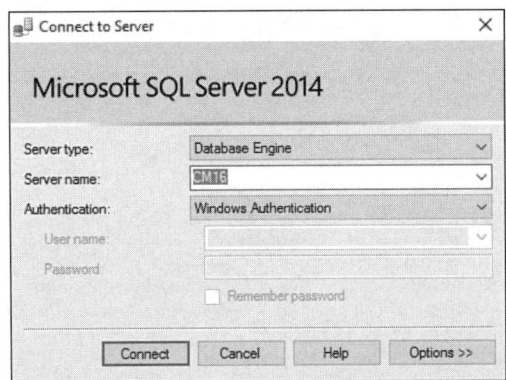

FIGURE 3.10   SQL Server Management Studio Connect to Server dialog.

TIP: PROBLEMS CONNECTING TO DATABASE

If you do not have the permissions required to connect to the database server, either run the SQL Server Management Studio tool using the RUN AS command and specify an account with the proper access or grant your user account the proper permissions on the SQL Server database.

---

2. Once connected, you see the main interface of SQL Server Management Studio, as shown in Figure 3.11.

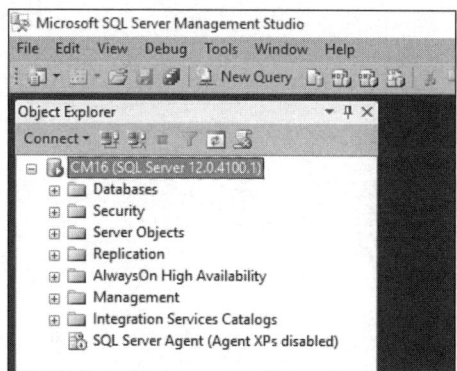

FIGURE 3.11   SQL Server Management Studio Object Explorer.

Executing a Query in SQL Server Management Studio

To create and execute a query, open a new query by clicking **New Query** in the SQL Server Management Studio menu bar. After the query page opens, it is important to make sure you change the database source to the ConfigMgr database. To do this, select the database from the dropdown menu, as shown in Figure 3.12.

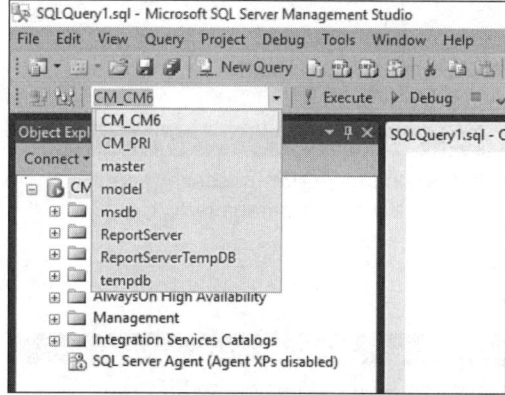

FIGURE 3.12   SQL Server Management Studio database dropdown menu.

Enter your query in the New Query page and click **Execute**. When you execute your query, the **Results** section appears at the bottom of your query page. Figure 3.13 shows an example of this section.

Using the Object Explorer

The Object Explorer, displayed on the left side of SQL Server Management Studio, provides the ability to drill down into the ConfigMgr database and get a list of all ConfigMgr views as well as the available columns that can be used within your queries. Notice that the expanded dbo.v_R_System_Valid view in Figure 3.14 contains many columns.

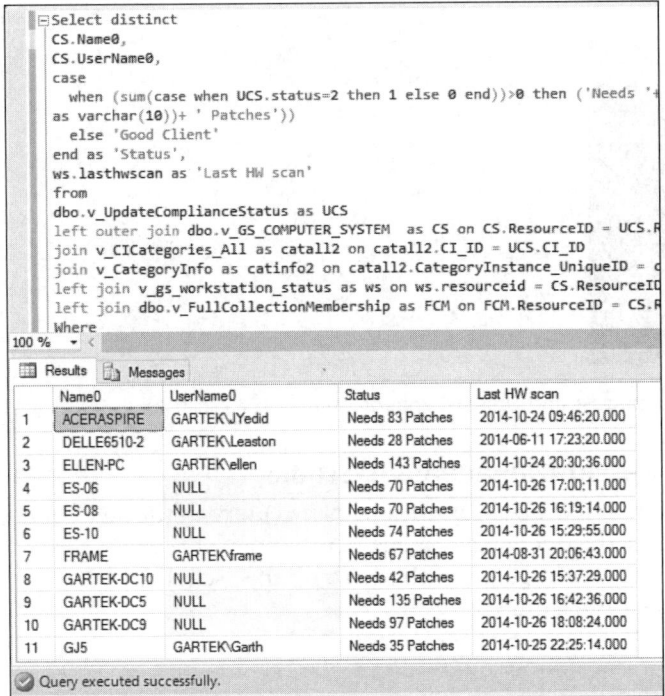

```
⊟Select distinct
  CS.Name0,
  CS.UserName0,
  case
    when (sum(case when UCS.status=2 then 1 else 0 end))>0 then ('Needs '+
  as varchar(10))+ ' Patches'))
    else 'Good Client'
  end as 'Status',
  ws.lasthwscan as 'Last HW scan'
  from
  dbo.v_UpdateComplianceStatus as UCS
  left outer join dbo.v_GS_COMPUTER_SYSTEM  as CS on CS.ResourceID = UCS.R
  join v_CICategories_All as catall2 on catall2.CI_ID = UCS.CI_ID
  join v_CategoryInfo as catinfo2 on catall2.CategoryInstance_UniqueID = c
  left join v_gs_workstation_status as ws on ws.resourceid = CS.ResourceID
  left join dbo.v_FullCollectionMembership as FCM on FCM.ResourceID = CS.R
  Where
```

	Name0	UserName0	Status	Last HW scan
1	ACERASPIRE	GARTEK\JYedid	Needs 83 Patches	2014-10-24 09:46:20.000
2	DELLE6510-2	GARTEK\Leaston	Needs 28 Patches	2014-06-11 17:23:20.000
3	ELLEN-PC	GARTEK\ellen	Needs 143 Patches	2014-10-24 20:30:36.000
4	ES-06	NULL	Needs 70 Patches	2014-10-26 17:00:11.000
5	ES-08	NULL	Needs 70 Patches	2014-10-26 16:19:14.000
6	ES-10	NULL	Needs 74 Patches	2014-10-26 15:29:55.000
7	FRAME	GARTEK\frame	Needs 67 Patches	2014-08-31 20:06:43.000
8	GARTEK-DC10	NULL	Needs 42 Patches	2014-10-26 15:37:29.000
9	GARTEK-DC5	NULL	Needs 135 Patches	2014-10-26 16:42:36.000
10	GARTEK-DC9	NULL	Needs 97 Patches	2014-10-26 18:08:24.000
11	GJ5	GARTEK\Garth	Needs 35 Patches	2014-10-25 22:25:14.000

Query executed successfully.

FIGURE 3.13   SQL Server Management Studio executed query with results.

TIP: INVALID OBJECT NAME ERROR MESSAGE

When executing a query, if you receive an "Invalid object name" error message (see Figure 3.15), it usually means that you forgot to change the target database to the ConfigMgr database (as shown in Figure 3.12).

TIP: CHANGING THE DEFAULT DATABASE IN SQL SERVER MANAGEMENT STUDIO

To permanently set the default SQL Server Management Studio database to be the ConfigMgr database, follow the instructions in the blog post at http://www.enhansoft.com/blog/invalid-object-name-in-sql-server-management-studio-ssms.

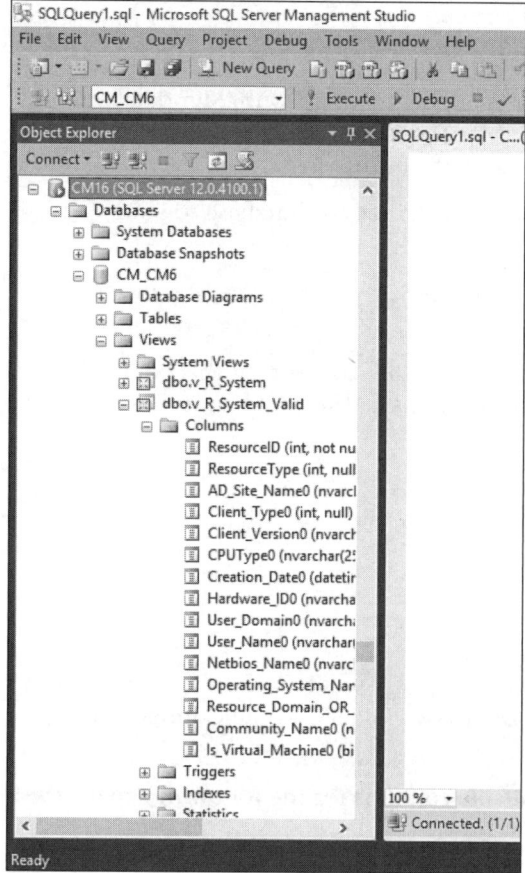

FIGURE 3.14   SQL Server Management Studio Object Explorer, showing columns.

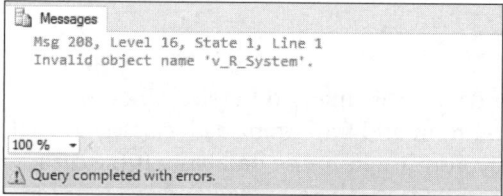

FIGURE 3.15   SQL Server Management Studio "invalid object name" error message.

Demonstrating SQL Server Management Studio

The purpose of this section is to help you become familiar with the SQL Server Management Studio tool discussed in this chapter. You will create and execute a query and look at views.

Creating and Executing a Query

Follow these steps to create and execute a query:

1. Open SQL Server Management Studio and connect to your ConfigMgr database server. See the "Connecting to the ConfigMgr Database Server" section of this chapter for detailed information on how to perform this step.

2. Using the dropdown list of available databases, change the database to your ConfigMgr site database.

3. Open a new query by clicking **New Query** in the SQL Server Management Studio menu bar.

4. Open the **PatchReport.txt** file provided in the online content for this book (see Appendix C for information) and then copy and paste the contents to the new query page.

5. Click **Execute** to execute the query.

6. Review the results.

Looking at Views

Follow these steps to look at a view:

1. Using the **Object Explorer**, expand the **Databases** folder and the ConfigMgr database.

2. Drill down into **Views** and note the available columns for the following table views:

   ▶ dbo.v_R_System

   ▶ dbo.v_GS_Computer_System

   ▶ dbo.v_Add_Remove_Programs

Summary

ConfigMgr gathers and stores a large amount of data across many different tables in its database. This chapter has reviewed the most common and important data classes, as well as their corresponding SQL data views, which are also stored in the database. It has also discussed how to launch and connect to the ConfigMgr database as well as execute some sample queries, using the SQL Server Management Studio tool.

Many sample queries have been provided in this chapter. Some of these queries are fairly simple and others a bit more complex. Don't worry about trying to understand how to write them just yet! Detailed explanations and examples about how to write SQL queries will be given in later chapters.

CHAPTER 4

Transact-SQL Primer

Transact-SQL, otherwise known as SQL or T-SQL, is the language used to query SQL Server databases. As a Configuration Manager (ConfigMgr) administrator, you should already be familiar with collection queries, which use Windows Management Instrumentation (WMI) Query Language (WQL). Since WQL is a subset of SQL, there are many similarities between the two languages. However, they are two separate and distinct languages.

This chapter is important for a couple of reasons:

▶ SQL Server Reporting Services (SSRS) uses SQL queries to create the reports that everyone from a ConfigMgr administrator to C-level managers will use to make informed decisions.

▶ SQL is a nondiscriminatory language; it allows you to create and execute queries that could have a serious impact on the performance of your SQL Server. Worse yet, it can provide you with inaccurate results.

This chapter discusses the basics of SQL queries. It provides an understanding of what is required to successfully write your own SQL queries. Using the guidance in this chapter, you can create SQL queries by incorporating best practices for ConfigMgr reporting, providing optimal performance and reliable and expected results.

The chapter also covers the structure of a basic SQL query; it discusses and demonstrates using operators such as DISTINCT and GROUP BY. It illustrates how to work with date and time functions and how to translate the resulting data into a more usable result. This chapter also discusses and demonstrates using JOIN statements. Appropriate use of the JOIN statement alone can provide the most significant performance improvement in SQL queries, ensuring that the results are appropriate and accurate yet with minimal performance impact on your SQL Server.

Understanding the Basic SQL Sections in a Query

SQL queries are composed of four major sections:

▶ SELECT

▶ FROM

▶ WHERE

▶ ORDER BY

These sections form the basic core of a SQL query. Not all these sections are mandatory to obtain results from a query, but they are strongly recommended for producing clear and easy-to-read results.

This chapter uses the query in the PatchReport.txt file introduced in Chapter 3, "Understanding Configuration Manager Data" (available as online content for this book; see Appendix C, "Available Online"), to break down and analyze each of these sections. The query is provided in Listing 4.1.

LISTING 4.1   Patch Report Sample

```
SELECT distinct
  CS.Name0,
  CS.UserName0,
  CASE
    when (sum(case when UCS.status=2 then 1 else 0 end))>0 then
      ('Needs '+(cast(sum(case when UCS.status=2 then 1
      else 0 end)as varchar(10))+ ' Patches'))
    else 'Good Client'
  end as 'Status',
  ws.lasthwscan as 'Last HW scan'
FROM
  dbo.v_UpdateComplianceStatus as UCS
  LEFT OUTER JOIN dbo.v_GS_COMPUTER_SYSTEM as CS
    on CS.ResourceID = UCS.ResourceID
  JOIN v_CICategories_All as catall2
    on catall2.CI_ID = UCS.CI_ID
  JOIN v_CategoryInfo as catinfo2
    on catall2.CategoryInstance_UniqueID
    = catinfo2.CategoryInstance_UniqueID
    and catinfo2.CategoryTypeName = 'UpdateClassification'
  LEFT JOIN v_gs_workstation_status as ws
    on ws.resourceid = CS.ResourceID
  LEFT JOIN v_FullCollectionMembership as FCM
    on FCM.ResourceID = CS.ResourceID
WHERE
  UCS.status = '2'
```

LISTING 4.1   Patch Report Sample

```
  and FCM.CollectionID = 'SMS00001'
GROUP BY
  CS.Name0,
  CS.UserName0,
  ws.lasthwscan,
  FCM.CollectionID
ORDER BY
  CS.Name0,
  CS.UserName0
```

Using the SELECT Statement

A SQL query starts with the SELECT section. This section is used to indicate the columns within a SQL view that will be included in the results of a query. Notice that you must separate columns with commas.

Listing 4.2 shows the SELECT section of the query shown in Listing 4.1. Executing the full query in Listing 4.1 displays the computer names, user names, count of missing software updates (status), and last hardware inventory scan data (Last HW scan) of systems in your environment. Each of these columns is identified in Listing 4.2.

> **TIP: SQL INTRODUCTION NOTE**
>
> This chapter is a general primer for T-SQL; it does not discuss every possible T-SQL feature, function, or option. This SQL primer is designed to provide an understanding of virtually everything you could need for ConfigMgr report writing. As such, T-SQL items that you would not normally see in a ConfigMgr environment are not covered in this book.

LISTING 4.2   The SELECT Section of a SQL Query

```
SELECT distinct
  CS.Name0,
  CS.UserName0,
  CASE
    when (sum(case when UCS.status=2 then 1 else 0 end))>0 then
      ('Needs '+(cast(sum(case when UCS.status=2 then 1
      else 0 end) as varchar(10))+ ' Patches'))
    else 'Good Client'
  end as 'Status',
  ws.lasthwscan as 'Last HW scan'
```

Using the FROM Statement

The FROM section of a query indicates the SQL views within the ConfigMgr database used to find the data. When you join multiple views together, this section also defines the common column between views, allowing the query results to display one row of data that spans multiple views.

Listing 4.3 shows the FROM section of the query shown in Listing 4.1. As shown, data is gathered from several SQL views and, as indicated by the ON statement, the views are linked together via a common column. This example is retrieving data from the v_UpdateComplianceStatus and v_GS_COMPUTER_SYSTEM views. In order for the results to have unique rows containing columns from both of these views, you should connect them on the ResourceID column, which is common to both.

LISTING 4.3   The FROM Section of a SQL Query

```
FROM
  dbo.v_UpdateComplianceStatus as UCS
  LEFT OUTER JOIN dbo.v_GS_COMPUTER_SYSTEM as CS
    on CS.ResourceID = UCS.ResourceID
  JOIN v_CICategories_All as catall2
    on catall2.CI_ID = UCS.CI_ID
  JOIN v_CategoryInfo as catinfo2
    on catall2.CategoryInstance_UniqueID
    = catinfo2.CategoryInstance_UniqueID
    and catinfo2.CategoryTypeName = 'UpdateClassification'
  LEFT JOIN v_gs_workstation_status as ws
    on ws.resourceid = CS.ResourceID
  LEFT JOIN v_FullCollectionMembership as FCM
    on FCM.ResourceID = CS.ResourceID
```

Defining Criteria with the WHERE Statement

The WHERE section allows you to narrow your query results by defining criteria or filtering out unwanted data. Although technically an optional section in a SQL query, its use is strongly recommended in order to focus your results to the information you want to relay.

Listing 4.4 shows the WHERE section of the query in Listing 4.1. In this case, the query is only gathering data where the status value is equal to 2 and the computer objects are in the ConfigMgr collection where the CollectionID is SMS00001, better known as the default All Systems collection.

LISTING 4.4   The WHERE Section of a SQL Query

```
WHERE
  UCS.status = '2'
  and FCM.CollectionID = 'SMS00001'
```

Using ORDER BY

The ORDER BY section allows for results to be sorted by columns, in a manner that makes sense to you. In most cases, each column is sorted in alphabetical order, from A to Z. Much like the WHERE section, ORDER BY is also optional in a SQL query; its use is also strongly recommended as it allows viewers to easily read the results because it can sort in alphabetical order. While incorporating ORDER BY may create a minimal delay in returning results as they must first be sorted, a sorted list is far more usable and readable than an unsorted list.

Listing 4.5 shows the ORDER BY section for the query in Listing 4.1. In this example, the results are sorted in alphabetical order, starting with the computer name (CS.Name0) column and then by the user name (CS.UserName0) column.

LISTING 4.5   The ORDER BY Section of a SQL Query

```
ORDER BY
  CS.Name0,
  CS.UserName0
```

Using Secondary Operators

Several secondary sections, or operators, can be used in SQL queries to further manipulate and focus the results. As you begin to use and become familiar with basic queries, incorporating these secondary operators will be key to further expanding and fine-tuning your reports:

▶ DISTINCT

▶ GROUP BY

▶ Aliases

▶ Operators

Once again, the query in Listing 4.1 demonstrates all these operators, and the following sections focus on each of them in turn.

Using the DISTINCT Keyword

The DISTINCT keyword is an operator used to remove any duplication of data from the results, thereby making each row unique. When writing ConfigMgr reports, you may need to search for a specific item, such as the display name of an application from Add/Remove Programs (v_Add_Remove_Programs). If you were to select all display names from v_Add_Remove_Programs, you would end up with hundreds of thousands of rows. When you add the DISTINCT operator after SELECT, as shown in Listing 4.6, only one unique row is returned for each display name.

LISTING 4.6   The DISTINCT Operator

```
SELECT DISTINCT
  CS.Name0,
  CS.UserName0,
  CASE
    when (sum(case when UCS.status=2 then 1 else 0 end))>0 then
      ('Needs '+(cast(sum(case when UCS.status=2 then 1
```

LISTING 4.6   The DISTINCT Operator

```
     else 0 end)as varchar(10))+ ' Patches'))
   else 'Good Client'
end as 'Status',
ws.lasthwscan as 'Last HW scan'
```

The GROUP BY Operator

You use the GROUP BY operator with a number of SQL actions, such as COUNT, SUM, AVG, MIN, and MAX. This section of a query allows you to combine rows together into groups. Listing 4.7 shows this operator grouping computer names (CS.Name0), user names (CS.UserName0), last hardware scan date (ws.lasthwscan), and collection ID (CollectionID) together so that they can be counted in the SELECT section to provide a numeric value for the missing updates.

LISTING 4.7   The GROUP BY Section of a SQL Query

```
GROUP BY
  CS.Name0,
  CS.UserName0,
  ws.lasthwscan,
  FCM.CollectionID
```

Using SQL View Aliases

Aliases allow you to temporarily rename a SQL view to something more meaningful and unique for the purpose of your query. In many cases, it is used to shorten the SQL view name to make it more manageable and easier to read. Aliases are identified as the text following as when specifying a SQL view under the FROM section. The boldface in Listing 4.8 indicates the use of aliases.

LISTING 4.8   Alias Examples

```
FROM
  dbo.v_UpdateComplianceStatus as UCS
  LEFT OUTR JOIN dbo.v_GS_COMPUTER_SYSTEM as CS
    on CS.ResourceID = UCS.ResourceID
  JOIN v_CICategories_All as catall2
    on catall2.CI_ID = UCS.CI_ID
  JOIN v_CategoryInfo as catinfo2
    on catall2.CategoryInstance_UniqueID
    = catinfo2.CategoryInstance_UniqueID
    and catinfo2.CategoryTypeName = 'UpdateClassification'
  LEFT JOIN v_gs_workstation_status as ws
    on ws.resourceid = CS.ResourceID
  LEFT JOIN v_FullCollectionMembership as FCM
    on FCM.ResourceID = CS.ResourceID
```

It is important to note that if you abbreviate a SQL view using an alias, you must refer to the view using the defined alias throughout the rest of the query. For example, if you shorten dbo.v_GS_COMPUTER_SYSTEM to CS, you must refer to CS in all sections of the query. If you use the original, long form instead of the alias in the SELECT section, you receive the error shown in Figure 4.1.

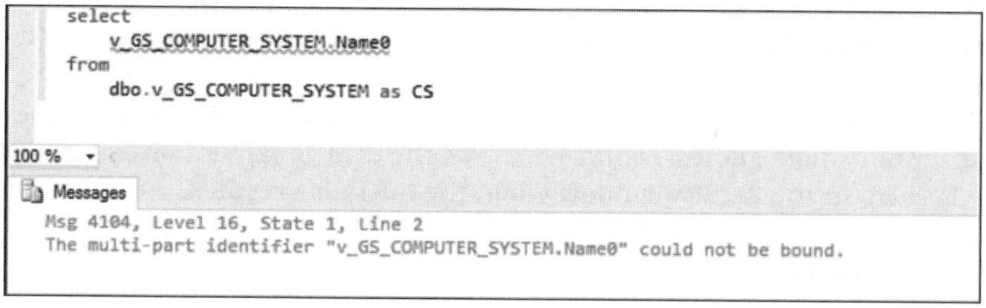

```
select
    v_GS_COMPUTER_SYSTEM.Name0
from
    dbo.v_GS_COMPUTER_SYSTEM as CS

100 %  ▾

Messages
  Msg 4104, Level 16, State 1, Line 2
  The multi-part identifier "v_GS_COMPUTER_SYSTEM.Name0" could not be bound.
```

FIGURE 4.1   Example of an alias error.

Using Operators

Operators allow you to perform arithmetic or logical operations within a query. They can help filter, identify, and manipulate data to return useful and more specific results. As in other programming languages, there are several different operators available for use. Table 4.1 lists the operators most commonly used in SQL queries.

TABLE 4.1   Common SQL Operators

Operator	Description
+	Addition
–	Subtraction
*	Multiplication
/	Division
=	Equals
>	Greater than
<	Less than
%	String wildcard, used in LIKE statements
AND	Logical AND, identifies multiple conditions that must be met
OR	Logical OR, identifies multiple conditions, one of which must be met
NOT	Logical NOT, opposite of the value or condition
LIKE	Logical LIKE, value matches a portion or pattern, used with wildcards
IN	Logical IN, equal to one of a list of values

TIP: COMPLETE LIST OF OPERATORS

For a complete list of available operators, see the SQL Operators section in the T-SQL online help, available at http://msdn.microsoft.com/en-us/library/ms174986(v=SQL.110).aspx.

Column Naming in Query Results

Every column in a SQL view has a default name. These names are assigned by developers and may not necessarily seem meaningful. Without clear column names, it could be challenging for readers who are not administrators or familiar with ConfigMgr to identify the results of a query.

For example, consider the `ws.Lasthwscan` column name, shown as part of the query in Listing 4.9. This column name is not meaningful for most report readers. However, you can give the column a more meaningful display name in the query results by using the AS operator after identifying a column in the SELECT section of the query, followed by the new display name, within single quotes. Figure 4.2 shows the display name `Last HW Scan`, instead of `ws.lasthwscan`, in the Results window when the query is executed.

LISTING 4.9   Column-Naming Example

```
SELECT DISTINCT
    CS.Name0,
    CS.UserName0,
    CASE
        when (sum(case when UCS.status=2 then 1 else 0 end))>0
        then ('Needs '+(cast(sum(case when UCS.status=2 then 1
        else 0 end)as varchar(10))+ ' Patches'))
        else 'Good Client'
    end as 'Status',
    ws.lasthwscan AS 'Last HW Scan'
```

CAUTION: QUOTATION MARKS WITH OPERATORS

Pay close attention to the single quotation marks when copying a query from a website or document as it might get replaced with a stylized (or "smart") single quote. You must be careful to always use ' instead of ' or '.

It might be difficult to notice the difference, but the last two quotes are stylized, and using either of them will result in an error.

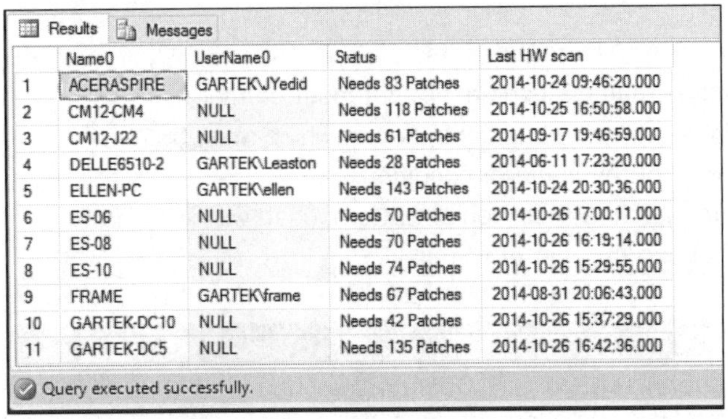

	Name0	UserName0	Status	Last HW scan
1	ACERASPIRE	GARTEK\JYedid	Needs 83 Patches	2014-10-24 09:46:20.000
2	CM12-CM4	NULL	Needs 118 Patches	2014-10-25 16:50:58.000
3	CM12-J22	NULL	Needs 61 Patches	2014-09-17 19:46:59.000
4	DELLE6510-2	GARTEK\Leaston	Needs 28 Patches	2014-06-11 17:23:20.000
5	ELLEN-PC	GARTEK\ellen	Needs 143 Patches	2014-10-24 20:30:36.000
6	ES-06	NULL	Needs 70 Patches	2014-10-26 17:00:11.000
7	ES-08	NULL	Needs 70 Patches	2014-10-26 16:19:14.000
8	ES-10	NULL	Needs 74 Patches	2014-10-26 15:29:55.000
9	FRAME	GARTEK\frame	Needs 67 Patches	2014-08-31 20:06:43.000
10	GARTEK-DC10	NULL	Needs 42 Patches	2014-10-26 15:37:29.000
11	GARTEK-DC5	NULL	Needs 135 Patches	2014-10-26 16:42:36.000

Query executed successfully.

FIGURE 4.2   Results of a column-naming query.

Understanding Aggregate Functions

Aggregate function is just a more technical name for a numeric function. From a non-programmer's perspective, an aggregate function simply returns numbers for the results rather than individual values. As you may know by now, ConfigMgr captures a considerable amount of data; instead of creating reports with hundreds or even thousands of rows and having to manually count each individual item, you can use aggregate functions to count, sum, or average those results.

In the "Demonstrating SQL Operators" section, later in this chapter, you will be asked how many times Adobe Reader XI is listed. This is the type of question you as a ConfigMgr administrator will often encounter, and it is a scenario where using aggregate functions can help provide the information you need without spending a significant amount of time trying to determine the answer.

Table 4.2 provides a list of aggregate functions. These functions are generally used in a summarized data report to give an overview of the results before drilling down into the details. Chapter 5, "Basic Report Design," explains summarized data reports.

It is important to note that aggregate functions use the GROUP BY section of a query, previously explained in the "Using Secondary Operators" section of this chapter.

The query shown in Listing 4.10 returns a list of system roles in the ConfigMgr environment, with a count of computers for each role; the minimum, average, and maximum RAM in each system role; and the total RAM for all systems within each specific system role. Using this query, you can further analyze each aggregate function. Figure 4.3 displays the results of this query.

TABLE 4.2 Aggregate Functions

Operator	Description
COUNT	Returns the number of items.
SUM	Returns the sum of all items.
AVG	Returns the average number of all items.
MIN	Returns the minimum number in a group of items.
MAX	Returns the maximum number in a group of items.

LISTING 4.10 Aggregate Functions Query

```
SELECT
  S.SystemRole0 as 'System Role',
  COUNT(S.SystemRole0) as 'Count of System Roles',
  MIN (Ram.TotalPhysicalMemory0) as 'Min RAM for a System Role',
  AVG (Ram.TotalPhysicalMemory0) as 'Avg RAM for a System Role',
  MAX (Ram.TotalPhysicalMemory0) as 'Max RAM for a System Role',
  SUM (Ram.TotalPhysicalMemory0) as 'Sum of RAM for a System Role'
```

LISTING 4.10   Aggregate Functions Query

```
FROM
  dbo.v_GS_X86_PC_MEMORY as RAM
  join dbo.v_GS_SYSTEM as S on S.ResourceID = RAM.ResourceID
GROUP BY
  S.SystemRole0
```

	System Role	Count	Min RAM for System Role	Avg RAM for System Role	Max RAM for System Role	Sum of RAM for System Role
1	Server	17	1560120	13310799	54462264	226283596
2	Workstation	15	1048120	4967231	10386796	74508468

FIGURE 4.3   Results from an aggregate functions query.

Using the COUNT Function

The COUNT function returns the total number of items. The example in Listing 4.10 looks for a count of the SystemRole0 column. The query returns the number of systems within the system role, shown in the second column.

Using the MIN (Minimum) Function

The MIN function returns the smallest number for a column. The example in Listing 4.10 looks for the smallest amount of TotalPhysicalMemory0 on a system for each SystemRole0. Using the results shown in Figure 4.3, you can tell that the lowest amount of RAM is 1.5GB in a server and 1GB in a workstation.

Using the AVG (Average) Function

The AVG function returns the average number for a column. The example in Listing 4.10 looks for the average TotalPhysicalMemory0 for each SystemRole0. From the results shown in Figure 4.3, you can determine that the average RAM for servers is 13GB, and it's over 4GB for a workstation.

Using the MAX (Maximum) Function

The MAX function returns the largest number for a column. The example in Listing 4.10 looks for the largest amount of TotalPhysicalMemory0 on a system for each SystemRole0. From the results shown in Figure 4.3, you can see that the most RAM is 54GB in a server and 10GB in a workstation.

Using the SUM Function

The SUM function returns the total value for a column. The example in Listing 4.10 looks for a sum of TotalPhysicalMemory0 for each SystemRole0. The results displayed in Figure 4.3 show that the total RAM for all servers is 226GB, and it's 74GB total for workstations.

Understanding Date and Time Functions

Date and time data is an important aspect of report writing. There will be many occasions when you need to return a date or compare one date to another within ConfigMgr data. You might, for example, need to display the install date for an application, compare an operating system (OS) install date to today in order to get the number of days since deployment, or show the date and time of the last hardware scan for a system.

The following sections discuss the most common date and time functions used in ConfigMgr reports.

TIP: LIST OF DATE AND TIME FUNCTIONS

The SQL online help at http://msdn.microsoft.com/en-us/library/ms186724.aspx contains a complete list of date and time functions.

Understanding Date Parts

Before starting to define date and time functions, let's explain the date format. Say you're working with the date July 6, 2014, at 9:44 AM; SQL displays this as `2014-07-06 09:44:59.120`. To use most date/time functions, you must first define what you are looking for, such as the number of years or the number of days between two dates. Transact SQL uses date parts to define this information. The most commonly used date parts in ConfigMgr reporting are listed in Table 4.3.

TABLE 4.3   Common Date Parts

Date Part	Abbreviations
Year	yy, yyyy
Month	mm, m
Day	dd, d
Hour	Hh
Minute	mi, n
Second	ss, s

TIP: FURTHER DATE PART INFORMATION

Refer to the SQL online help at http://msdn.microsoft.com/en-us/library/ms174420.aspx for a complete list of available date parts.

Using Common Date and Time Functions

Table 4.4 lists and describes the common date and time functions; it also provides the proper syntax to use for each function within queries and ConfigMgr reports. Listing 4.11 further demonstrates the use of these functions in a sample SQL query. Figure 4.4 shows the results of this query.

TABLE 4.4   Common Date and Time Functions

Function	Description	Syntax
GETDATE	Returns the current date and time.	GETDATE ()
DATEDIFF	Returns the difference between the start date and end date provided. The value returned is based on the defined date part.	DATEDIFF(*date part, start date, end date*)
DATEPART	Returns the date part value for a given date/time.	DATEPART(*date part, date*)

TIP: DATE VALUES

ConfigMgr stores date values differently, depending on where the date originates. For example, the last hardware inventory scan date and time is based on the computer's clock, whereas status messages are generally recorded using Universal Coordinated Time (UTC).

LISTING 4.11   Date and Time Sample Query

```
SELECT
  R.Netbios_Name0,
  GETDATE () as 'Today Date',
  OS.InstallDate0 as 'OS install date',
  DATEDIFF (dd, OS.InstallDate0, getdate()) as '# of Days since installed',
  DATEPART (mm, OS.InstallDate0) as 'Month installed'
FROM
  v_R_System as R
  JOIN dbo.v_GS_OPERATING_SYSTEM as OS on R.ResourceID = OS.ResourceID
ORDER BY
  R.Netbios_Name0
```

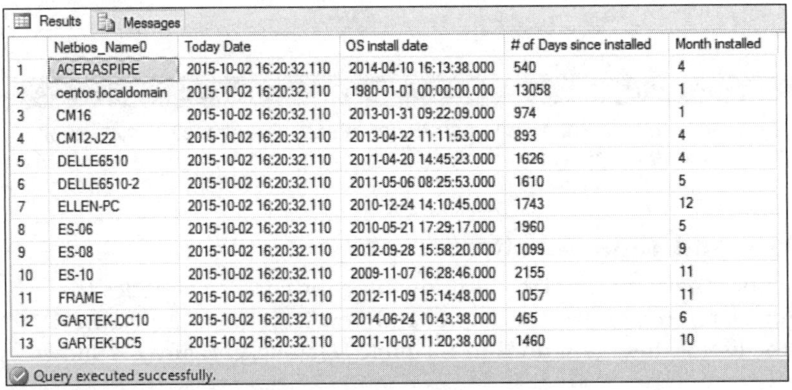

	Netbios_Name0	Today Date	OS install date	# of Days since installed	Month installed
1	ACERASPIRE	2015-10-02 16:20:32.110	2014-04-10 16:13:38.000	540	4
2	centos.localdomain	2015-10-02 16:20:32.110	1980-01-01 00:00:00.000	13058	1
3	CM16	2015-10-02 16:20:32.110	2013-01-31 09:22:09.000	974	1
4	CM12-J22	2015-10-02 16:20:32.110	2013-04-22 11:11:53.000	893	4
5	DELLE6510	2015-10-02 16:20:32.110	2011-04-20 14:45:23.000	1626	4
6	DELLE6510-2	2015-10-02 16:20:32.110	2011-05-06 08:25:53.000	1610	5
7	ELLEN-PC	2015-10-02 16:20:32.110	2010-12-24 14:10:45.000	1743	12
8	ES-06	2015-10-02 16:20:32.110	2010-05-21 17:29:17.000	1960	5
9	ES-08	2015-10-02 16:20:32.110	2012-09-28 15:58:20.000	1099	9
10	ES-10	2015-10-02 16:20:32.110	2009-11-07 16:28:46.000	2155	11
11	FRAME	2015-10-02 16:20:32.110	2012-11-09 15:14:48.000	1057	11
12	GARTEK-DC10	2015-10-02 16:20:32.110	2014-06-24 10:43:38.000	465	6
13	GARTEK-DC5	2015-10-02 16:20:32.110	2011-10-03 11:20:38.000	1460	10

Query executed successfully.

FIGURE 4.4   Results from the date and time sample query.

TIP: DATETIME FORMAT

The functions mentioned in this section work only with data stored in datetime format. It is important to note that some dates and times within the ConfigMgr database are recorded in string format. Before using these functions for string data, you must first convert the values to datetime format. Converting data is further discussed in the "Transforming Data Stored in the ConfigMgr Database" section of this chapter.

Transforming Data Stored in the ConfigMgr Database

Many items in ConfigMgr are stored in a SQL database either in short form or as codes. This method of storing data is useful because it saves space; however, from a reporting standpoint, the meaning or description of these codes may not always be clear. For example, if a query returns a chassis type value of 3, what does this mean? The following sections detail how to use functions to transform that data to make it more meaningful to the report reader.

Using the CASE Function

You use the CASE function to evaluate an expression and translate the data based on the results. For example, the CASE function could be used to translate the value 1 to January. Listing 4.12 shows the proper syntax for the CASE function.

LISTING 4.12   CASE Syntax

```
CASE <Expression>
    When 1 then 'January'
    When 2 then 'February'
    When 3 then 'March'
    ...
    Else 'Winter'
End as 'column name'
```

The sample query provided in Listing 4.13 uses a CASE function to return all system names, today's date, the last hardware scan date, the month of the last hardware scan, and a translated value for the month. Figure 4.5 display the results of this query.

LISTING 4.13   CASE Sample Query

```
SELECT
  R.Netbios_Name0,
  GETDATE() as 'Today Date',
  WS.LastHWScan as 'Last HW Scan date',
  datepart(mm,WS.LastHWScan) as 'Month',
  CASE DATEPART (mm,WS.LastHWScan)
    When 1 then 'January'
    When 2 then 'February'
```

LISTING 4.13   CASE Sample Query

```
    When 3 then 'March'
    When 4 then 'April'
    When 5 then 'May'
    When 6 then 'June'
    When 7 then 'Summer'
    When 8 then 'Summer'
    When 9 then 'Fall'
    When 10 then 'Fall'
    Else 'Winter'
  End as 'time of year'
FROM
  v_R_System as R
  join dbo.v_GS_WORKSTATION_STATUS as WS on R.ResourceID = WS.ResourceID
ORDER BY
  R.Netbios_Name0
```

	Netbios_Name0	Today Date	Last HW Scan date	Month	time of year
1	ACERASPIRE	2015-10-02 16:26:40.857	2014-10-24 09:46:20.000	10	Fall
2	centos.localdomain	2015-10-02 16:26:40.857	2014-08-21 14:00:04.000	8	Summer
3	CM16	2015-10-02 16:26:40.857	2014-10-25 16:50:58.000	10	Fall
4	CM12-J22	2015-10-02 16:26:40.857	2014-09-17 19:46:59.000	9	Fall
5	DELLE6510	2015-10-02 16:26:40.857	2014-03-27 11:32:46.000	3	March
6	DELLE6510-2	2015-10-02 16:26:40.857	2014-06-11 17:23:20.000	6	June
7	ELLEN-PC	2015-10-02 16:26:40.857	2014-10-24 20:30:36.000	10	Fall
8	ES-06	2015-10-02 16:26:40.857	2014-10-26 17:00:11.000	10	Fall
9	ES-08	2015-10-02 16:26:40.857	2014-10-26 16:19:14.000	10	Fall
10	ES-10	2015-10-02 16:26:40.857	2014-10-26 15:29:55.000	10	Fall
11	FRAME	2015-10-02 16:26:40.857	2014-08-31 20:06:43.000	8	Summer

Query executed successfully.

FIGURE 4.5   CASE function results.

TIP: CASE FUNCTION INFORMATION

For more information about the CASE function, see the SQL online books at
http://msdn.microsoft.com/en-us/library/ms181765.aspx.

Converting Data with the CONVERT and CAST Functions

The CONVERT and CAST functions convert data from one type to a different data type that
you specify. For example, if data is returned as a string, these functions allow you to
convert the data to datetime format. As mentioned in the "Understanding Date and Time
Functions" section earlier in this chapter, certain functions can be used only with specific
data types.

Table 4.5 shows the proper syntax for the CONVERT and CAST functions. The sample query
provided in Listing 4.14 returns computer names, all installation dates from Add/Remove
Programs (v_Add_Remove_Programs), the same installation date in datetime format (using the

CAST function), and the installation date converted from datetime to string format (using the CONVERT function). Notice the display difference between datetime format and string format.

TABLE 4.5 CONVERT and CAST Functions

Function	Syntax
CONVERT	CONVERT(data type, column/value, *style*)
	Note that *style* is an optional field.
CAST	CAST(column/value AS data type)

LISTING 4.14 CONVERT and CAST Sample Query

```
SELECT
  R.Netbios_Name0 as 'PC',
  ARP.InstallDate0 as 'ARP Install Date',
  CAST (ARP.InstallDate0 as datetime) AS 'ARP Date/Time',
  CONVERT (Char(19), Cast(ARP.InstallDate0 AS DATETIME), 0) as 'ARP Date string'
FROM
  v_R_System as R
  join v_Add_Remove_Programs as ARP on R.ResourceID = ARP.ResourceID
  join v_GS_SYSTEM as S on R.ResourceID = S.ResourceID
WHERE
  S.SystemRole0 = 'Workstation'
  and isdate(ARP.InstallDate0)=1
  and ARP.InstallDate0 is not Null
ORDER BY
  R.Netbios_Name0
```

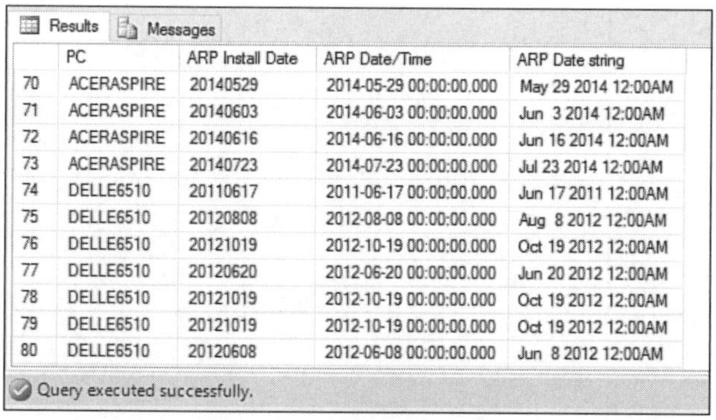

	PC	ARP Install Date	ARP Date/Time	ARP Date string
70	ACERASPIRE	20140529	2014-05-29 00:00:00.000	May 29 2014 12:00AM
71	ACERASPIRE	20140603	2014-06-03 00:00:00.000	Jun 3 2014 12:00AM
72	ACERASPIRE	20140616	2014-06-16 00:00:00.000	Jun 16 2014 12:00AM
73	ACERASPIRE	20140723	2014-07-23 00:00:00.000	Jul 23 2014 12:00AM
74	DELLE6510	20110617	2011-06-17 00:00:00.000	Jun 17 2011 12:00AM
75	DELLE6510	20120808	2012-08-08 00:00:00.000	Aug 8 2012 12:00AM
76	DELLE6510	20121019	2012-10-19 00:00:00.000	Oct 19 2012 12:00AM
77	DELLE6510	20120620	2012-06-20 00:00:00.000	Jun 20 2012 12:00AM
78	DELLE6510	20121019	2012-10-19 00:00:00.000	Oct 19 2012 12:00AM
79	DELLE6510	20121019	2012-10-19 00:00:00.000	Oct 19 2012 12:00AM
80	DELLE6510	20120608	2012-06-08 00:00:00.000	Jun 8 2012 12:00AM

Query executed successfully.

FIGURE 4.6 Results from using the CONVERT and CAST functions.

TIP: CONVERT AND CAST FUNCTION INFORMATION

For more information about the CONVERT and CAST functions, refer to the SQL online books at http://msdn.microsoft.com/en-us/library/ms187928.aspx.

Using the ISNULL Function

The ISNULL function checks to see if the data returned contains NULL values; if so, ISNULL returns either the actual value or a value specified as its replacement. The sample query in Listing 4.15 returns all system names (R.Netbios_Name0), their last logon time stamp (R.Last_Logon_Timestamp), and a third column where all NULL values for R.Last_Logon_Timestamp are replaced with 1980-04-05, identified by the black arrows in Figure 4.7. Following is the proper syntax for the ISNULL function:

```
ISNULL(Column Name, 'Replacement Value')
```

LISTING 4.15   ISNULL Sample Query

```
SELECT distinct
    R.Netbios_Name0,
    R.Last_Logon_Timestamp0,
    isnull(R.Last_Logon_Timestamp0, '1980-04-05')
FROM
    v_R_System as R
ORDER BY
    R.Netbios_Name0
```

> **TIP:** ISNULL **FUNCTION INFORMATION**
>
> For more information about the ISNULL function, refer to the SQL online books at http://msdn.microsoft.com/en-us/library/ms184325.aspx.

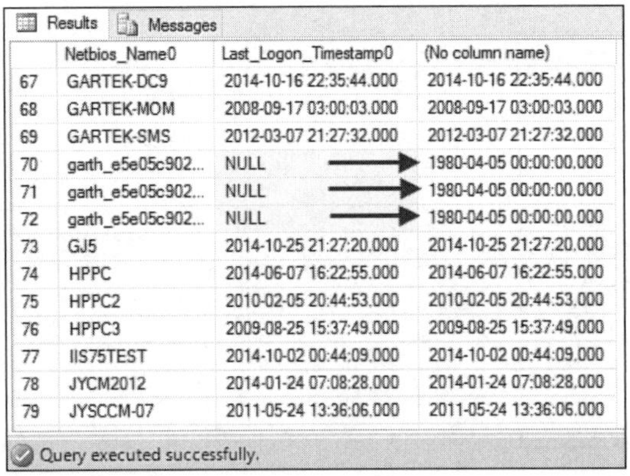

	Netbios_Name0	Last_Logon_Timestamp0	(No column name)
67	GARTEK-DC9	2014-10-16 22:35:44.000	2014-10-16 22:35:44.000
68	GARTEK-MOM	2008-09-17 03:00:03.000	2008-09-17 03:00:03.000
69	GARTEK-SMS	2012-03-07 21:27:32.000	2012-03-07 21:27:32.000
70	garth_e5e05c902...	NULL	1980-04-05 00:00:00.000
71	garth_e5e05c902...	NULL	1980-04-05 00:00:00.000
72	garth_e5e05c902...	NULL	1980-04-05 00:00:00.000
73	GJ5	2014-10-25 21:27:20.000	2014-10-25 21:27:20.000
74	HPPC	2014-06-07 16:22:55.000	2014-06-07 16:22:55.000
75	HPPC2	2010-02-05 20:44:53.000	2010-02-05 20:44:53.000
76	HPPC3	2009-08-25 15:37:49.000	2009-08-25 15:37:49.000
77	IIS75TEST	2014-10-02 00:44:09.000	2014-10-02 00:44:09.000
78	JYCM2012	2014-01-24 07:08:28.000	2014-01-24 07:08:28.000
79	JYSCCM-07	2011-05-24 13:36:06.000	2011-05-24 13:36:06.000

Query executed successfully.

FIGURE 4.7   Results from using the ISNULL function.

Understanding the SQL JOIN Statement

There are many places to report on data within ConfigMgr. All the SQL views are independent of each other, and each one stores specific data. For example, v_Add_Remove_Programs stores the Add/Remove Programs data (also known as Programs and Features in Windows Vista and later) that is inventoried from each computer. If you were to query both v_R_System and v_Add_Remove_Programs within one query without joining them, the results from your query would be huge.

To get an idea what we mean by *huge*, assume that you have a small lab with 200 computers within the v_R_System SQL view. Also assume that v_Add_Remove_Programs contains only 4,000 entries. If you query the two views without any joining information, you have 200 computers × 4,000 ARP entries, which would equal 800,000 rows of data. Listing 4.16 shows two queries to support the previous example and a third query that does not join any views together. Figure 4.8 shows the results of these queries; the numbers are similar to those in the previous example.

LISTING 4.16   Sample Query Without a JOIN Statement

```
SELECT
  count(R.ResourceID) as '# of computers'
FROM
  dbo.v_R_System as R


SELECT
  count(ARP.ResourceID) as '# of ARP entries'
FROM
  dbo.v_Add_Remove_Programs AS ARP


SELECT
  R.Netbios_Name0 as 'Computer',
  ARP.DisplayName0 as 'ARP Display Name'
FROM
  dbo.v_R_System as R,
  dbo.v_Add_Remove_Programs AS ARP
ORDER BY
  R.Netbios_Name0 DESC,
  ARP.DisplayName0 DESC
```

More important than the actual results of the query is the impact of running a query without any joins. As you can see in Figure 4.9, it took the query 2 minutes 13 seconds to execute (see the first black arrow, on the left), and it returned 927,303 rows (see the second black arrow). Not only did this query take a long time to run, the amount of data returned is so large that it is not usable by anyone.

The following sections discuss how to join SQL views to each other, the different types of joins available, and when to use them all.

	Results	Messages	
	# of computers		
1	169		

	# of ARP entries		
1	5487		

	Computer	ARP Display Name
1	XP-VM	Языковой пакет Microsoft ReportViewer 2010 Redi...
2	XP-VM	Zune Language Pack (SVE)
3	XP-VM	Zune Language Pack (RUS)
4	XP-VM	Zune Language Pack (PTG)
5	XP-VM	Zune Language Pack (PTB)
6	XP-VM	Zune Language Pack (PLK)
7	XP-VM	Zune Language Pack (NOR)
8	XP-VM	Zune Language Pack (NLD)
9	XP-VM	Zune Language Pack (MSL)
10	XP-VM	Zune Language Pack (KOR)
11	XP-VM	Zune Language Pack (JPN)

Query executed successfully.

FIGURE 4.8   Results of a query without a JOIN statement.

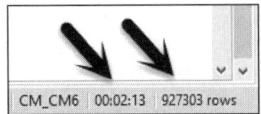

CM_CM6 | 00:02:13 | 927303 rows

FIGURE 4.9   Impact of a query without a JOIN statement.

What Is a JOIN?

A SQL JOIN allows you to combine information from two or more SQL views and to specify how to link the tables together. The sample query in the "Understanding the SQL JOIN Statement" section of this chapter does not use any joins, and therefore SQL assumes that all rows of data from the first view must apply to each row of data in the second view. When you use joins to define how the two views link together, the query returns rows of data that contain results from both views combined.

Using the ResourceID Column

For most ConfigMgr views, you use the ResourceID column from one SQL view to join another. This column is a unique ID given to each system in ConfigMgr and allows you to link data rows together for results that pertain to each system. Using the example in the "Understanding the SQL JOIN Statement" section, let's adjust the query to join the SQL views together and see how this affects the results. The query in Listing 4.16 returns a huge number of rows that are unusable because it does not join any views together. Listing 4.17 adds the appropriate JOIN to the query to provide the desired results. Figure 4.10 shows the results of this new query.

LISTING 4.17   Sample Query Using JOIN

```
SELECT
  R.Netbios_Name0 as 'Computer',
  ARP.DisplayName0 as 'ARP Display Name'
FROM
  dbo.v_R_System as R
  JOIN dbo.v_Add_Remove_Programs AS ARP ON R.ResourceID = ARP.ResourceID
ORDER BY
  R.Netbios_Name0 DESC,
  ARP.DisplayName0 DESC
```

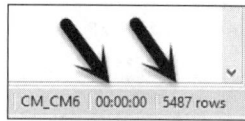

FIGURE 4.10   Impact of executing a query using JOIN.

Notice in Figure 4.10 that it took less than one second (see the first black arrow, on the left) to execute the query (from Listing 4.17), and the number of rows returned is only 5487 (see the second black arrow). This is a much more valuable and efficient query than the one in Listing 4.16, which does not use a JOIN statement.

REAL WORLD: USER VERSUS COMPUTER

It would seem logical to join the user's ResourceID with a computer's ResourceID. However, this is one of the few cases where ResourceID should not be joined together as it represents completely different information in the two tables, and the two are not relevant to each other.

When joining views on a user account, it is best to use the user's unique ID. The user's unique ID in the v_R_System_Valid view would be the combination of the User_Domain0 and User_Name0 columns with a \ in-between; on the other hand, for v_R_User, the matching unique ID that can be joined is stored in the Unique_User_Name0 column. You will see this later in the chapter, in Listing 4.19.

Using the v_R_System_Valid View

The v_R_System_Valid view is very important when you're writing SQL queries for a couple of reasons:

▶ The underlying data in this view is indexed, which makes your query faster and much more efficient.

▶ This view shows only active clients in ConfigMgr. This is important in ConfigMgr because when someone deletes a client, all its references are not immediately deleted as well. Instead, ConfigMgr keeps the data until it is automatically purged from the database, approximately five days later.

For these reasons, the authors recommend using the `v_R_System_Valid` view instead of `v_R_System` when writing queries.

Explaining the `JOIN` Statements

The following sections use the RGB color wheel shown in Figure 4.11 to help explain all the different variations of the `JOIN` statement. The color names and index letters are listed in Table 4.6.

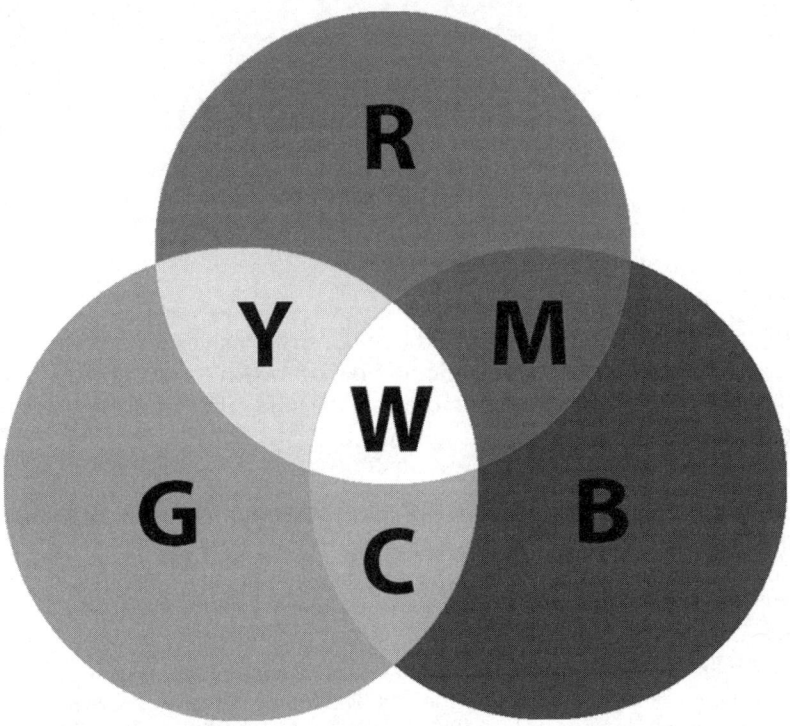

FIGURE 4.11   RGB color wheel.

TABLE 4.6   RGB Colors

Index	Color
R	Red
G	Green
B	Blue
Y	Yellow
M	Magenta
C	Cyan
W	White

The INNER JOIN **Statement**

INNER JOIN, or in its short form simply JOIN, is the most commonly used join statement. It returns all common items between two or more SQL views.

To help visualize how an INNER JOIN works, let's assign colors to each SQL view in the query shown in Listing 4.18, based on the RGB color wheel:

▶ **Green:** v_R_System_Valid (RV)

▶ **Red:** v_GS_X86_PC_MEMORY (RAM)

▶ **Blue:** v_HS_X86_PC_MEMORY (HRAM)

This query performs a JOIN (INNER JOIN) between all three SQL views, as shown in Figure 4.12. This means it is looking for data where all three of the views intersect. The column that is joining the views (RV.ResourceID) must contain matching data in each view for the column to be returned in the results. Since the three views in the query represent the green, red, and blue sections of the RGB color wheel, the results from the query represent the white area.

LISTING 4.18   Sample INNER JOIN Statement

```
SELECT
    RV.Netbios_Name0 as 'PC Name',
    RV.User_Domain0 as 'User Name',
    RAM.TotalPhysicalMemory0 as 'Current RAM',
    HRAM.TotalPhysicalMemory0 as 'Historic RAM'
FROM
    dbo.v_R_System_Valid RV
    JOIN dbo.v_GS_X86_PC_MEMORY RAM on RV.ResourceID = RAM.ResourceID
    JOIN dbo.v_HS_X86_PC_MEMORY HRAM on RV.ResourceID = HRAM.ResourceID
WHERE
    RAM.TotalPhysicalMemory0 <> HRAM.TotalPhysicalMemory0
    and RV.Is_Virtual_Machine0 = 0
ORDER BY
    RV.Netbios_Name0
```

FIGURE 4.12   Results from INNER JOIN RGB color query.

The LEFT OUTER JOIN Statement

The LEFT OUTER JOIN statement takes all data from the left side of the JOIN equation and joins it to any common data on the right side of the equation. Again, using the RGB color wheel, let's assign colors to each SQL view in the query in Listing 4.19:

▶ **Green:** v_R_System_Valid (RV)

▶ **Blue:** v_R_User (RU)

The v_R_System_Valid view (green) is on the left side of the equation. All data rows in this view are returned as part of the results. Any data from the v_R_User view (blue) that matches with a row (containing the same user name) from v_R_System_Valid is joined and included in the results. The final results from this query are the green circle in addition to the cyan section from the blue circle, shown in Figure 4.13.

LISTING 4.19   Sample LEFT OUTER JOIN Statement

```
SELECT
  RV.Netbios_Name0 as 'PC Name',
  RV.User_Domain0+'\'+RV.User_Name0 as 'User Name',
  RU.Unique_User_Name0 as 'Unique User Name'
FROM
  dbo.v_R_System_Valid RV
  LEFT OUTER JOIN dbo.v_R_User RU
    on RV.User_Domain0+'\'+RV.User_Name0 = RU.Unique_User_Name0
ORDER BY
  RV.Netbios_Name0,
  RU.Unique_User_Name0
```

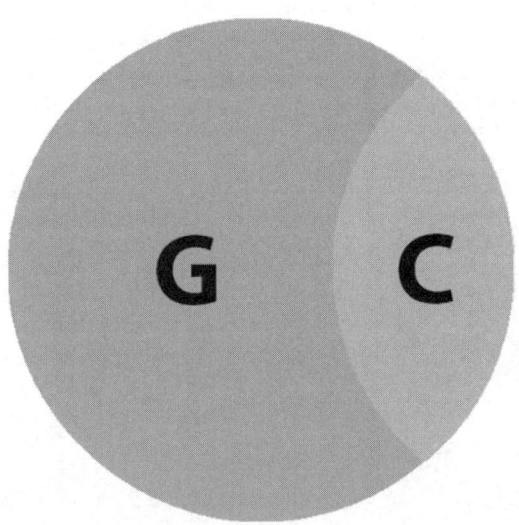

FIGURE 4.13   Results from LEFT OUTER JOIN RGB color query.

When executing this query, notice in Figure 4.14 that rows 16, 17, 22, and 27 have NULL values for the unique user name. This is because the right side of the equation has no common data for that row.

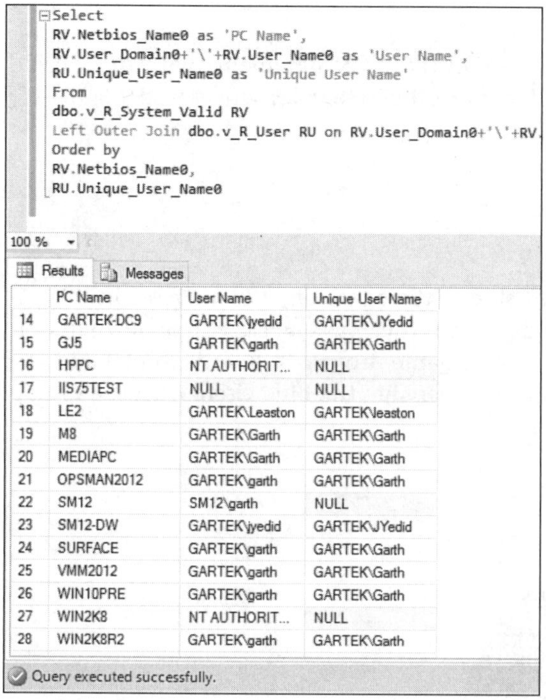

```
⊟Select
    RV.Netbios_Name0 as 'PC Name',
    RV.User_Domain0+'\'+RV.User_Name0 as 'User Name',
    RU.Unique_User_Name0 as 'Unique User Name'
    From
    dbo.v_R_System_Valid RV
    Left Outer Join dbo.v_R_User RU on RV.User_Domain0+'\'+RV.
    Order by
    RV.Netbios_Name0,
    RU.Unique_User_Name0
```

100 % ▼

Results Messages

	PC Name	User Name	Unique User Name
14	GARTEK-DC9	GARTEK\jyedid	GARTEK\JYedid
15	GJ5	GARTEK\garth	GARTEK\Garth
16	HPPC	NT AUTHORIT...	NULL
17	IIS75TEST	NULL	NULL
18	LE2	GARTEK\Leaston	GARTEK\leaston
19	M8	GARTEK\Garth	GARTEK\Garth
20	MEDIAPC	GARTEK\Garth	GARTEK\Garth
21	OPSMAN2012	GARTEK\garth	GARTEK\Garth
22	SM12	SM12\garth	NULL
23	SM12-DW	GARTEK\jyedid	GARTEK\JYedid
24	SURFACE	GARTEK\garth	GARTEK\Garth
25	VMM2012	GARTEK\garth	GARTEK\Garth
26	WIN10PRE	GARTEK\garth	GARTEK\Garth
27	WIN2K8	NT AUTHORIT...	NULL
28	WIN2K8R2	GARTEK\garth	GARTEK\Garth

Query executed successfully.

FIGURE 4.14   Results from LEFT OUTER JOIN query.

The RIGHT OUTER JOIN Statement

The RIGHT OUTER JOIN, as you might guess, is the mirror-opposite of a LEFT OUTER JOIN: It takes all data from the right side of the equation and any common data on the left side of the equation.

Notice that the only change to the query in Listing 4.20 is that the LEFT OUTER JOIN statement now reads RIGHT OUTER JOIN.

LISTING 4.20   Sample RIGHT OUTER JOIN Statement

```
SELECT
    RV.Netbios_Name0 as 'PC Name',
    RV.User_Domain0+'\'+RV.User_Name0 as 'User Name',
    RU.Unique_User_Name0 as 'Unique User Name'
FROM
    dbo.v_R_System_Valid RV
    RIGHT OUTER JOIN dbo.v_R_User RU
     on RV.User_Domain0+'\'+RV.User_Name0 = RU.Unique_User_Name0
```

LISTING 4.20   Sample RIGHT OUTER JOIN Statement

```
ORDER BY
   RV.Netbios_Name0,
   RU.Unique_User_Name0
```

Much as in the example in the section "The LEFT OUTER JOIN Statement" with the sample code in Listing 4.19, let's assign the same colors from the RGB color wheel to the SQL views in Listing 4.20:

- ▶ **Green:** v_R_System_Valid (RV)

- ▶ **Blue:** v_R_User (RU)

Since the v_R_User view (blue) is on the right side of the equation, all data rows in this view are returned as part of the results. Any data from the v_R_System_Valid view (green) that matches with a row, containing the same user name, from v_R_User is joined and included in the results. The final results from this query are the blue circle with the cyan section from the green circle, shown in Figure 4.15.

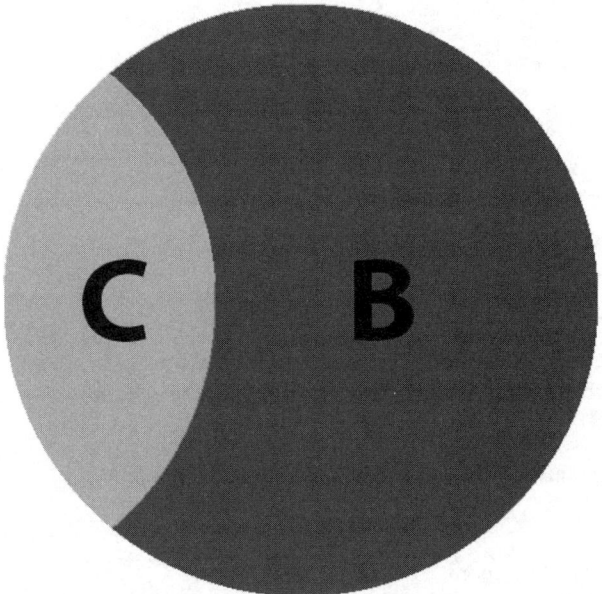

FIGURE 4.15   Results from RIGHT OUTER JOIN RGB color query.

When you execute this query, notice in Figure 4.16 that rows 1 through 49 have NULL values for the PC name and user name. This is because the left side of the equation has no common data for that row.

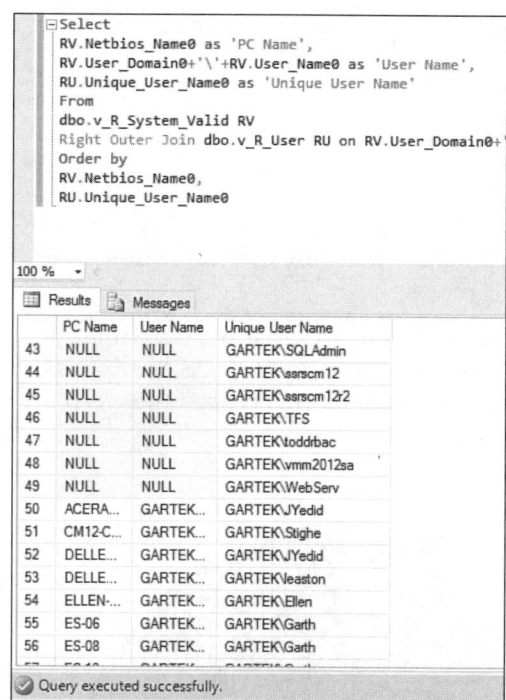

```
⊟Select
  RV.Netbios_Name0 as 'PC Name',
  RV.User_Domain0+'\'+RV.User_Name0 as 'User Name',
  RU.Unique_User_Name0 as 'Unique User Name'
  From
  dbo.v_R_System_Valid RV
  Right Outer Join dbo.v_R_User RU on RV.User_Domain0+
  Order by
  RV.Netbios_Name0,
  RU.Unique_User_Name0
```

100 %   ▾

🔳 Results   🗎 Messages

	PC Name	User Name	Unique User Name
43	NULL	NULL	GARTEK\SQLAdmin
44	NULL	NULL	GARTEK\ssrscm12
45	NULL	NULL	GARTEK\ssrscm12r2
46	NULL	NULL	GARTEK\TFS
47	NULL	NULL	GARTEK\toddrbac
48	NULL	NULL	GARTEK\wmm2012sa
49	NULL	NULL	GARTEK\WebServ
50	ACERA...	GARTEK...	GARTEK\JYedid
51	CM12-C...	GARTEK...	GARTEK\Stighe
52	DELLE...	GARTEK...	GARTEK\JYedid
53	DELLE...	GARTEK...	GARTEK\easton
54	ELLEN-..	GARTEK...	GARTEK\Ellen
55	ES-06	GARTEK...	GARTEK\Garth
56	ES-08	GARTEK...	GARTEK\Garth

✅ Query executed successfully.

FIGURE 4.16   RIGHT OUTER JOIN query results.

The FULL JOIN Statement

A FULL JOIN statement does exactly what its name tells you it does: It takes everything from both sides of the equation and displays that as the results.

Notice that the only change to the query in Listing 4.21 is that the RIGHT OUTER JOIN statement now reads FULL JOIN.

LISTING 4.21   Sample FULL JOIN Statement

```
SELECT
  RV.Netbios_Name0 as 'PC Name',
  RV.User_Domain0+'\'+RV.User_Name0 as 'User Name',
  RU.Unique_User_Name0 as 'Unique User Name'
FROM
  dbo.v_R_System_Valid RV
  Full Join dbo.v_R_User RU on RV.User_Domain0+'\'+RV.User_Name0 =
    RU.Unique_User_Name0
ORDER BY
  RV.Netbios_Name0,
  RU.Unique_User_Name0
```

Once again, let's assign the same colors to the SQL views, as previously done in the examples in Listing 4.19 and Listing 4.20:

▶ **Green:** v_R_System_Valid (RV)

▶ **Blue:** v_R_User (RU)

In the FULL JOIN statement, the results shown include all green and blue circles, with the cyan section represents a row where the results contain a matching user name from both views, meaning no NULL values, as illustrated in Figure 4.17.

When you execute the query in Listing 4.21, notice in Figure 4.18 that there are some rows containing NULL values on the left side, some rows with NULL values on the right side, and some rows without any NULL values—indicating the differences between the green, blue, and cyan sections of the RGB color wheel.

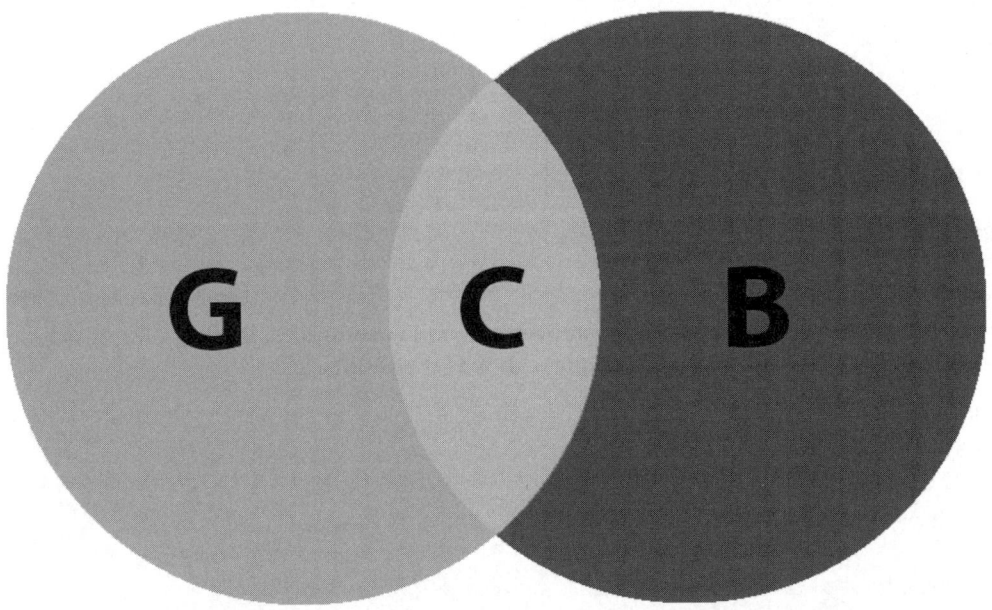

FIGURE 4.17   Results from FULL JOIN RGB color query.

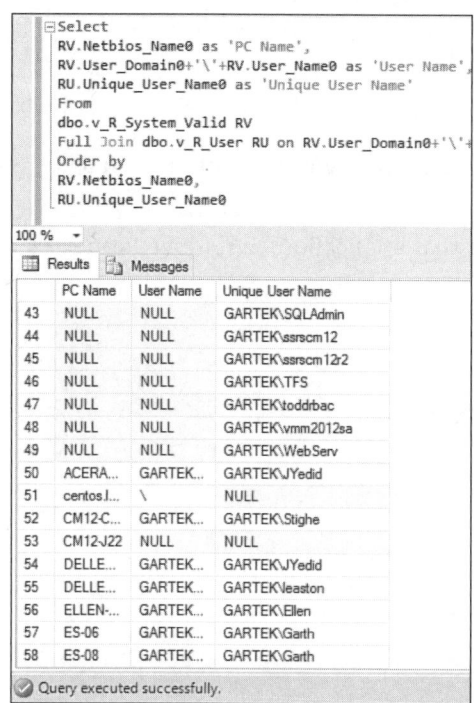

```
⊟Select
  RV.Netbios_Name0 as 'PC Name',
  RV.User_Domain0+'\'+RV.User_Name0 as 'User Name',
  RU.Unique_User_Name0 as 'Unique User Name'
  From
  dbo.v_R_System_Valid RV
  Full Join dbo.v_R_User RU on RV.User_Domain0+'\'+
  Order by
  RV.Netbios_Name0,
  RU.Unique_User_Name0
```

	PC Name	User Name	Unique User Name
43	NULL	NULL	GARTEK\SQLAdmin
44	NULL	NULL	GARTEK\ssrscm12
45	NULL	NULL	GARTEK\ssrscm12r2
46	NULL	NULL	GARTEK\TFS
47	NULL	NULL	GARTEK\toddrbac
48	NULL	NULL	GARTEK\vmm2012sa
49	NULL	NULL	GARTEK\WebServ
50	ACERA...	GARTEK...	GARTEK\JYedid
51	centos.l...	\	NULL
52	CM12-C...	GARTEK...	GARTEK\Stighe
53	CM12-J22	NULL	NULL
54	DELLE...	GARTEK...	GARTEK\JYedid
55	DELLE...	GARTEK...	GARTEK\leaston
56	ELLEN-...	GARTEK...	GARTEK\Ellen
57	ES-06	GARTEK...	GARTEK\Garth
58	ES-08	GARTEK...	GARTEK\Garth

Query executed successfully.

FIGURE 4.18   Results from a FULL JOIN query.

Demonstrating SQL Operators

The purpose of this section is to help you become familiar with many of the secondary SQL operators discussed in this chapter. In each of the following sections, you will modify a query based on the required results. Use the information explained throughout this chapter to return the requested data.

Running the Sample SQL File

To get started, load a sample SQL file into SQL Server Management Studio and execute the SQL query. Then follow these steps:

1. Open SQL Server Management Studio.

2. Connect to your ConfigMgr database server. (See the "Connecting to the ConfigMgr Database Server" section in Chapter 3 for information on how to perform this step.)

3. Using the dropdown list of available databases, change the database to your ConfigMgr site database.

4. Open a new query window by clicking **New Query**.

5. Open the Chapter4Demo.SQL file in Windows Notepad (provided as online content for this book; see Appendix C) and then copy and paste the contents to the new query window.

6. Execute the query by clicking **Execute**.

7. Review the results:

▶ How many rows are there?

▶ Take note of how many versions are listed for a single application, such as Adobe Reader, in your environment.

▶ How many times is a specific version of that application, say Adobe Reader XI, listed?

Editing the Sample Query

To edit the sample query, perform the following steps:

1. Edit the query to add the following items:

▶ DISTINCT

▶ An alias named ARP for the view dbo.v_Add_Remove_Programs

▶ Results filtered to the following publishers:

Dell

Microsoft Corporation

Adobe Systems Incorporated

▶ Results ordered by Publisher, Display Name, and Version

▶ A viewer-friendly display name for each column with the trailing 0s removed and spaces added between separate words instead of underscores

2. Execute the query by clicking **Execute**.

3. Review the results:

▶ How many rows are now there?

▶ Using an application installed in your environment, say Adobe Reader, note which versions are present.

▶ After making the changes to the query, how many times is this application listed now?

▶ How are the results ordered?

Creating a Query with Aliases

Write a new query with the following result criteria:

▶ List the computer names (PC), user names (User), application names (Application), and versions (Version) of systems with Adobe Reader installed. (The column names that should appear in the results are listed here in parentheses.)

▶ Order the results alphabetically by computer name.

Demonstrating Aggregate Functions

The purpose of this section is to help you become familiar with the different aggregate functions and their use within ConfigMgr queries. These functions, COUNT in particular, appear throughout this book, and you will utilize them as you begin creating your own queries. These demonstrations begin by asking you to modify existing queries to incorporate and analyze the different aggregate functions discussed to this point.

TIP: AGGREGATE QUERY ANSWERS

Answers for these aggregate queries can be found in Appendix B, "Demonstration Outcomes."

Creating a New Query

To get started, create a query that returns the minimum, average, and maximum hard disk sizes for system roles. Perform the following steps:

1. Open SQL Server Management Studio.

2. Connect to your ConfigMgr database server.

3. Using the dropdown list of available databases, change the database to your ConfigMgr database.

4. Open a new query window by clicking **New Query**.

5. Create a query to find the minimum, average, and maximum hard disk sizes for each system role.

TIP: DEMONSTRATING AGGREGATE FUNCTIONS

Use the example from Listing 4.10 as a starting point.

Using the COUNT Function

To add the COUNT function to your query, follow these steps:

1. Open SQL Server Management Studio.

2. Connect to your ConfigMgr database server.

3. Using the dropdown list of available databases, change the database to your ConfigMgr database.

4. Open a new query window by clicking **New Query**.

5. Open the Chapter4Demo.SQL file in Windows Notepad (provided as online content for this book; see Appendix C) and then copy and paste the contents to the new query window.

6. Modify this query to show the COUNT of each installed application (DisplayName0).

7. Execute the query.

8. Review the results. How many times is Adobe Reader XI installed?

Demonstrating Date and Time Functions

This section is meant to help you become familiar with the different date and time functions. Create a new query to find the following information from all systems in your environment:

▶ The current date

▶ The date of the last hardware inventory scan

▶ The number of minutes since the last hardware inventory scan

▶ The day of the month on which the last hardware inventory scan occurred

To become familiar with using date and time functions, follow these steps:

1. Open SQL Server Management Studio.

2. Connect to your ConfigMgr database server.

3. Using the dropdown list of available databases, change the database to your ConfigMgr database.

4. Open a new query window by clicking **New Query**.

5. Copy the sample query from Listing 4.11 and paste it into the New Query window.

6. Modify the query to include the following details:

    ▶ The current date

    ▶ The date of the last hardware inventory scan

▶ The number of minutes since the last hardware inventory scan

▶ The day of the month on which the last hardware inventory scan occurred

---

TIP: DATE AND TIME DEMONSTRATION

See Listing 4.1 to find the view and column for the last hardware inventory scan (Last HW Scan).

Demonstrating Data Transforms

The following sections will help you become familiar with the CASE, CAST, CONVERT, and ISNULL SQL functions. In each section, start with the following steps and then apply the required changes and functions to achieve the requested results:

1. Open SQL Server Management Studio.

2. Connect to your ConfigMgr database server.

3. Using the dropdown list of available databases, change the database to your ConfigMgr database.

4. Open a new query window by clicking **New Query**.

Applying the CASE Function

Create a query to display all computer names and system enclosure chassis types. Convert the chassis type numeric codes to their descriptions, provided in Table 4.7.

TIP: LOCATING CHASSIS TYPE

Use the dbo.v_GS_SYSTEM_ENCLOSURE SQL view in the ConfigMgr database to find the ChassisType column.

TABLE 4.7   Chassis Type Codes

Code	Description
1	Other
2	Unknown
3	Desktop
4	Low-profile desktop
5	Pizza box
6	Mini tower
7	Tower
8	Portable
9	Laptop
10	Notebook

TABLE 4.7   *continued*

Code	Description
11	Handheld
12	Docking station
13	All-in-one
14	Sub-notebook
15	Space-saving
16	Lunch box
17	Main system chassis
18	Expansion chassis
19	Subchassis
20	Bus expansion chassis
21	Peripheral chassis
22	Storage chassis
23	Rack mount chassis
24	Sealed-case PC

Applying the CAST and CONVERT Functions

Create a query to get all system names and the last hardware scan date. Convert the last hardware scan date to ANSI date format *YYYY.MM.DD*.

> **TIP:** CAST AND CONVERT **HINT**
>
> The ANSI date format *YYYY.MM.DD* is style 102.

Applying the ISNULL Function

Create a query to return all system names and user names (User_Name0) from the v_R_System_Valid view. Have the query replace any NULL values in the v_R_System_Valid User_Name0 column with the value n/a.

Demonstrating JOIN Statements

The purpose of this section is to help you become familiar with the different type of JOIN statements. For each example, start with the following steps and then apply the necessary changes to achieve the requested results.

1. Open SQL Server Management Studio.

2. Connect to your ConfigMgr database server.

3. Using the dropdown list of available databases, change the database to your ConfigMgr database.

4. Open a new query window by clicking **New Query**.

Executing an Inefficient Query

Execute the query in Listing 4.22 to show the impact and results of an inefficient query that does not use JOIN statements. Take note of the number of rows as well as the time it takes to execute the query.

LISTING 4.22   Demonstrating an Inefficient Query

```
SELECT
  R.Netbios_Name0 as 'Computer',
  ARP.DisplayName0 as 'ARP Display Name'
FROM
  dbo.v_R_System as R,
  dbo.v_Add_Remove_Programs AS ARP
ORDER BY
  R.Netbios_Name0 DESC,
  ARP.DisplayName0 DESC
```

4

Writing an Efficient Query

Modify the query from Listing 4.22 to join both views. Use the appropriate join to get all data from the v_R_System view as well as matching data (ResourceID) from the v_Add_ Remove_Programs view.

Working with the Different JOIN Statements

To become familiar with the different joins, read through this chapter again and execute the queries provided as examples for the INNER JOIN, LEFT OUTER JOIN, RIGHT OUTER JOIN, and FULL JOIN statements. Take note of the variations and locations of the NULL results for each type of join. Are there any NULL results in an INNER JOIN?

Summary

The foundation of ConfigMgr reporting is writing good and efficient SQL queries. This chapter has reviewed many aspects of SQL queries to help you not only write but understand the underlying SQL language of ConfigMgr reports. Most queries you create will incorporate many of the topics in this chapter.

Many demonstrations are provided throughout the chapter. Although this might seem like repetition or recaps, run these queries in your lab environment and take note of the results, variations, and similarities. As you become familiar and comfortable with writing SQL queries, these queries will become second nature; but until then, be sure to take your time and understand each section of this chapter.

The next chapters of this book focus on the design, concepts, and features of ConfigMgr reports rather than the underlying SQL queries themselves.

PART III

Using SSRS for Configuration Manager Reporting

IN THIS PART

Basic Report Design

Part II of this book, "About Data and Retrieval," discussed the data that can be gathered from SQL queries. Now it is time to consider overall report design. Before getting your hands dirty with SQL Server Data Tools Business Intelligence (SSDT-BI) for Visual Studio 2013 and beginning to create reports, you should understand what you will be creating, how you will create it, what you want your report to look like, and how you want individuals viewing the report to interact with it.

Here's why this is important: New Configuration Manager (ConfigMgr) administrators often do not spend enough time upfront on basic report design—such as templates, styles, and functionality—before beginning to create and publish reports. As an administrator's skills with the reporting tool mature, his or her reports start to include additional features, such as drillthroughs, interactive sorting, charts, and more. While these newer reports are often more useful, they differ from the earlier ones in their look, feel, and functionality.

The lack of a standard look and feel can make it difficult for those viewing reports to become comfortable using them, particularly if some may allow sorting by columns or using a drillthrough to view detailed reports, while others do not include any interaction. As a result, the administrator needs to update older reports or templates or re-create old reports from scratch if the design files were not saved.

To help avoid such growing pains, the authors strongly recommend spending the time to learn the basics of report design, detailed in this chapter. The next chapter, "Building a Basic Report," introduces you to the report-writing tool SSDT-BI for Visual Studio 2013 and walks through creating actual reports.

Understanding the Purpose of a Report Series

One of the challenges a ConfigMgr administrator faces is how to display all important data in a useful manner to everyone who might use the report, particularly when you will have a wide range of report viewers, including service desk staff, service desk managers, chief technology officers (CTOs), and end users. Reports can range from simple to very complicated, depending on what you want them to show. The key is having your report design and writing start with a good foundation and a well-thought-out query. Once this base is established, you can build on the query to create a functional, easy-to-read report that addresses the needs of multiple audiences.

One way to display all important data in a useful manner to everyone who might use the report is to build a summarized data report that contains a drillthrough to individual reports containing more specific information. This is referred to as a *report series*. Following is an overview of a sample report series:

▶ **Count of MS Office SKUs:** This report shows all the Microsoft Office products installed in your environment by stock-keeping unit (SKU).

▶ **List of PCs by MS Office SKU:** This report provides a list of computers with a particular Office SKU installed.

▶ **MS Office Details:** This report shows a detailed list of all Microsoft Office products installed on a specific computer.

Using a general report series design works for everyone from your CTO to your end users. Here's why:

▶ The CTO is able to see high-level information necessary to make upgrade/purchase decisions about the environment.

▶ The service desk manager can use a drillthrough to see additional details such as the computers or users that will be affected.

▶ The frontline service desk technologist can view what software products are installed on the specific computer he is troubleshooting or upgrading.

Using a Summarized Data Report

A *summarized data report* is intended to present a high-level view (or summary) of the data. This type of report is useful for obtaining an overview of the environment without needing to see specific details. For example, say you want to determine the number of installations of a product for purposes of license purchasing or performing a true-up. Management often needs such information, and it might also be included in presentations. Figure 5.1 shows an example of a summarized data report. In most cases, this type of report includes the following features:

▶ A chart for visual representation of the data

▶ A table with the following characteristics:

  ▶ Several columns that help explain the chart

  ▶ Interactive sorting enabled on each column

  ▶ Shading applied to alternate rows to improve readability

▶ Ability to navigate to more detailed reports

▶ Standard page format, such as letter size (8.5×11in) or A4 size

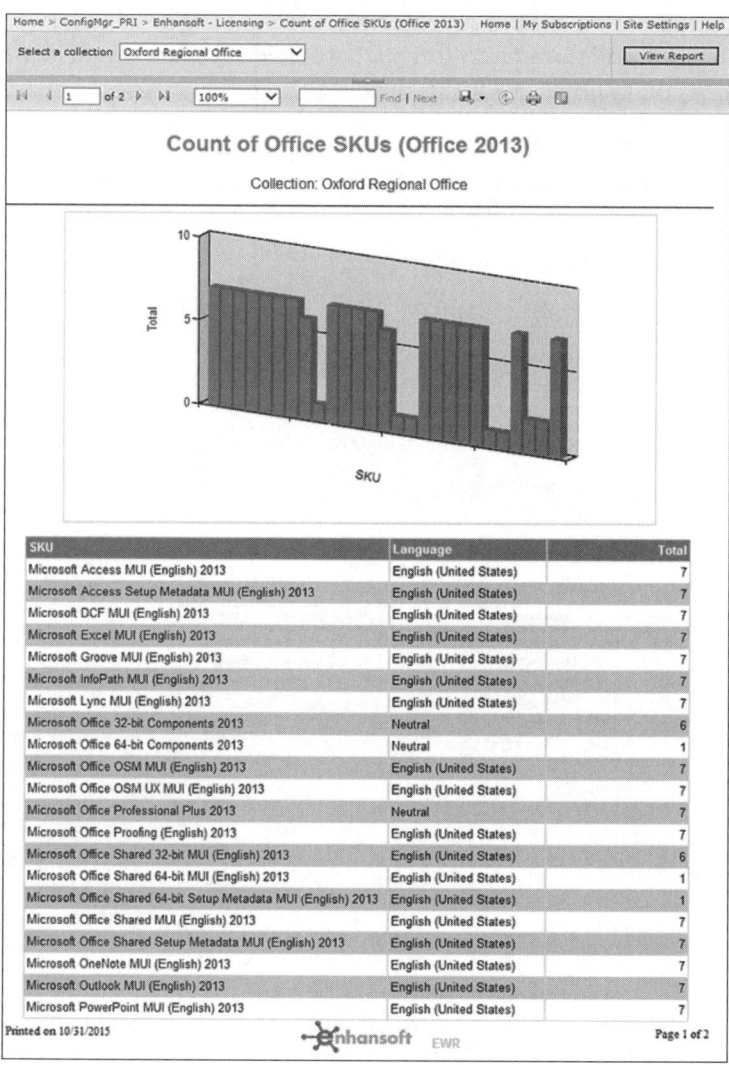

FIGURE 5.1   Example of a summarized data report.

TIP: PAPER SIZES

The letter paper size is the standard in the United States and is roughly equivalent to the A4 paper size in Europe. Regardless of the paper sizes that may be applicable for you, the same general guidelines and suggestions apply. For a comparison of paper sizes, see http://www.prepressure.com/library/paper-size.

Using a List Report

A *list report* is intended to expand on the information contained within the summarized data report. It provides additional data to help complete a picture as it pertains to the previous type of report. For example, say you want to see a list of systems with Microsoft Office Standard 2013 installed. This report is useful for administrators to see what systems or users would be impacted with a version upgrade. An example of a list report is shown in Figure 5.2.

A list report's design contains the following features:

▶ Typically uses the landscape page orientation with a paper size of either 11×8.5in (letter) or 14×8.5in (legal)

▶ Includes a table with the following characteristics:

    ▶ All columns on one page (width)

    ▶ Typically fewer than eight columns

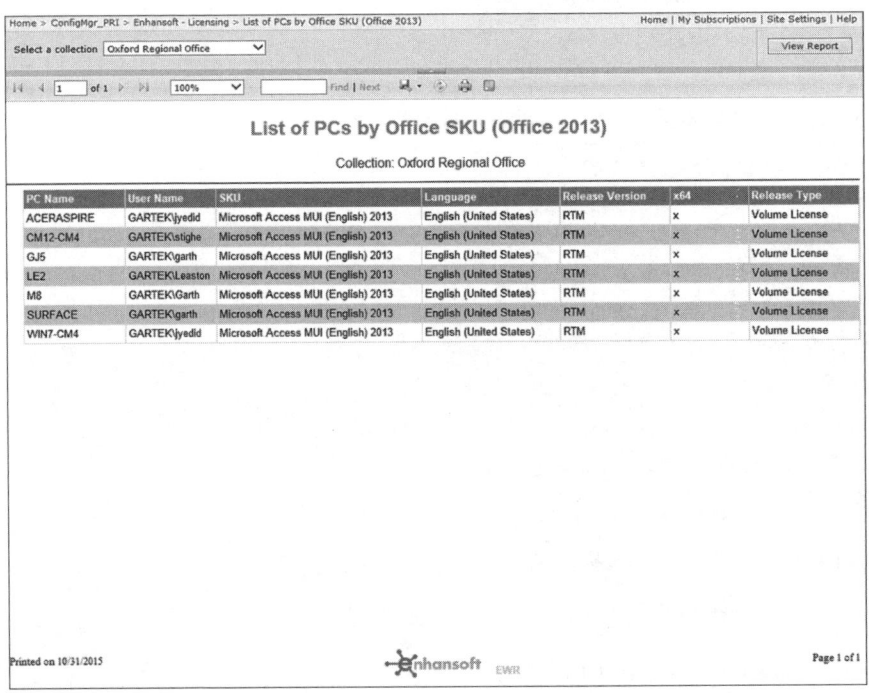

FIGURE 5.2   Example of a list report.

- ▶ Interactive sorting enabled on each column

- ▶ Shading applied to alternate rows to improve readability

▶ If necessary, provides the ability to navigate to another report for more details

Using a Detailed PC Report

A *detailed PC report* provides information about a specific computer. It may include information such as a list of installed software, hardware information, operating system details, history, and more. When linked from a summarized data report, it typically contains details about a single computer as it pertains to the summary information, such as all installed applications from a specific vendor. Figure 5.3 shows an example of a detailed PC report, listing all Microsoft Office 2013 products installed on the computer named CM12-CM4. A good detailed report usually has the following features:

▶ A table with the following characteristics:

- ▶ All columns on one page (width)

- ▶ Typically fewer than six columns

- ▶ Interactive sorting enabled on each column

- ▶ Shading applied to alternate rows to improve readability

▶ Similar page size/orientation to the list report (landscape 11×8.5in (letter) or 14×8.5in)

▶ Different sections within the report (header, body, footer) containing variable details

Microsoft Office 2013 Details

| PC Name: | CM12-CM4 | | | Top Console User: | | GARTEK\stighe | |

SKU	Language	Release Version	x64	Release Type
Microsoft Access MUI (English) 2013	English (United States)	RTM	x	Volume License
Microsoft Access Setup Metadata MUI (English) 2013	English (United States)	RTM	x	Volume License
Microsoft DCF MUI (English) 2013	English (United States)	RTM	x	Volume License
Microsoft Excel MUI (English) 2013	English (United States)	RTM	x	Volume License
Microsoft Groove MUI (English) 2013	English (United States)	RTM	x	Volume License
Microsoft InfoPath MUI (English) 2013	English (United States)	RTM	x	Volume License
Microsoft Lync MUI (English) 2013	English (United States)	RTM	x	Volume License
Microsoft Office 32-bit Components 2013	Neutral	RTM	x	Volume License
Microsoft Office OSM MUI (English) 2013	English (United States)	RTM	x	Volume License
Microsoft Office OSM UX MUI (English) 2013	English (United States)	RTM	x	Volume License
Microsoft Office Professional Plus 2013	Neutral	RTM	x	Volume License
Microsoft Office Proofing (English) 2013	English (United States)	RTM	x	Volume License
Microsoft Office Shared 32-bit MUI (English) 2013	English (United States)	RTM	x	Volume License
Microsoft Office Shared MUI (English) 2013	English (United States)	RTM	x	Volume License
Microsoft Office Shared Setup Metadata MUI (English) 2013	English (United States)	RTM	x	Volume License
Microsoft OneNote MUI (English) 2013	English (United States)	RTM	x	Volume License
Microsoft Outlook MUI (English) 2013	English (United States)	RTM	x	Volume License
Microsoft PowerPoint MUI (English) 2013	English (United States)	RTM	x	Volume License
Microsoft Publisher MUI (English) 2013	English (United States)	RTM	x	Volume License
Microsoft Word MUI (English) 2013	English (United States)	RTM	x	Volume License

Printed on 11/1/2015   Enhansoft EWR   Page 1 of 1

FIGURE 5.3   Example of a detailed PC report.

Understanding Report Design Considerations

A couple major design considerations are important for SSRS report writing:

▶ Reports should look consistent. It is important that custom reports be consistent in features such as drillthroughs, interactive sorting, and so on, in addition to having a consistent look and feel.

▶ The page layout should be consistent between the screen and printed versions. A report that displays properly on a computer screen may not be readable on paper due to information being cut off from the page. This could cause table columns and data to fall on separate pages and make the report almost impossible to follow when reading page to page. To prevent this from occurring, you should test and preview your reports on paper or by using the Export to PDF option.

To save time and ensure that your reports display properly, consider creating a template for each common page layout. Using these templates, you can quickly create a new report without having to worry about the initial page setup, margins, or report size. The templates can include other general settings and items to help save you time, including your company logo, custom color codes, and header and footer sections.

Providing a Consistent Look and Feel

A major pain point for someone using ConfigMgr reports is inconsistencies in look and feel. The built-in ConfigMgr reports that are installed with the reporting services point system role provide a similar look and feel and include some consistent basic features. Figure 5.4 presents two, side-by-side, built-in ConfigMgr reports as a comparison.

As shown by both of the reports in Figure 5.4 and any other built-in report, it is important to have consistency in the color style, table layout, and report header information. Each of these reports contains Microsoft System Center Configuration Manager as the component name in the top-right corner on a light blue background, followed by the report name in a dark, bolded font. An expandable Description section is also included in the header to describe the purpose of the report.

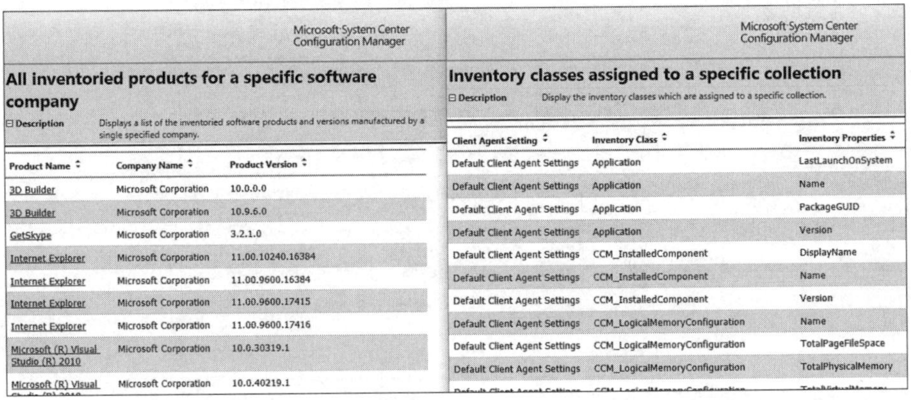

FIGURE 5.4   ConfigMgr built-in reports.

Notice the similarities between the tables shown in the two reports in Figure 5.4. Although each displays different data, the font of the header row is boldface, and each column allows for interactive sorting, indicated by the up and down arrows next to the column name. Each data row of the table alternates between a white background and a gray background, making it easier to read and follow a single row between each column. One last observation is the underlined data within the Product Name column, indicating that this is a hyperlink that opens a more detailed information report for that specific product. (The report on the right-hand side of Figure 5.4 does not contain hyperlinks on any column because there are no further details to provide.)

Now compare these reports to two different custom reports that were created for ConfigMgr, shown in Figure 5.5.

With a quick glance at these two custom reports, you can quickly see that they look very dissimilar. Not only do these reports look unprofessional, it is clear that they have quite a bit of room for improvement. They would be much better if they had a common header with a company logo and font and table styles with alternating row colors. It's difficult to say whether these reports were created by the same person or in the same company or where this data originated.

These are only two examples of reports. Imagine if every custom report available in this environment were completely different, with different styles or features. For a manager or technician trying to get valuable information from ConfigMgr, it can quickly become frustrating and confusing to try to locate and find the right report and to determine which report has the right combination of needed data. It is also difficult to understand how to navigate or use features of these reports. A feature such as interactive sorting can easily go unnoticed since it is only available on the Application Name column on the right-hand side of the report.

When presented with such different report styles, a user typically resorts to exploring and using the built-in reports to try to locate or piece together the desired data rather than coming to you for reports that contain the required data. The danger here is that non-administrators who don't understand ConfigMgr or its data are interpreting the output of reports they might stumble upon, potentially making important and costly decisions around it.

PC Name	Missing Software Updates	Last Hardware scan date		Applications		
ACERASPIRE	Needs 83 Patches	10/24/2014 9:46:20 AM				
CM12-J22	Needs 61 Patches	9/17/2014 7:46:59 PM				
CM16	Needs 118 Patches	10/25/2014 4:50:58 PM				
DELLE6510-2	Needs 28 Patches	6/11/2014 5:23:20 PM		Application Name	Version	Install Date
ELLEN-PC	Needs 143 Patches	10/24/2014 8:30:36 PM		Adobe Reader X (10.1.12)	10.1.12	20140923
ES-06	Needs 70 Patches	10/26/2014 5:00:11 PM		Adobe Reader X (10.1.9)	10.1.9	20140116
ES-08	Needs 70 Patches	10/26/2014 4:19:14 PM		Adobe Reader X (10.1.9)	10.1.9	20140222
ES-10	Needs 74 Patches	10/26/2014 3:29:55 PM		Adobe Reader X MUI	10.0.0	20111107
FRAME	Needs 67 Patches	8/31/2014 8:06:43 PM		Adobe Reader XI (11.0.03)	11.0.03	20130517
GARTEK-DC10	Needs 42 Patches	10/26/2014 3:37:29 PM		Adobe Reader XI (11.0.07)	11.0.07	20140515
GARTEK-DC5	Needs 135 Patches	10/26/2014 4:42:36 PM		Adobe Reader XI (11.0.07)	11.0.07	20140729
GARTEK-DC9	Needs 97 Patches	10/26/2014 6:08:24 PM		Adobe Reader XI (11.0.09)	11.0.09	20140923
GJ5	Needs 35 Patches	10/25/2014 10:25:14 PM		Adobe Reader XI (11.0.09)	11.0.09	20141003
HPPC	Needs 23 Patches	6/11/2014 9:15:28 PM		Adobe Reader XI (11.0.09)	11.0.09	20141007
IIS75TEST	Needs 138 Patches	9/17/2014 9:37:19 PM		Adobe Reader XI (11.0.09) MUI	11.0.09	20140918

FIGURE 5.5   Examples of custom ConfigMgr reports.

For example, someone without ConfigMgr experience could easily click on the Software File report, retrieve information regarding the quantity of photoshop.exe installations, and purchase enough licenses to accommodate the number shown in the report. However, he or she may not have taken into account that this number included all file shares where the source files are stored to allow administrators to install the software and any USB sticks connected to systems being used as installation media. The purchase now is for a far greater number of licenses than the actual number of installations, but the correct number could have been accurately gathered by running a report of Photoshop installations discovered from Programs and Features (v_Add_Remove_Programs). The built-in reports are good at providing general, high-level information, regardless of the environment or implementations you may have, but they rarely provide the specific data that may be pertinent or requested.

Printed Versus Interactive Reports

When you are building a report, you generally view it within the design tool you are using by using the preview option or through the SSRS Configuration Manager website. This is referred to as *interactive* mode. However, there are times when it is necessary to print a report or export it from the website. When this occurs, you need to be aware of the page layout and where there are page breaks in the report. A report may look great in interactive mode but may cut off at the wrong places when printed or exported.

The example shown in Figure 5.6 is taken from interactive mode, where the report looks great and all columns are visible.

However, as Figure 5.7 shows, when this report is printed, the last column is not on the same page. The Last Hardware scan date column is cut off and appears on page 2 of the report. This is due to page sizing and must be addressed to make the report useful in interactive mode and as well as when printed. An easy way to avoid this situation is to create a template report for each page size and ensure that it does not exceed the width of the page.

The Benefits of Using Report Templates

Templates can ensure proper printing and exporting of reports, and they can also contain most custom configurations to provide a consistent experience in different reports. When you are creating templates to fit page sizes, you should also include the header and footer configurations, custom color codes (explained in Chapter 8, "SSRS Reporting Features"), your company logo, and any other desired features. In addition to enabling the creation of reports that have a consistent look and feel—even those created by different administrators—using templates can significantly reduce the time and effort required to create a new report.

Begin planning your templates around the page sizes you want to support. The following templates are based on the most commonly used paper sizes for printing:

▶ **Letter Portrait template (8.5×11in):** This template is the letter page size with a portrait orientation. This layout is preferred for summarized data reports containing charts, graphs, and tables with only several columns (typically four or fewer). Since this page layout is not very wide, the authors do not recommend using it with detailed reports that contain large tables with many columns.

PC Name	User Name0	Missing Software Updates	Last Hardware scan date
ACERASPIRE	GARTEK\JYedid	Needs 83 Patches	10/24/2014 9:46:20 AM
CM12-J22		Needs 61 Patches	9/17/2014 7:46:59 PM
CM16		Needs 118 Patches	10/25/2014 4:50:58 PM
DELLE6510-2	GARTEK\Leaston	Needs 28 Patches	6/11/2014 5:23:20 PM
ELLEN-PC	GARTEK\ellen	Needs 143 Patches	10/24/2014 8:30:36 PM
ES-06		Needs 70 Patches	10/26/2014 5:00:11 PM
ES-08		Needs 70 Patches	10/26/2014 4:19:14 PM
ES-10		Needs 74 Patches	10/26/2014 3:29:55 PM
FRAME	GARTEK\frame	Needs 67 Patches	8/31/2014 8:06:43 PM
GARTEK-DC10		Needs 42 Patches	10/26/2014 3:37:29 PM
GARTEK-DC5		Needs 135 Patches	10/26/2014 4:42:36 PM
GARTEK-DC9		Needs 97 Patches	10/26/2014 6:08:24 PM
GJ5	GARTEK\Garth	Needs 35 Patches	10/25/2014 10:25:14 PM
HPPC	NT AUTHORITY\SYSTEM	Needs 23 Patches	6/11/2014 9:15:28 PM
IIS75TEST		Needs 138 Patches	9/17/2014 9:37:19 PM
LE2	GARTEK\Leaston	Needs 98 Patches	10/23/2014 4:22:08 PM
M8	GARTEK\Garth	Needs 120 Patches	10/26/2014 3:03:37 PM
MEDIAPC	GARTEK\Garth	Needs 72 Patches	10/26/2014 3:19:59 PM
OPSMAN2012	GARTEK\garth	Needs 144 Patches	8/19/2014 5:30:30 PM
SURFACE	GARTEK\Garth	Needs 84 Patches	10/13/2014 7:45:53 PM
VMM2012		Needs 150 Patches	8/19/2014 3:29:54 PM
WIN10PRE		Needs 5 Patches	10/23/2014 10:12:52 AM
WIN2K8	NT AUTHORITY\SYSTEM	Needs 68 Patches	10/25/2014 7:04:32 PM
WIN2K8R2		Needs 94 Patches	10/25/2014 6:58:59 PM
WIN7-CM4		Needs 344 Patches	10/25/2014 11:04:47 PM
WIN8	GARTEK\Stighe	Needs 116 Patches	10/24/2014 5:10:50 PM
win81-cm4		Needs 49 Patches	10/26/2014 3:32:45 PM

FIGURE 5.6   Report view in interactive mode.

▶ **Letter Landscape template (11×8.5in):** This page template uses the letter paper size with a landscape orientation. This layout is ideal for list and detailed PC types of reports containing tables with several columns, as it is wider than the Letter Portrait template.

▶ **Legal Landscape template (14×8.5in):** This template uses legal paper size with a landscape orientation. This size is slightly wider and allows you to create reports that contain tables with a large number of columns that will not easily fit on an 11×8.5 inch sheet of paper. But beware: Not all printers have the ability to use or are outfitted with legal-sized paper. If your environment doesn't allow for this size, it may be best not to create reports using this template.

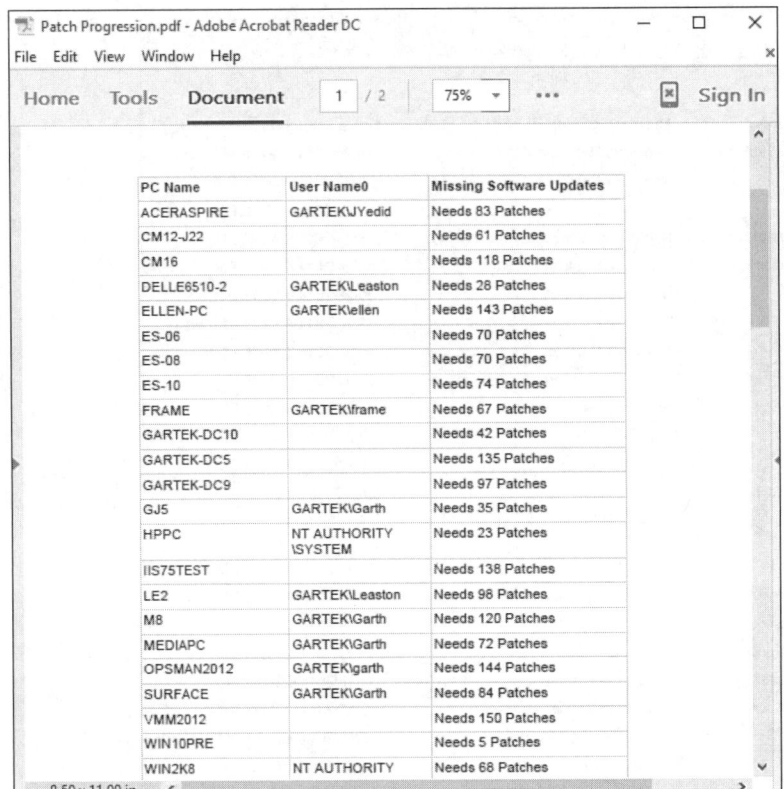

FIGURE 5.7   Example of the same report shown in Figure 5.6, now printed and missing the last column on the right.

TIP: USING LEGAL-SIZE PAPER

The authors strongly recommend that you notify users when reports are created using a legal paper size. This can be done either in the report comments in SSRS or as a note on the report itself. Such notification can prevent someone from accidentally sending these reports to the wrong printer tray or to a printer that does not have legal size sheets of paper.

The Ability to Export Reports

SSRS reports can easily be exported to different formats directly from the report website. The same is true for exporting reports from SSDT-BI. There are several reasons an administrator might want to export a report. The following sections highlight some of the most common reasons and export formats used for SSRS reports.

Exporting to PDF

Exporting directly from SSDT-BI is a practical way to test the viewability of a report to ensure that it is printer friendly before adding it to the SSRS website. Exporting to PDF format is the recommended way to ensure that a report displays properly on a page without any columns or data being cut off. You might also need to export a report to PDF when you want to keep the layout and style of the report but not allow the data to be altered or modified—so you can, for example, share it with a client.

Exporting to CSV
Reports are often exported to provide data to someone who might not have sufficient permissions to access the reports directly from the report website, either because this is a one-time request or the data is being used for audit purposes. If you want to export a report's data only in plain text, with no formatting or styles, you can choose Export to CSV (comma-separated values).

Exporting to Excel
If you need to provide a report to someone and want to maintain the layout and style as it appears in SSRS but want to allow the data to be manipulated, select the Export to Excel option. This option allows you to use and apply Microsoft Excel features on the report data, such as copying/pasting, highlighting, removing columns or rows, filtering table data, adding or modifying chart properties, incorporating formulas and functions, and more. This format can allow someone using an existing report to slightly customize it or make use of the data.

5

> **TIP: USING EXCEL TO MODIFY A REPORT**
>
> If someone is using Microsoft Excel to modify or customize a report on a regular basis, the authors recommend that you create an SSRS report to suit his or her needs. Doing so can prevent constant frustration or wasted time and effort from requiring the user to export and modify the data manually.

Exporting to XML File
The Export to XML export option returns an XML-formatted report that contains only data. Layout information and page breaks are not maintained in this export format. The XML file can be used to import the data into a database or within a custom application that supports data input from XML.

Exporting to MHTML (Web Archive)
The Export to MHTML (web archive) option provides a fully formed HTML page of a report. This is the same format used to view a report from the SSRS website using a web browser. The file output from this export is a fully formed HTML page containing the HTML, HEAD, and BODY tags. The HTML file output from the report is supported by Internet Explorer, Firefox, Chrome, Safari, and other modern browsers.

Exporting to TIFF File
Exporting using the TIFF format generates a report as an image file with a .tif extension. This image file can be used to display the report in an image viewer and then print it. The report can also be converted from this format to many other image formats, including .bmp, .gif, .jpeg, and .png. The TIFF format can be useful for adding a report as a picture on a website, in a presentation, or in a Word document.

Exporting to Word

Select the Export to Word option to export a report in .docx format, supported by Word 2007 and higher. From the exported document, the contents of the report as well as styles can be modified using Microsoft Word. The Word page size of the export is set by the report properties. Not all features of the report are supported with this format; for example, interactive sorting is not supported, and data will be sorted in Word as it was when the report was exported. Hyperlink and drillthrough links are supported on text box and image items as hyperlinks; however, they are not supported on chart or map items. Charts, images, and map report items are converted as static images in Word. For additional information on the Word format, see https://msdn.microsoft.com/en-us/library/dd283105.aspx.

Using SSRS Report Subscriptions

It is important not to overlook the reporting export features and to make sure your reports function properly even if you don't believe they will be printed. The SSRS report website provides a *subscription* feature that allows users with access to reports to subscribe to individual reports that are executed according to a scheduled date and time and delivered via email or file sharing. When creating a subscription, a user specifies a delivery method, format, and schedule. The report is run, exported to the specified format, and delivered to the user based on the defined schedule. Note that if a report doesn't fit on a page or isn't scaled properly for a regular page size, this may cause issues if someone wants a report to be automatically run and be made available at certain intervals. Further information, along with instructions for setting up subscriptions, is provided in Chapter 8.

Using Custom Report Requests

Some reports are easy and fairly straightforward, such as the All applications installed on a system or All systems with a specified application reports. As you start creating custom reports, publishing them on the SSRS website, and sharing their links with various people and groups, you will realize that many people are interested in the data gathered by ConfigMgr. Service desk technicians will want to see reports for deployed hardware makes/ models along with driver versions and client health. Software licensing departments may want to know the applications that are deployed, the number of installs for each, and their usage to forecast budgets and true-up agreements. Development teams may want to know the frequency and time of use as well as how many systems are using an application that they plan to replace. Security officers will be interested in software update compliance, the impact of vulnerable software versions, and antivirus installation confirmation. The list of requests for ConfigMgr data can soon begin to feel overwhelming.

Rather than deal with each request one at a time as each request is brought forward, consider spending some time before you begin creating and publishing reports to come up with a solid report request process.

Gathering Report Information

A good foundation for a request process provides a clear and easy way to gather information from the requestor. At first it may be easy to sit down with each requestor and discuss each individual request one at a time. However, this individual gathering of information becomes very time-consuming and is not maintainable in the real world.

The best way to avoid this situation and to be proactive is to develop a checklist or a request form. This way, when you receive a request, it already includes most of the information you need to start planning and creating the report.

The authors include a sample request form, Requesting a Report, available as online content for this book (see Appendix C, "Available Online"), to help you get started. Figure 5.8 shows an example of this request form. You can modify the sample form as required to suit your needs and environment. The following sections describe the fields in this form to provide you with further information on its use.

Report Information	
TICKET NUMBER	
REQUESTOR	
REQUESTOR'S EMAIL ADDRESS	
REQUESTOR'S TELEPHONE #	
REPORT TITLE	
DESCRIPTION	
INTENDED USAGE	
PROMPTS	Yes / No
CHART	Yes / No
TABLE	Yes / No
PAGE ORIENTATION	
PAPER SIZE	
REPLACING A REPORT	
PRIMARY DATA EXIST WITHIN CONFIGMGR CONSOLE	Example being: • Resource Explorer • Collections • Device properties
AVAILABLE MOCK-UP OF THE REPORT	Yes / No
LOCATION OF MOCK-UP	

FIGURE 5.8   Sample request form example.

Report Information

This section of the form requests general information about the requested report. These questions are high level and typically require simple yes/no answers, and other sections of the form get into details about these areas. The Report Information section includes the following fields:

▶ **Ticket Number:** Requires an IT service management (ITSM) ticket number as a tracking mechanism for the requested report.

▶ **Requestor:** Identifies the individual requesting the report. Any follow-up questions, as well as the report delivery, should be done with the individual listed here.

▶ **Requestor's Email Address:** Identifies the email address of the requestor for further follow-up or delivery of the completed report.

▶ **Requestor's Telephone Number:** Identifies the telephone number of the requestor for further follow-up regarding the requested report.

▶ **Report Title:** Identifies the name of the report that will be used on the SSRS website and in the report's header section.

▶ **Description:** Provides a short overview of the report and should identify the type of report and its purpose. This information is listed on the SSRS website by the report title. You can also include it in the report header.

▶ **Intended Usage:** Identifies the purpose of the report, how it will be used, what the report is aiming to accomplish, and the questions answered by this report's data. This field should help you understand the intent of the request, as well as ensure that the request is aligned with its purpose. More information regarding this field is provided further in the "Questioning Report Requirements" section of this chapter.

▶ **Prompt:** Uses a simple Yes/No value to identify whether the report will prompt the viewer for a parameter value to filter or tailor the data output. If the value is Yes, further information for the prompt should be answered in the Parameters section.

▶ **Chart:** Uses a simple Yes/No value to identify whether the report will include a chart item. If the value is Yes, further information regarding the chart should be provided in the Chart Details section.

▶ **Table:** Uses a simple Yes/No value to identify whether the report will include a table item. If the value is Yes, further information regarding the table should be provided in the Table Details section.

▶ **Page Orientation:** Identifies the page orientation the report should use. This could be either portrait or landscape. Consider this field a suggestion; if the client is asking for a large table or a lot of information, you may have no choice but to provide the report in landscape orientation.

▶ **Paper Size:** Indicates the desired paper size of the report. You can provide a check box for each paper size supported in your templates. Again, this field should be considered a suggestion and not a requirement.

▶ **Replacing a Report:** Identifies whether this request is to update or replace an existing report. Information on the report life cycle is provided in the "Report Life Cycle and Maintenance" section of this chapter.

▶ **Primary Data Exists Within ConfigMgr Console:** (Optional) Helps identify the requested data and where it can be found within the ConfigMgr console. Not all requestors may be able to answer this item, but if populated, this could save you time by helping you understand what the requestor is looking for and therefore help you locate the correct SQL view for use by the query in the report.

▶ **Available Mock-up of the Report:** Uses simple `Yes/No` value to identify whether a mock-up or sample of the requested report exists. If the value is `Yes`, the Location of Mock-up field should be completed.

▶ **Location of Mock-up:** Identifies the location of a sample or mock-up of the requested report. This is an optional field. If provided, the mock-up can help save you time designing the report and understanding the request.

Parameters

The Parameters section of the request form collects additional details regarding each required prompt of the report. This section should be duplicated for each parameter that is to be included in the report. As you may notice, this section includes an extra column, Further Details/Comments. This column is included to help provide additional details for the requested field. The Parameters section includes the following fields:

▶ **Name:** Specifies a unique name for the parameter. This information is used when creating the report parameter and to identify the parameter's value within the report.

▶ **Subtitle with Prompt Details:** Uses a simple `Yes/No` value to identify whether a subtitle for the prompt and the selected value should be shown in the report's header section, under the report title. `Yes` is assumed on all reports by default. Further information can be provided to identify the subtitle name and location.

▶ **Prompt Text:** Indicates the prompt text displayed immediately after running a report, before the query is executed and any data is provided. This should indicate to the report viewer what input is required in order to provide tailored data output from this report. An example is provided as `Select a collection`.

▶ **Optional Prompt:** Uses a simple `Yes/No` value to identify whether the prompt is optional, allowing the report to be run without the viewer providing any prompt value.

▶ **Default Value:** Indicates the default value for the prompt, if any. If a value is provided, the prompt's value field is prepopulated at runtime.

▶ **Prompt Type:** Identifies the type of prompt displayed when running the report. Possible values are `text box`, which provides free-form value entry; `drop down`, which displays a list of values to choose from; and `multi-select`, which provides a list of values to choose from when multiple values can be selected.

▶ **Cascade Prompt:** Uses a simple `Yes/No` value to identify when multiple prompts are required and any subsequent prompt values should be based on, or filtered on, the value of the initial prompt. If the value is `Yes`, the cascade prompt hierarchy should be identified under the Further Details/Comments column.

Chart Details

The Chart Details section of the request form collects additional information regarding each chart required for the report. If multiple charts are requested, this section should be duplicated and answered for each individual chart. As you may notice, there is an extra column in this section, Further Details/Comments. This column is included to help provide additional details for the requested field. The Chart Details section contains the following fields:

▶ **Chart Name:** Specifies the name of the chart. The name must be unique, and by default it is set to `Chart<ID>` (for example, `Chart1`). This name is used as a reference between report items and is not visible when running the report.

▶ **Chart Title:** (Optional) Specifies the label that appears above the chart itself.

▶ **Type of Chart:** Identifies the type of chart item to use to represent the data. Possible options include pie chart, bar chart, line chart, pyramid chart, donut chart, and more. To make it easier for the requestor to choose, provide a list of check boxes to choose from for each chart type.

▶ **Include Legend:** Uses a simple `Yes/No` value to specify whether to include a legend. If `Yes` is chosen, a legend can be placed either to the left, right, above, or below the chart to show the different data values along with their colors in the chart.

▶ **Include Labels:** Uses a simple `Yes/No` value to specify whether to include labels. `Yes` indicates that labels should be shown on the chart. A label can be displayed either inside or outside a bar, line, or pie section to identify the data value of that indicator.

▶ **Custom Fill Colors:** Uses a simple `Yes/No` value to specify whether to allow custom fill colors. If the requestor requires custom fill colors for the chart, the RGB color codes to use should be provided in the Further Details/Comments column. The standard colors used in the template are used by default.

▶ **Drillthrough on Chart Items:** Uses a simple `Yes/No` value to specify whether the items in the chart can contain an action that allows each chart item to be clicked to redirect to a detailed report of the data. Typically the detailed report contains a table listing all individual items that comprise that specific chart item.

▶ **Table Will Provide More Details of Chart:** Uses a simple `Yes/No` value to indicate whether a table should follow the chart to describe the results. If `Yes` is selected, the table details should be provided in the next section of the form, Table Details.

Table Details

The Table Details section of the request form collects additional information regarding each required table. Like the Chart Details section, this section should be duplicated for each table that is to be included in the report. An extra part to this section, Table Layout, outlines exactly how the table item in the report should be created. The Table Details section includes the following fields:

▶ **Table Name:** Specifies the name of the table item in the report. The name must be unique, and by default it is set to `Table<ID>` (for example, `Table1`) This name is used as a reference between report items and is not visible when running the report.

▶ **Table Title:** Uses a simple Yes/No value to specify whether to include a table title. If Yes is selected, a label is added above the chart with the desired title, indicated in the Further Details/Comments column.

▶ **Number of Columns:** Indicates the total number of columns to be included in the table. Further details about the columns are provided in the Table Layout section of the form. Note that the number of columns can affect the page layout required for the report.

▶ **Interactive Sorting:** Offers the options Yes/Some/No. If Yes is chosen, all columns of the table will have the interactive sorting option enabled, allowing the columns to be sorted manually by the report viewer. If Some is selected, the columns where interactive sorting are desired should be listed in the Further Information/Comments column.

▶ **Alternating Row Colors:** Specifies the color to use for alternating rows. The default value is White/Silver. If different alternating colors are desired, they should be indicated in the Value field.

▶ **Match Chart Colors (if Applicable):** Specifies whether the chart colors match the table background. If a chart is included in the report, the chart colors that are used will match the table background colors by default. If this is not desired, select No and specify the color details for use in the table.

▶ **Drillthrough:** Specifies whether the user can use a drillthrough in a table to view a more detailed report. For count and list reports, the default value is Yes. However for computer detail reports, the default is No. If Yes is selected, the reader of the report will be able to click on a field in the table to open a more detailed report, such as a System Name field linking to a computer detail report.

Table Layout

The Table Layout subsection of the Table Details section collects layout details for the table item. Based on the desired number of columns, indicated in the Table Details section, fill out this section to provide the following for each column:

▶ **Column #:** Specifies the column number and is prefilled with numbers 1 through 8. The fields below should be completed for each column included in the table.

▶ **Column Title:** Indicates the name for the column, which will appear in the header row.

▶ **Column Data:** Indicates the information that will be provided by this column.

▶ **Column Action (Link):** Specifies the action, or link, that will be set on the column data. The action can be either a drillthrough to a detailed report or a URL to a website.

Export

The Export section of the request form collects additional information regarding the intended use of the report. It confirms whether the report is intended to be exportable, and if so, the formats that should be validated before the report is published to the SSRS website. The Export section includes the following fields:

▶ **Exportable:** Uses a simple `Yes/No` value to indicate whether the report will be used in an exported format. If `Yes`, ensure that the layout of the report is functional and maintained against the formats indicated in this section. SSRS allows all reports to be exported; this field is intended to provide insight into how the report will be used and to double-check that the format renders the report properly and as intended.

▶ **Select Export Formats:** Provides a selection of all formats that are expected to be used when running and exporting the report. By default, all reports should be rendered and validated in TIFF and PDF formats, as these are typically the most commonly used types.

Security

The Security section is intended to collect details around any specific required access or restrictions to run the report and any subscription information. Requestors may not know the answers to some of these fields; based on the data of the report and SQL views used in your query, you will be able to determine whether extra permissions within ConfigMgr are required to view the data. The Security section includes the following fields:

▶ **Required Role-Based Administration (RBA):** Specifies any extra permissions required for ConfigMgr, through role-based administration, required to view the report data. This is optional for requestors, as most are not aware of required permissions; however, this should be filled out by the report author for tracking purposes. More information regarding role-based administration is provided in Chapter 9, "Role-Based Administration and Reporting."

▶ **Restrict Access to an AD Group:** Indicates all groups that will require access if access to the report should be restricted. When the report is added to the SSRS website, only members of those indicated groups will see the report listed.

▶ **Access Required to ConfigMgr Collection:** Indicates the collection if the data requires additional access to a ConfigMgr collection. Once again, most requestors may not know if access to a collection is required. However, this should be completed by the report author for tracking and auditing purposes.

▶ **Configure Subscription:** Uses a simple `Yes/No` value to indicate whether any subscriptions should be configured for this report in SSRS. Clients may be able to configure their own subscriptions in SSRS; however, it is much easier to have the subscriptions created by an administrator once the report is published to SSRS.

▶ **Subscription Type:** Provides two options: `Email` and `File share`. By default, `Email` is selected if subscriptions are requested.

▶ **Subscription Run Schedule:** Indicates when the subscription should be run for the report as well the recurrence (for example, the first of every month).

▶ **Subscribers/Location:** Indicates a list of email addresses to be used if the subscription type is `Email` or the report path location if the subscription type is `File share`.

For `Email`, the list of email addresses is set as the recipients of the report; these people will receive an email with the report as an attachment from SSRS, based on the run schedule.

Report Customizations

The Report Customizations section is included for the requestor to provide any details around settings or items that should not follow the default or template styles and settings used in most reports. Many fields in this section look for justification as to why a customization is required in order to determine whether the extra time and effort incurred by not following the default template is valid. The Report Customizations section includes the following fields:

▶ **Include Subreports:** Uses a simple `Yes`/`No` value to indicate whether the report should include a subreport. If a subreport is chosen, provide the requested subreport name under the further details/comments column. By default, reports do not include any subreports; this value is considered a customization because the requested report must be the correct paper size and orientation to match the subreport.

▶ **Images:** Uses a simple `Yes`/`No` value to indicate whether additional images are to be included in the body of the report. This is not a typical request; therefore, the default value is `No`.

▶ **Customization Required from the Default Template Report:** Indicates whether any changes or customizations are required to the report template. These can include changes to the header and/or footer sections of the report and may include different logos, URLs, colors, font styles, and more. If any changes are required, justifications must be provided, as explained next.

▶ **Justification:** Provides justification for the requested customizations to the default template. Using a template saves a considerable amount of time, and any customizations can significantly increase the amount of effort required. Always ensure that justifications are valid. Some examples could include reports for external clients or different branding for regions or customers.

▶ **Detail Each Customization Required:** Provides specific details for each customization to the template that is required. If different logos are required, they should be provided here, or a location for them should be specified. If colors should be different, the RGB color codes and details where they should be used are to be provided in this field.

Sample Report Form with Examples

To help illustrate how each field in the sample request form relates to a completed report, the next few figures contain numbered items, as follows:

▶ Figure 5.9 shows the completed report in the folder view of the SSRS website.

▶ Figure 5.10 shows the report's prompts immediately after execution.

▶ Figure 5.11 shows the executed report once a prompt has been provided.

The numbered items on these figures relate to the request form's fields and the values listed below:

- ▶ Report Title (1): Count of Operating System Versions
- ▶ Description (2): Summarized data view of all Operating System versions by Collection
- ▶ Prompts: Yes
    - ▶ Name: Coll01
    - ▶ Prompt Text (3): Select a collection
    - ▶ Prompt Type (4): Dropdown
    - ▶ Subtitle with Prompt Details (5): Yes
    - ▶ Optional Prompt: No
    - ▶ Default Value: None
    - ▶ Cascade Prompt: No
- ▶ Chart (6): Yes
    - ▶ Chart Name: Chart1
    - ▶ Chart Title (7): Count of Operating Systems
    - ▶ Type of Chart (8): Stacked Column
    - ▶ Include Legend: No
    - ▶ Include Labels (9): Yes (inside labels are shown)
    - ▶ Custom Fill Colors (10): No (default template colors are used)
    - ▶ Drillthrough on Chart Items: No
    - ▶ Table Will Provide More Details of Chart: Yes
- ▶ Table (11): Yes
    - ▶ Table Name: Table1
    - ▶ Table Title: No
    - ▶ Number of columns: 3
    - ▶ Interactive Sorting (12): Yes (all columns)
    - ▶ Alternating Row Colors (13): White/Silver
    - ▶ Drillthrough: Yes—Systems with specified Operating System (link to existing report)
    - ▶ Table Layout: See Table 5.1.

TABLE 5.1   Table Layout: Sample Request Form

	#1	#2	#3
Column Title	Operating System	Service Pack	Total
Column Data	OS name	Service pack version	Total count of installs
Column Action (Link)	None	None	None

▶ Page Orientation: Portrait

▶ Paper Size: Letter (8.5×11in)

▶ Replacing a Report: No

▶ Primary Data Exists Within ConfigMgr Console: Resource Explorer (Hardware | Operating System | Caption)

TIP: WHERE TO PUBLISH THE REQUEST FORM

If your environment or help desk has already published request forms, whether for hardware, software, or as part of another request process, try to combine or add the report request form that you will create to this same process. You can save time by using an already defined process for client requests and also facilitate report creation.

Keep in mind that only the main fields and options of the request form are described in the preceding list, as some fields provide background information for follow-ups, and not every field applies to every report. The request form itself is available as online content (see Appendix C).

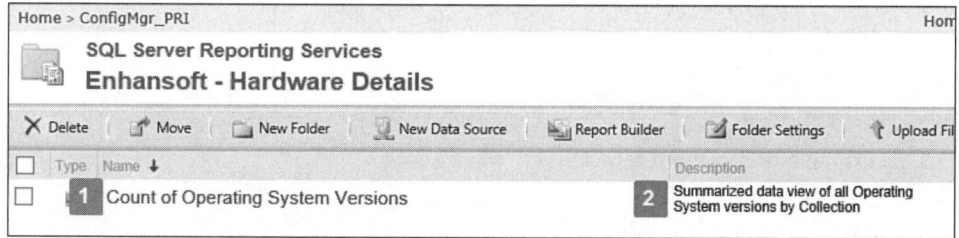

FIGURE 5.9   Report in the list view on the SSRS website.

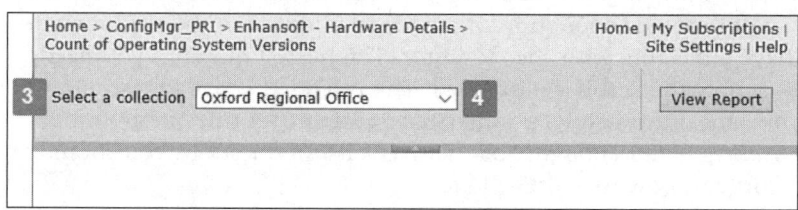

FIGURE 5.10   The report's prompts after execution.

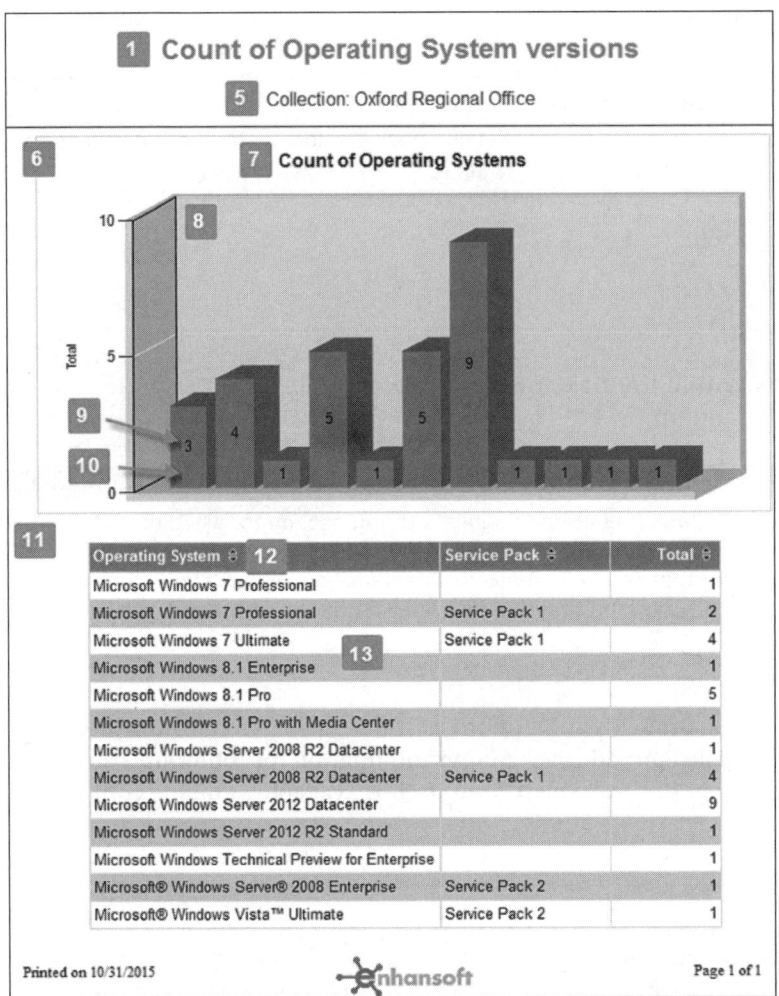

FIGURE 5.11   Example of a custom report.

Questioning Report Requirements

Before blindly creating a report based on a completed request form, take the time to go through the requirements to fully understand the request and to ensure that it is practical. Some request forms may not provide enough information to understand the requirements, and you may need to have a meeting with the requestor. The biggest question you need to ask—and challenge—is how the report will be used. The Intended Usage (or Purpose) field of the request form is meant to help you understand and answer this question, but sometimes the answer you get is not enough. Following is a list of questions you should ask before creating a report and how to address them:

▶ Is the request asking for too much data or too many fields to be properly displayed on a page?

  ▶ This may be the case if a request is asking for too much data, such as too many fields or columns; asking for information that does not go well together (for example, all applications installed on all systems, with versions, hardware information, operating system version, and patch compliance); or asking for a query that will return so many rows that it will be unusable.

  ▶ When too much data or too many fields are requested, propose to break up the report into a report series that contains a summary report of the data with drillthrough links to go into detailed reports that provide further information. This way the viewers get a high-level view of the information they want, and from that information, they can choose to click on the data where they want to see more information (such as system names to see their hardware details).

▶ How frequently will this report be used?

  ▶ Try to determine the frequency or usage of the report. For example, if the purpose of the report is to satisfy an audit from a vendor on license information, chances are it will only be used one time.

  ▶ If the report is only to be used once or very infrequently, it is not worth the time and effort required to create a full report. Instead, create and execute the SQL query in SQL Server Management Studio and save the results in Microsoft Excel. This way you can save time and avoid wasting effort on a report that will be used a few times and then forgotten.

▶ Do the description and intended usage/purpose of the report align with the requested data and items?

  ▶ Sometimes a requestor does not know what information he wants to see, so he adds a lot of details or is unclear on the specific need.

  ▶ In this scenario, when the usage or description does not match up with the data requested, it is best to sit down to understand what the requestor wants to get from the report. Always begin by understanding what the report will be used for and then propose to the requestor what data should be included in the report.

REAL WORLD: UNDERSTANDINGING REPORT REQUESTS

Keep in mind that requestors do not always know what they want to see. As an administrator and report creator, it is also your job to ensure that a report is usable and meets the overall purpose. Just because someone asks for certain data does not mean that is what is needed. Always ask questions to clarify requests when you are unsure or when requests aren't clear. This saves you a lot of time that you might spend creating useless reports and going back and forth with the requestor.

Report Verification and Delivery

Once the data has been gathered and you have created the requested report, it is important to confirm that everything functions as it should and that all requested elements have been addressed. A problem with unplanned and unorganized report writing is the amount of back and forth required with the report requestor, which often leads to wasted time and effort. Not only is it important to proactively gather all necessary information to create a report, it is equally important to have a good checklist and ensure the proper delivery of the report. Before providing the requestor with his requested report, take the time to verify all elements of the report both within SSDT-BI and once it is published from the SSRS website. Following is a checklist of items to help you verify that a report is ready for requestor testing and approval:

▶ The report has been created using a template that matches the paper type and page orientation requested.

▶ The report title is visible in the header portion of the report.

▶ If applicable, the prompt values are listed in the header section of the report.

▶ If applicable, required parameters and prompts appear when the report is run.

    ▶ If a dropdown list of available parameters was requested, the expected dropdown list is populated and functional.

    ▶ If a default value was specified, this value appears when running the report.

▶ If a chart was requested, the report contains a chart.

    ▶ The requested chart type is used to represent the data.

    ▶ The legends and labels appear as requested on the chart item.

▶ The report owner has been identified in a tracking system, either in the report description or knowledge base.

▶ The report is sorted by default on the requested fields.

▶ If requested, the data is grouped by the specified data field.

▶ Any requested drillthrough links and hyperlinks function as intended.

▶ Any desired conditional formatting functions as requested.

▶ All identified file types have been tested for accuracy, page breaks, and style formatting.

▶ Access to the report has been granted to all requested user accounts, security groups, and distribution lists.

▶ The report subscription feature has been tested with your account to ensure that the report type is as requested, delivery is functioning, and formatting is correct.

TIP: REPORT SUBSCRIPTIONS

Do not worry about configuring subscriptions or security roles until the client has signed off and tested the report. Only then should you create the requested security roles and subscriptions to ensure that the report isn't inadvertently used or emailed with incorrect data.

Once you have walked through this checklist and ensured that all elements of the report are functioning and to your liking, have the report requestor validate it to ensure that the report is to his satisfaction and is what he wanted. Always provide the requestor with a link to the report so the requestor can run it independently when he wants. Once the report is accepted, ensure that the proper subscription details are created based on the request. Creating new subscriptions can be difficult or confusing for some users, and for reports that are scheduled for infrequent recurrence, it may take quite some time for a user to realize it didn't run properly. It is usually easier and quicker to create a subscription on behalf of the user in such a case.

These recommendations can help ensure that a user is satisfied with his reports, and they show a mature reporting process.

Report Life Cycle and Maintenance

Over the life of ConfigMgr, many reports will be created, replaced, retired, or no longer required. Keeping track of these reports over time can become cumbersome, and old reports that are no longer needed can begin to add up. The authors recommend that you keep track of custom reports and ensure that any reports that are no longer required or used are removed from the report website. Clients will often be satisfied with a report once it is created; however, due to the fast rate of change and product version releases, the needs of a report may change as well. This can lead to modifying reports or completely replacing them. In these cases, it is important that you verify and consult with identified report owners before removing published reports. When possible, try to consolidate similar reports and remove reports that are no longer required. The authors recommend reviewing all custom reports every 6 to 12 months to ensure that they are still valid and being used.

TIP: REPORT LIFE CYCLE

It is important to include both the Owner and Replacing an Existing Report fields in the report request form. This can help you keep your reports current and eliminate any old reports that are no longer required.

When removing a report from the SSRS website, rather than actually delete it, it is best to be cautious and copy the report to a file share. If at a later time a report is requested that is similar to one that has been retired, you will be glad you have this backup.

To assist with maintenance and cut down on the time required to modify and create new reports, the authors strongly recommend creating one central SSDT-BI report server project location, stored on a file share that is backed up regularly. The steps to create a report server project are described in Chapter 6, "Building a Basic Report." When multiple administrators are creating reports, having a central location greatly reduces the time and effort required to modify existing reports as the reports are stored and available immediately when opening the report server project, regardless of who created the initial report. This method also ensures that all reports are created from the same templates and follow the same basic formatting and styles, and it allows for collaboration and sharing of features previously created and tested from existing reports. Utilizing this central report server project, any updates or modifications can simply be uploaded to replace the existing report on the SSRS website.

TIP: PROVIDING FOR REPORT BACKUPS

ConfigMgr does not back up custom reports (.rdl files) as part of its backup task. Make sure that you plan for this and configure a recurring backup job for either the .rdl files or the report server database.

Creating separate folders on the SSRS website to store custom reports also greatly helps report viewers find and run their reports. When the reporting services point role is installed, ConfigMgr automatically creates a reporting folder structure where out-of-the-box reports are placed. This can sometimes get overwhelming or confusing for end users trying to find custom reports they have requested. To alleviate this problem, create a new folder to store custom reports. This also helps with report maintenance for administrators, as all the custom reports can be easily identified from the default ConfigMgr reports.

FIGURE 5.12 Custom SSRS report folders.

REAL WORLD: MULTIPLE CUSTOM REPORT FOLDERS

If you want to create multiple folders to store different groups or types of reports, use a common identifier to start the folder name, such as your company's name or initials. This helps with sorting and finding the folders that contain your reports. An example is shown in Figure 5.12, where all custom reports are stored within Enhansoft folders.

Summary

This chapter has discussed many concepts that are crucial to basic report design. It is important to understand the different types of reports within a series: the summarized data report, list report, and detailed report. As you begin to create reports in the upcoming chapters, you will see how different data fits into the different series and how clients interact and navigate between them. While creating ConfigMgr reports, always remember and keep in mind the following design rules that have been covered throughout this chapter:

▶ When you are satisfied with the look of a report, export it to PDF to simulate a printed copy for final review. As you review it, consider the following:

  ▶ Verify that the font is easy to read and all table rows are easy to follow; use different colors for alternating rows.

  ▶ Check that the page breaks are in appropriate locations (for example, not cutting off the footer or a chart).

  ▶ Ensure that no columns are cut off from the page (width).

  ▶ Confirm that table headers are repeated on each page.

▶ Ensure that the report does not contain too many columns or too much. Ensure that everything fits on a single page width (either in portrait or landscape orientation). As you review it, consider the following:

  ▶ If columns break onto a second page, it becomes difficult to read the data and keep track of individual rows.

  ▶ If the number of pages within a report is excessively large, the report will not be readable. Consider creating summary reports instead.

  ▶ Watch your row heights and line wrapping. If you see wrapping, you might need to change page sizes, adjust column widths, or remove columns altogether.

▶ Be consistent from one report to the next, using templates and existing reports as starting points. This consistency makes the readers feel comfortable with the data that is being presented. Use the same consistent formats for the following areas:

  ▶ Report titles

  ▶ Header and footer areas

  ▶ Color schemes

  ▶ Fonts

▶ Always save a copy of a report. This reduces the time required to make simple adjustments and helps you when you create new reports as you can copy an existing report to use as a starting point.

Over the next few chapters, you will have chances to practice and put these design concepts to use while creating reports. All report items will be explained and detailed, giving you opportunities to see them first hand. Chapter 6 walks you through the design tool and has you create a new report server project and your first set of SSRS reports. Chapter 7, "Intermediate Reporting Concepts," explains, among many other concepts, how to create report templates that have been introduced in this chapter, and Chapter 8 discusses how to create report subscriptions in the SSRS website.

Building a Basic Report

This chapter discusses using SQL Server Data Tools 2014 Business Intelligence (SSDT-BI) for Visual Studio 2013 and shows how to create a new project to build a basic report. Chapter 1, "Installing SQL Server Reporting Services," discussed installing the SSDT-BI tool, which is used to demonstrate creating reports throughout this book. This chapter steps through creating a basic report. It describes the available report items, how to change item property values, and how to add page header and footer sections. It also discusses the basic settings to use when adding a table to display query data within a report. You will learn how to customize a report based on the recommended concepts discussed in Chapter 5, "Basic Report Design," to present a simple and professional look. Chapter 7, "Intermediate Report Concepts," dives further into these concepts, showing you how to add additional complex features, including prompts, charts, and actions.

The authors are often asked whether the preferred tool for building SQL Server Reporting Services (SSRS) reports is SSDT-BI or Report Builder. Table 6.1 compares the capabilities of these two tools and shows that SSDT-BI is a more feature-rich tool that allows you to work on multiple reports at once. These are the basic differences:

▶ SSDT-BI works best when you intend to create many reports and want to keep them organized and easily accessible.

▶ Consider Report Builder if you only plan to quickly create several reports with basic features. This tool has a familiar style, and you use it much the way you use Microsoft Office products, such as Microsoft Word.

TABLE 6.1   Comparing SSDT-BI and Report Builder

SSDT-BI	Report Builder
Can open and work on multiple reports at a time.	Can work on only a single report at once.
Can cut/copy and paste between reports.	Because only one report can be open at once, copy and paste is not available.
Can easily create drillthrough links in reports.	Although it is possible to create drillthrough links, it is very cumbersome.
Can control every feature and setting within a report.	Some features are missing and cannot be modified or controlled within Report Builder.

You should note that there are multiple versions of report authoring tools available, including several versions of SSDT-BI and Business Intelligence Development Studio (BIDS), as well as multiple versions of the Report Builder tool. Understanding report compatibility for the different versions of Reporting Services can be challenging. Table 6.2 identifies the different SSRS versions and the compatible Report Definition Language (RDL) generated from the various tools. It is important to create reports using a tool that generates files supporting the installed SQL Server Reporting Services version in your environment.

TABLE 6.2   SSRS-Compatible Reports

SSRS Version	SSDT-BI and BIDS Versions	Report Builder
SQL Server 2014	SSDT-BI 2014 for Visual Studio 2013 SSDT-BI 2012 for Visual Studio 2012 BIDS 2008 R2, BIDS 2008, BIDS 2005	Report Builder 1.0, 2.0, 3.0
SQL Server 2012	SSDT-BI 2014 for Visual Studio 2013 SSDT-BI 2012 for Visual Studio 2012 BIDS 2008 R2, BIDS 2008 BIDS 2005	Report Builder 1.0, 2.0, 3.0
SQL Server 2008 R2	SSDT-BI 2014 for Visual Studio 2013 SSDT-BI 2012 for Visual Studio 2012 BIDS 2008 R2, BIDS 2008 BIDS 2005	Report Builder 1.0, 2.0, 3.0
SQL Server 2008	BIDS 2008 BIDS 2005	Report Builder 1.0, 2.0
SQL Server 2005	BIDS 2005	Report Builder 1.0

TIP: AUTHORING TOOL RECOMMENDED VERSION

The authors recommend installing the highest version of SSDT-BI or BIDS that supports the lowest version of SQL Server Reporting Services in your environment. This book uses SSDT-BI 2014 for Visual Studio 2013 and SQL Server 2014 Reporting Services.

Don't be concerned if you are using a different version. You can still follow along, but you should be aware that the tools may look slightly different, and some options or items may not be in exactly the same locations as demonstrated in this chapter.

Creating a Project

Before creating your first report in SQL Server Data Tools 2014 Business Intelligence (referred to as SSDT-BI from here on) for Visual Studio 2013, you must create a new project. All the reports inside a project can use common settings, such as a shared data source to connect to the Configuration Manager (ConfigMgr) database. In addition, a project establishes a common folder to store your created reports and provides a simple, organized view of all the reports you create from within Solution Explorer in Visual Studio.

In this section you will create a project for a fictional company named SSRS US. Perform the following steps to create this new project:

1. From the Windows Start menu, navigate to **Microsoft SQL Server 2014 -> SQL Server Data Tools for Visual Studio 2013**.

2. On the Microsoft Visual Studio Start Page, click **File -> New -> Project** (see Figure 6.1) to create a new project.

3. In the New Project dialog, shown in Figure 6.2, select **Report Server Project** from among the Business Intelligence templates. At the bottom of the dialog box, enter a name for the project (which automatically populates the Solution name field) and specify a location to store the project.

   Notice that the **Create directory for solution** check box is checked by default. This option creates a folder in the location you have specified that will contain the project files, configuration, and reports. Click **OK** to create the project.

TIP: RECOMMENDED PROJECT LOCATION

The authors recommend storing a project on a network share where all ConfigMgr administrators and report creators can access the project. This enables sharing of already created reports as well as report templates among all report creators.

The authors also suggest including this network share in any backup solution available to ensure that it is recoverable if the data is lost or corrupted.

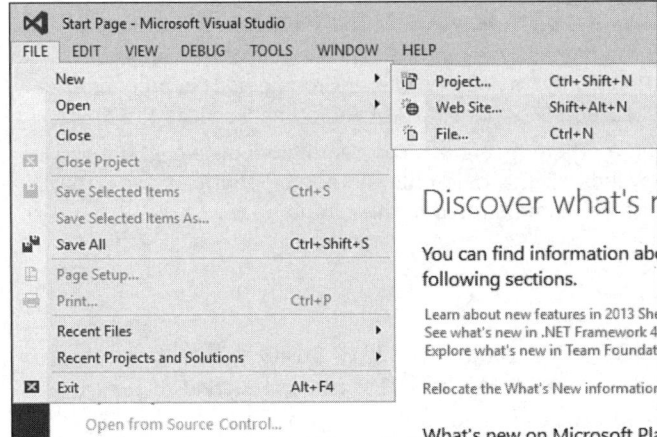

FIGURE 6.1   Creating a new project from the Microsoft Visual Studio Start Page.

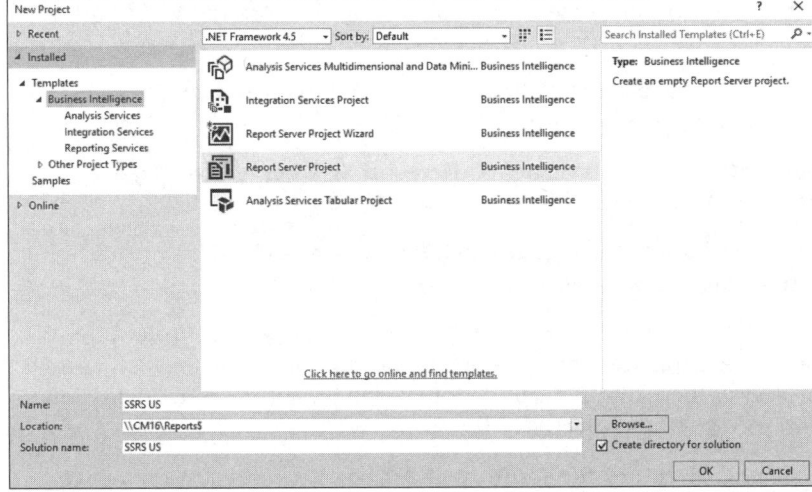

FIGURE 6.2
The New Project dialog.

4. Once the project is created, add a new shared data source. In the Solution Explorer, on the top right-hand side of the Visual Studio page, right-click **Shared Data Sources** and select **Add New Data Source**, as shown in Figure 6.3.

5. On the Shared Data Source Properties dialog, specify a Name for the shared data source and configure a connection string by clicking **Edit**.

6. In the Connection Properties dialog, specify the server name of the SQL Server that contains the ConfigMgr database and then, using the dropdown, specify the ConfigMgr database name under the Select or enter a database name field, as shown in Figure 6.4. Click **Test Connection** to ensure that the connection is successful and then click **OK** to close the Connection Properties dialog.

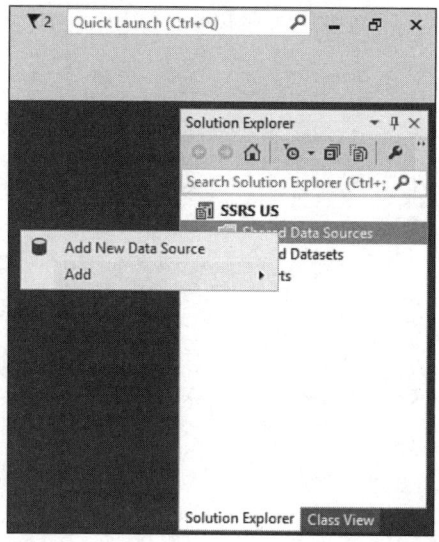

FIGURE 6.3   Selecting **Add New Data Source**.

Connection Properties   ?   ✕

Data source:

| Microsoft SQL Server (SqlClient) | Change... |

Server name:

| CM16 | ⌄ | Refresh |

Log on to the server

◉ Use Windows Authentication

○ Use SQL Server Authentication

User name: [   ]

Password: [   ]

☐ Save my password

Connect to a database

◉ Select or enter a database name:

| CM_CM6 | ⌄ |

○ Attach a database file:

[   ] Browse...

Logical name:

[   ]

Advanced...

| Test Connection | | OK | Cancel |

FIGURE 6.4   The Connection Properties dialog.

7. Confirm that the settings in the Shared Data Source Properties dialog (see Figure 6.5) are correct and click **OK**.

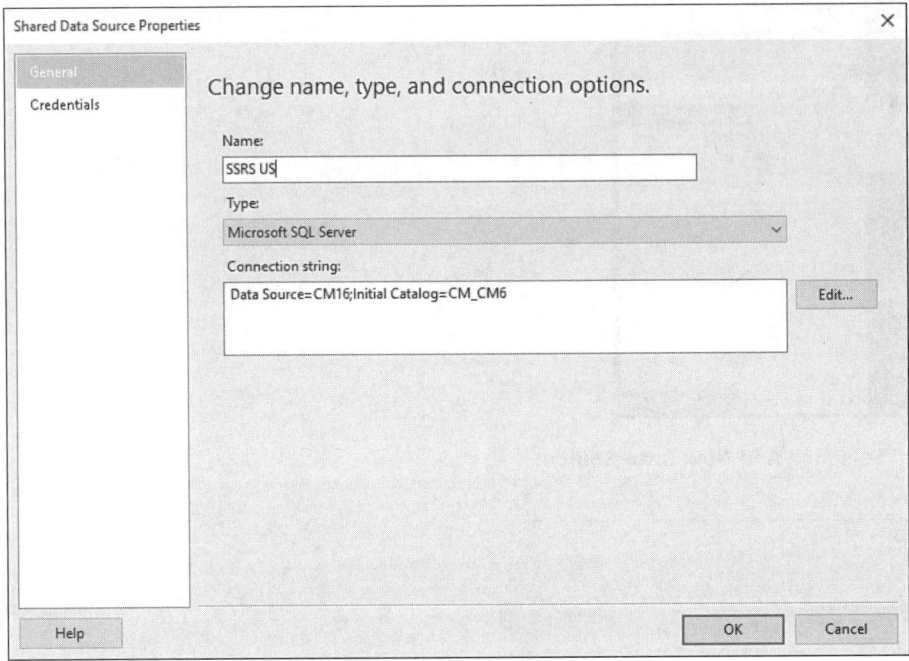

FIGURE 6.5   The Shared Data Source Properties dialog.

Creating a Basic Report

Now that you have created a project, you can start creating your own reports. Going forward, to access any reports created using this project, you can simply launch SSDT-BI and open the saved project. All your settings will be restored, and your reports will be listed and available from the Reports folder in the Solution Explorer.

Building on the steps in the previous section, this section walks through the basics of creating a new report using SSDT-BI. Follow these steps:

1. In the Solution Explorer section, on the far right side of SSDT-BI, right-click the **Reports** folder and select **Add -> New Item**, as shown in Figure 6.6.

2. In the Add New Item dialog, shown in Figure 6.7, select **Report** from the list of items, specify a name for the report (such as **Patch Compliance Progression**), and click **Add**.

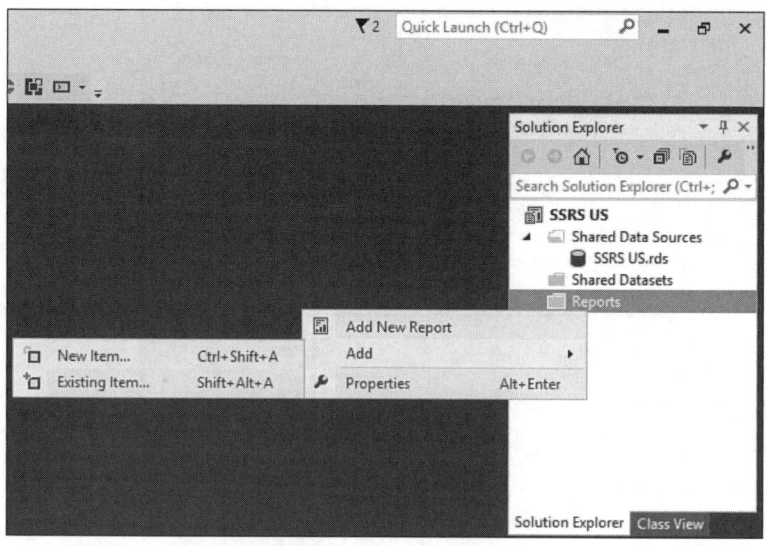

FIGURE 6.6   Selecting **Add** -> **New Item**.

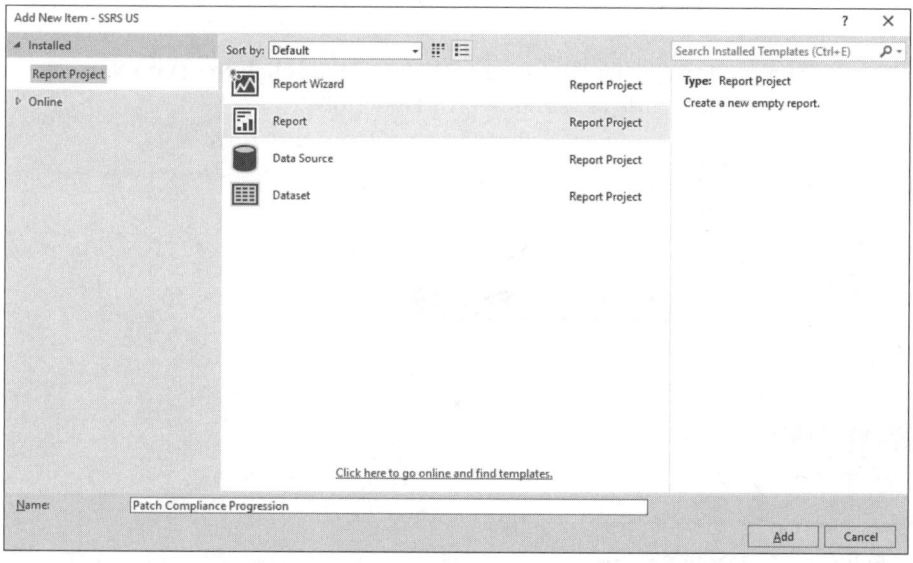

FIGURE 6.7   The Add New Item dialog.

You now have a new blank report. As Figure 6.8 shows, the center section of SSDT-BI now contains the new blank report, ready to be populated.

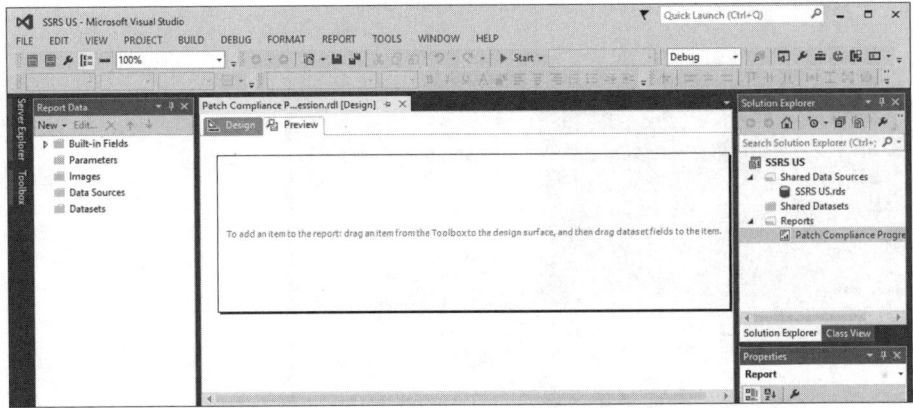

FIGURE 6.8   A blank report in SSDT-BI.

Creating a Data Source

Before adding report items such as tables or charts, you must add a data source to a report. The *data source* is the connection information to the ConfigMgr database, indicating where the report gets its information. Perform the following steps to add a data source for your ConfigMgr database:

1. In the Report Data section on the left side of SSDT-BI, right-click the **Data Sources** folder and select **Add Data Source**, as shown in Figure 6.9.

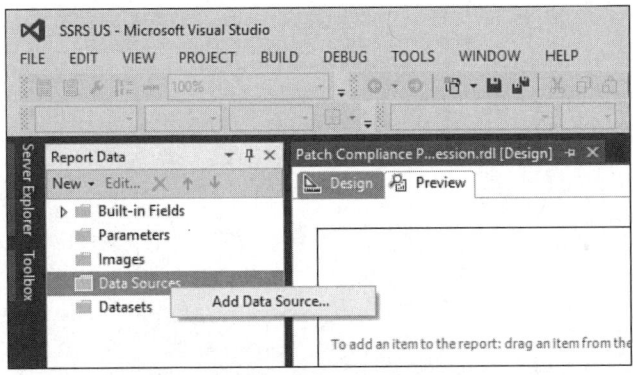

FIGURE 6.9   Selecting **Add Data Source**.

2. In the Data Source Properties dialog, as shown in Figure 6.10, specify a name for the data source and select **Use shared data source reference**. From the dropdown, select the shared data source added in the "Creating a Project" section of this chapter (for example, **SSRS US**) and click **OK**.

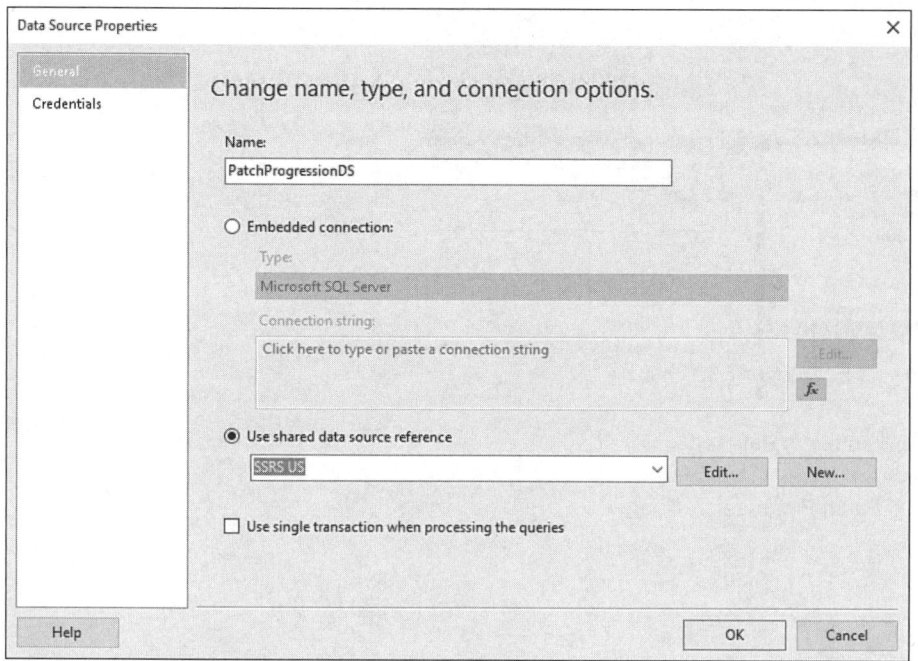

FIGURE 6.10   Specifying data source properties.

Creating a Dataset

A *dataset* is an actual query used to get data for a report. Creating a query in SQL Server Management Studio allows you to quickly see the specified columns and results and to easily make any necessary changes to the query before creating a full report and running it in SSDT-BI. Once you are satisfied with your query and the results, simply copy it from SQL Server Management Studio and paste it in the Query field of the dataset, as demonstrated in this section. Follow these steps:

1. From the Report Data section on the left side of SSDT-BI, right-click the **Datasets** folder and select **Add Dataset**, as shown in Figure 6.11.

2. In the Dataset Properties dialog, as shown in Figure 6.12, specify a name for the dataset and select **Use a dataset embedded in my report**. For the Data source field, select the data source you created in the "Creating a Data Source" section of this chapter. In the Query field, paste the query previously created in SQL Server Management Studio. This example uses the query shown in Listing 6.1, patchcompliance.sql, which is included as online content for this book for your convenience (see Appendix C, "Available Online"). Then click **OK** to create the dataset.

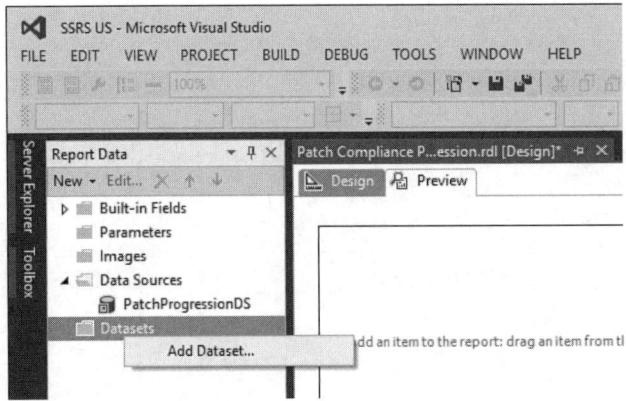

FIGURE 6.11   Adding a dataset.

LISTING 6.1   Patch Progression Query

```
SELECT Distinct
  CS.Name0,
  CS.UserName0,
  CASE
    When (sum(case when UCS.status=2 then 1 else 0 end))>0 then
        ('Needs '+(cast(sum(case when UCS.status=2 then 1 else 0 end)
        as varchar(10))+ ' Patches'))
    Else 'Good Client'
  End as 'Status',
  ws.lasthwscan as 'Last HW scan'
FROM
  v_UpdateComplianceStatus UCS
  LEFT OUTER JOIN dbo.v_GS_COMPUTER_SYSTEM CS on CS.ResourceID = UCS.ResourceID
  JOIN v_CICategories_All catall2 on catall2.CI_ID = UCS.CI_ID
  JOIN v_CategoryInfo catinfo2 on catall2.CategoryInstance_UniqueID =
      catinfo2.CategoryInstance_UniqueID and
      catinfo2.CategoryTypeName = 'UpdateClassification'
  LEFT JOIN v_gs_workstation_status ws on ws.resourceid = CS.resourceid
  LEFT JOIN v_fullcollectionmembership FCM on FCM.resourceid = CS.resourceid
WHERE
  UCS.Status = '2'
  and FCM.collectionid = 'SMS00001'
GROUP BY
  CS.Name0,
  CS.UserName0,
  ws.lasthwscan,
  FCM.collectionID
ORDER BY
  CS.Name0,
  CS.UserName0
```

Once the dataset is created, notice that all the columns returned from the query are listed below the dataset name (PatchDataset), as shown in Figure 6.13. The columns of the dataset will be used in report items that are added to the report. This is explained further in the "Adding a Table to a Report" section, later in this chapter.

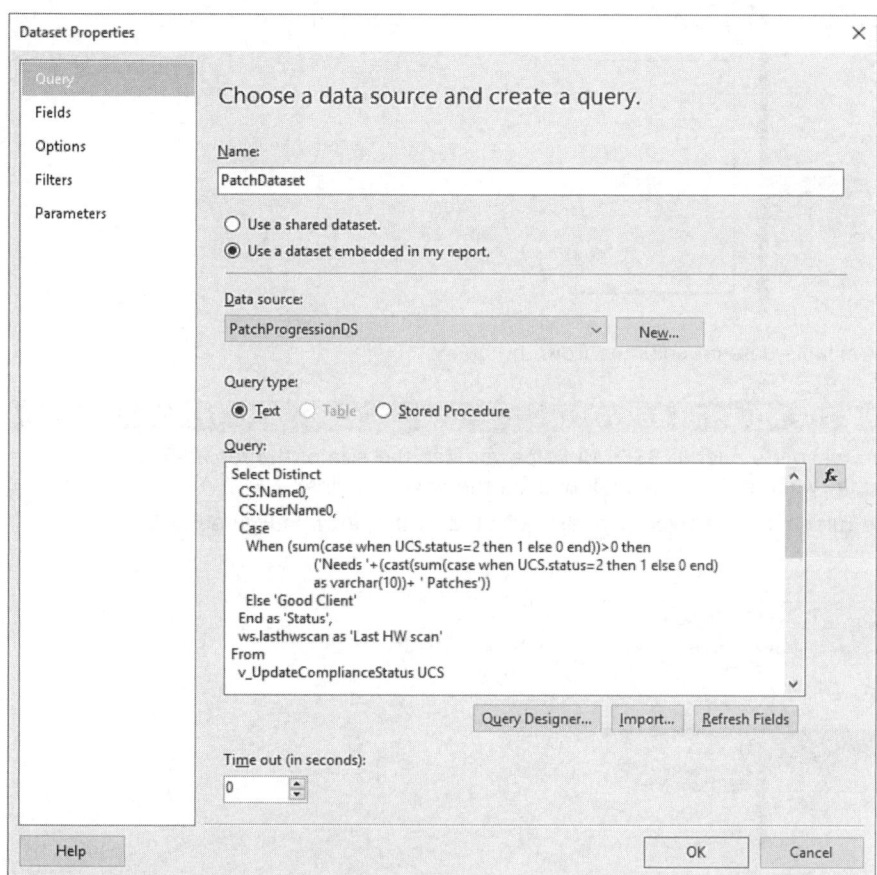

FIGURE 6.12   Specifying dataset properties.

Setting the Size of a Report

As discussed in Chapter 5, when you're considering the size of a report, it generally is more important to pay attention to the width of the report than to the height. If a report spans multiple pages in height, it is easy to follow as the data flows down onto a second page, much as when you're reading a document. However, if the report spans multiple pages in width, when viewed in a browser or printed on paper, it becomes difficult to follow the data across multiple pages.

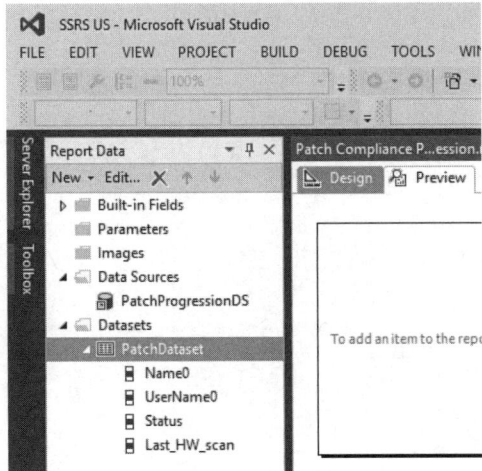

FIGURE 6.13   Available dataset columns from the query.

TIP: ENABLING THE RULER IN SSDT-BI

Turning on the taskbar's ruler in SSDT-BI helps you see the size of the report. This also helps you identify whether items will fall outside the page margins.

To turn on the ruler, click the ruler icon, as indicated by the arrow in Figure 6.14.

FIGURE 6.14   Enabling the ruler in SSDT-BI.

Follow these steps to configure the report size and margins to fit on an 8.5×11-inch sheet of paper:

1. From the Properties section, on the bottom-right side of SSDT-BI, select the **Body** property from the dropdown and expand the **Size** node.

2. Under the Size node, set the Width value to **8in**, as shown in Figure 6.15. This allows for a total half-inch margin between the left and right sides of your report.

NOTE: THE SSDT-BI PROPERTIES SECTION

Most objects in SSDT-BI can be adjusted or customized by editing their property values using the SSDT-BI Properties section. As your selections change to different items in a report, notice that the available properties change for the specific item that is selected.

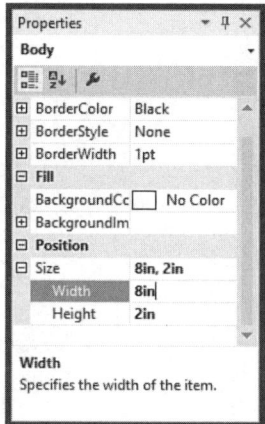

FIGURE 6.15   Expanding the Size node in the SSDT-BI Properties section.

Accessing Report Items

Report items, much like tables, charts, and text boxes, are available under the Toolbox menu by the Report Data section on the far left side of SSDT-BI. By default, the Toolbox menu is automatically hidden when not in use, and it is displayed only when you click on the tab shown in Figure 6.16. If you prefer to always have the Toolbox menu visible, showing the available report items, simply click the pin icon highlighted in Figure 6.17.

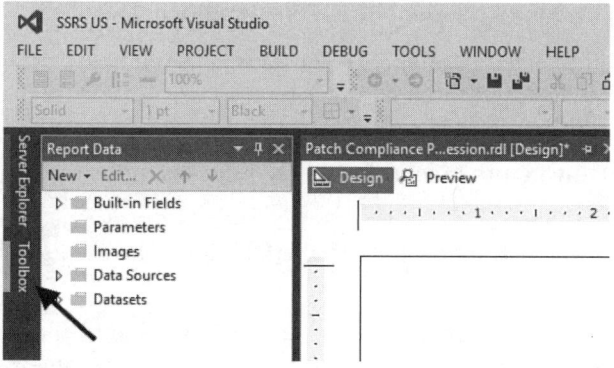

FIGURE 6.16   Opening the Toolbox menu to display report items.

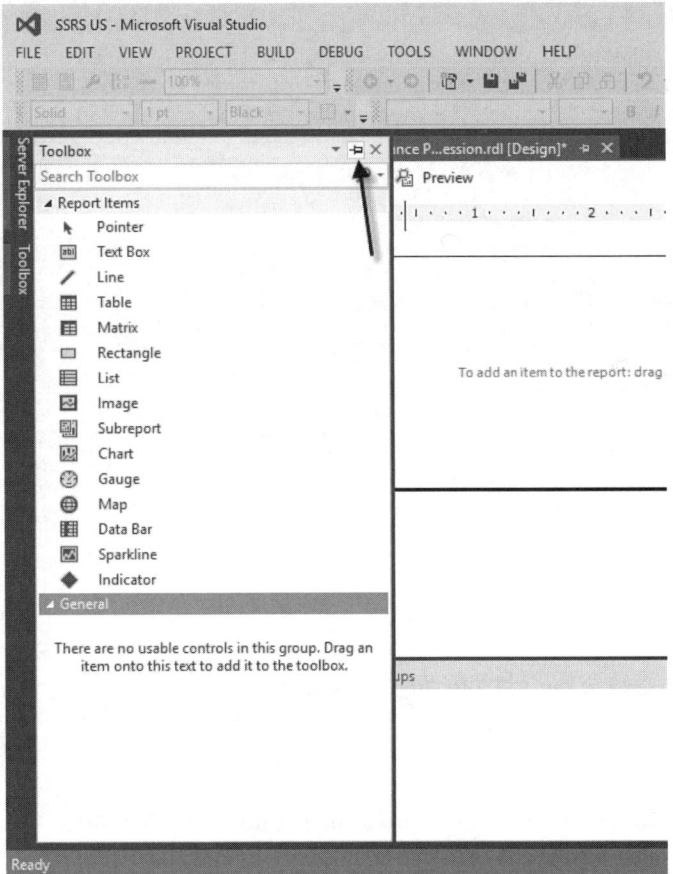

FIGURE 6.17   Pinning the Toolbox menu to keep it visible in SSDT-BI.

As Figure 6.17 shows, there are many report items you can add to a report. The following are the various items, with a brief description of the use of each one within a report:

▶ **Pointer:** The pointer is the default selected item in SSDT-BI. This is the simple mouse pointer that allows you to select items in a report.

▶ **Textbox:** This item allows you to enter simple text into a report, such as a label, or specify expressions to be populated when the report is executed (for example, the current date or page number).

▶ **Line:** The line item adds a simple line to a report for visual effect. It can be used to separate sections or information.

▶ **Table:** The table item is similar to an Excel spreadsheet. In an SSDT-BI table, you can group data together, identify header columns and rows, and more. Tables are some of the most popular items used in reporting.

▶ **Matrix:** A matrix is a special type of table, similar to a pivot table in Microsoft Excel. Data in a matrix can be grouped together and can grow both by columns and rows.

▶ **Rectangle:** The rectangle item allows you to group other report objects together and treat them as a single object within a report.

▶ **List:** A list is a grouping of report items. It allows you to add items from other reports within the list and display them in free form rather than within a grid.

▶ **Image:** The image item allows you to import images or pictures into a report. This item is commonly used to display a company logo in the header or footer section of a report.

▶ **Subreport:** This item allows you to embed another report within the current report. The body section of the targeted report is displayed within this item when the report is executed.

▶ **Chart:** This item creates a chart within a report to represent your data. Various types of charts can be selected, such as bar, line, pie, or pyramid charts. Charts are further explained and demonstrated in Chapter 7.

▶ **Gauge:** The gauge item can display a value, an expression, or a field in either a radial or linear type of gauge. Gauges are similar to charts; however, they are intended to display summary data.

▶ **Map:** This item allows you to display data against a map. There are two types of map charts:

  ▶ A marker map allows you to pinpoint a location.

  ▶ A bubble map shows the number of items for a given area.

▶ **Data Bar:** This item displays a visual indicator of a value. It tends to be used within a table item.

▶ **Sparkline:** Much like a data bar, a sparkline is often used within a table. This is a miniature line chart without any labels.

▶ **Indicator:** An indicator is similar to a gauge; it displays minimal information so that at a quick glance, a user can determine the value that is represented. In most cases, indicators are used in tables.

Adding a Table to a Report

To display the results of a query (dataset), you need to add a table to your report. Then, within the table, you can add the individual columns you want to display. When the report is executed, the query results populate the table item. Follow these steps to add a table and populate the query columns of the report:

1. From the toolbox, drag the table item to the blank report. Notice that by default the table item is created with three columns, as shown in Figure 6.18. You must add another column to the table to display all four columns from your dataset.

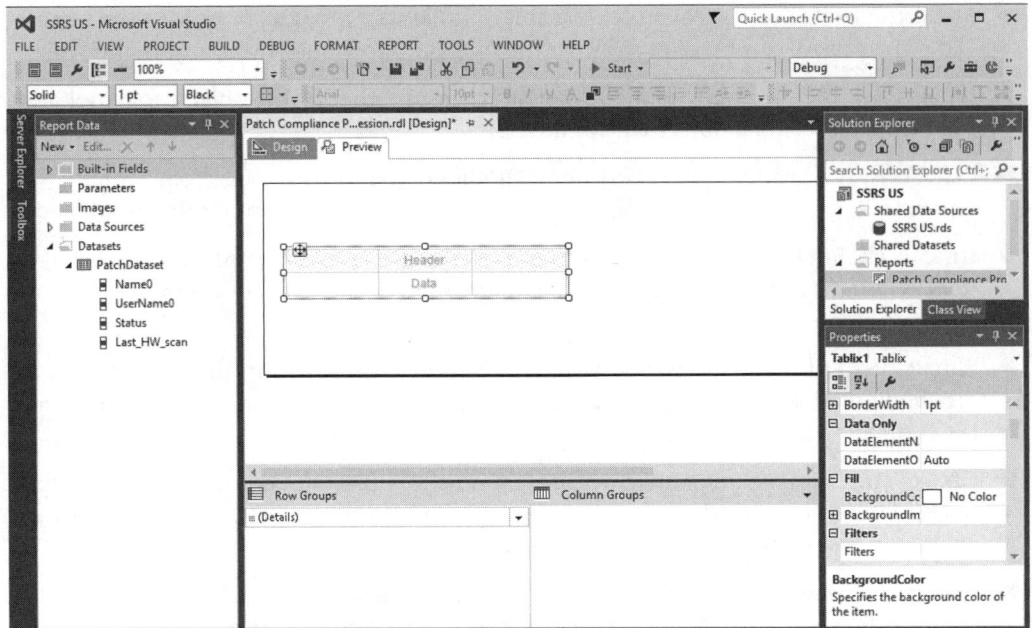

FIGURE 6.18   Adding a table item to a report.

2. To add a fourth column to the table, right-click the last (in this case third) column and select **Insert Column -> Right**, as shown in Figure 6.19.

3. Now add the dataset to the table. Under the Report Data section, expand the **Datasets** folder and expand the dataset you created (in this case, PatchDataset). Drag each column from the dataset into the corresponding column in the table. When complete, your table should look like the one shown in Figure 6.20.

4. With the dataset added to the table item, you can properly format the table. To do so, make the following changes to the table:

▶ Modify the labels of the headers in the first row to add appropriate titles that represent the data. Accomplish this by double-clicking the cell and replacing the current text (Name0, UserName0, Status, and Last_HW_scan).

▶ Set the font style of the header row to bold.

▶ Adjust the widths of the table columns so that the data is well displayed. Avoid cutting off information or having the row expand vertically to fit the data output.

▶ Adjust the table size to have it stretch the width of the entire page; however, ensure that doing this does not affect the width of the page. The page width should not exceed 8in.

Figure 6.21 shows the table with these changes made.

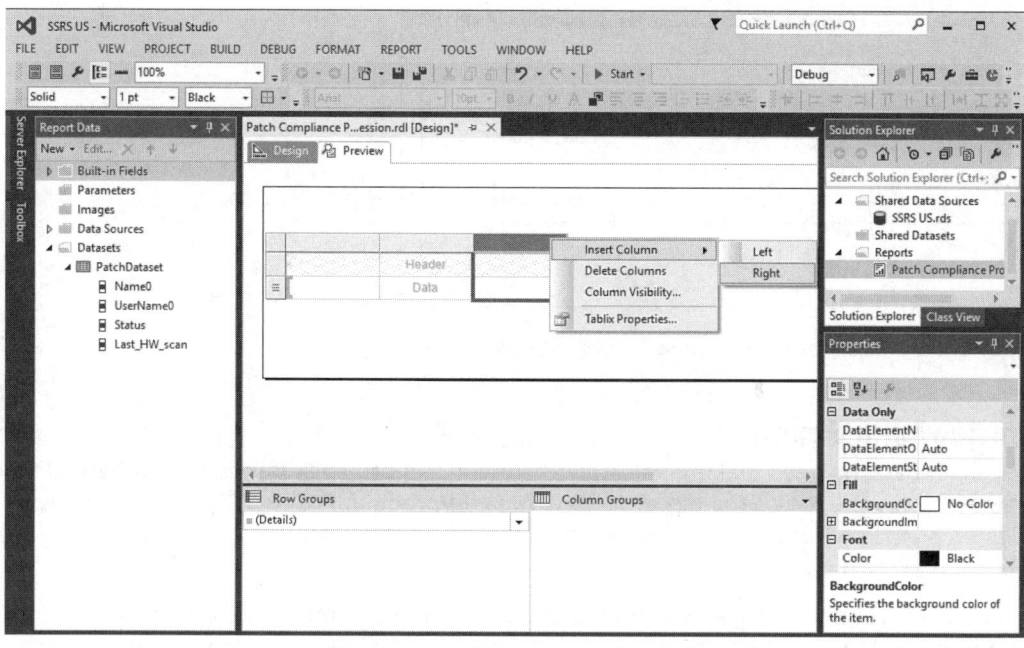

FIGURE 6.19   Clicking **Insert Column** -> **Right** to add an additional column on the right of the table.

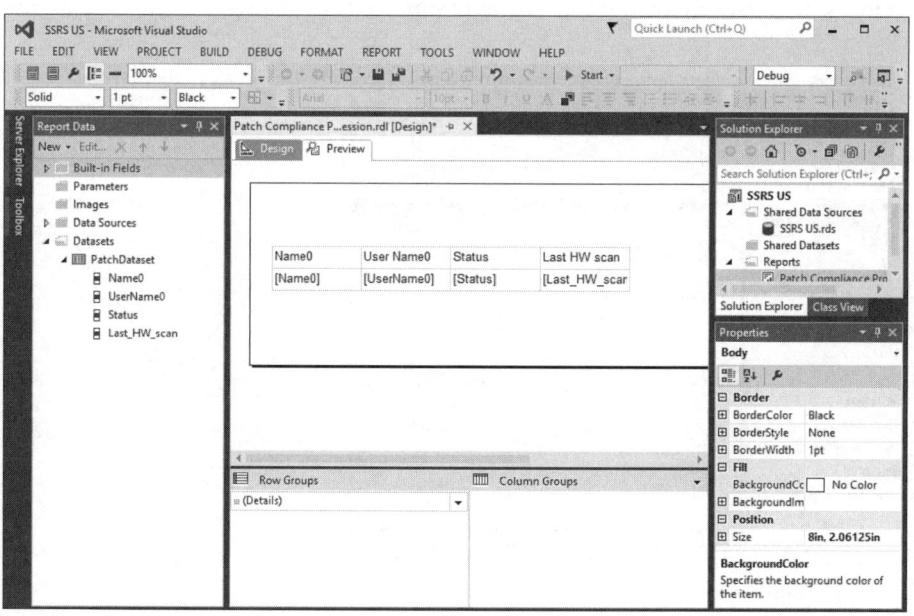

FIGURE 6.20   Dataset columns added to the table item of the report.

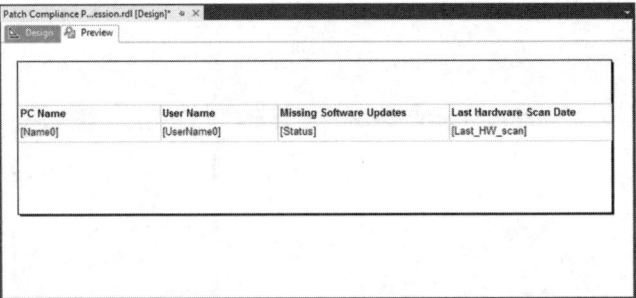

FIGURE 6.21   Formatting the table size and header labels.

Previewing a Report

Once you have finished making adjustments to your report, click **Preview** (highlighted in Figure 6.22) at the top of the report to view the end product. Figure 6.23 shows a preview of the report. Previewing a report executes the query in the dataset and populates the report items with data.

Ensure that everything displays as intended and that the columns are appropriate widths, such that no information is cut off or missing. If additional changes are required after previewing your report, make any necessary adjustments and preview your report again to ensure that those issues are resolved. To return to Design mode after you finish previewing, simply click **Design** at the top of the report.

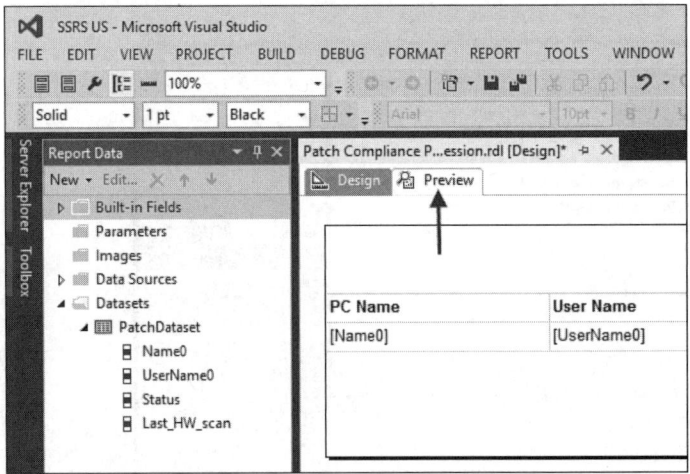

FIGURE 6.22   Clicking the Preview tab.

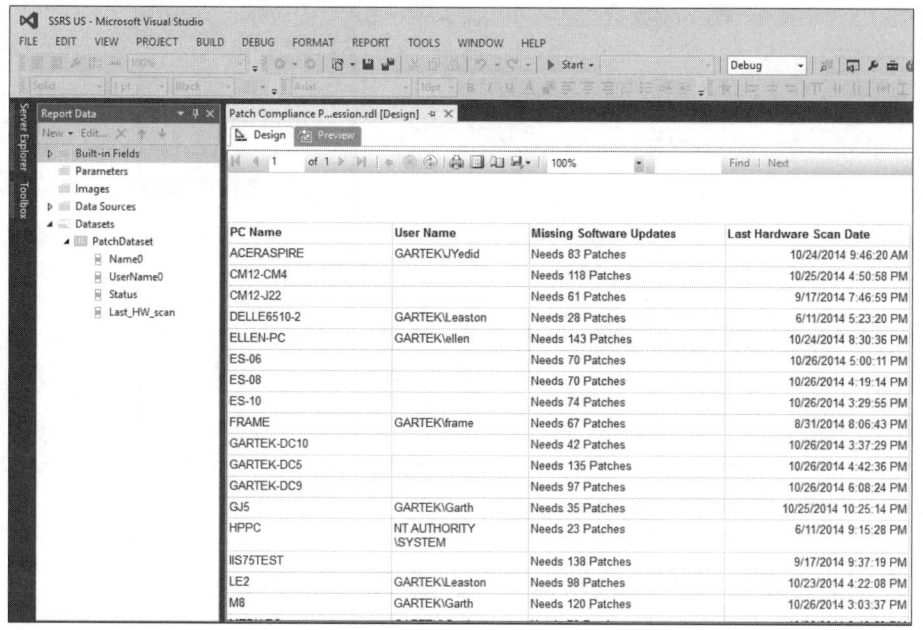

FIGURE 6.23   Report running in Preview mode.

Customizing a Report

At this point, you have a report with a dataset and a table item to return the query results. The output is still a very simple report without color, customization, or company branding. You can now customize the report by adding some color to the table, adding interactive sorting on the table columns, and creating header and footer sections with a company logo. These elements, discussed in the following sections, will help you create professional-looking reports.

Adding Background Color to Rows

To add visual appeal and help users identify important rows, such as the header, you can add background colors to the table. Adding a color to the header row helps draw attention to the table without overwhelming the report reader. Follow these steps to add a background color:

1. Highlight the header row of the table by selecting all cells in the first row. In the Properties section of the Solution Explorer, located in the bottom right of SSDT-BI, find the **BackgroundColor** property, as shown in Figure 6.24.

2. Click the dropdown next to the No Color value (see Figure 6.25) and select a color of your choice. The color **Red** is chosen for this example. The background color of the header row is now changed to the color red, as shown in Figure 6.26.

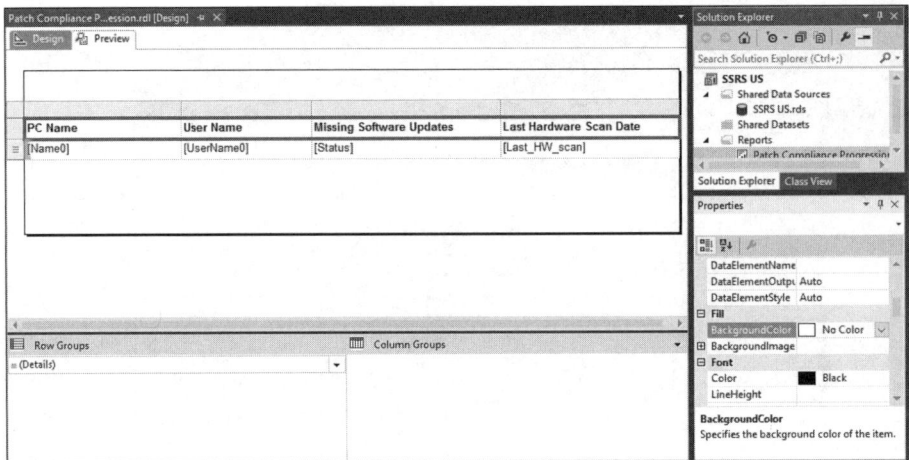

FIGURE 6.24   Selecting the **BackgroundColor** property.

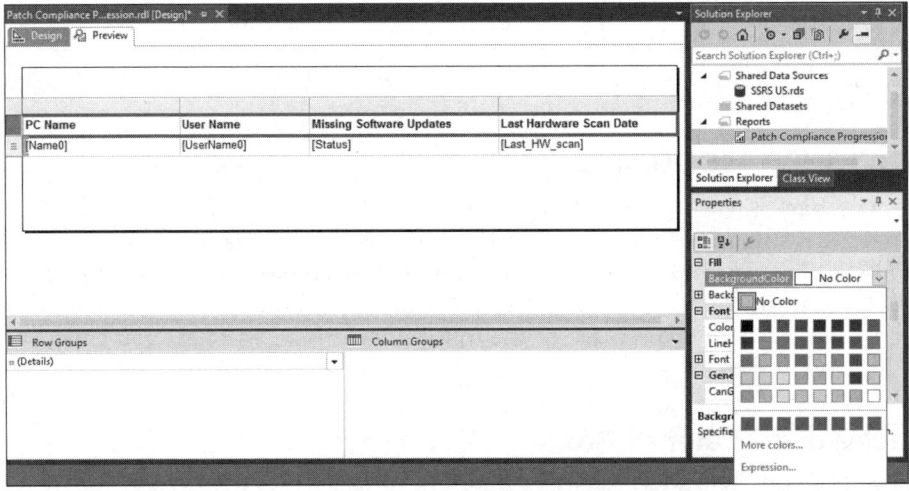

FIGURE 6.25   Available values for BackgroundColor.

TIP: ADDITIONAL COLORS

There are several options available in terms of choosing a color for an item that is outside the basic palette available from the property dropdown (displayed in Figure 6.25):

▶ Select the **More Colors** option and then select colors from defined palettes, select from color circles, or manually enter the RGB values.

▶ Select **Expression** and enter the color name (Red) or hexadecimal color value (#FF0000).

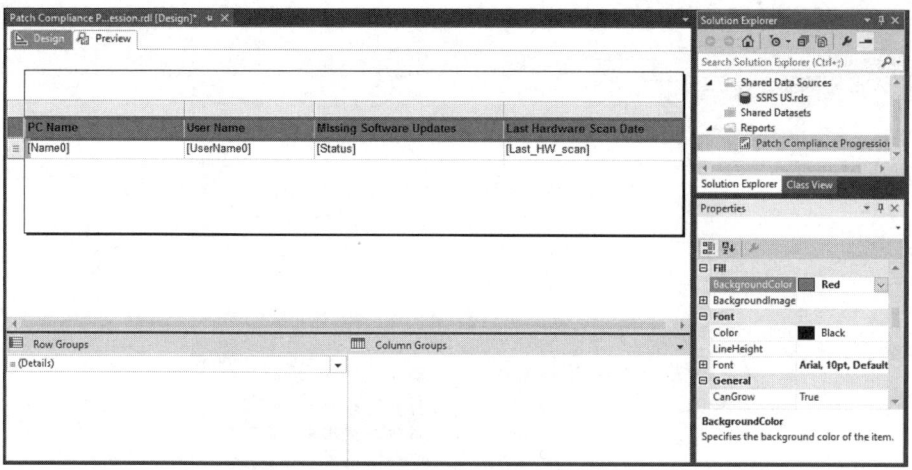

FIGURE 6.26   Red background set on a header row.

Alternating Data Row Colors

If you view your report in Preview mode (as previously shown in Figure 6.23), you might notice that it can be difficult to follow the data in each individual row. This most often occurs with large tables that contain multiple columns and rows. By default, there is no easy way to identify and follow a single row from beginning to end. While adjusting the background color is a good approach, if you have dozens—or even hundreds—of rows in a report, it would be far too time-consuming to manually alternate the background colors for all the rows. Thankfully, there is a built-in function called **RowNumber** that returns the current row count of a table. By combining this function with others, you can automatically have a report alternate the colors of the rows. Applying the expression shown in Listing 6.2 as the BackgroundColor value for the dataset row sets all odd-numbered rows to white and all even-numbered rows to silver. To apply this expression, follow these steps:

LISTING 6.2   Alternate Row Color Expression

```
=iif(RowNumber(Nothing) Mod 2, "White", "Silver")
```

1. Select the second row of the table. In the Properties section, located in the bottom right of SSDT-BI, find the **BackgroundColor** property. Click the dropdown next to the No Color value and select **Expression**.

2. In the Expression dialog, enter the expression from Listing 6.2 (and also shown in Figure 6.27) and click **OK**.

3. To ensure that the expression is properly set and working as intended, select **Preview** in the report and confirm that the data rows are alternating colors between white and silver. Notice the output in Figure 6.28. It is now much easier to read and follow the data for each individual row of the table.

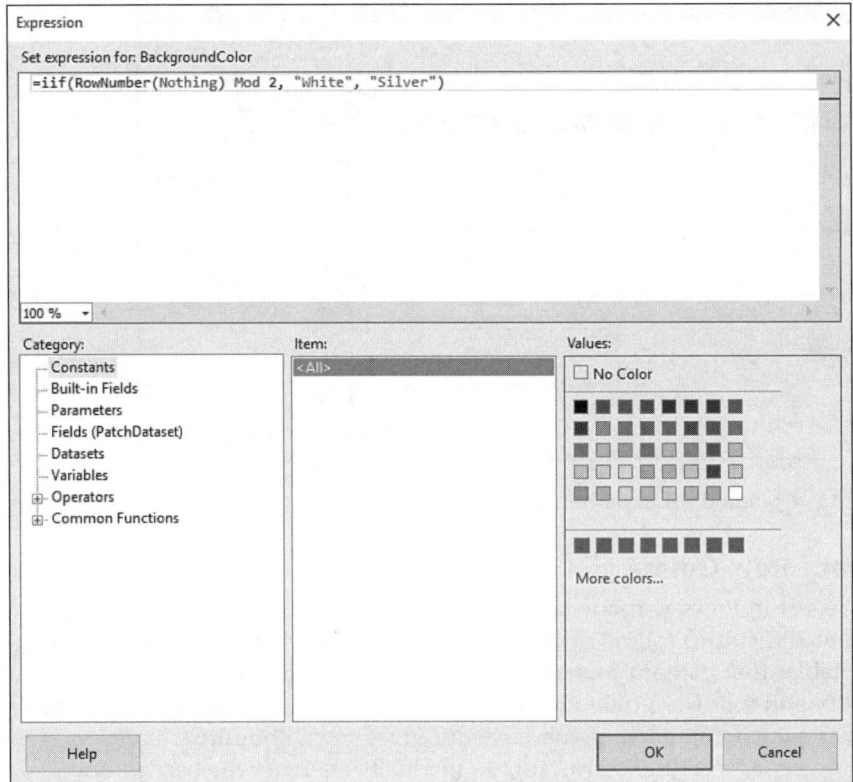

FIGURE 6.27   Entering the expression as the BackgroundColor value.

Adding Interactive Sorting

A feature most report readers find very helpful is the ability to sort a table by individual columns while viewing the report. For example, you might want to be able to sort the report shown in Figure 6.28 by the Missing Software Updates column. You can add this functionality by enabling the interactive sorting feature. Unfortunately, this feature is not global for the entire table and must be set for each individual column where you want to add the ability to sort the data. Chapter 5 recommended enabling interactive sorting on every table column to provide the best experience for readers. To enable this feature, ensure that your report is in Design mode by selecting **Design** and then perform the following steps:

1. Right-click the header cell of the **Missing Software Updates** column and select **Text Box Properties**, as shown in Figure 6.29.

2. In the Text Box Properties dialog, select **Interactive Sorting** on the left side and click the **Enable interactive sorting on this text box** check box. In the **Sort by** dropdown box, select the appropriate column from the dataset. The **[Status]** column is selected for this example (see Figure 6.30), as this value corresponds with the Missing Software Updates data column. Click **OK** to apply these settings and close the dialog.

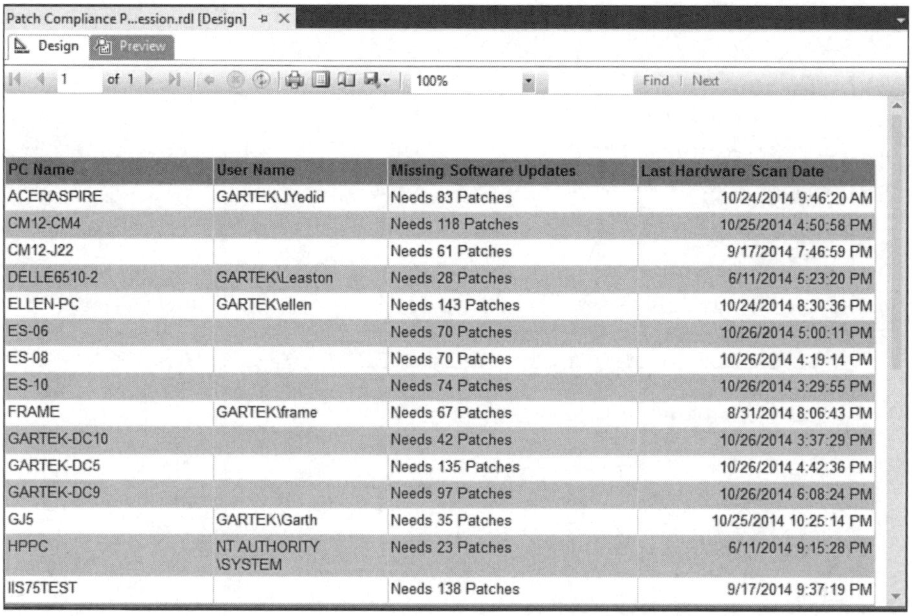

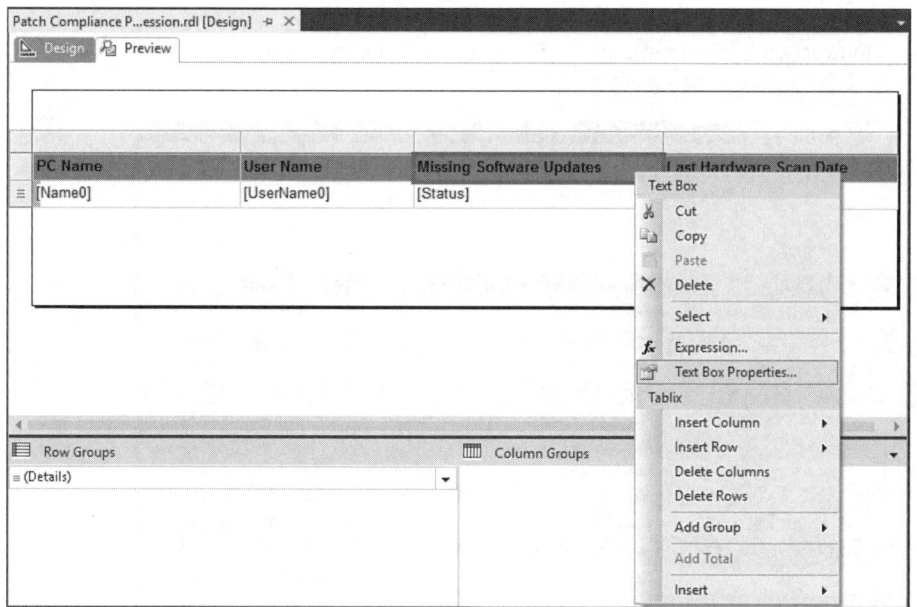

FIGURE 6.28   Report preview with alternating data row colors.

FIGURE 6.29   Selecting **Text Box Properties** from the right-click menu.

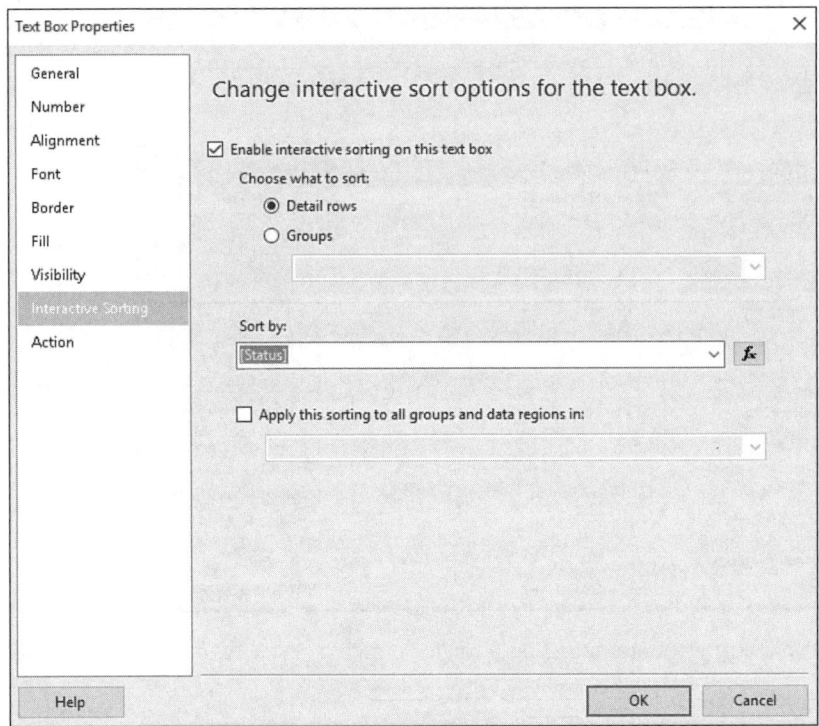

FIGURE 6.30   Interactive sorting settings in the Text Box Properties dialog.

PC Name	User Name	Missing Software Updates	Last Hardware Scan Date
ACERASPIRE	GARTEK\JYedid	Needs 83 Patches	10/24/2014 9:46:20 AM
CM12-CM4		Needs 118 Patches	10/25/2014 4:50:58 PM
CM12-J22		Needs 61 Patches	9/17/2014 7:46:59 PM
DELLE6510-2	GARTEK\Leaston	Needs 28 Patches	6/11/2014 5:23:20 PM
ELLEN-PC	GARTEK\ellen	Needs 143 Patches	10/24/2014 8:30:36 PM
ES-06		Needs 70 Patches	10/26/2014 5:00:11 PM
ES-08		Needs 70 Patches	10/26/2014 4:19:14 PM
ES-10		Needs 74 Patches	10/26/2014 3:29:55 PM
FRAME	GARTEK\frame	Needs 67 Patches	8/31/2014 8:06:43 PM
GARTEK-DC10		Needs 42 Patches	10/26/2014 3:37:29 PM
GARTEK-DC5		Needs 135 Patches	10/26/2014 4:42:36 PM
GARTEK-DC9		Needs 97 Patches	10/26/2014 6:08:24 PM
GJ5	GARTEK\Garth	Needs 35 Patches	10/25/2014 10:25:14 PM
HPPC	NT AUTHORITY \SYSTEM	Needs 23 Patches	6/11/2014 9:15:28 PM
IIS75TEST		Needs 138 Patches	9/17/2014 9:37:19 PM

FIGURE 6.31   Sorting arrows available with the Missing Software Updates column header.

3. Select **Preview** to view the changes to the report and ensure that the interactive sorting feature is working properly. Notice that the sorting arrows now appear next to the Missing Software Updates column header shown in Figure 6.31. Click the sorting arrows and notice that you can now sort the data by the Missing Software Updates column, in alphabetical and descending order.

4. Repeat steps 1–3 to enable the interactive sorting feature on all columns of the table. When you are finished, preview the report to ensure that the sorting arrows appear for all columns, as shown in Figure 6.32.

PC Name	User Name	Missing Software Updates	Last Hardware Scan Date
ACERASPIRE	GARTEK\JYedid	Needs 83 Patches	10/24/2014 9:46:20 AM
CM12-CM4		Needs 118 Patches	10/25/2014 4:50:58 PM
CM12-J22		Needs 61 Patches	9/17/2014 7:46:59 PM
DELLE6510-2	GARTEK\Leaston	Needs 28 Patches	6/11/2014 5:23:20 PM
ELLEN-PC	GARTEK\ellen	Needs 143 Patches	10/24/2014 8:30:36 PM
ES-06		Needs 70 Patches	10/26/2014 5:00:11 PM
ES-08		Needs 70 Patches	10/26/2014 4:19:14 PM
ES-10		Needs 74 Patches	10/26/2014 3:29:55 PM
FRAME	GARTEK\frame	Needs 67 Patches	8/31/2014 8:06:43 PM
GARTEK-DC10		Needs 42 Patches	10/26/2014 3:37:29 PM
GARTEK-DC5		Needs 135 Patches	10/26/2014 4:42:36 PM
GARTEK-DC9		Needs 97 Patches	10/26/2014 6:08:24 PM
GJ5	GARTEK\Garth	Needs 35 Patches	10/25/2014 10:25:14 PM
HPPC	NT AUTHORITY \SYSTEM	Needs 23 Patches	6/11/2014 9:15:28 PM
IIS75TEST		Needs 138 Patches	9/17/2014 9:37:19 PM
LE2	GARTEK\Leaston	Needs 98 Patches	10/23/2014 4:22:08 PM

FIGURE 6.32   Interactive sorting available for all columns of the table.

Setting the Table Header Row to Repeat on All Pages

When using table items, you can set the header row to repeat on every page. This is a convenient feature for reports that contain a large number of rows that will span multiple pages. Repeating header rows allows the viewer to refer to the column names without having to go back and reference the first page of the report. Perform the following steps to set this behavior on the report:

1. Ensure that your report is in Design mode. Select the header row of the table and right-click the gray border cell to the left of the first column header cell. Click **Tablix Properties**, as shown in Figure 6.33.

2. In the Row Headers section, check the **Repeat header rows on each page** check box (shown in Figure 6.34). Click **OK** to apply the settings.

3. Preview the report. If there are multiple pages, view each page to confirm that the table header is shown on every page that contains rows from the table item.

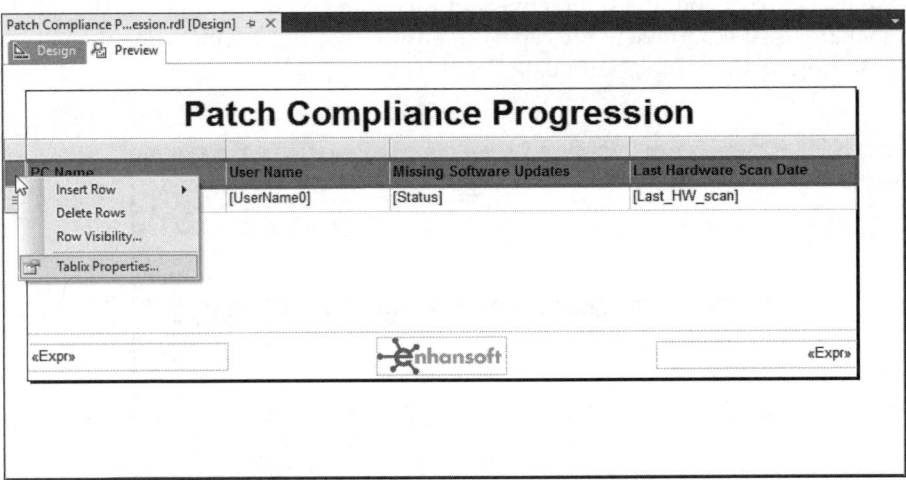

FIGURE 6.33   Selecting **Tablix Properties**.

Adding a Page Header to a Report

Page headers are displayed on each page of your report. You can use the header area to add details about your report. Items such as the report name help readers identify which report they are viewing, particularly when you add links to other reports. Follow these steps to add a header section to the report:

1. Ensure that your report is in Design mode. From the SSDT-BI toolbar, select the **Report** menu and click **Add Page Header** (as shown in Figure 6.35). The header section now appears in the Design mode of your report, as shown in Figure 6.36. The header and body sections are separated by a thin dotted line.

2. Begin populating the page header with a report title. From the toolbox, drag the text box item into the header section of the report. Double-click the text box item and type **Patch Compliance Progression**. Place the text box in the top-left corner of the page. Using the Properties section in the bottom-right corner of the screen, find and change the Size value to **8in, 0.5in**. Change the font of the text box to **Bold**, set the font size to **24pt**, and set the alignment to **Center**.

   Modifying text formatting is simple in SSDT-BI and is performed in the same way as with other Microsoft Office products. The report should now look similar to the one displayed in Figure 6.37.

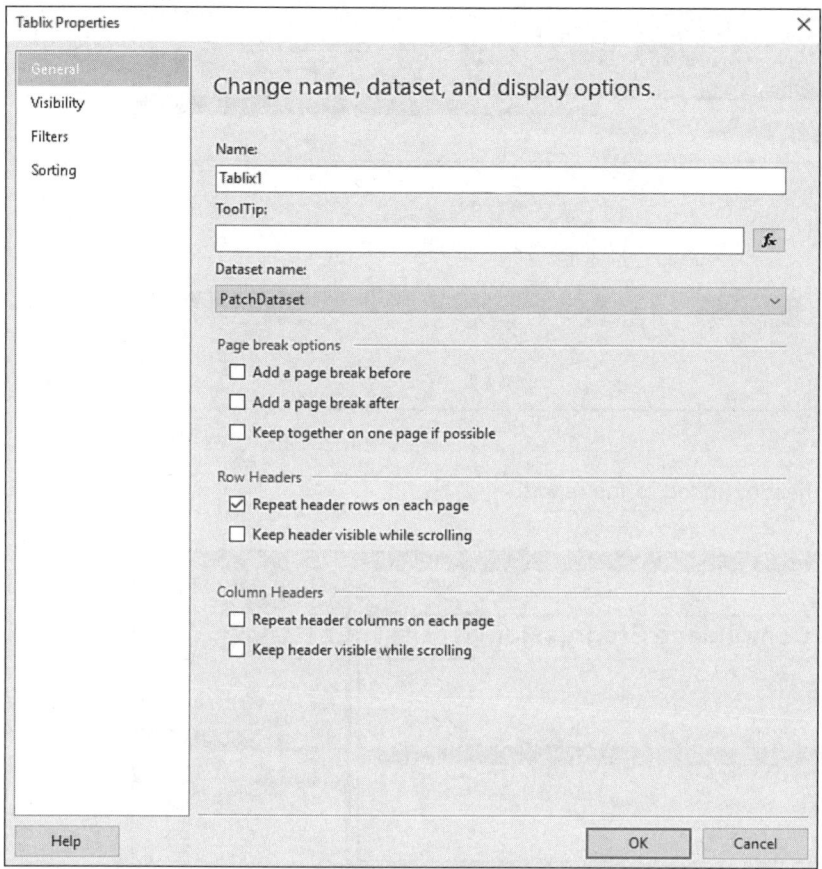

FIGURE 6.34   Checking the box **Repeat header rows on each page**.

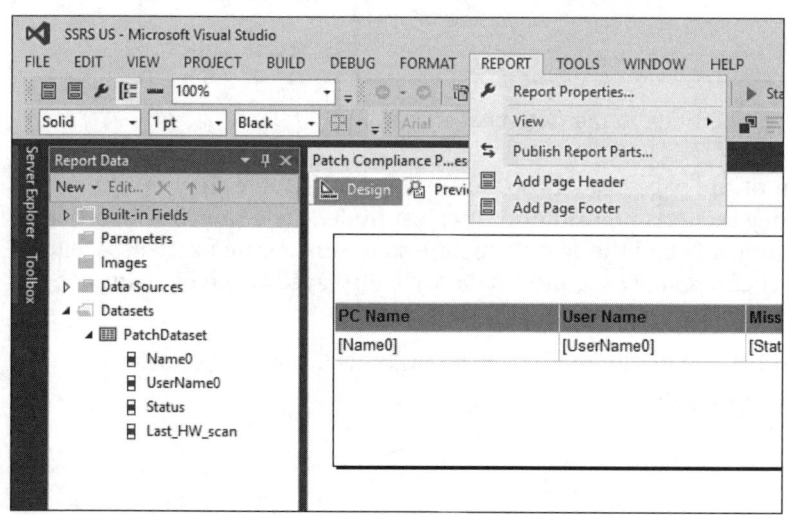

FIGURE 6.35   Selecting **Report -> Add Page Header**.

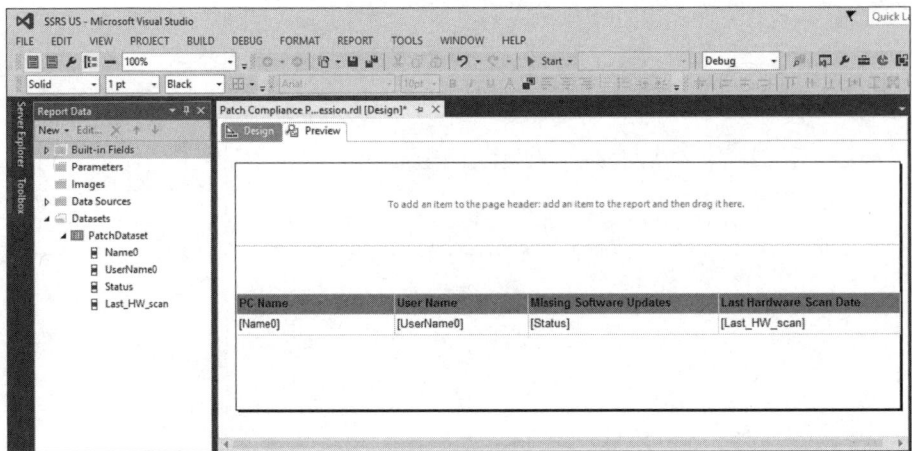

FIGURE 6.36   Page header added to the report.

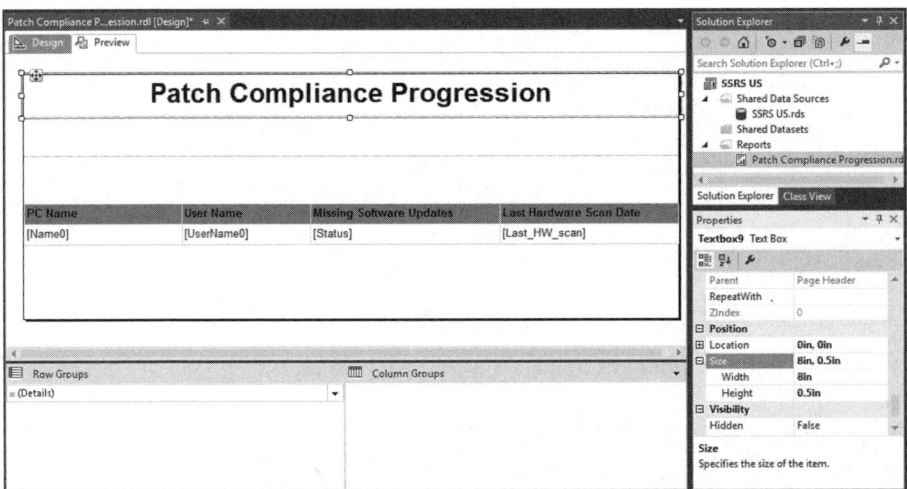

FIGURE 6.37   Adding the report title to the page header.

3. Modify the height of the page header by dragging the dotted line that separates the header and body sections upward until it is just under the report title text box. Drag the table item just below the separating line to minimize the wasted space in the report. These changes allow the most data to be displayed while reducing the number of pages generated.

4. Preview the report by clicking **Preview** to ensure that it displays and functions as expected, as shown in Figure 6.38.

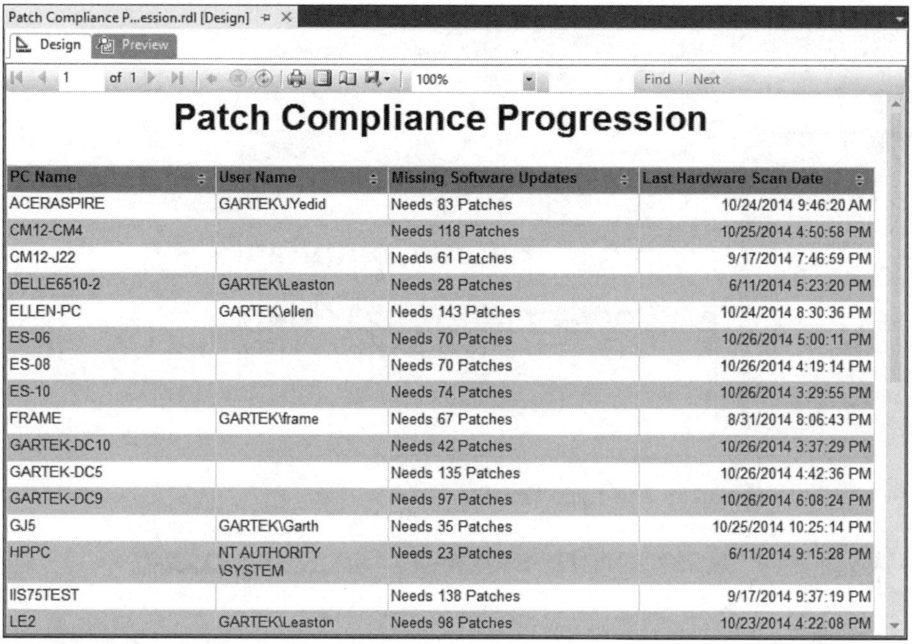

PC Name	User Name	Missing Software Updates	Last Hardware Scan Date
ACERASPIRE	GARTEK\JYedid	Needs 83 Patches	10/24/2014 9:46:20 AM
CM12-CM4		Needs 118 Patches	10/25/2014 4:50:58 PM
CM12-J22		Needs 61 Patches	9/17/2014 7:46:59 PM
DELLE6510-2	GARTEK\Leaston	Needs 28 Patches	6/11/2014 5:23:20 PM
ELLEN-PC	GARTEK\ellen	Needs 143 Patches	10/24/2014 8:30:36 PM
ES-06		Needs 70 Patches	10/26/2014 5:00:11 PM
ES-08		Needs 70 Patches	10/26/2014 4:19:14 PM
ES-10		Needs 74 Patches	10/26/2014 3:29:55 PM
FRAME	GARTEK\frame	Needs 67 Patches	8/31/2014 8:06:43 PM
GARTEK-DC10		Needs 42 Patches	10/26/2014 3:37:29 PM
GARTEK-DC5		Needs 135 Patches	10/26/2014 4:42:36 PM
GARTEK-DC9		Needs 97 Patches	10/26/2014 6:08:24 PM
GJ5	GARTEK\Garth	Needs 35 Patches	10/25/2014 10:25:14 PM
HPPC	NT AUTHORITY \SYSTEM	Needs 23 Patches	6/11/2014 9:15:28 PM
IIS75TEST		Needs 138 Patches	9/17/2014 9:37:19 PM
LE2	GARTEK\Leaston	Needs 98 Patches	10/23/2014 4:22:08 PM

FIGURE 6.38 Preview of the report with page header and title.

Adding a Page Footer to a Report

Like the header, the page footer is repeated on every page of the report. This is a good area for including details such as the date the report was executed, the company logo, and the page number. The steps to add a page footer are almost identical to the steps for the page header:

1. Ensure that the report is in Design mode. From the SSDT-BI toolbar, select the **Report** menu and click **Add Page Footer** (as shown in Figure 6.39). The footer section now appears in the Design mode of your report, as shown in Figure 6.40. As with the header and body sections, the footer and body sections are now separated by a thin dotted line.

2. Add the date to the page footer of the report. To do this, from the toolbox, drag the text box item into the footer section of the report. Place the text box on the far left side of the page, double-click it, and enter the expression shown in Listing 6.3.

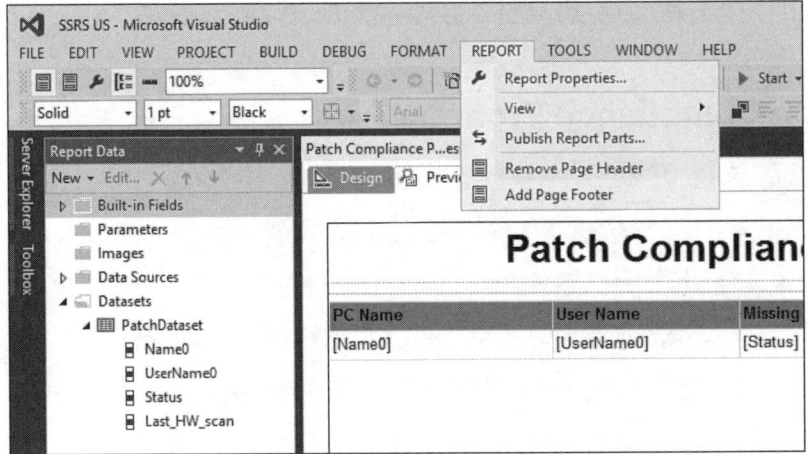

FIGURE 6.39   Selecting **Report -> Add Page Footer**.

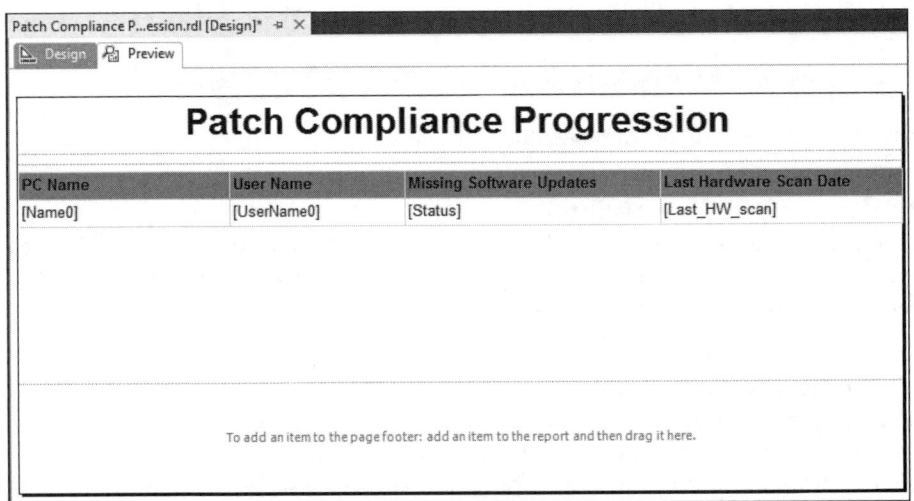

FIGURE 6.40   Page footer added to the report.

LISTING 6.3   Expression to Display the Date

```
="Printed on " & Today
```

3. Add the page number to the page footer of the report. To do this, from the toolbox, drag a second **Text Box** item into the footer section. Place this second text box item on the far-right side of the page, double-click it, and enter the expression shown in Listing 6.4. Set the font alignment to **Right**.

LISTING 6.4   Expression to Add the Page Number

```
=String.Format("Page {0} of {1}", Globals!PageNumber,Globals!TotalPages)
```

4. Reduce the height of the page footer by dragging the bottom of the report page upward. Because both the page header and footer sections are fixed sizes and will not grow, you are allowing for the maximum height to be used by the page body and reducing the number of pages generated.

5. Preview the report by clicking **Preview** to ensure that it displays and functions as expected. Figure 6.41 shows an example of a preview with the page footer.

Patch Compliance Pession.rdl [Design]			
IIS75TEST		Needs 138 Patches	9/17/2014 9:37:19 PM
LE2	GARTEK\Leaston	Needs 98 Patches	10/23/2014 4:22:08 PM
M8	GARTEK\Garth	Needs 120 Patches	10/26/2014 3:03:37 PM
MEDIAPC	GARTEK\Garth	Needs 72 Patches	10/26/2014 3:19:59 PM
OPSMAN2012	GARTEK\garth	Needs 144 Patches	8/19/2014 5:30:30 PM
SURFACE	GARTEK\Garth	Needs 84 Patches	10/13/2014 7:45:53 PM
VMM2012		Needs 150 Patches	8/19/2014 3:29:54 PM
WIN10PRE		Needs 5 Patches	10/23/2014 10:12:52 AM
WIN2K8	NT AUTHORITY \SYSTEM	Needs 68 Patches	10/25/2014 7:04:32 PM
WIN2K8R2		Needs 94 Patches	10/25/2014 6:58:59 PM
WIN7-CM4		Needs 344 Patches	10/25/2014 11:04:47 PM
WIN8	GARTEK\Stighe	Needs 116 Patches	10/24/2014 5:10:50 PM
win81-cm4		Needs 49 Patches	10/26/2014 3:32:45 PM
Printed on 11/12/2015			Page 1 of 1

FIGURE 6.41   Preview of the report with the page footer, including the date and page number.

Adding an Image to a Report

When creating reports, it is common to add company branding such as a company logo. This is a good way to add a unique, customized feel to your reports. You can place an image item anywhere in a report; however, for a more professional feel, the authors recommend adding an image with a company logo to either the page footer or header. This section demonstrates how to add a company logo to the page footer area of the report. Perform the following steps:

1. Ensure that your report is in Design mode. From the toolbox, drag the image item into the page footer of the report.

2. In the Image Properties page, as shown in Figure 6.42, enter a name for the image under the Name field and click **Import**. Browse to the appropriate location and select the image you want to add to the report and then click **Open**. Click **OK** to add the image to the report.

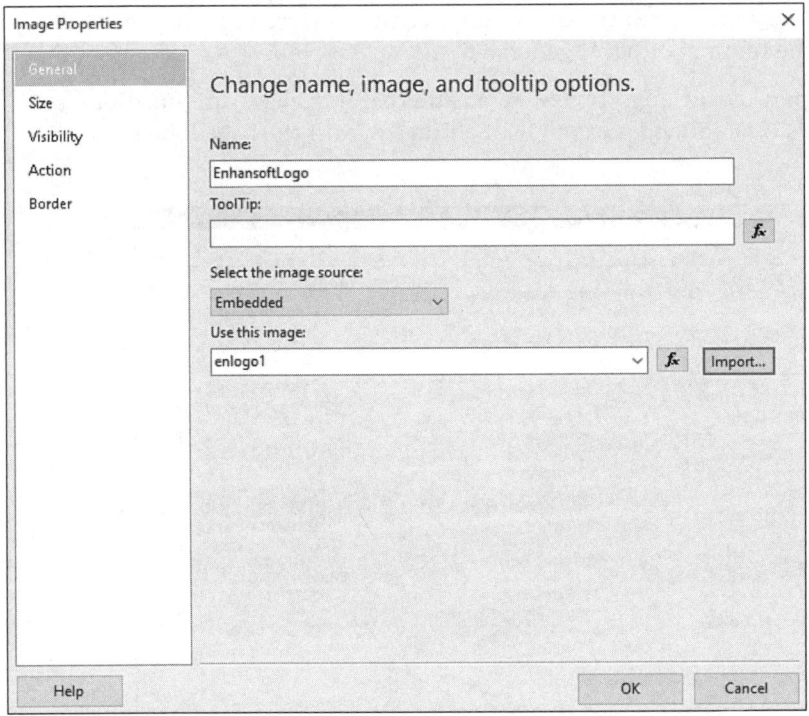

FIGURE 6.42   Completed Image Properties page.

3. After adding an image, you often need to adjust the size and location of the image item. You can either stretch the image item directly by clicking and dragging the item's edges or you can adjust the Size Width and Height values in the Properties section in the bottom right of the page.

4. When the image is the appropriate size, center it both horizontally and vertically in the page footer. To easily center an item, click the item to select it and then click the **Center Horizontally** and **Center Vertically** icons on the toolbar, as shown in Figure 6.43.

5. Preview the report to ensure that the image is displayed properly and will be the desired size when the report is executed.

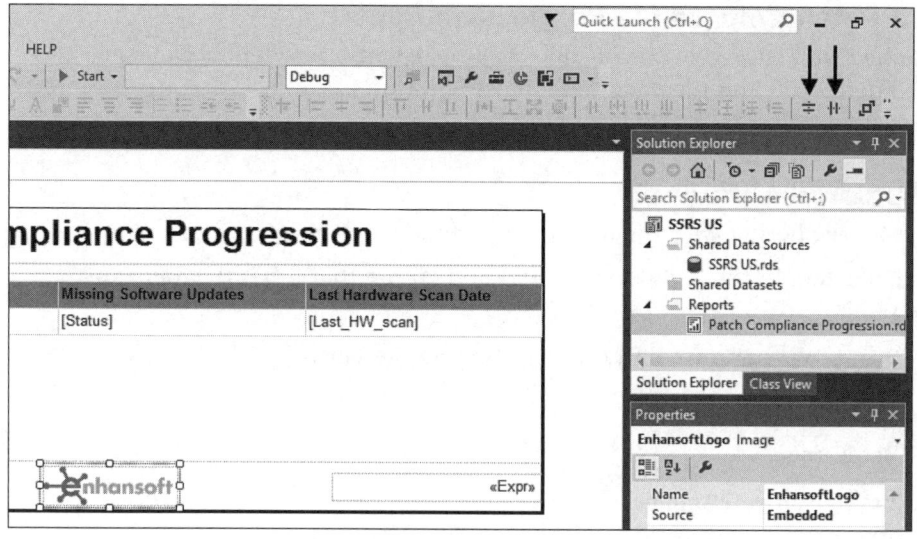

FIGURE 6.43   The Center Horizontally and Center Vertically icons.

Demonstrating Basic Report Creation

The purpose of this demonstration is to give you practice creating a project, creating basic reports, and customizing these items. You will create a new project and two separate reports in this demonstration. Each report will contain all the features discussed to this point. Follow the criteria required for each report and refer to previous sections of this chapter as required to complete the reports.

Creating a New Project

Create a new report server project in SSDT-BI. This project will be used for all further demonstrations in this book. Create the project using the following criteria:

▶ Create the project using the Report Server Project template.

▶ Select a name of your choice for the project.

▶ Set the project location to a folder on your local hard drive.

▶ Create a shared data source and connect it to your ConfigMgr database.

Be sure to test the shared data source connection and ensure that it is successful before continuing to the next section, as this will be used for the remaining demonstrations in this book.

Creating a Patch Compliance Progression Report

Inside the project you created in the previous section, create a new report named Patch Compliance Progression and then add the following features:

▶ Create a dataset using the query shown in Listing 6.1, earlier in this chapter.

▶ Set the page width to 8 inches.

▶ Include a page header with the report name centered on the page.

▶ Add a table item in the body of the report and ensure that it has the following features:

    ▶ Give it four columns with the following header labels:

    PC Name

    User Name

    Missing Software Updates

    Last Hardware Scan Date

    ▶ Make the header row bold with a red background color.

    ▶ Have the data rows alternate background colors between white and silver.

    ▶ Enable interactive sorting on every column.

▶ Add a page footer that contains the following items:

    ▶ The date of report execution on the left side of the page

    ▶ A logo in the center of the page

    ▶ The page number on the right side of the page

▶ Create a shared data source and connect it to your ConfigMgr database.

Be sure to preview your report once it is complete to confirm that all settings and features are functioning as intended and display properly on the page. You will use this report again in the next chapter to add advanced features and functionality.

Creating a Computer Hardware Information Report

Once again, inside the project you created in this demonstration, create a new report named Computer Hardware Information. Use SQL Server Management Studio to create a new query to get the required data before creating the report in SSDT-BI. Do the following for this report:

▶ Using SQL Server Management Studio, create a query to get the computer name, user name, make, model, and last hardware scan date for all systems in your environment.

▶ Hint: Turn to Chapter 3, "Understanding Configuration Manager Data," to find the correct SQL views for getting this information. Note that WHERE statements are not required to get this data.

▶ Create a dataset using the query you created in SQL Server Management Studio.

▶ Set the page width to 8 inches.

▶ Add a page header that contains the report name centered on the page.

▶ Add a table item in the body of the report and ensure that it has the following features:

 ▶ Give it five columns with the following header labels:

 PC Name

 User Name

 Make

 Model

 Last Hardware Scan Date

 ▶ Make the header row font bold with a background color of your choice.

 ▶ Have the data rows alternate background colors between white and silver.

 ▶ Enable interactive sorting on every column.

▶ Add a page footer that contains the following items:

 ▶ Date of execution on the left side of the page

 ▶ A logo in the center of the page

 ▶ The page number on the right side of the page

▶ Create a shared data source and connect it to your ConfigMgr database.

Be sure to preview your report once it is complete to confirm that all settings and features are functioning as intended and display properly on the page. You will build on this report in the demonstrations in Chapter 7.

Summary

This chapter has shown hands-on illustrations building on some of the basic design concepts discussed in Chapter 5. In this chapter you have learned about the multiple versions of tools available for creating new SSRS reports for ConfigMgr. This information should help you determine which tool is best for creating reports that will be compatible with the version of SSRS implemented in your environment.

Using the latest version of SSDT-BI for Visual Studio 2013, the chapter has demonstrated basic features, including how to create a new project and shared data sources and how to create new reports within a project. The chapter has covered available report items and demonstrated creating a dataset for a table item. It has discussed core features of reports, such as the page header, footer, size, and some basic items.

The remaining chapters of this book expand on the report basics explained in this chapter. Chapter 7 discusses advanced features such as report prompts and actions and how to create templates. It also introduces more advanced report items, such as charts. Chapter 7 continues to build on the reports created in this chapter.

Intermediate Reporting Concepts

Intermediate reporting concepts build on the foundational information discussed throughout Chapter 5, "Basic Report Design," and Chapter 6, "Building a Basic Report." This chapter describes how to create report templates and how to use those templates when fulfilling new report requests. A key component to report writing, as mentioned in Chapter 5, is ensuring that the report data fits the width of a single page. This chapter walks through how to export a report to verify that no items are cut off from the page—and if they are, how to fix the report.

Another essential feature of report writing is the ability to add parameters to reports. Using parameters produces reports that prompt viewers for details to filter and tailor the resulting data. Using parameters allows you to create more generic reports and lessens the need to write reports for specific requests. Several different styles of parameters can be utilized, including simple, dropdown, and multi-value. Each type of parameter has different capabilities to help the reader find the needed data. Each of these styles is described and demonstrated in this chapter.

This chapter also describes various types of chart items, which you can use to provide a visual representation of the data being returned from a report. A chart, the main report item used in summarized data reports, gives readers a high-level overview of the requested data. You can use several types of chart items to represent different types of data. From these reports, you can add actions to allow the reader to drill into the data to get further detailed information. Actions can build on general reports by passing along parameter values; these are useful for adding flow to the reports without requiring the reader to run several individual reports.

Creating Report Templates

Chapter 5 discussed the benefits of creating and using report templates and the common paper sizes typically used when building templates. Not only can templates provide a consistent look and feel to your reports, they save time when you're creating a new report. The following sections discuss how to create template reports for common page sizes to ensure that data does not get cut off the width of the page and how to copy and use templates to create a new report. Note that you can also create other templates to fit any paper size, using the same methods and steps detailed here.

Creating a Report Template (8.5×11in)

You can create report templates to match any paper size used in your environment. The steps to create a report template are the same for any page size. To illustrate the process, this section discusses how to create a letter portrait (8.5×11) template. Follow these steps:

1. If you have not already done so, in SQL Server Data Tools 2014 Business Intelligence (SSDT-BI) for Visual Studio 2013, open the project containing your Patch Compliance Progression report. This example uses the project created in Chapter 6, named SSRS US.

2. To create a new report, right-click the **Reports** folder under the Solution Explorer in the top-right section of the screen and select **Add -> New Item**.

3. In the Add New Item dialog shown in Figure 7.1, select **Report** from the list of items. Under the Name field, enter **_Template (8.5x11).rdl** and click **Add**.

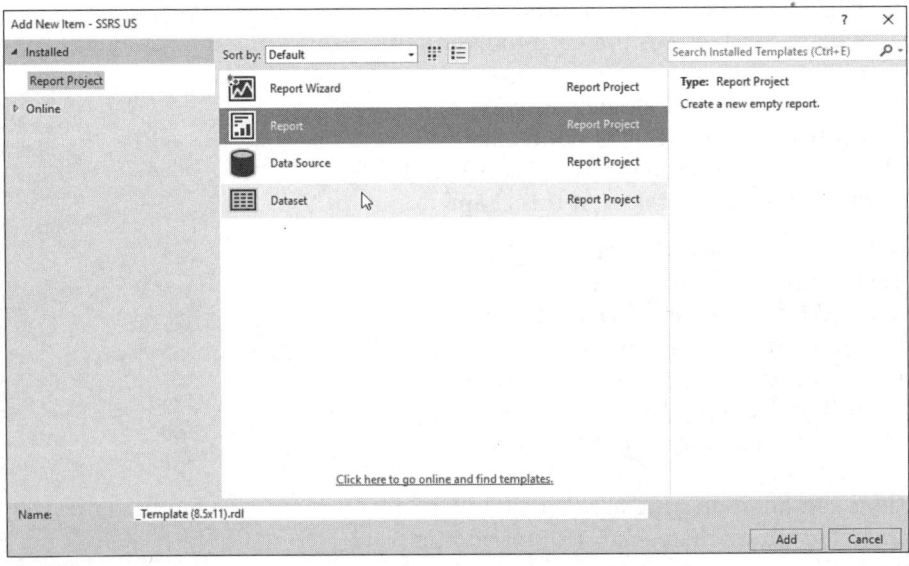

FIGURE 7.1   Creating a new report named **_Template (8.5x11).rdl**.

4. In the Properties section at the bottom right, use the dropdown to change the focus from Body to **Report**, as shown in Figure 7.2.

5. Scroll down in the Properties section and expand the **InteractiveSize** property so you can configure the values to match the paper size. Set the Width value to **8.5in** and the **Height** value to **11in**, as shown in Figure 7.3.

6. Below the InteractiveSize section expand the **Margins** property and set the Left, Right, Top, and Bottom values to **0.25in** each, as shown in Figure 7.4.

TIP: MARGIN SIZES

Regardless of the paper size being used, the authors recommend using 0.25in margins on each side of the page. This allows the maximum space of the page to be used for the report while maintaining a small, professional-looking border around the page when printed or exported to Word and PDF formats.

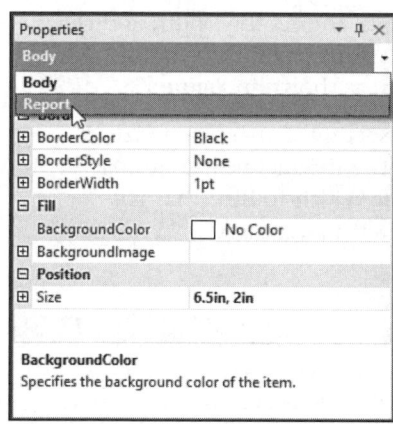

FIGURE 7.2   Changing the Properties section focus to **Report**.

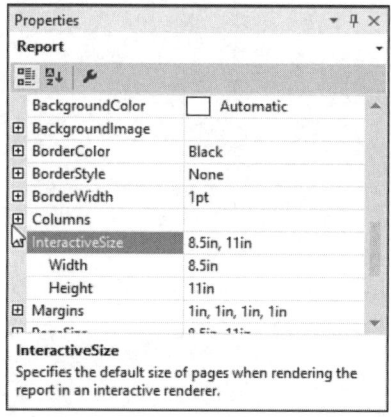

FIGURE 7.3   Setting the InteractiveSize property values to the paper size.

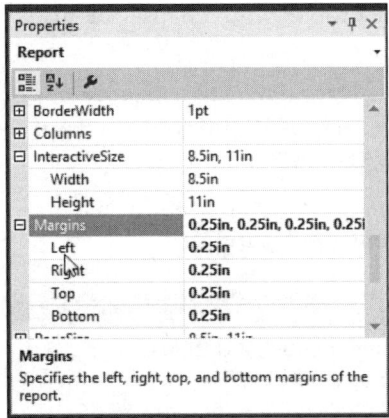

FIGURE 7.4   Setting all margin property values to 0.25in.

7. Below the Margins section, expand the PageSize property and set the Width and Height values to the same size as the InteractiveSize property set in step 5. For this example, set the Width value to **8.5in** and the Height value to **11in**, as shown in Figure 7.5.

8. Change the focus in the Properties section to **Body** section. Expand the **Size** property. Set the Width value to the same width as the InteractiveSize minus the Left and Right margin sizes. For this example, set Width to **8in** (that is, InteractiveSize Width of 8.5in minus 0.25in for the left margin and 0.25 for the right margin), as shown in Figure 7.6.

TIP: ENSURE THAT THE REPORT WIDTH DOES NOT EXPAND

As you add and resize report items, the size of your body section may change and expand. Keep an eye on the width to ensure that it does not exceed the InteractiveSize minus both left and right margins, or data will be split onto a separate page. To help with this, enable the ruler on your report by right-clicking the body of the report and selecting **View** -> **Ruler**.

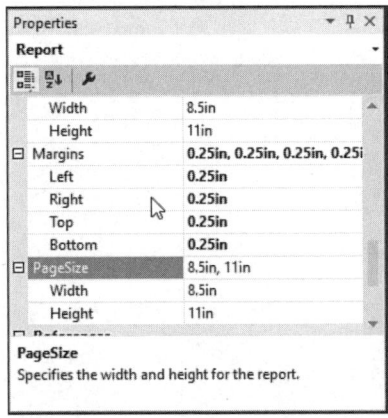

FIGURE 7.5   Setting PageSize values to the same size as for the InteractiveSize property.

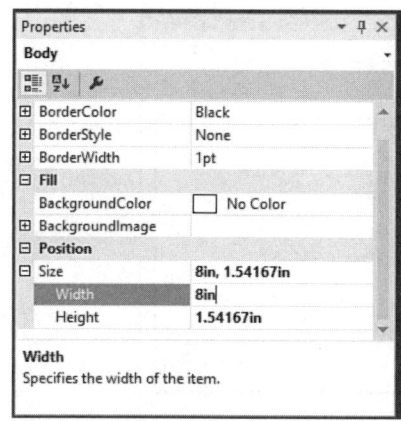

FIGURE 7.6   Setting the body size Width value.

9. Add header and footer sections to the report. Configure the desired style and formatting that will be common for every report in your environment. This can include adding a Report Title text box as a placeholder in your header and text boxes for the page count and date expressions in the footer section. Don't forget to add any desired logos and background colors to the report. When you're done with this, save the report. Figure 7.7 shows an example of a template report.

REAL WORLD: REPORT HEIGHT SIZE

The authors have mentioned the report size multiple times to ensure that data does not surpass the page width and get cut off to another page. The only consideration regarding the report height size is to make certain that items in the Design mode do not exceed the InteractiveSize height minus the top and bottom margins (10.5in for the example in this section).

Table rows automatically continue to flow onto following pages; however, if your design includes items that exceed the height size, they will get cut to following pages and will become out of sync on paper. When a report is executed, items in the Body section of the report are fully populated in the order in which they appear in Design mode. As an example, if your report includes a table above a chart, the chart item will not appear in the report until all rows of the table are populated.

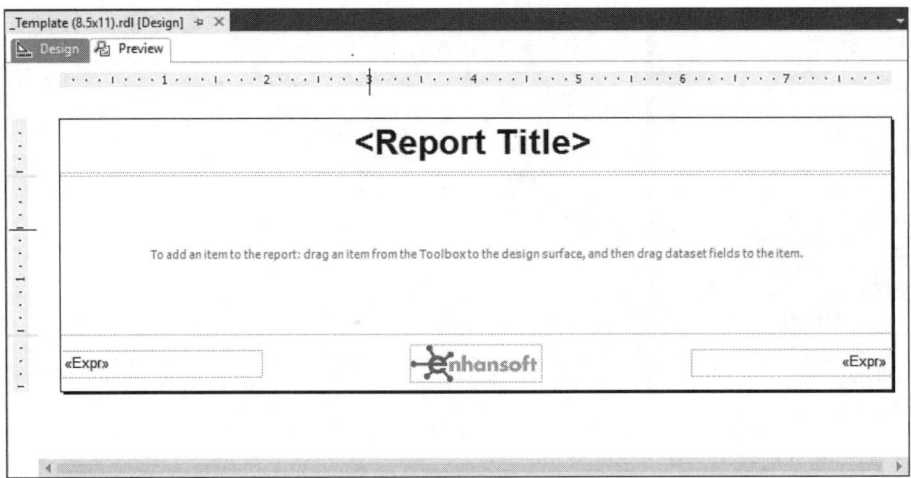

FIGURE 7.7   Example of a completed template report.

Creating a New Report from a Template

You can use template reports to build new reports. To create a new report using a template, simply make a copy of the template and rename it to the desired title of your new report. Perform the following steps to create a copy of a report:

1. In the Solution Explorer on the right side of SSDT-BI, under the Reports folder, right-click your template report. This example uses the **_Template (8.5x11).rdl** report created in the previous section. Select **Copy**, as shown in Figure 7.8.

2. On the SSDT-BI toolbar, select **Edit** and click **Paste**, as shown in Figure 7.9.

3. Notice the new report named **Copy of _Template (8.5x11).rdl** in the Solution Explorer, under Reports. Right-click this report and select **Rename**. Enter the name of the new report, as shown in Figure 7.10.

4. Double-click the new report to open it in Design mode. Notice the tab at the top of the main section of SSDT-BI, above the Design and Preview buttons, indicating the name of the report you are currently viewing and editing (see Figure 7.11).

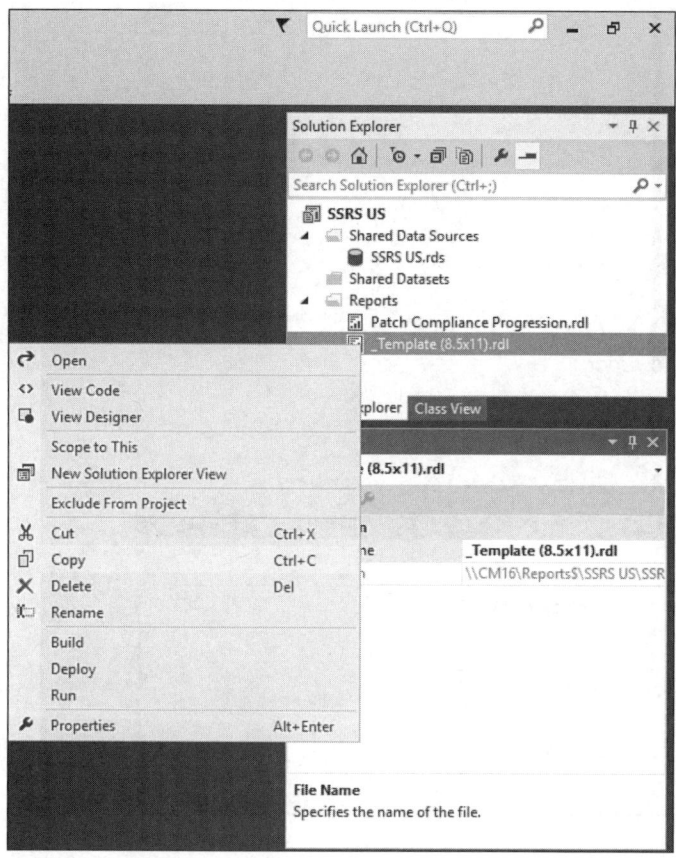

FIGURE 7.8   Right-clicking the template report and selecting **Copy**.

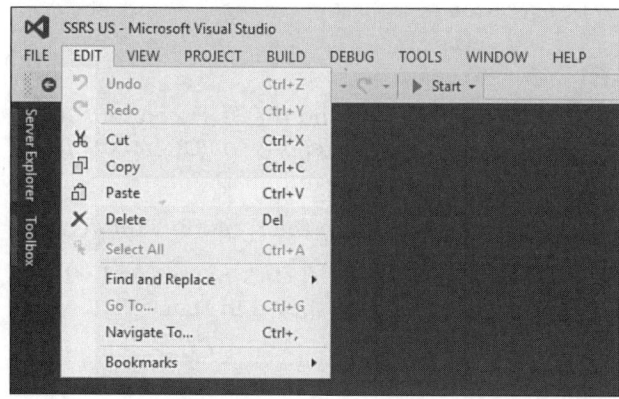

FIGURE 7.9   Selecting **Edit** -> **Paste** from the SSDT-BI toolbar.

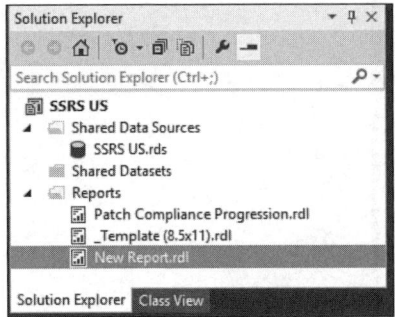

FIGURE 7.10   Renaming the copied report.

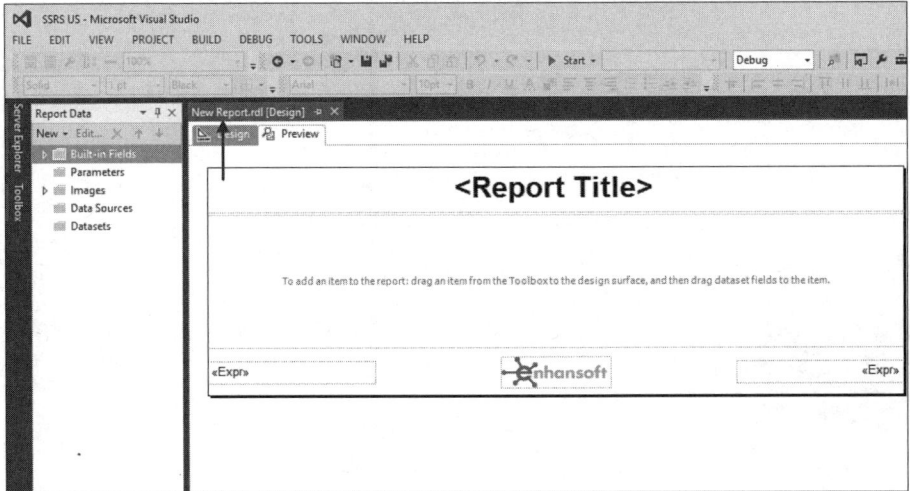

FIGURE 7.11   Verifying which report is in Design mode by looking at the report name tab.

Exporting Reports from SSDT-BI

To confirm that a report is the proper width for the page size and that data columns from a table will not be cut off onto separate pages, you can export reports to PDF from SSDT-BI Preview mode. Perform the following steps to export a report within SSDT-BI:

1. Open the **Patch Compliance Progression.rdl** report from the Solution Explorer.

2. Click **Preview** at the top of the report. From Preview mode, click **Export** and select a file type. For this example, the **PDF** option is selected, as shown in Figure 7.12.

3. In the **Save As** dialog, select a location to save the report and click **Save**.

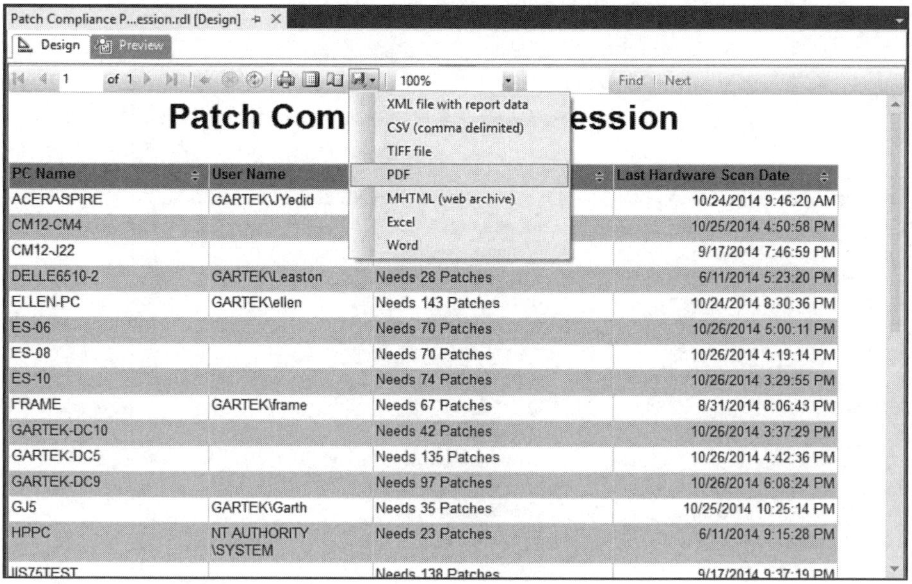

FIGURE 7.12   Exporting the report to a PDF file from Preview mode.

Modifying the Page Size of an Existing Report

The PDF export of the report, displayed in Figure 7.13, shows that the last column of the table does not fit within the first page and gets cut to the second page. Keep in mind that viewing a report in PDF format provides an accurate representation of how the report will appear when printed on paper. The page width problem is not noticeable when you preview the report in SSDT-BI, as you can see in Figure 7.12, where SSDT-BI displays all four columns. To correct the page width issue with the Patch Compliance Progression report, the Report and Body sizes must be adjusted to match the values detailed in the template creation steps. Follow these steps to modify the size of an existing report:

1. In Design mode, in the bottom-right corner of the Properties section, change the focus to **Report**.

2. Ensure that both the InteractiveSize and PageSize properties are set to **8.5in, 11in**. Expand the Margins property and set the values for the Left, Right, Top, and Bottom properties to **0.25in**.

3. In the Properties section, change the focus to **Body**.

4. Expand the **Size** property and ensure that the Width property value is set to **8in**.

5. Once all the settings are properly set and verified, preview the report. In Preview mode, click **Export** and select **PDF**.

6. In the Save As dialog, select a location to save the report and click **Save**.

7. Open the newly saved report to validate that all columns appear properly on a single page width, as shown in Figure 7.14.

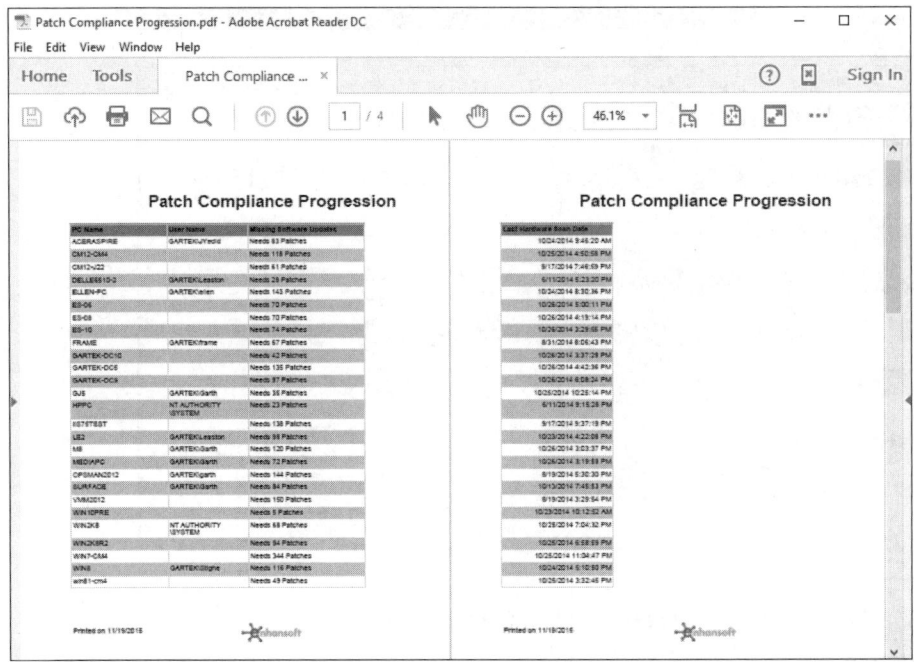

FIGURE 7.13   Patch Compliance Progression report data does not fit within a page width.

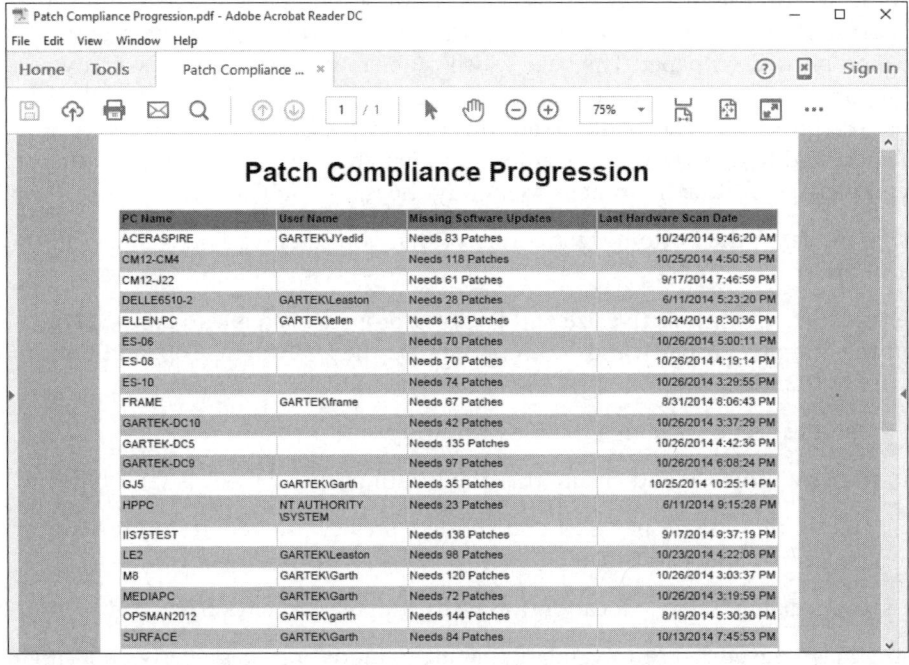

FIGURE 7.14   All table columns now appear within a page width.

TIP: MARGIN AND PAGE SIZES

When items do not fit within a column width, the problem is usually the margin values and the body size values. Always validate that the BodySize value is equal to the paper width (InteractiveSize width) minus the left and right margin values.

Using Report Parameters

This section of the chapter explains parameters, their available options, and how to use them in a report to prompt the reader for information. Adding a prompt by using a parameter allows the report to adapt and tailor the data to specific information requested by the reader. It is also a great way to reduce the number of individual reports that need to be created. For example, rather than creating one report to show the patch compliance progression for all systems, a second report to show patch compliance for desktops only, and a third for server systems, you can add a simple prompt to a single report to let the user specify the data he or she wants to see.

Understanding the Value and Label Fields

It is easy to get confused by the value and the label fields because they are very similar. However, they each play a very important role when it comes to defining a parameter:

▶ **Value:** The value field contains the data that is passed to a parameter (variable) in the query. Think of the value field as the ResourceID or CollectionID column data.

▶ **Label:** The label field is the user-friendly name that is displayed as part of the prompt. It is translated or linked to the value field, which is passed to the query.

For example, the reader would see the computer name or the collection name. The label field for a collection would show as All Systems, and its value would be SMS00001, which would be passed to the query to run the report.

Using Default Values

The default values of a parameter are used to define the initial values that appear when a report runs. If the user does not change a value, the report is executed using the defined default value. This field is helpful when a report is most often used with the same parameter value and requires only infrequent changes.

An example of a default value would be the SMS00001 value to identify the All Systems collection for the Patch Compliance Progression report. A majority of the time this report would run to view the compliance of all systems. Running the report to see all systems does not require changes to the prompt value; however, for the occasional time that you need to compare the compliance only for your server fleet, you can change the value from the default.

Understanding Cascade Prompts

You use a cascade prompt when a report requires multiple parameters. It allows the value of one prompt to feed or limit the values available for the next prompt(s). For example, say that there are two dropdown boxes that contain lists of values:

▶ The first dropdown box prompts the reader to select a country.

▶ Based on the country selected, the second prompt provides a list of states or provinces to be selected.

Using Multi-Value Parameters

You use a multi-value parameter to provide additional flexibility for your readers when running a report. As its name suggests, a multi-value parameter allows readers to specify more than one value to be passed to a query. For example, if you have a report that lists computers in a collection that has a parameter and a prompt for the collection name, you can enable the option **Allow multiple values** on the parameter. This way, readers can select more than one collection when running the report. It is important to note that your report query must accept the parameter using the IN criteria instead of = or LIKE.

Adding a Simple Prompt

When creating reports, you may sometimes want to be able to slightly modify the report's dataset (query) by adding another column or adding a prompt to make your report more practical or reader-friendly. Whatever the change, you can modify the dataset directly in SSDT-BI without needing to go back to SQL Server Management Studio. In this section you will add a prompt to the Patch Compliance Progression report created in Chapter 6 to select a collection so you don't have to specify the CollectionID value of SMS00001 directly in the query. The change makes for a much more versatile report. Follow these steps to add the prompt:

1. In SSDT-BI, open the Patch Compliance Progression report by double-clicking the report item in the Solution Explorer in the top-right corner.

2. In the Report Data section in SSDT-BI, expand the Datasets folder. Right-click **PatchDataset** (or the name of the dataset you created) and select **Dataset Properties**, as shown in Figure 7.15.

3. In the Query section, scroll down to find the WHERE section and locate the line from Listing 7.1 specifying the CollectionID as SMS00001.

LISTING 7.1   Original WHERE Section Specifying the SMS00001 Collection

```
And FCM.CollectionID = 'SMS00001'
```

4. Modify the line shown in Listing 7.1 to use @Coll as a parameter for CollectionID, as shown in Listing 7.2. After modifying the query (as shown in Figure 7.16), click **OK** to apply the changes and close the Dataset Properties dialog.

LISTING 7.2   Modified WHERE Section Using the @Coll Parameter for CollectionID

```
And FCM.CollectionID = @Coll
```

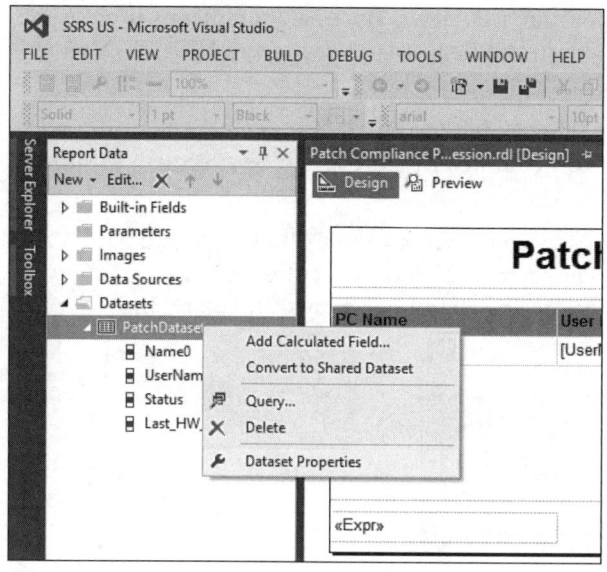

FIGURE 7.15   Selecting Dataset Properties.

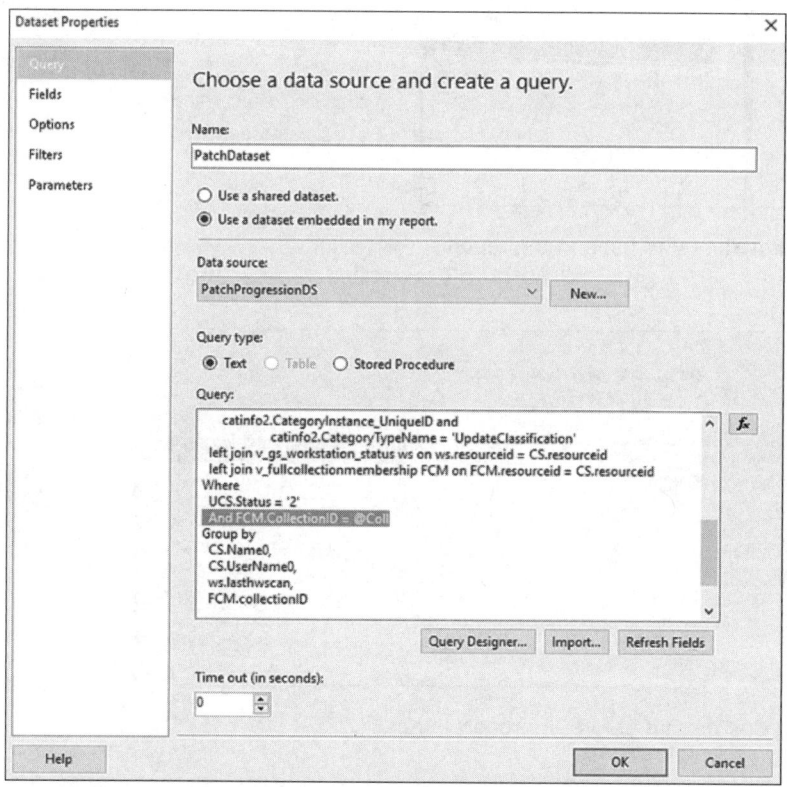

FIGURE 7.16   Modified dataset query.

5. To confirm that the change is successful and view a list of all parameters used in the report, expand the Parameters folder in the Report Data section in SSDT-BI. Notice the new @Coll parameter, shown in Figure 7.17.

6. Preview the report by clicking the Preview tab to view the parameter prompt. Notice that the report prompts for the @Coll parameter before it can be executed, as shown in Figure 7.18.

7. To view the report, enter **SMS00001** as the value for the Coll prompt and click **View Report** on the far right of the Preview tab. The report executes and displays query results from the SMS00001 (All Systems) collection, as shown in Figure 7.19.

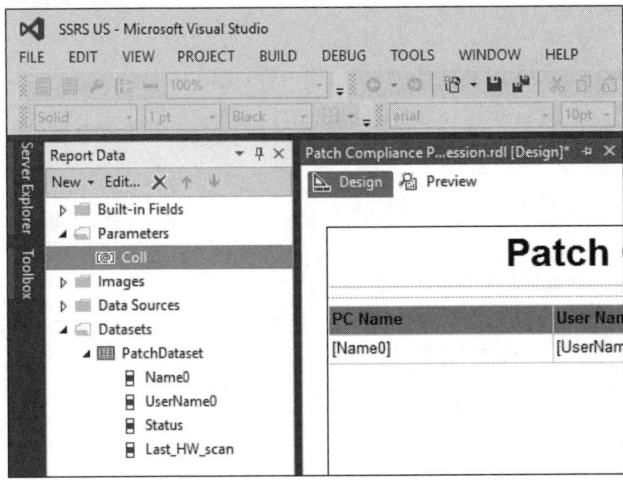

FIGURE 7.17   List of all parameters used in the report.

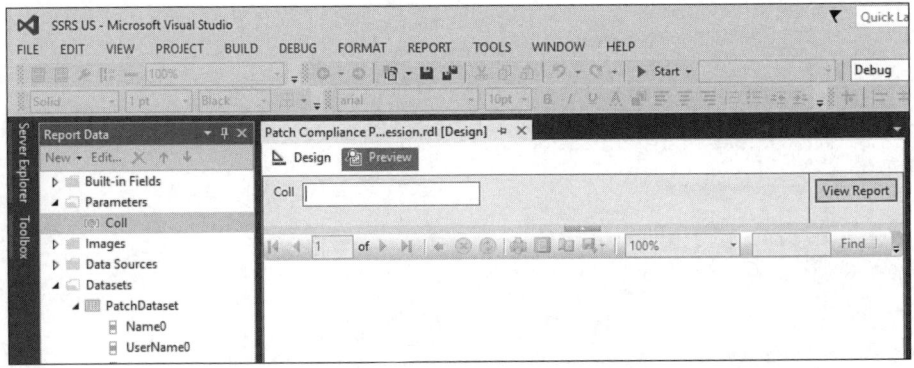

FIGURE 7.18   Required Coll prompt before the report is run.

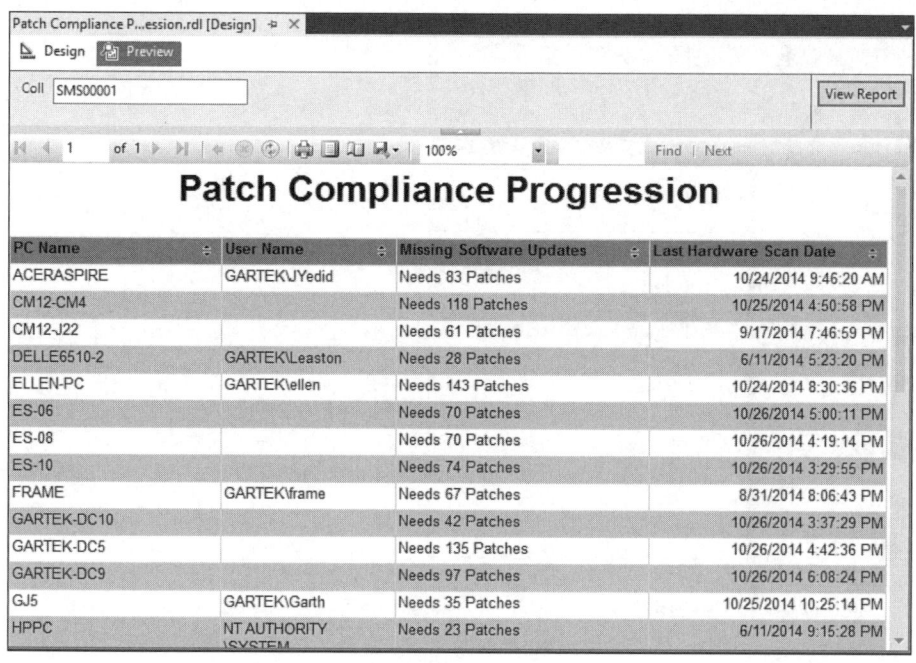

FIGURE 7.19   Report executed with SMS00001 value.

Adding a Dropdown Prompt

In the previous section you added a simple prompt to a report to tailor the query for a specified ConfigMgr collection. To identify the targeted collection, the CollectionID had to be manually keyed at the report prompt in order to view the resulting data. Unfortunately, it is not easy to remember specific collection IDs; most readers who are not ConfigMgr administrators may not even know what a collection ID represents or how to find one. To make it easier for everyone reading the report, you could add to the report a dropdown list of collection names from ConfigMgr rather than displaying a simple prompt. To do so, you would start by adding a second dataset to get all collection names and their matching collection IDs and then you would change the parameter to get available values from a query in the new dataset. Perform the following steps to create the dataset and modify the parameter:

1. In the Report Data section in SSDT-BI, right-click the **Datasets** folder and select **Add Dataset**, as shown in Figure 7.20.

2. In the Dataset Properties dialog, enter a name for the dataset. For this example, use the name PromptColl. Select the option **Use a dataset embedded in my report**. Under the Data source field, using the dropdown, select your data source. Under the Query field, enter the query shown in Listing 7.3 to get a list of all collection names and their associated CollectionIDs. (For your convenience, this listing is available as online content; see Appendix C, "Available Online," for details.), Figure 7.21 shows the completed Dataset Properties dialog. Click **OK** to create the new dataset.

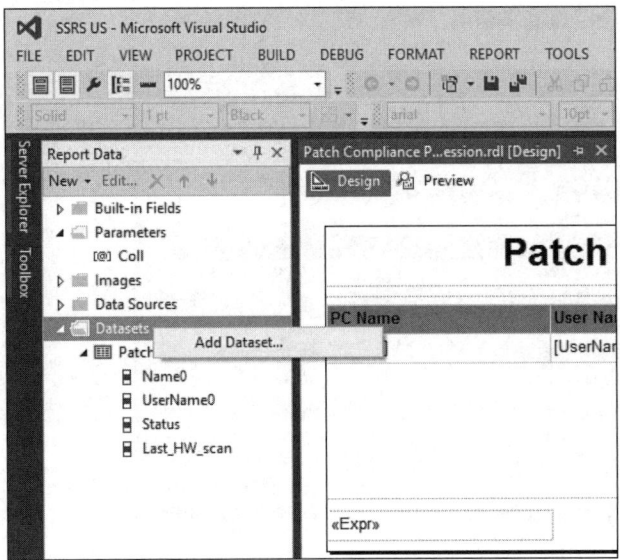

FIGURE 7.20   Right-clicking **Datasets** and selecting **Add Dataset**.

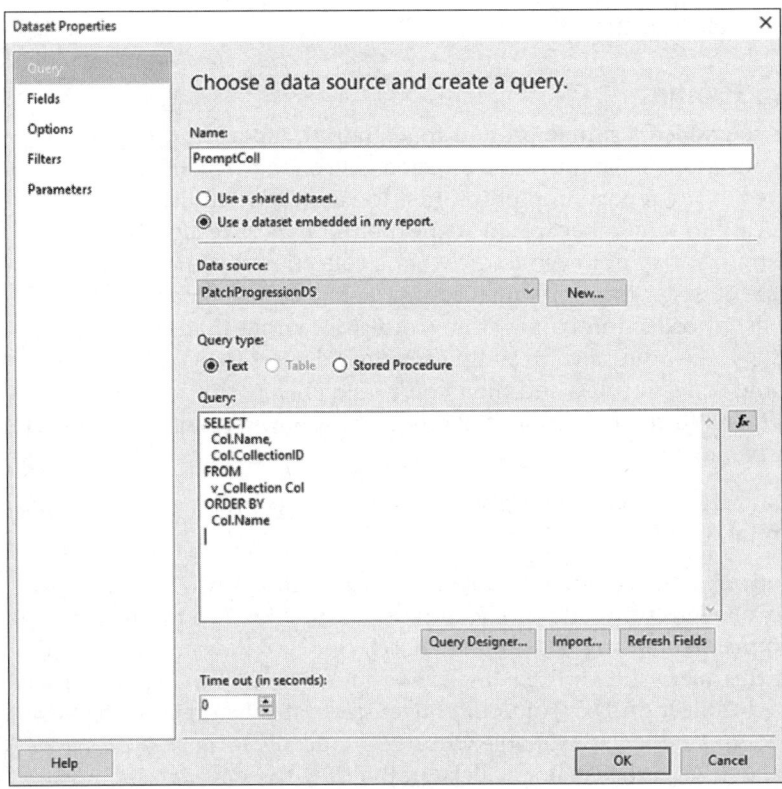

FIGURE 7.21   Completed Dataset Properties dialog.

LISTING 7.3   Query for All Collection Names and IDs

```
SELECT
  Col.Name,
  Col.CollectionID
FROM
  v_Collection Col
ORDER BY
  Col.Name
```

3. In the Report Data section in SSDT-BI, expand the Parameters folder, right-click the **Coll** parameter, and select **Parameter Properties**, as shown in Figure 7.22.

4. In the Report Parameter Properties dialog, on the General tab under the Prompt field, enter a reader-friendly prompt title such as **Select a Collection**, as shown in Figure 7.23.

5. Click the **Available Values** tab on the left side of the Report Parameter Properties dialog and select the **Get values from a query** option. Using the dropdown under the Dataset field, select the PromptColl dataset created in step 2. Set the **Value** field to **CollectionID**. This is the value that is passed to the query when the report is executed. Under the **Label** field, select **Name** to identify the dataset column that will appear in the dropdown list for the reader to select.

When the Report Parameter Properties dialog is complete, as shown in Figure 7.24, click **OK** to apply the changes and close the dialog.

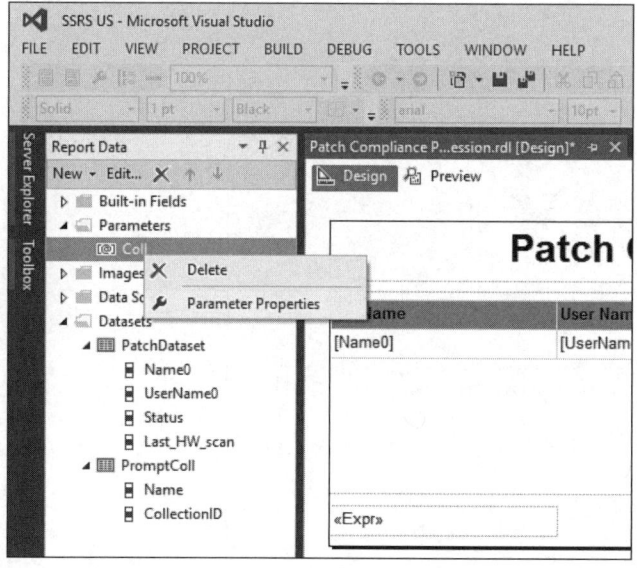

FIGURE 7.22   Selecting **Parameter Properties** from the right-click menu.

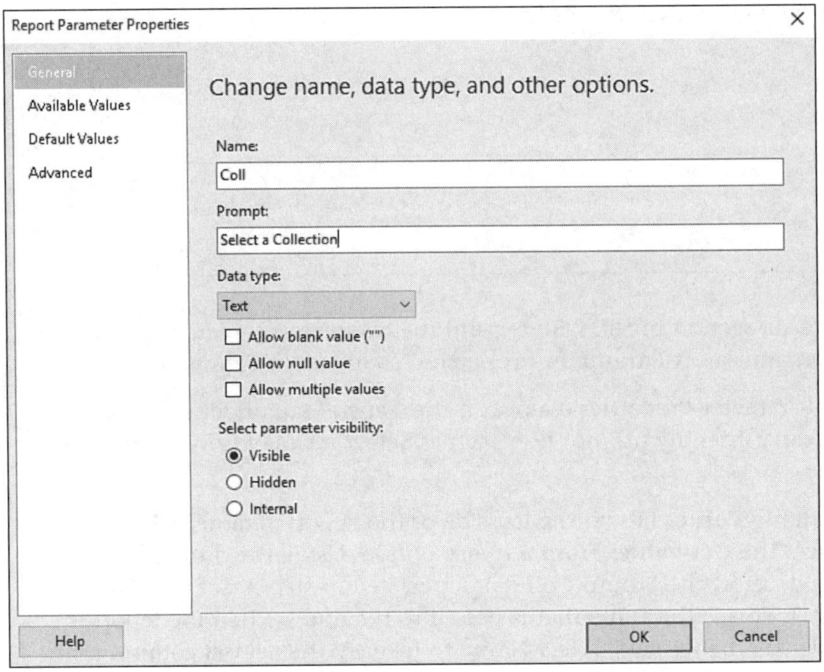

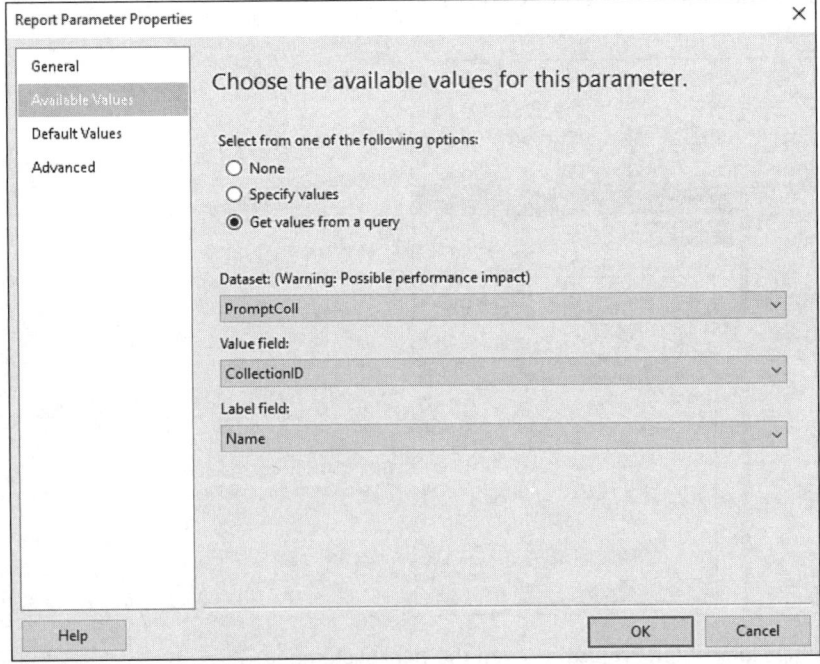

FIGURE 7.23   Entering a reader-friendly prompt title.

FIGURE 7.24   Completing the Available Values tab of the Report Parameter Properties dialog.

6. Preview the report; notice that the prompt title now shows **Select a Collection** and the prompt is now a dropdown menu of all available collections from ConfigMgr displayed by Name, as shown in Figure 7.25. When a collection is selected, the CollectionID is passed to the query, and the results are displayed.

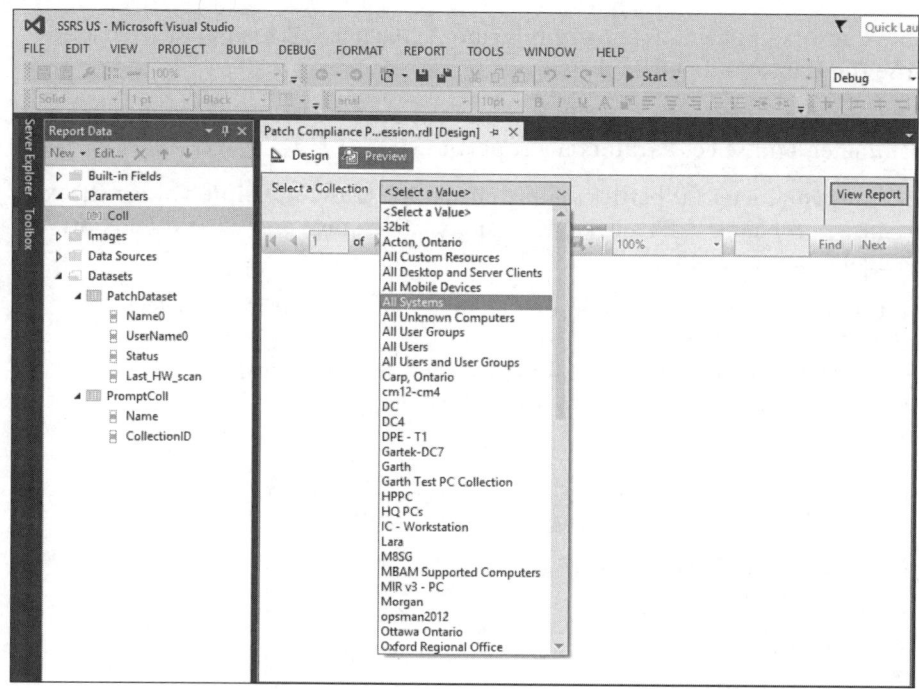

FIGURE 7.25   Report containing an updated title and dropdown prompt.

Adding a Multi-Value Parameter

Adding a multi-value parameter is a good way to add flexibility to a report. A report with a simple parameter that accepts only a single value requires that the reader run the same report multiple times to get data from different collections. Using a multi-value parameter removes this requirement by allowing the reader to select multiple collections at once. You must modify the dataset slightly before enabling this feature. Follow these steps to modify the dataset and enable the multi-value feature:

1. In the Report Data section in SSDT-BI, expand the **Datasets** folder. Right-click **PatchDataset** (or the name of the dataset you created) and select **Data Properties**.

2. In the Query section, scroll down to find the WHERE section and locate the line from Listing 7.4, which indicates that the CollectionID is using the @Coll parameter.

LISTING 7.4   Original WHERE Section Specifying the @Coll Parameter

```
And FCM.CollectionID = @Coll
```

3. Replace the = criteria with IN, as shown in Listing 7.5.

LISTING 7.5   Updated WHERE Section Using IN Criteria for the CollectionID Parameter

---
And FCM.CollectionID IN (@Coll)
---

4. Once the query is updated, as shown in Figure 7.26, click **OK** to apply the changes and close the Dataset Properties dialog.

5. In the Report Data section in SSDT-BI, expand the **Parameters** folder, right-click the **Coll** parameter, and select **Parameter Properties**.

6. In the Report Parameter Properties dialog, check the **Allow multiple values** check box, as shown in Figure 7.27. Click **OK** to apply the change and close the Report Parameters Properties dialog.

7. Preview the report to view the parameter changes. Notice that in the Select a Collection dropdown there are now check boxes next to the collection names, as shown in Figure 7.28. Adding checks next to multiple collections and clicking **View Report** gets results from all the selected values.

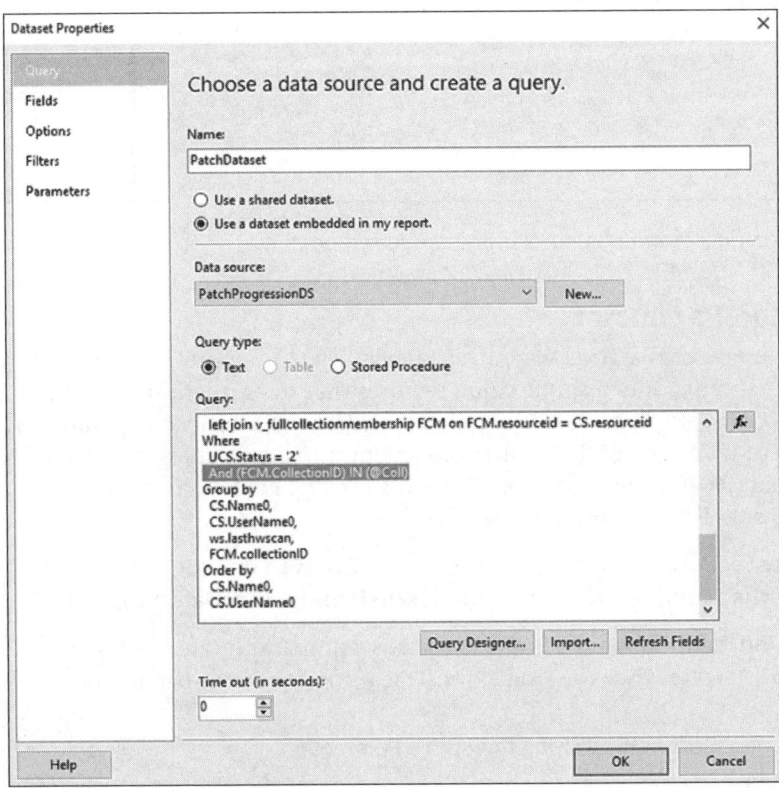

FIGURE 7.26   Updated dataset query using the IN criteria.

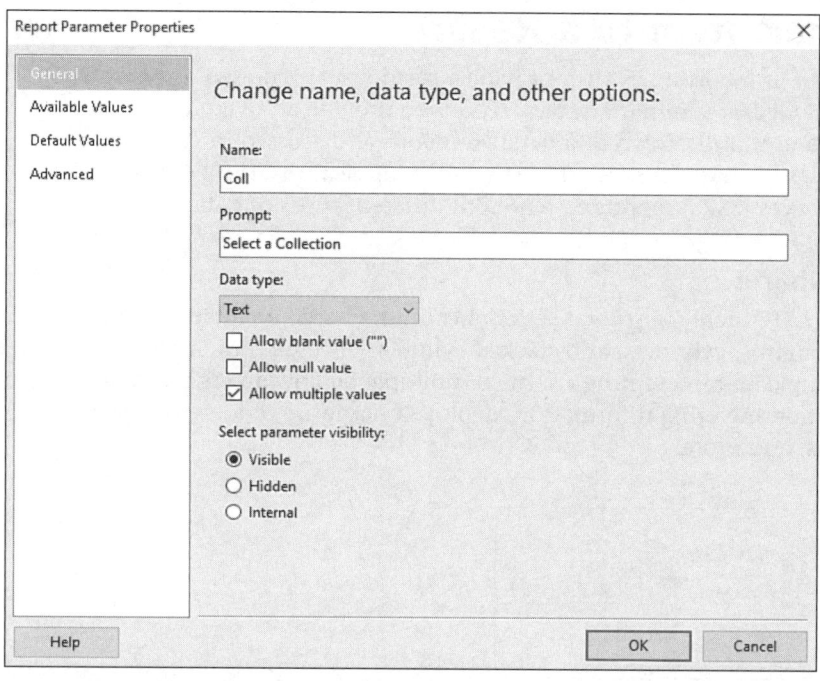

FIGURE 7.27   Enabling **Allow multiple values** in the Report Parameter Properties dialog.

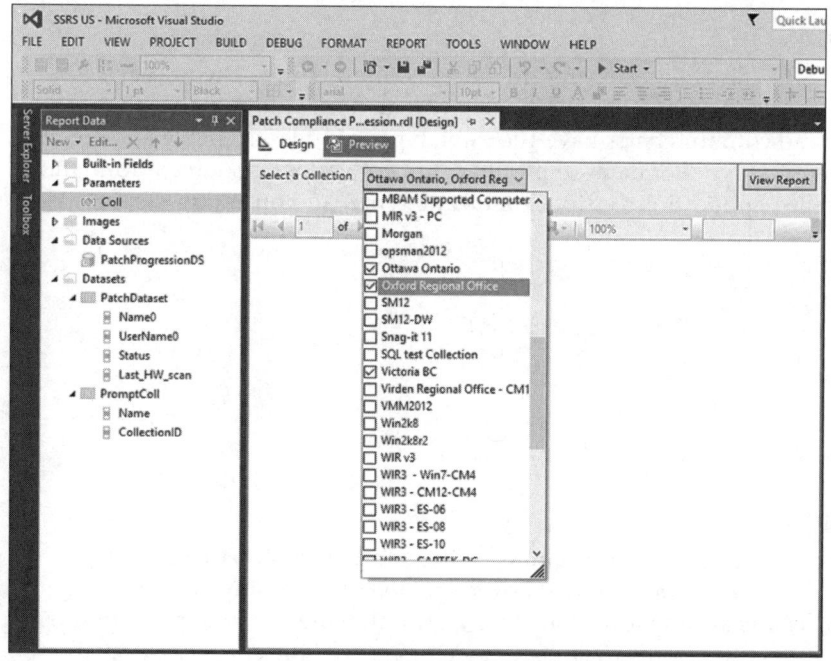

FIGURE 7.28   Report prompt allowing multiple collections to be selected.

Adding a Chart Item to a Report

Charts are very useful in reporting as they provide a clean visual representation of data. Charts are often included in summarized data reports to provide an overview of the information before a user drills down to a detailed report, as discussed in Chapter 5. Several different styles of charts, discussed in the following sections, can be used in SQL Server Reporting Services (SSRS) reports to represent different types of data.

Using Column Charts

As shown in Figure 7.29, there are several styles of column charts, including simple columns, stacked columns, cylinders, and stacked cylinders. These types of charts are useful for showing data representing counts of multiple deployed versions of an application, application metering information, deployed hardware models, operating system (OS) versions, and more.

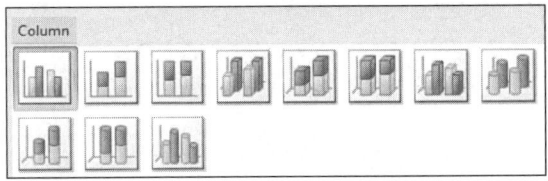

FIGURE 7.29   Available column charts.

Using Bar Charts

As shown in Figure 7.30, bar charts are very similar to column charts. The primary difference between the two is that a bar chart displays data horizontally rather than vertically. Both bar and column charts have the same types of styles available and are also useful for showing similar types of data—typically counts of various resource information, including total installed application versions, hardware types, and operating systems.

FIGURE 7.30   Available bar charts.

Using Line Charts

Line charts display data as a set of points connected by a line. Typically these types of charts are used to show large amounts of data over a period of time. Some examples of reports ideal for line charts are application metering (monthly usage of an application over a year) and monthly successful software updates by OS version. Line charts are available in different styles, including basic lines, smooth lines, stepped lines, 3D lines, lines with markers, and smooth lines with markers. Figure 7.31 shows these different styles.

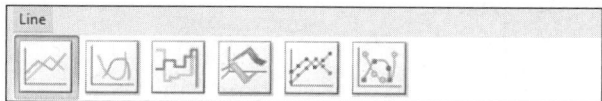

FIGURE 7.31   Available line charts.

Using Pie Charts

A pie chart, as the name suggests, displays data as a wedge or section of a pie. Pie charts are common in SSRS reporting for showing data as a percentage, as in deployments (complete vs. incomplete or success vs. failed), application upgrades and patching status (compliant vs. noncompliant), and breakdowns of hardware models or operating system versions. The pie chart is available in the different styles shown in Figure 7.32: the standard pie, exploded pie, 3D, and 3D exploded pie.

It is important to note that it becomes very difficult to read a pie chart if there are a large number of unique data wedges in the pie. In cases where it is difficult to read a pie chart, it is usually best to change the type to either a column or bar chart.

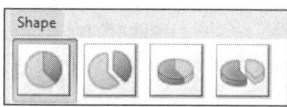

FIGURE 7.32   Available pie charts.

Using Doughnut Charts

A doughnut chart is identical to a pie chart with the exception that it shows data as sections, or bites, of a doughnut instead of wedges of a pie. This type of chart is available in two styles: standard doughnut and exploded doughnut (see Figure 7.33). Both pie and doughnut charts are part of the Shapes chart section in SSDT-BI.

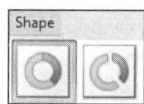

FIGURE 7.33   Available doughnut charts.

Using Other Chart Types

There are several other SSRS-supported chart types and styles to choose from within SSDT-BI, including pyramid, funnel, area, range, scatter, and polar charts. These other chart types are not often used to represent ConfigMgr data; however, they are available and can be used if you desire. Figure 7.34 shows these remaining chart types.

Adding a Chart to a Report

Adding a chart item to a report in SSDT-BI is a simple process, although getting the chart to display the proper information requires a bit more effort than with a table item. To demonstrate adding a chart to a report, in this section you will modify the Patch

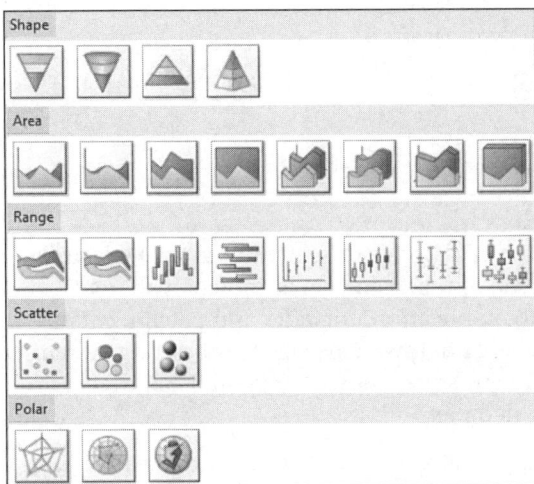

FIGURE 7.34   All other available chart types.

Compliance Progression report to remove the existing table and add a pie chart in its place. In this way, you will transform the report into a summarized data report. Follow these steps to add and configure a chart item:

1. Create a copy of the Patch Compliance Progression report and rename the copy **Patch Compliance Progression Chart.rdl**.

2. Double-click the new report to open it. Notice the tab above Design/Preview that indicates the report you currently have open.

3. Before adding the chart item, delete the existing table from the report by selecting the table item in the body section, right-clicking the top-left corner of the table where the column and row frames meet, and selecting **Delete** (see Figure 7.35).

4. Add a chart item to the report. From the toolbox, drag the chart item to the body of the report.

5. In the Select Chart Type dialog select the desired chart—in this case the exploded pie chart, under the Shapes type (see Figure 7.36)—and click **OK** to add the item. The exploded pie chart is now added to the body of the report. Notice that the chart is populated with sample wedges to let you see how it will look when you run your report.

6. Before adding data to the chart, the dataset must be modified slightly to have the Status field return only the number of missing patches for a machine. By showing only the integer value, the pie chart's wedge size accurately represents the number of patches required for each system. Under the PatchDataset folder, right-click PatchDataset (created in Chapter 6) and select **Properties**. In the Query section, find the CASE statement that identifies the Status column shown in Listing 7.6.

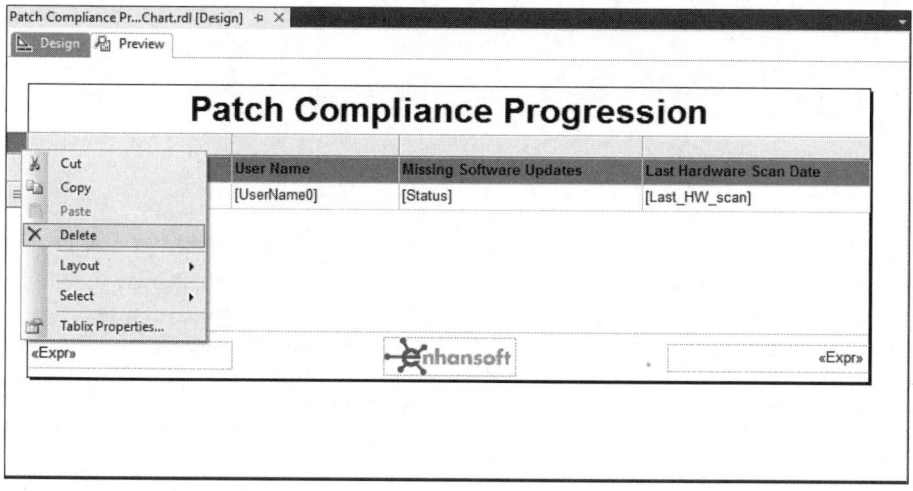

FIGURE 7.35   Deleting the existing table item from the new report.

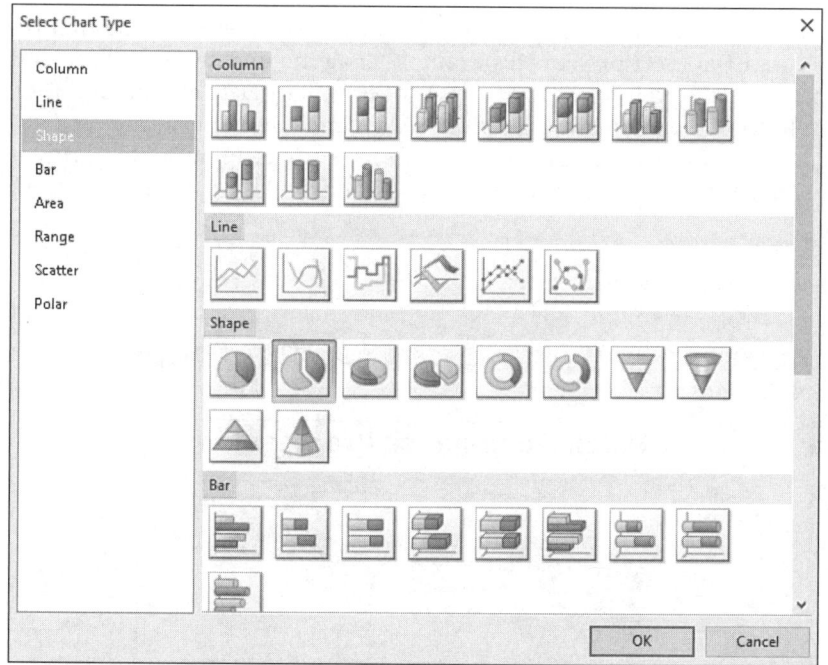

FIGURE 7.36   Selecting the exploded pie chart item.

LISTING 7.6   Original CASE Statement Identifying the Status Column

```
CASE
   When (sum(case when UCS.status=2 then 1 else 0 end))>0 then
        ('Needs '+(cast(sum(case when UCS.status=2 then 1 else 0 end)
        as varchar(10))+ ' Patches'))
   Else 'Good Client'
End as 'Status',
```

7. Replace the code in Listing 7.6 with the new, simpler status column shown in Listing 7.7. This new column returns only the total (sum) number of missing patches for a system. Click **OK** to close the Dataset Properties dialog.

LISTING 7.7   Replacement Status Column in the SELECT Section

```
sum(case when UCS.status=2 then 1 else 0 end) as 'Status',
```

8. Select the chart in the body of the report to view the Chart Data section shown in Figure 7.37. Notice that there are currently no values associated with the chart.

9. To add data to the chart, drag and drop columns from your dataset to the desired sections in the Chart Data section. For this example, drag the updated Status column, under PatchDataset, into the Values area of the Chart Data section and the Name0 column to the Category Groups section (see Figure 7.38). This results in a wedge of the pie for each system name, where the wedge size is appropriate to the number of missing patches for that system.

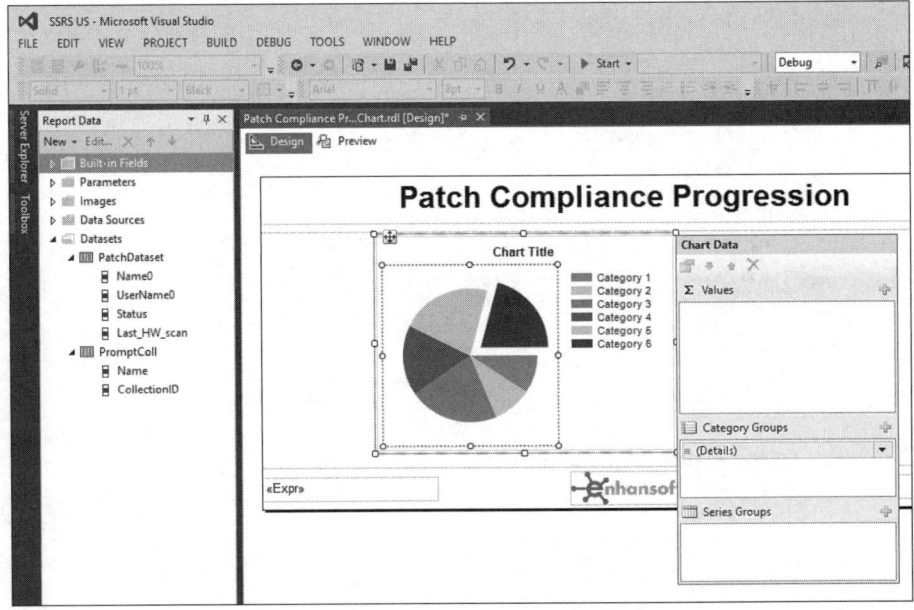

FIGURE 7.37   Selecting the chart item to see the Chart Data section.

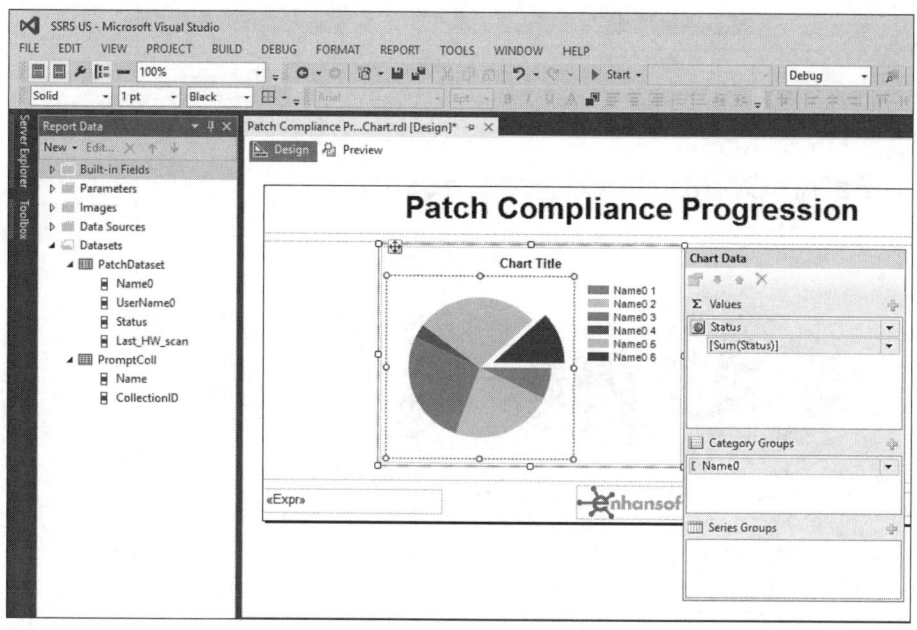

FIGURE 7.38   Completed Chart Data section.

10. Increase the size of the chart by selecting the item and stretching the outside edges of the object or by modifying the size values in the Properties section in the bottom-right corner of the screen. Also, center the chart within the report by clicking **Center Horizontal** in the SSDT-BI toolbar.

TIP: SIZING THE CHART ITEM

The chart size when running a report is the same size as it appears in Design mode. This allows you to accurately size the chart in the body of your report without needing to preview the results to confirm the chart's size and placement in the report.

---

11. When you're satisfied with the size and placement of the chart, preview the report by selecting a collection from the dropdown prompt in order to view the report data (see Figure 7.39).

Customizing Chart Items

The previous section discussed adding to a report a simple chart item with default settings. Chart items contain many modifiable features and areas. These modifications include enabling 3D effects for the chart to improve individual wedge visibility, adding data labels to the chart to identify the value represented by each wedge, and placing the legend and title areas. In this section you'll learn how to enable 3D effects, remove the chart title, and move the legend to the bottom of the chart. Follow these steps:

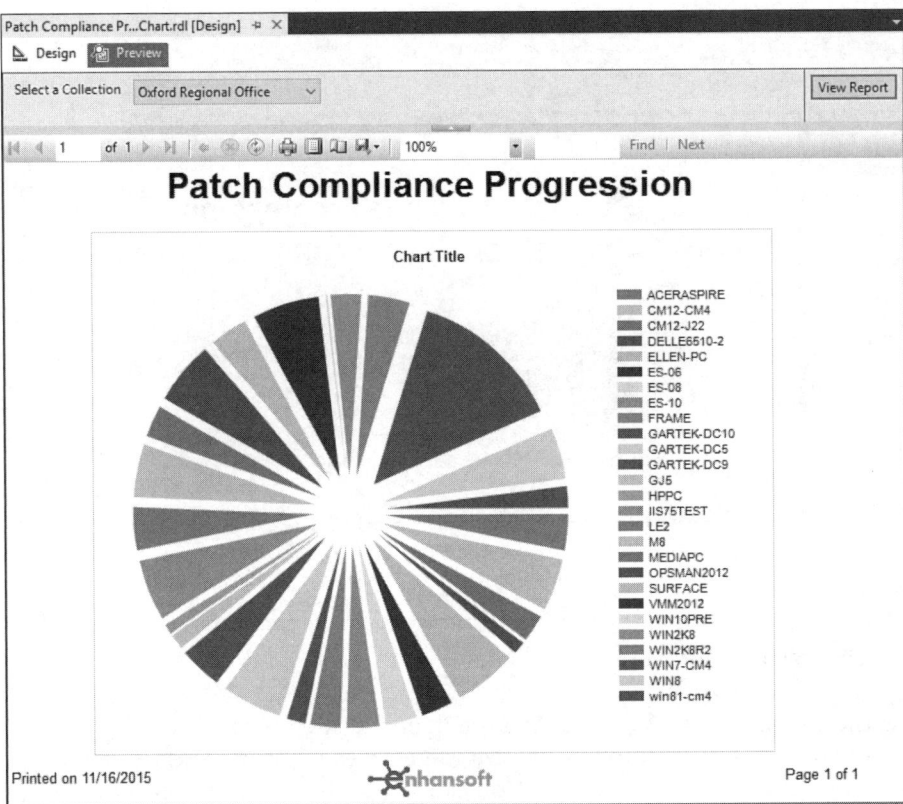

FIGURE 7.39   Previewing exploded pie chart data.

1. In Design mode, right-click the pie section of the chart and select **3D Effects**.

2. In the Chart Area Properties dialog, check the **Enable 3D** option, shown in Figure 7.40. You can also modify the Rotation (degrees) and Inclination (degrees) values. When you are finished, click **OK** to apply the changes and close the Chart Area Properties dialog. The 3D effects are immediately visible in Design mode, so you can see that the settings were applied successfully.

3. Remove the title area by right-clicking the **Chart Title** label and selecting **Delete Title**, as shown in Figure 7.41.

4. To move the location of the legend within the chart item, right-click the legend area of the chart and select **Legend Properties**.

5. On the General tab of the Legend Properties dialog, select the placement of the legend by selecting a radio button under Legend position. Three different positions are available for each of the four sides of the chart item. For this example, the bottom center position is selected, as shown in Figure 7.42. Click **OK** to apply your changes. The legend is immediately moved to the selected location of the chart, and you don't need to preview the report.

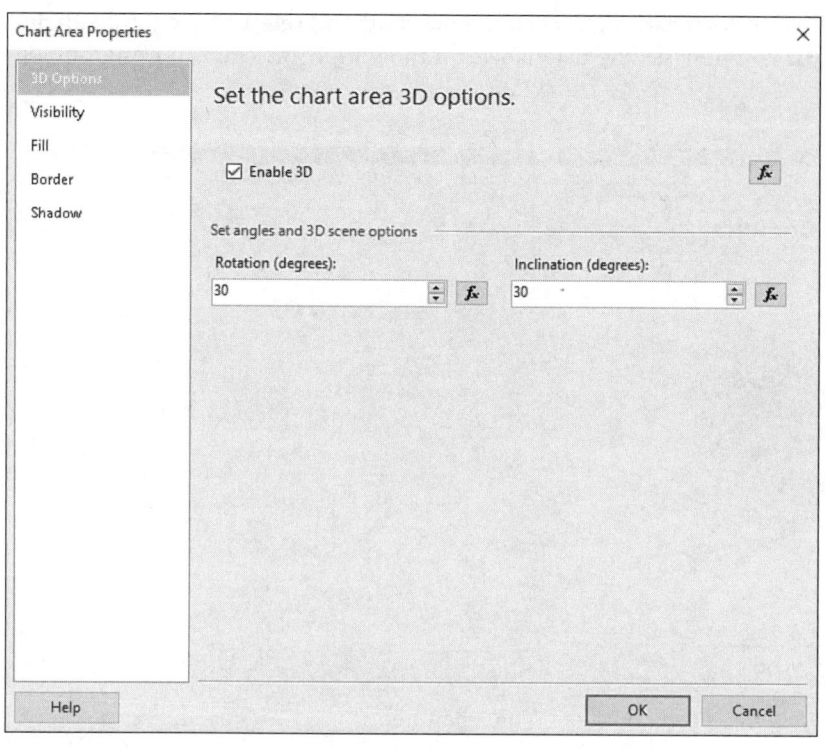

FIGURE 7.40   Enabling the 3D option for a chart.

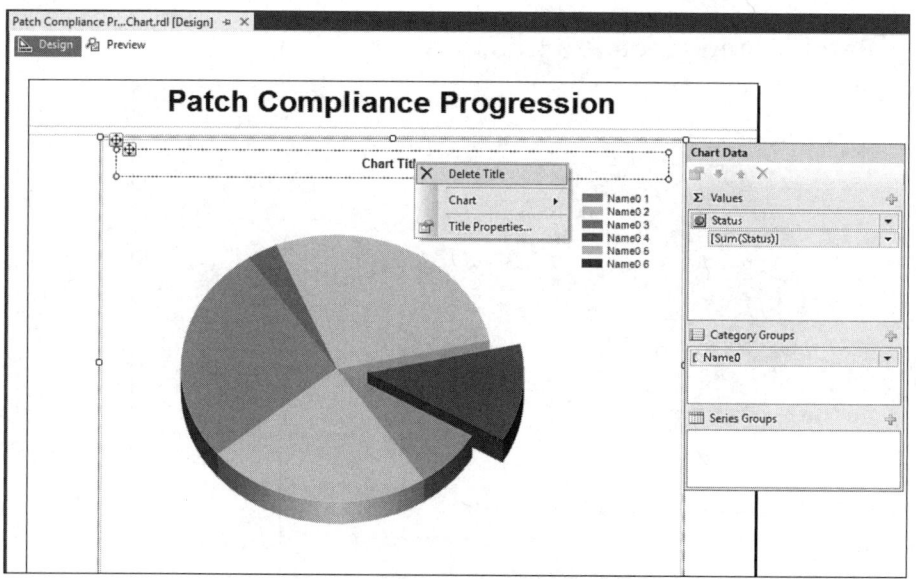

FIGURE 7.41   Deleting the title area of the chart.

6. To add data labels to the chart, right-click the pie chart and select **Show Data Labels** (see Figure 7.43). You now see the data labels on the sample pie chart in Design mode.

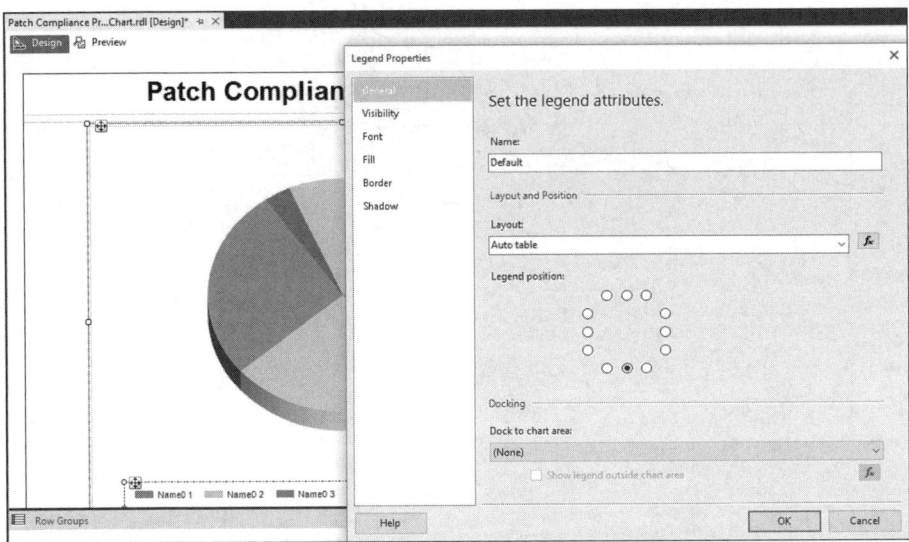

FIGURE 7.42   Modifying the legend position in the chart item.

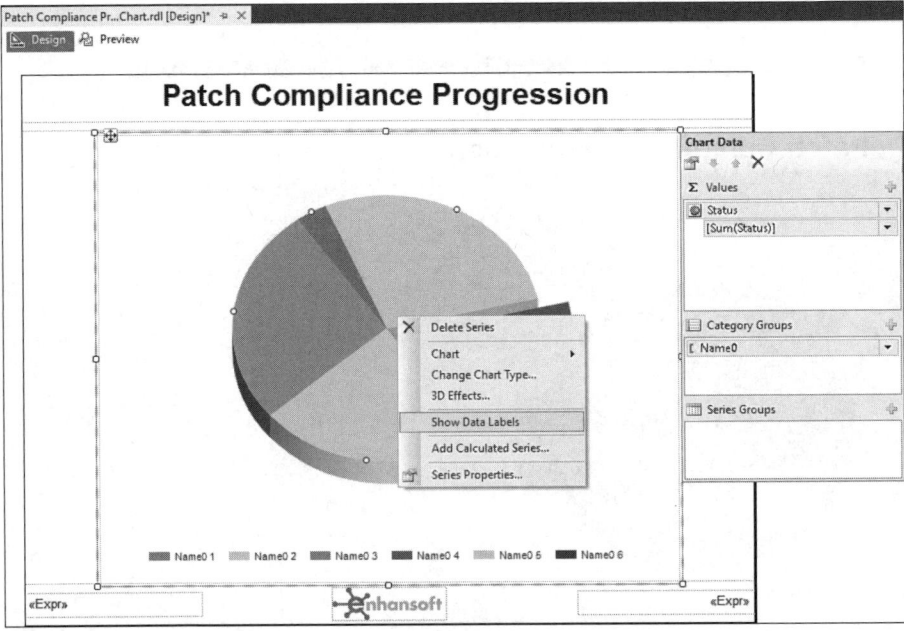

FIGURE 7.43   Selecting **Show Data Labels** on the chart.

7. To make the labels easier to read, left-click a data label in the chart to select it. Notice that all labels are selected automatically. Set the font of the labels to bold by clicking Bold in the SSDT-BI toolbar or by changing the FontWeight value under the Font section of the Properties area in the bottom right of the screen and shown in Figure 7.44.

8. Preview the report to see all the changes with actual data populating the chart, as shown in Figure 7.45. Notice the 3D effect on the chart and the legend displayed below the pie chart. Because there are so many individual wedges in the pie chart, the labels are difficult to read and often overlap each other because they are displayed within each wedge.

9. To properly read the data labels of a chart when there are multiple wedges, add a label to the outside of the pie wedge by returning to Design mode and selecting the pie chart. In the Properties area in the bottom-right corner of the screen, expand the CustomAttributes section and change the value of PieLabelStyle from Inside to **Outside**, as shown in Figure 7.46.

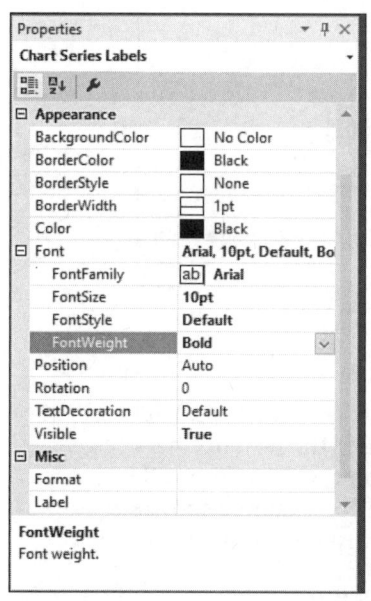

FIGURE 7.44   Setting the FontWeight value to **Bold** for the data labels.

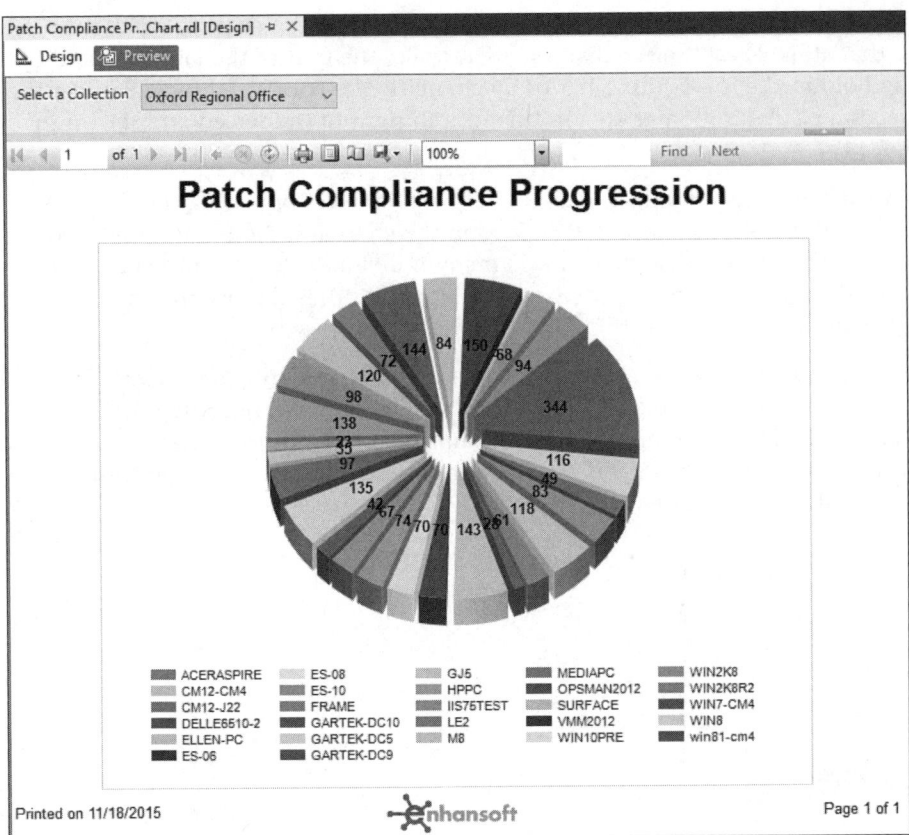

FIGURE 7.45   Previewing the report to validate the changes to the chart.

10. Notice that the data labels are now displayed outside the chart, and each is linked to its respective wedge with a line. To increase or reduce the distance between the data labels and the chart, in the same Properties area, change the value of 3DLabelLineSize to a number between 30 and 200. In the example shown in Figure 7.47, the value is changed to **30**, reducing the distance of the label.

11. Preview the report to view the changes using actual ConfigMgr data, as shown in Figure 7.48. Notice that the labels now appear outside the individual wedges, making it much easier to read the data.

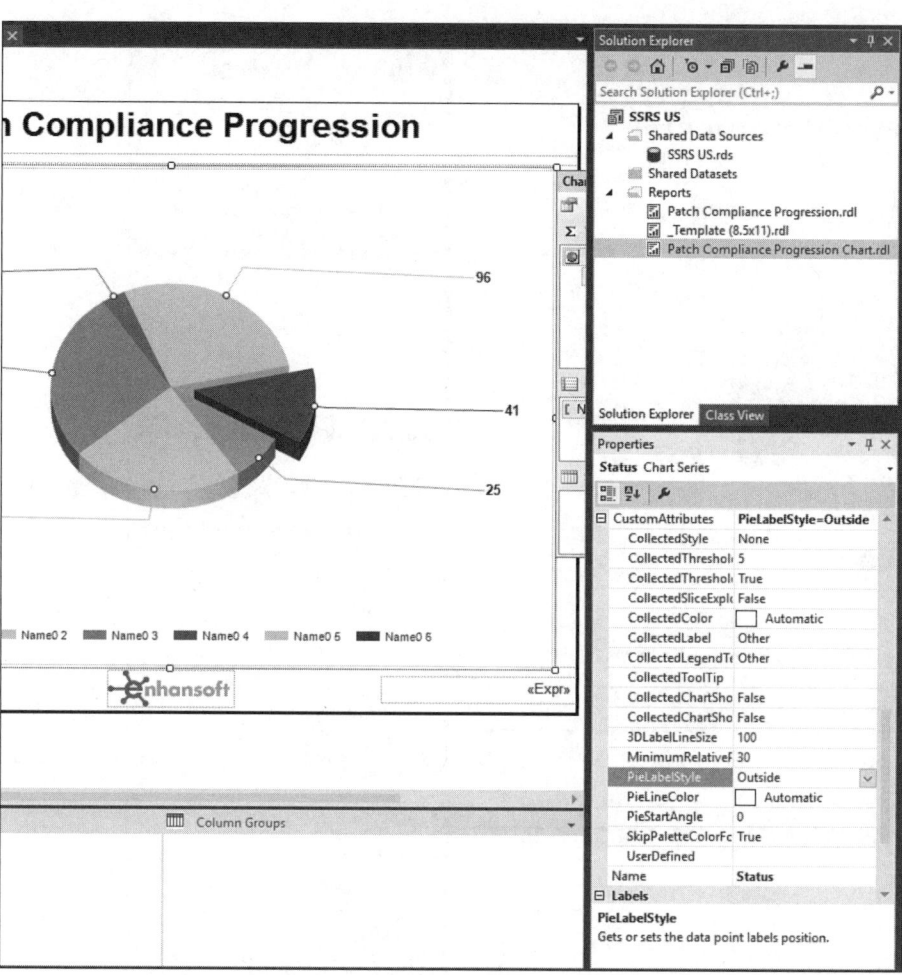

FIGURE 7.46   Displaying the data labels outside the pie chart.

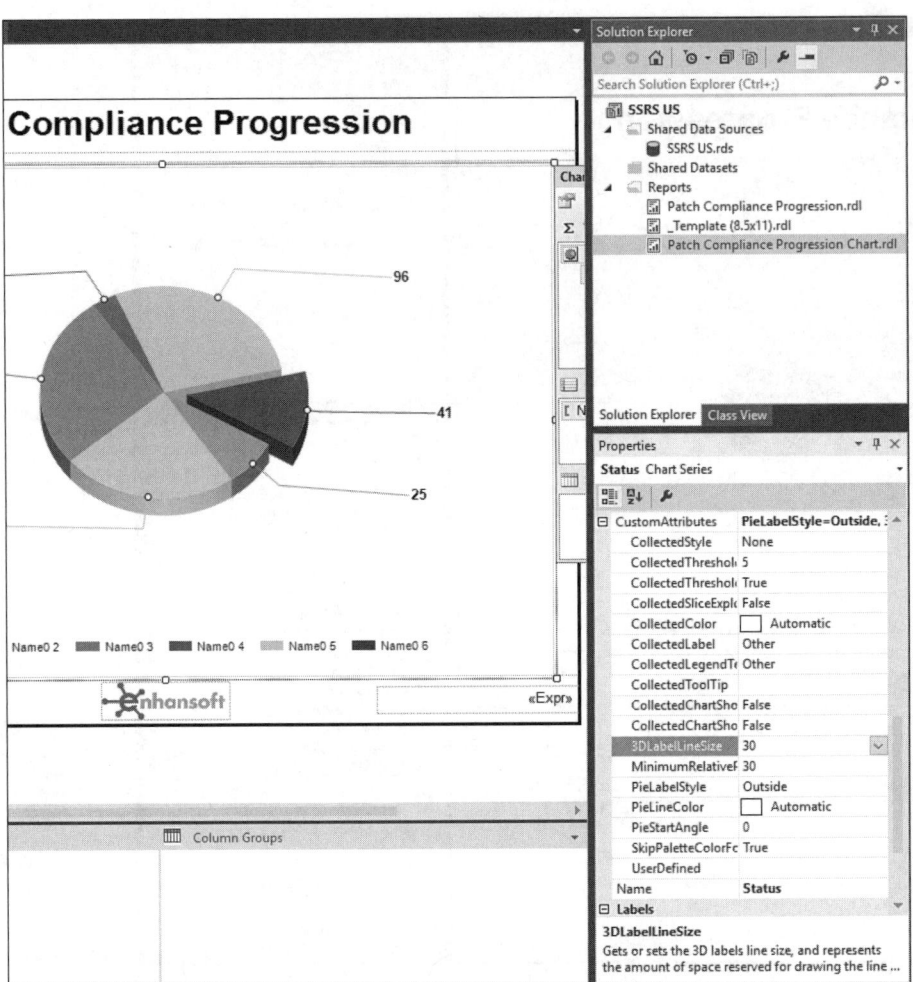

FIGURE 7.47   Reducing the distance of the data labels.

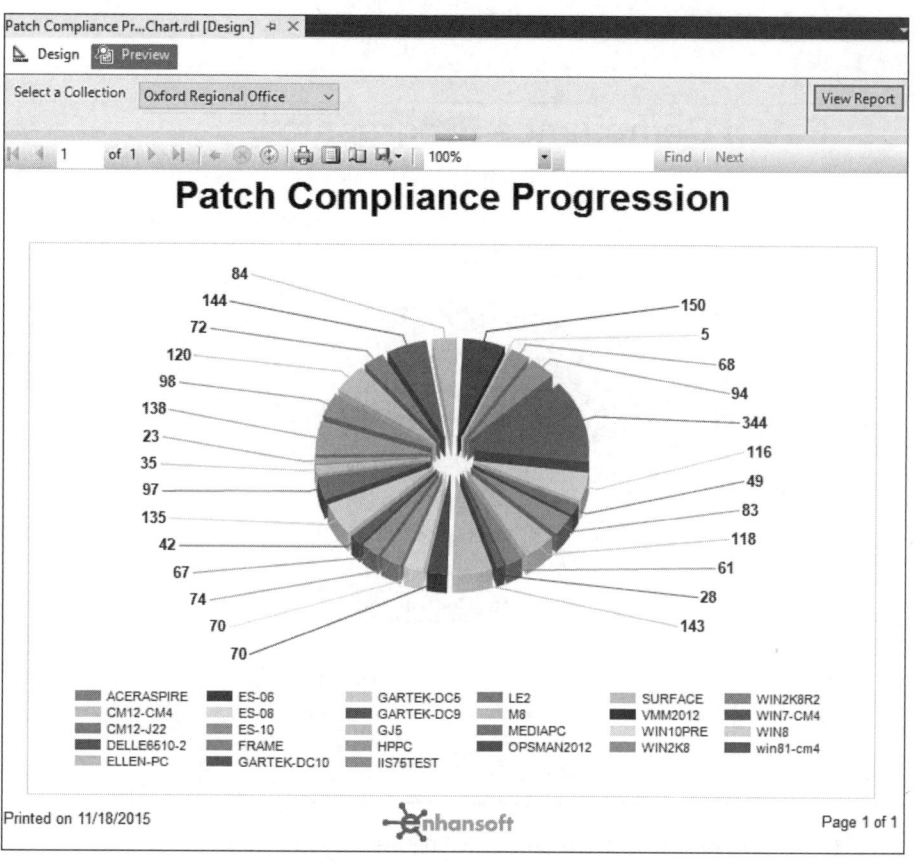

FIGURE 7.48   Previewing the report to view the chart populated with ConfigMgr data.

TIP: CUSTOMIZING CHARTS

Although a pie chart item was used here to demonstrate and explain the different customizations, you can use the same procedure to apply customizations to all other chart items in SSDT-BI. As you create reports using different chart types, try exploring the different settings to find a style that suits you and your report readers.

Adding an Action to a Chart

Adding an action on a chart allows you to link the chart's data to another report to provide further details. Say you want to view the updates of a specific computer. If you use an action, the reader can click on a pie chart's wedge for a specific computer name to be taken to a detailed report showing a list of patches. Follow these steps to add an action to a chart:

1. In Design mode, right-click the pie section of the chart and select **Series Properties**, as shown in Figure 7.49.

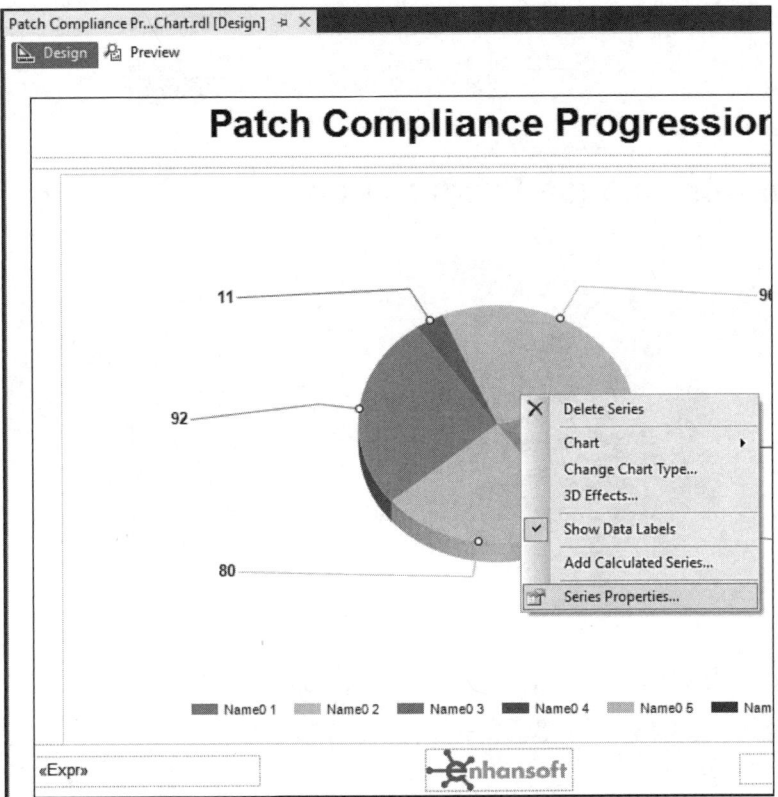

FIGURE 7.49   Right-clicking the pie section and selecting **Series Properties**.

2. In the Series Properties dialog, select the **Action** tab on the left. Under Enable as an action, select **Go to report**. Under Specify a report, using the dropdown, select the **Patch Compliance Progression** report.

   In order to pass along the same collection parameter, under Use these parameters to run the report, click **Add**. As the Name field, use the dropdown and select **Coll**. As the Value field, click the **Function (fx)** button to the right of the dropdown.

3. In the Expression dialog, select the **Parameters** category. Double-click **Coll** under Values to add it to the expression, as shown in Figure 7.50, and click **OK**.

4. Now that the Series Properties dialog is complete (as shown in Figure 7.51), click **OK** to apply the action.

5. Preview the report and hover over a pie wedge. Notice that the cursor changes to identify that the pie wedge contains a link and can be clicked. Click on any pie wedge. You are now taken to the report identified in the action, the Patch Compliance Progression report, as shown in Figure 7.52. Notice that the second report is displayed without a prompt to select a collection. This is because of the expression configured in step 3, where the value of the Coll parameter was selected. This passed the value selected in the original chart report to the Patch Compliance Progression report.

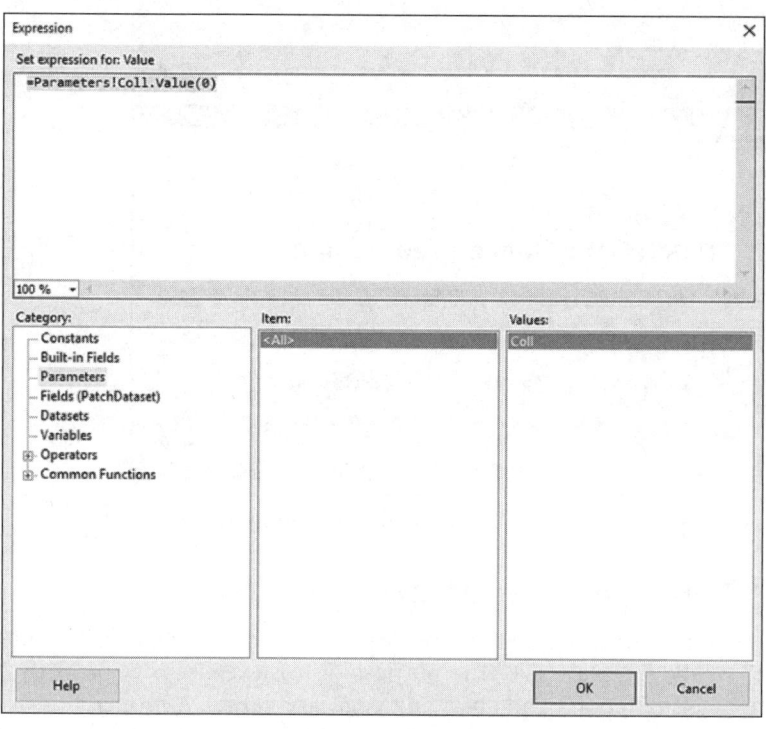

FIGURE 7.50   Completed Expression dialog for the parameter value.

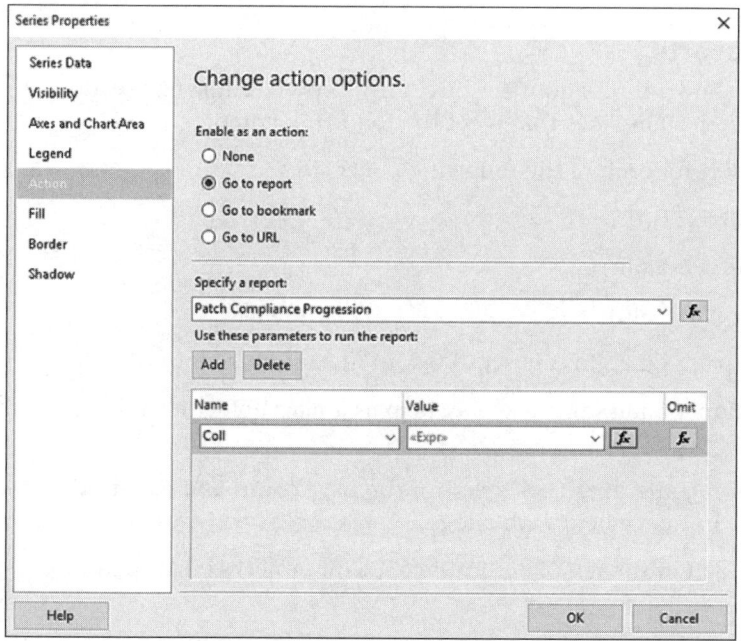

FIGURE 7.51   Action properties for a chart item.

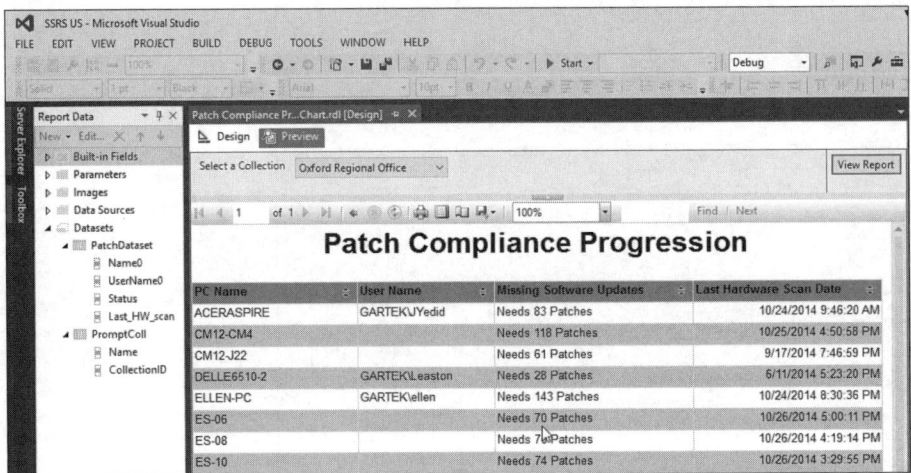

FIGURE 7.52   The action on the chart opens the Patch Compliance Progression report.

Demonstrating Template Creation

In this demonstration you will create a template report for three common paper sizes and modify existing reports to fit the template size. The purpose of this exercise is to practice and become familiar with creating reports and changing page size values. A properly created template provides a strong foundation for all reports in your environment and allows report creators to be efficient when creating newly requested reports.

Creating Template Reports

Following the instructions shown throughout the "Creating Report Templates" section of this chapter, create three report templates that meet the following criteria:

▶ Create a template report for each of the following paper sizes:

  ▶ Letter portrait (8.5×11in)

  ▶ Letter landscape (11×8.5in)

  ▶ Legal landscape (14×8.5in)

▶ Ensure that each template's margins are set to 0.25in, 0.25in, 0.25in, 0.25in.

▶ Include a header section containing a text box item as a placeholder for the report's title.

▶ Include a footer section containing text boxes for the page count and current date expressions. Also add an image item with a logo.

Be sure to create and save each of the templates in the SSDT-BI project you created in Chapter 6.

Modifying Page Sizes for Existing Reports

Using the guidelines for creating report templates, modify the existing reports to meet the specified page sizes. Ensure that both the Patch Compliance Progression and Computer Hardware Information reports are updated to meet the following criteria:

▶ Modify the Patch Compliance Progression report to fit a paper size of 8.5×11in.

▶ Modify the Computer Hardware Information report to fit a paper size of 11×8.5in.

▶ Modify the table item in the Computer Hardware Information report to span the full width of the report. Stretch the individual column widths accordingly.

▶ Preview the completed report and export it to PDF. View the PDF report to ensure that all columns fit on the width of a page without any columns being cut off. Fix any problems you find and then export and examine the report again.

▶ Export the reports to Excel and CSV and compare the features of the different formats.

Make sure to save both reports once everything is complete, as these versions will be used in the following demonstrations.

Demonstrating Report Parameters

The purpose of this demonstration is to help you become familiar with modifying datasets, adding parameters, and adding report prompts. Understanding how to create different types of prompts is important when you're creating reports. The demonstrations in this section ask you to create and use multi-value prompts, which provide more options than simple and dropdown prompts. Note, however, that using multi-value prompts is not always a desired solution. Sometimes you need simple prompts with free-form values, and other times you might simply want a dropdown list.

When creating reports with prompts, use your best judgment about the type of prompt based on the type of report and its intended audience. Your goal is to make it easiest to use for readers who are not ConfigMgr administrators.

Updating the Patch Compliance Progression Report

Following the instructions in the "Using Report Parameters" sections of this chapter, make the following modifications to the Patch Compliance Progression report:

▶ Add a prompt for a multi-value parameter named Coll.

▶ Have the Coll parameter identify the CollectionID to filter the report data.

▶ Make the prompt a dropdown list, allowing for multiple values to be selected. Ensure that the dropdown list includes all collection names from ConfigMgr.

NOTE: DISPLAYING COLLECTION NAMES IN THE DROPDOWN LIST

Remember to add a new dataset to get a list of all CollectionIDs and their matching names. Only the collection names should be visible in the dropdown prompt.

Preview the completed report to confirm that all settings and features are functioning properly, as detailed in this section. Save this report as it will be used in upcoming demonstrations.

Updating the Computer Hardware Information Report

Make a copy of your Computer Hardware Information report and name it **Computer Hardware Information Prompt.rdl**. Using the new copy of the report, modify the dataset as follows:

▶ Add a parameter named `Manu` to the dataset query.

▶ Have this new parameter identify the Manufacturer value to filter the report data.

▶ Make the prompt a dropdown list, allowing for multiple values to be selected.

▶ Ensure that the dropdown list includes all manufacturer names from the ConfigMgr environment.

NOTE: ADDING THE MANUFACTURER PROMPT

Because the manufacturer prompt does not already exist, you need to modify the dataset query by adding a WHERE statement.

Preview the completed report to confirm that all settings and features are functioning properly, as described in this section. Save this report as it will be used in the upcoming demonstrations.

Demonstrating Adding Chart Items

The purpose of this demonstration is to become familiar with adding chart items to reports. Chart items are very useful for providing summarized data reports, giving the reader a high-level view of the data. When you add actions to a chart, the reader can choose to see additional information about the data provided.

Adding a Chart to the Patch Compliance Progression Report

Following the instructions in the "Adding a Chart Item to a Report" section of this chapter, make the required modifications to the Patch Compliance Progression report. Modify the report as follows:

▶ Make a copy of the Patch Compliance Progression report and name it Patch Compliance Progression Chart.rdl.

- ▶ Modify the query to change the `Status` column to return only the integer of the number of required updates.

- ▶ Replace the table in the body section with a 3D exploded pie chart item.

- ▶ Set the `Name0` column as the Category Groups field of the chart.

- ▶ Set the `Status` column as the Values field of the chart.

- ▶ Add an action on the chart to link to the Patch Compliance Progression report.

- ▶ Ensure that when a user clicks a pie wedge, the Patch Compliance Progression report opens and uses the CollectionID value selected in the Compliance Progression Chart report.

Preview the completed report to confirm that all settings and features are functioning properly, as detailed above. Save this report as it will be used in upcoming demonstrations.

Adding a Chart to the Computer Hardware Information Report

Make a copy of the Computer Hardware Information report, created in Chapter 6, and name the copy Computer Hardware Information Chart.rdl. Modify the new chart report as follows:

- ▶ Replace the table in the body section with a 3D exploded pie chart to show all computer manufacturers and their representation (count) in the environment. Make the following changes in the table:

  - ▶ Set the `Manufacturer` column as the Category Groups field of the chart.

  - ▶ Set `COUNT` `(Manufacturer0)` as the Value field of the chart.

  - ▶ Add data labels, in bold font, to the chart to show the count of systems for each manufacturer.

  - ▶ Add an action on the chart to go to the Computer Hardware Information Prompt report.

- ▶ Ensure that when a user clicks a pie wedge, the report opens and passes the Manufacturer value to the Computer Hardware Information Prompt report.

TIP: ACTION TO PASS SELECTED PIE WEDGE VALUE AS PARAMETER

To pass the specific manufacturer name of the pie wedge that is selected to the Computer Hardware Information Prompt report's parameter, specify the [Manufacturer0] column as the parameter value, instead of a function, on the Action tab of the pie chart.

Preview the completed report to confirm that all settings and features function properly, as detailed in this section. Notice that when you click a pie wedge, the prompt report does not ask for a parameter, and the report contains only systems belonging to the selected manufacturer. Save this report as it will be used in upcoming demonstrations.

Summary

In this chapter you have added features and customizations to the reports you created in Chapter 6. You have also created several report templates to use as a basis for new reports for your environment. This chapter has shown you how to create parameters by building on the Patch Progression Report created in Chapter 6, as well as the Computer Hardware Information report created in the demonstrations. You have learned how to add simple parameters to the report, including a free-form text box for specifying values; you have also learned how to adapt those parameters to a dropdown prompt of values populated from a query and also a prompt that supports selecting multiple values.

As you create more reports, you will begin to see which types of prompts you prefer, based on the data returned and the intended audience. If a prompt should allow for wildcards, a simple prompt is required; however, if a value should be a specific result, you want to use a dropdown or multi-value prompt from a query to eliminate the potential for mistakes and typos.

This chapter has also detailed the various chart types. It has described each type and its typical use, and it has walked you through adding pie charts to the demonstration reports. From these charts, you applied customizations such as 3D effects, data labels, and actions with links to different reports.

To further these concepts, Chapter 8, "SSRS Reporting Features," describes advanced color codes that can be added to SSRS reports. It also walks through adding and publishing the reports created throughout the book to an SSRS website and creating report subscriptions.

SSRS Reporting Features

SQL Server Reporting Services (SSRS) allows you to integrate advanced features into reports. This chapter discusses several of these features, including drilling through to different reports, setting custom color palates, and adding reports to your SSRS website.

You can use actions on items to allow drillthrough to different reports. When you do this, you enable the reader to navigate from an overview of data to a detailed view on a specific item or area without having to navigate through the SSRS website or close and open separate reports. Parameter values for reports can also be passed through such an action, based on the value selected in the parent report.

You can further customize the look of reports to better match your company's branding by setting custom color palettes. You can set a color palette to include a list of colors that are cycled through when set on chart items. You can also use custom color palettes to associate colors with specific values in a report. You can set an expression on any color property in a report, and based on the returned value in the item, the matching color can be used; for example, you might set a table row's background color to red to identify systems that are missing patches.

Another useful feature is the ability to add reports to your SSRS website for your readers to view. This chapter discusses two methods of adding reports: manually adding a report from the SSRS website and publishing a report from SQL Server Data Tools Business Intelligence (SSDT-BI) directly to SSRS. Once a report is available in SSRS, subscriptions can be added if required. Subscriptions can send reports through email or place reports on file shares.

Using Report Drillthroughs

A report *drillthrough* provides a way to navigate from one report to another without requiring the user to exit and launch separate reports individually. Chapter 7, "Intermediate Reporting Concepts," used a pie chart to show how to add an action to go to a more detailed report. The associated demonstration asked you to create an action to go to a detailed report while passing a parameter to see specific hardware information. Not only can actions be set on chart items, they can be added on any object in SSDT-BI for Visual Studio 2013, such as a table's cell, text boxes, image items, and so on.

Adding an Action on a Table Cell's Value

To help you understand the steps to set an action on different objects, this section discusses creating an action on the cells under the PC Name column of the Patch Compliance Progression report. The action's purpose is to open a new report that provides the computer hardware information specific to the selected system. Begin by making a copy of the **_Template (8.5x11in).rdl** report that you created in Chapter 7 and renaming the copy **Detailed Computer Information.rdl**. After copying and renaming the report, perform the following steps to create a detailed report that will be drilled through from another report:

1. In the Solution Explorer, double-click the Detailed Computer Information.rdl report to open it.

2. In Design mode, rename the report title placeholder **Detailed Computer Information**.

3. To create a new data source, in the Report Data section in SSDT-BI, right-click the **Data Sources** folder and click **Add Data Source**. In the Data Source Properties dialog, enter a name for the data source, such as **DetailedPCDS1**. Select **Use shared data source reference** and use the dropdown to select your shared data source (**SSRS US** in this example). When you are done with this dialog, as shown in Figure 8.1, click **OK**.

4. To add a new dataset to the report, in the Report Data section in SSDT-BI, right-click the **Datasets** folder and click **Add Dataset**. In the Dataset Properties dialog, set the name to **PCDataset**, and select **Use a dataset embedded in my report**. Under Data source, use the dropdown to select the data source created in step 3. Under the Query section, enter the query shown in Listing 8.1. Click **OK** when the Dataset Properties dialog is complete, as shown in Figure 8.2.

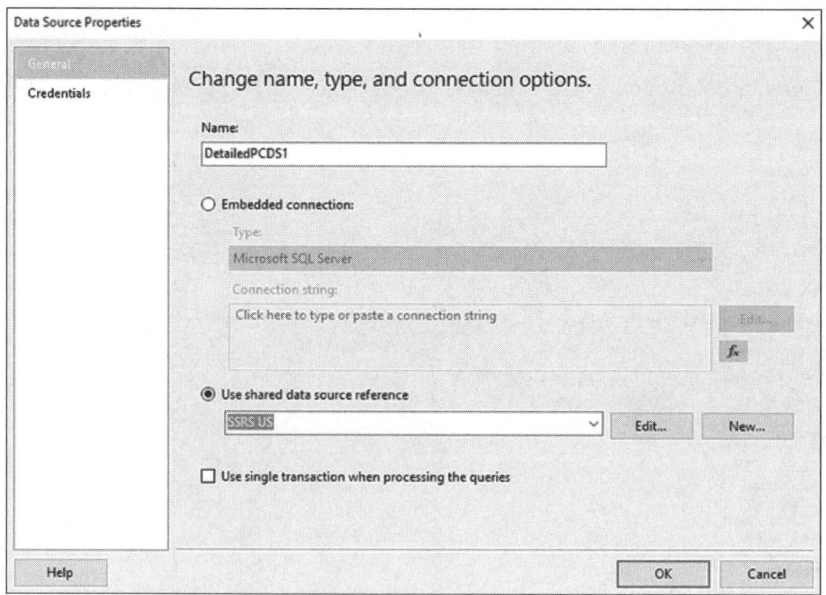

FIGURE 8.1   Creating a new data source.

LISTING 8.1   Detailed Computer Query

```
SELECT DISTINCT
    CS.Name0,
    CS.UserName0,
    CS.Manufacturer0,
    CS.Model0,
    ws.LastHWScan
FROM
    v_GS_COMPUTER_SYSTEM CS
    LEFT JOIN v_gs_workstation_status ws on ws.resourceid = CS.resourceid
WHERE
    CS.Name0 = @PC
```

5. To add a customized table item to the body section of the report, from the toolbox on the left, drag the table item into the report. Make the following changes to the table (see Figure 8.3):

   ▶ Add two extra columns to the table, for a total of five, and drag each column of the dataset to the table.

   ▶ Modify the labels of the headers for each column to appropriate titles that represent the data. Add spaces between words and remove the trailing 0.

   ▶ Set the font style of the header row to bold and the background color to red.

   ▶ Adjust the widths of the column so the table spans the width of the report.

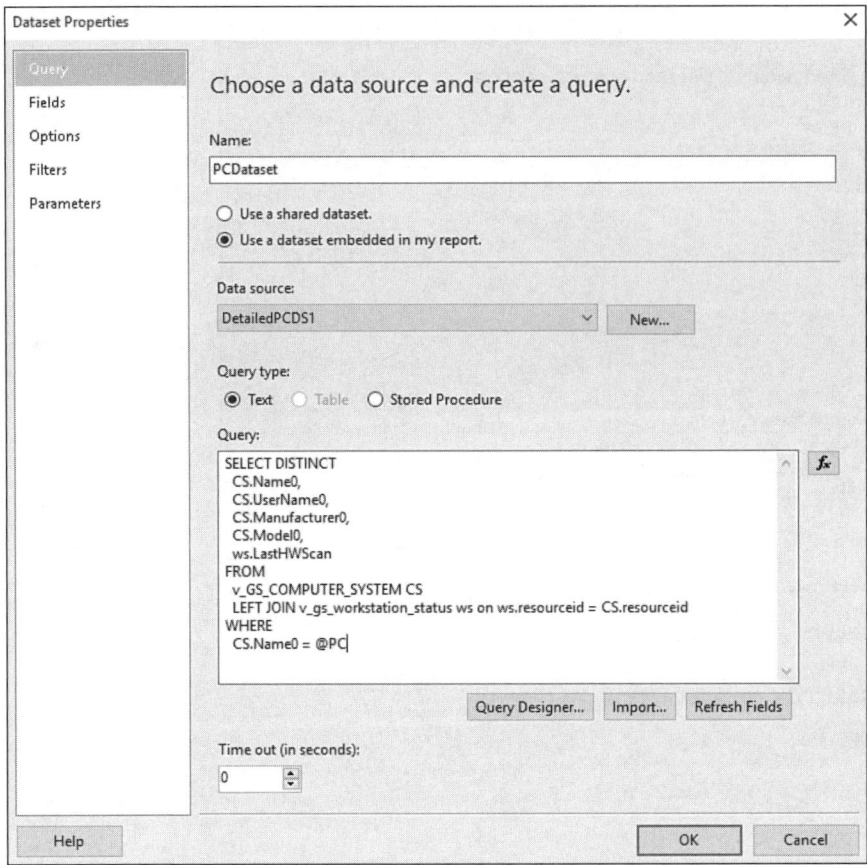

FIGURE 8.2   Creating a dataset for a report.

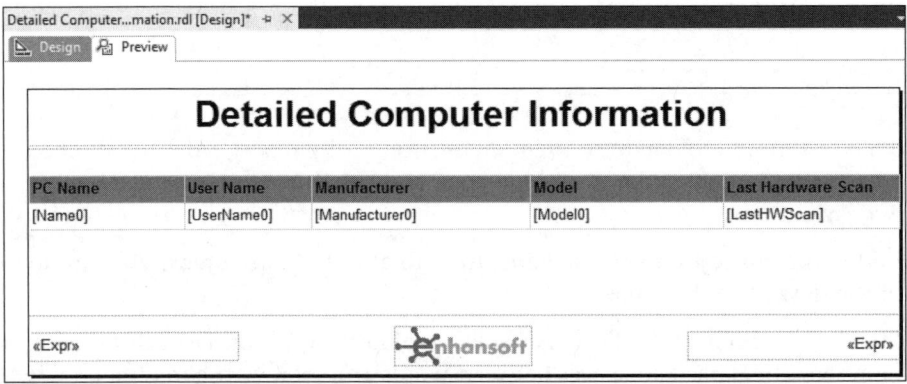

FIGURE 8.3   Adding and customizing a table item to the body of the report.

6. Save the report and open the Patch Compliance Progression report.

7. In the Patch Compliance Progression report, right-click the [Name0] cell and select **Text Box Properties**, as shown in Figure 8.4.

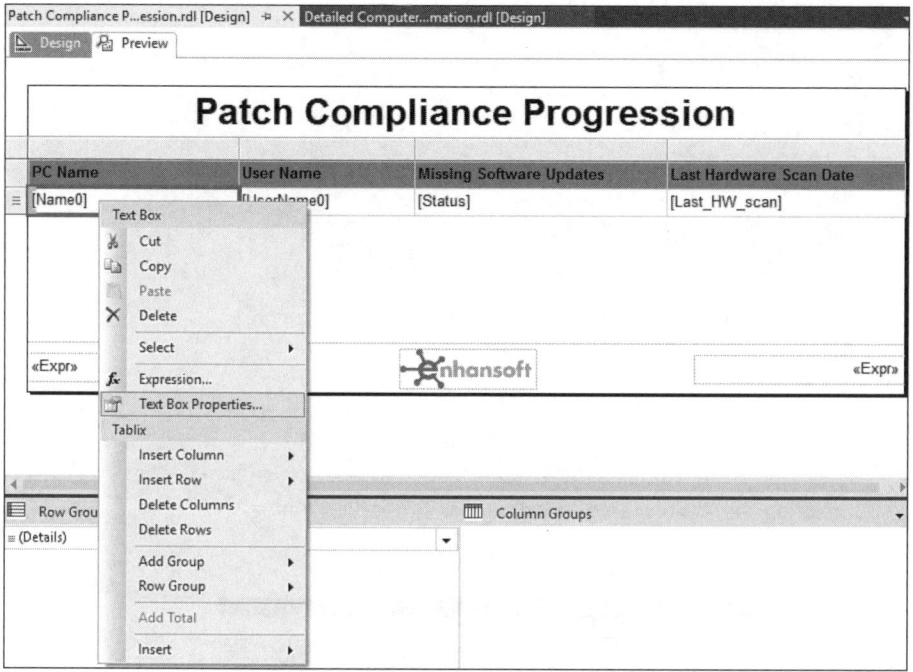

FIGURE 8.4   Selecting Text Box Properties.

8. In the Text Box Properties dialog, select the **Action** tab and then select the **Go to report** option. Under Specify a report, select **Detailed Computer Information** from the dropdown list. Select **Add** under Use these parameters to run the report. At the Name field, select the **PC** parameter and as the Value field select the **[Name0]** value from the dropdown list. Click **OK** when you're done with these changes, as shown in Figure 8.5.

9. Preview the Patch Compliance Progression report. At the prompt, select a collection and click **View Report** to execute the report. When the report is populated, click a PC name in the table. You are now redirected to the Detailed Computer Information report, which displays information specific to the PC name you clicked, without requiring any additional prompts (see Figure 8.6).

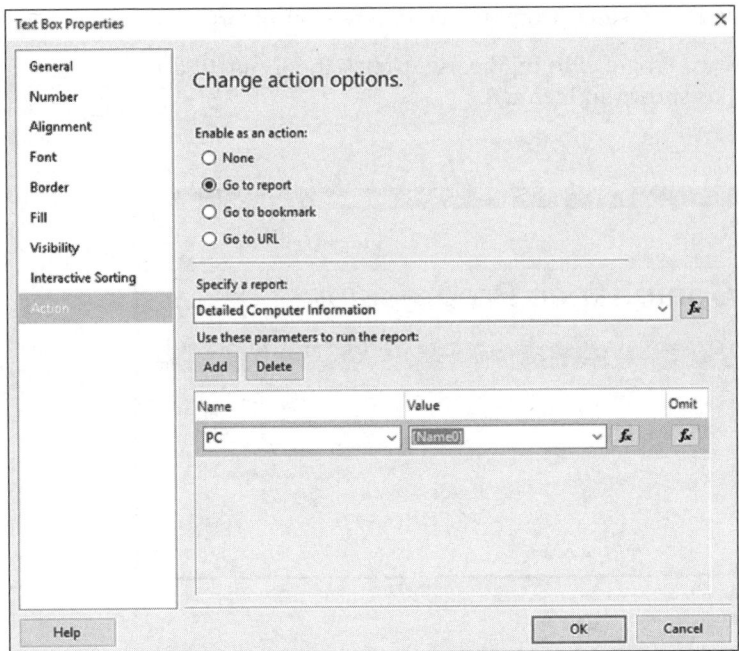

FIGURE 8.5   Completing the Action tab of the Text Box Properties dialog.

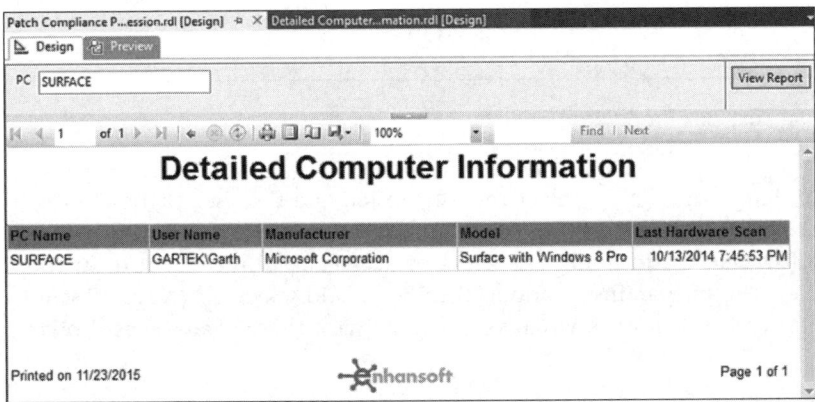

FIGURE 8.6   Being redirected to the new Detailed Computer Information report.

Adding Hyperlinks to a Report Item

Hyperlinks are very similar to report drillthroughs, but rather than navigating to a different report, a hyperlink provides a link to a website. Hyperlinks are typically set on logos to provide a link to a company's website. They are also often found on software updates from a patching report to link a patch to its Microsoft Knowledge Base article for additional information (as demonstrated in the next section, "Adding a Subreport Item"). To set a hyperlink on a logo for a company website, follow these steps:

1. Open the Patch Compliance Progression Chart report by double-clicking it in the Solution Explorer.

2. In Design mode, right-click the company logo in the footer section and select **Image Properties**, as shown in Figure 8.7.

3. In the Image Properties dialog, select the **Action** tab. Select the **Go to URL** action, and in the Select URL field, enter the company website address, as shown in Figure 8.8. Click **OK** to apply the changes.

4. Preview the report and click on the company logo in the footer where the action was added. Confirm that the company's website is launched from your browser.

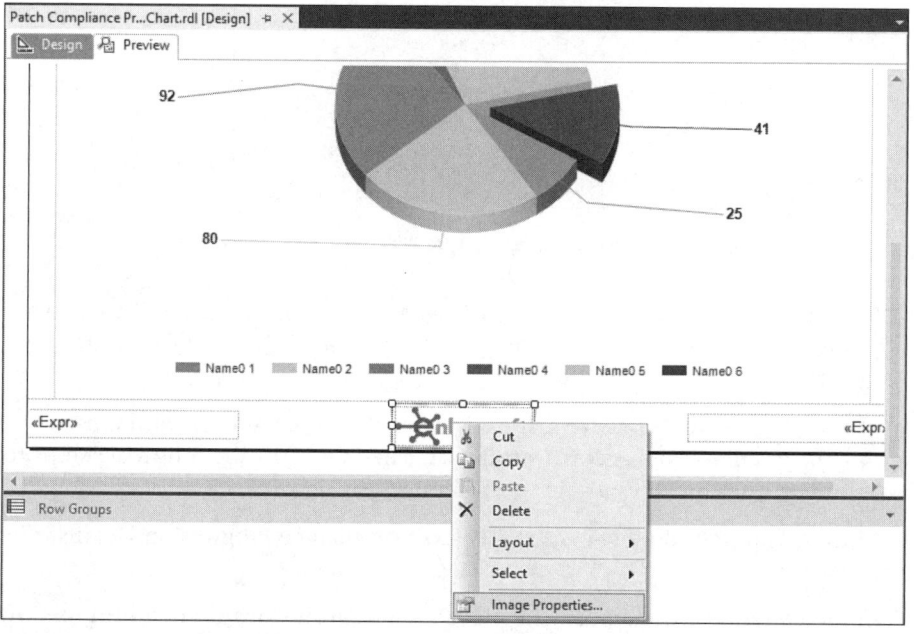

FIGURE 8.7   Right-clicking the image item and selecting **Image Properties**.

Adding a Subreport Item

Subreport items provide the ability to display a report within the body of a parent report. A subreport can contain parameters that are passed from its parent. Using subreports is very convenient when you want to provide additional information in a detailed report without having to add additional queries or parameters to the parent report or have the reader navigate to a separate report. To demonstrate subreport items, this section shows you how to create a new report, Patch Compliance Progression Details, that provides a list

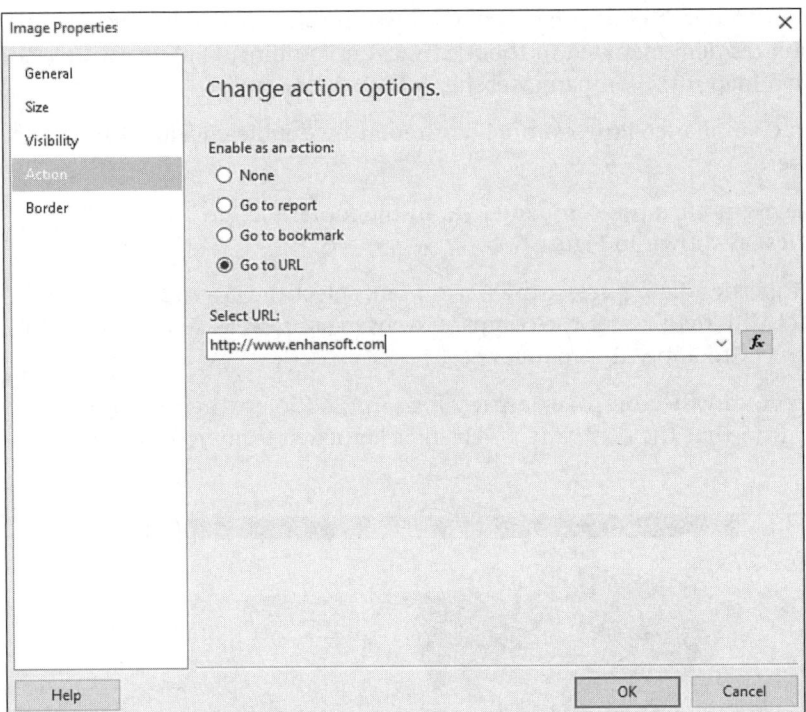

FIGURE 8.8   Completing the action tab using **Go to URL**.

of missing patches for a specific computer. You will give this report a subreport to display the computer hardware information, using the previously created Detailed Computer Information report.

Make a copy of the **_Template (8.5x11in).rdl** report, created in Chapter 7, and rename the copy **Patch Compliance Progression Details.rdl**. Then perform the following steps to create a detailed report that includes a subreport item:

1. In the Solution Explorer, double-click the Patch Compliance Progression Details.rdl report to open it.

2. In Design mode, rename the report title placeholder **Patch Compliance Progression Details**.

3. To create a new data source, in the Report Data section in SSDT-BI, right-click the **Data Sources** folder and select **Add Data Source**. In the Data Source Properties dialog, enter a name for the data source, such as **DetailedPatchDS**. Select **Use shared data source reference** and use the dropdown to select your shared data source (**SSRS US** in this example). When you are done with this dialog, click **OK**.

4. To add a new dataset to the report, in the Report Data section in SSDT-BI, right-click the **Datasets** folder and select **Add Dataset**. In the Dataset Properties dialog, set the name to **PatchDataset** and select **Use a dataset embedded in my report**.

Under Data source, use the dropdown to select the data source created in step 3. In the Query section, enter the query shown in Listing 8.2. Click **OK** when the Dataset Properties dialog is complete, as shown in Figure 8.9.

LISTING 8.2   Detailed Patch Compliance Query

```
SELECT DISTINCT
  ui.BulletinID,
  ui.ArticleID,
  ui.Title,
  ui.dateposted,
  ui.InfoURL
FROM
  v_UpdateComplianceStatus UCS
  LEFT OUTER JOIN dbo.v_GS_COMPUTER_SYSTEM  CS on CS.ResourceID = UCS.ResourceID
  JOIN v_CICategories_All catall2 on catall2.CI_ID = UCS.CI_ID
  JOIN v_CategoryInfo catinfo2 on catall2.CategoryInstance_UniqueID =
          catinfo2.CategoryInstance_UniqueID
          and catinfo2.CategoryTypeName = 'UpdateClassification'
  LEFT JOIN v_fullcollectionmembership FCM on FCM.resourceid = CS.resourceid
  JOIN v_UpdateInfo ui on ui.CI_ID = UCS.CI_ID
WHERE
  UCS.Status = '2'
  AND cs.Name0 = @PC
ORDER BY
  ui.ArticleID
```

5. Add a text box item to the top-left corner of the body section. Change the text in the text box to **Computer Information**. Increase the font size to **16pt** and set the style to bold. If required, expand the text box item's size so that it displays the entire value, as shown in Figure 8.10.

6. From the toolbox, add a subreport item to the body section of the report. Move the subreport item to the top-left corner, below the Computer Information text box created in step 5. Select the subreport item and from the Properties section, in the bottom-right corner of the screen, expand the **Size** property, and set the Width value to **8in** and the Height value to **0.3in**, as shown in Figure 8.11.

7. Right-click the subreport item and select **Subreport Properties**. From the General tab of the Subreport Properties dialog, use the dropdown under the **Use this report as a subreport** field to select the **Detailed Computer Information** report (see Figure 8.12).

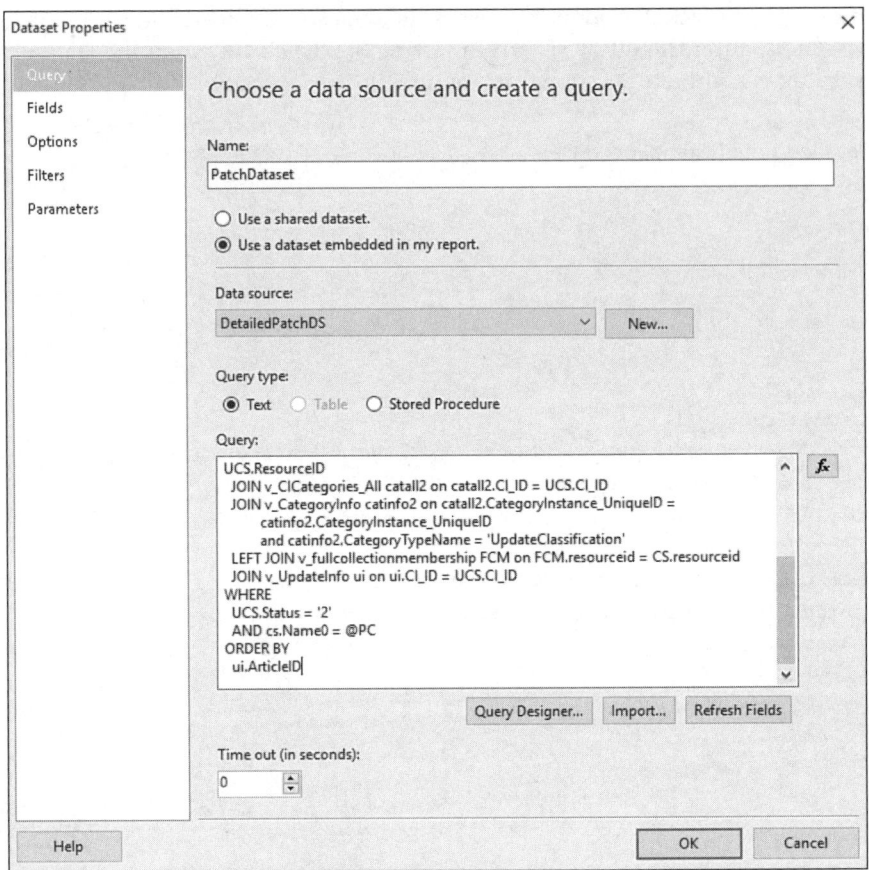

FIGURE 8.9   Creating a dataset for a report.

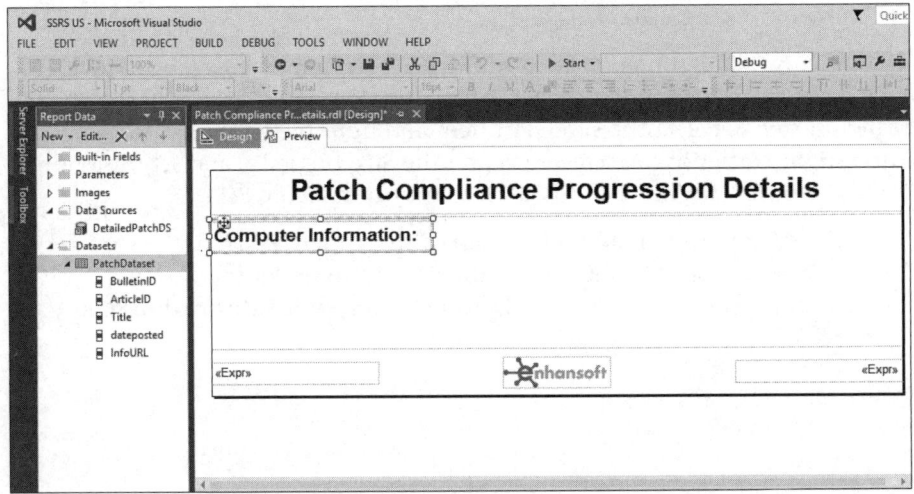

FIGURE 8.10   Adding a text box containing the text **Computer Information**.

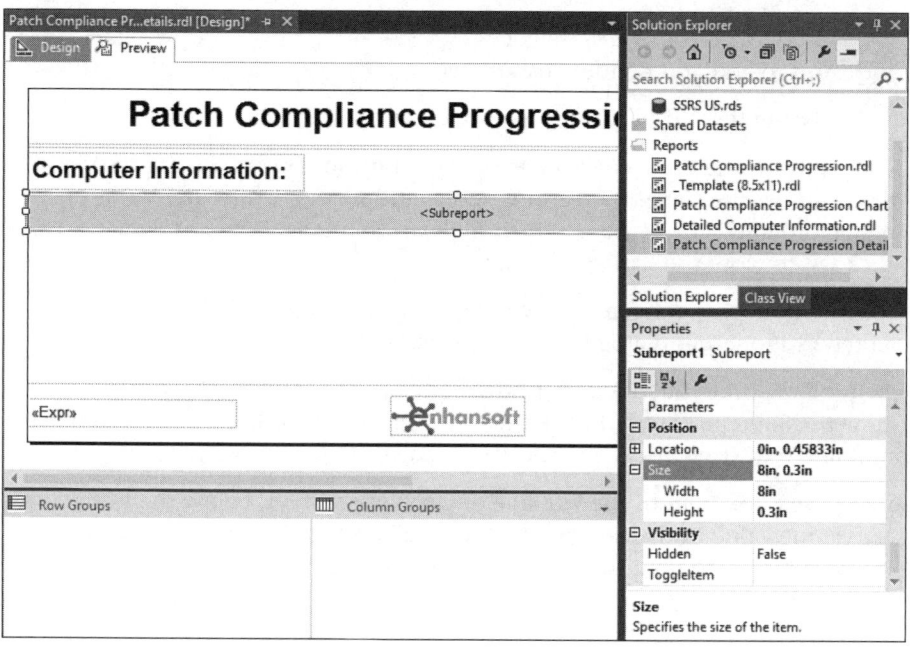

FIGURE 8.11   Setting the subreport item's Size properties.

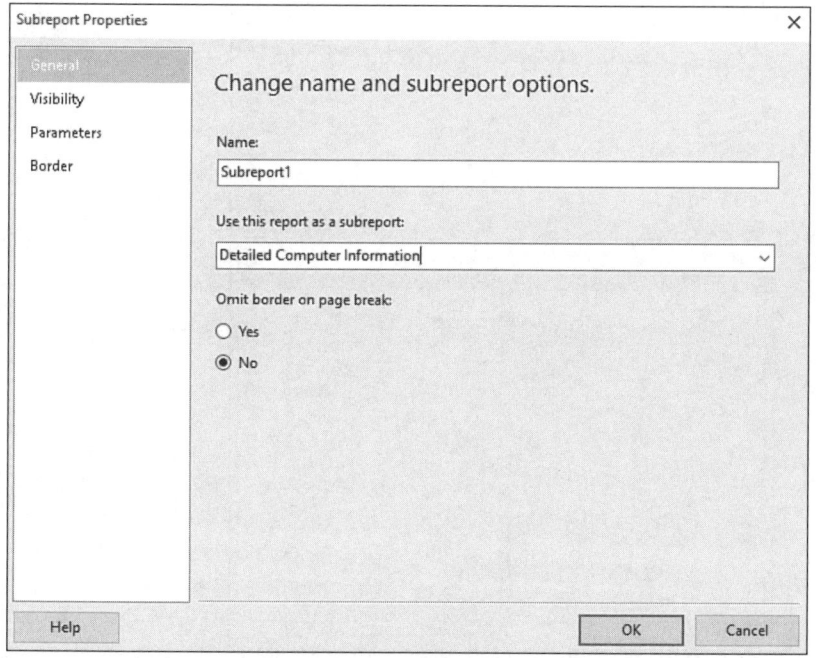

FIGURE 8.12   Selecting the Detailed Computer Information report as the subreport.

8. Select the **Parameters** tab of the Subreport Properties dialog and change as follows:

▶ Click **Add** to add and define a parameter.

▶ Set the Name field to **PC** using the dropdown lists.

▶ Next to the Value field, click the expression button (**fx**). In the Expression dialog, under the Category section, select **Parameters**. Under the Values section, double-click **PC** to add it to the expression, as shown in Figure 8.13. Click **OK** to close the Expression dialog.

▶ Confirm that the parameter value field is set to [@PC]. Click **OK** when the Subreport Properties dialog looks similar to Figure 8.14.

9. From the toolbox, drag the line item to the body of the report. Position the line item below the Subreport item. Resize the line item by stretching its edges to make a horizontal line that stretches across the report page, as shown in Figure 8.15.

10. Add another text box item to the left side of the body section, below the horizontal line. Change the value of the text box to **Missing Patches**. Increase the font size to **16pt** and set the style to bold. If required, expand the text box item's size so that it displays the entire value.

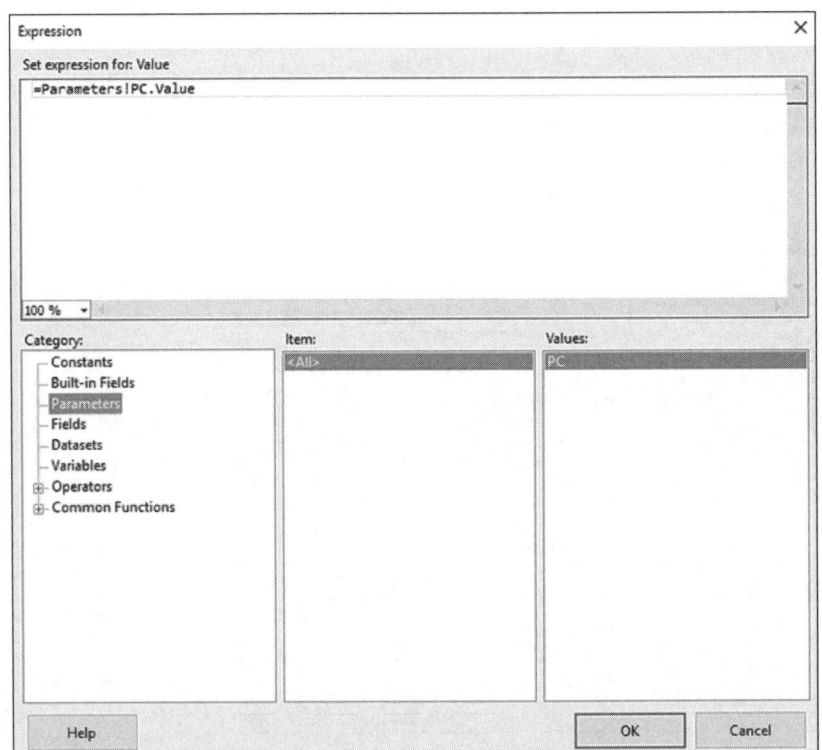

FIGURE 8.13   Setting an expression to pass the PC parameter value to the subreport.

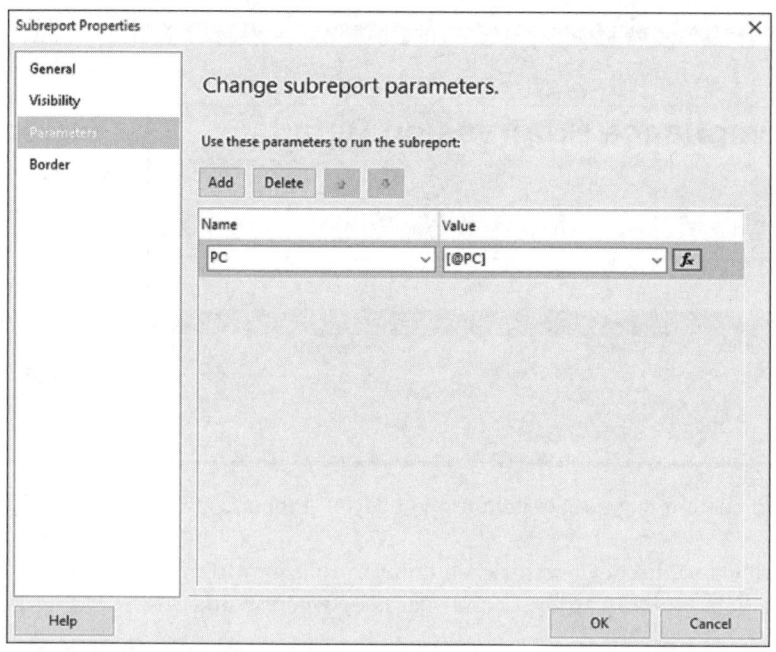

FIGURE 8.14   Setting the subreport parameters.

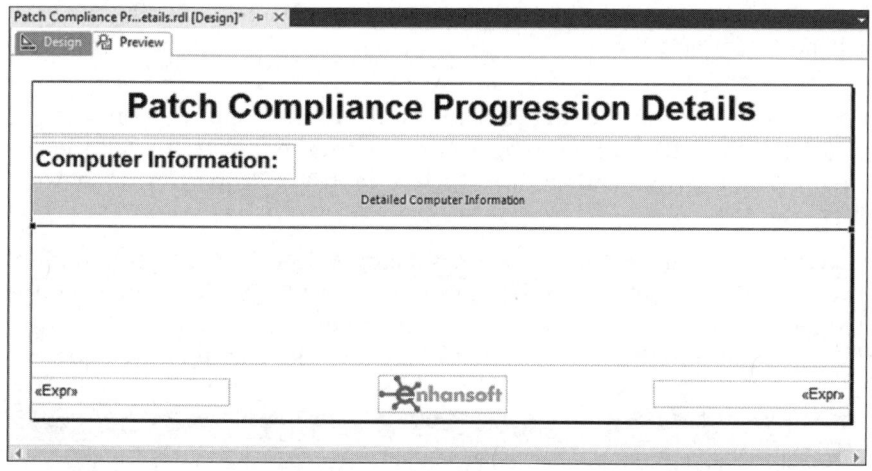

FIGURE 8.15   Adding a horizontal line to a report to visually separate the subreport.

11. To add a customized table item to the body section of the report, from the toolbox on the left side, drag the **Table** item into the report. Make the following changes to the table (see Figure 8.16):

▶ Add an extra column to the table, for a total of four columns, and drag these columns of the dataset to the table: BulletinID, ArticleID, Title, and dateposted.

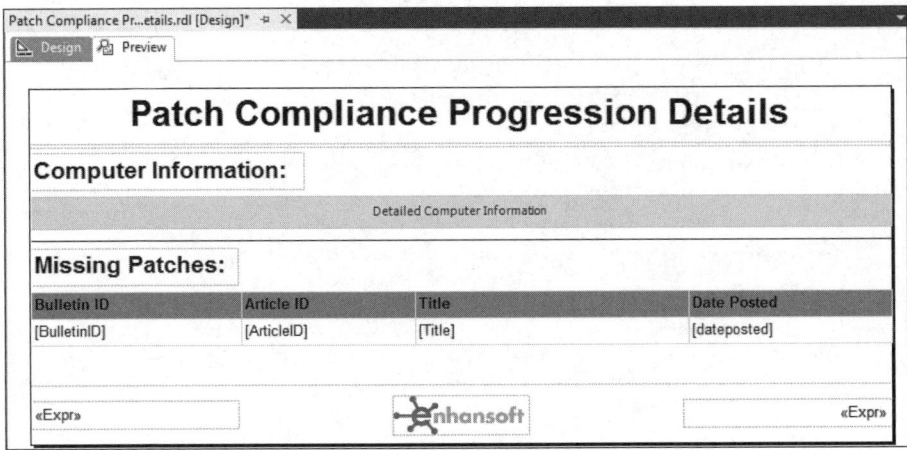

FIGURE 8.16   Adding and customizing a table item to the body of a report.

> ▶ Modify the labels of the headers for each column to appropriate titles that represent the data and add any required spaces between words.

> ▶ Set the font style of the header row to bold and the background color to red.

> ▶ Adjust the widths of the columns so the table spans the width of the report.

> ▶ Add interactive sorting on each column header; see Chapter 6, "Building a Basic Report," for details.

12. As previously discussed in the "Adding Hyperlinks to a Report Item" section, add a hyperlink on the ArticleID column to open the URL for the update. To add the hyperlink, right-click the **[ArticleID]** cell and select **Text Box Properties**, as shown in Figure 8.17.

13. Select the **Action** tab in the Text Box Properties dialog. Select the **Go to URL** option. Under the Select URL field, select **[InfoURL]** from the dropdown. Click **OK** when the Text Box Properties dialog is complete, as shown in Figure 8.18. A link is now added on the ArticleID column to the URL provided in the InfoURL column of the query.

TIP: ACTION VISIBILITY

To help readers identify which columns or cells in a table contain actions, the authors recommend setting the font style on cells that contain actions to underline. When running a report, readers will easily notice values that are underlined and will be aware that these values contain clickable links. Notice in Figure 8.19 that the Underline style has been set for the **[ArticleID]** cell.

14. Save the Patch Compliance Progression Details report and open the Patch Compliance Progression.rdl report.

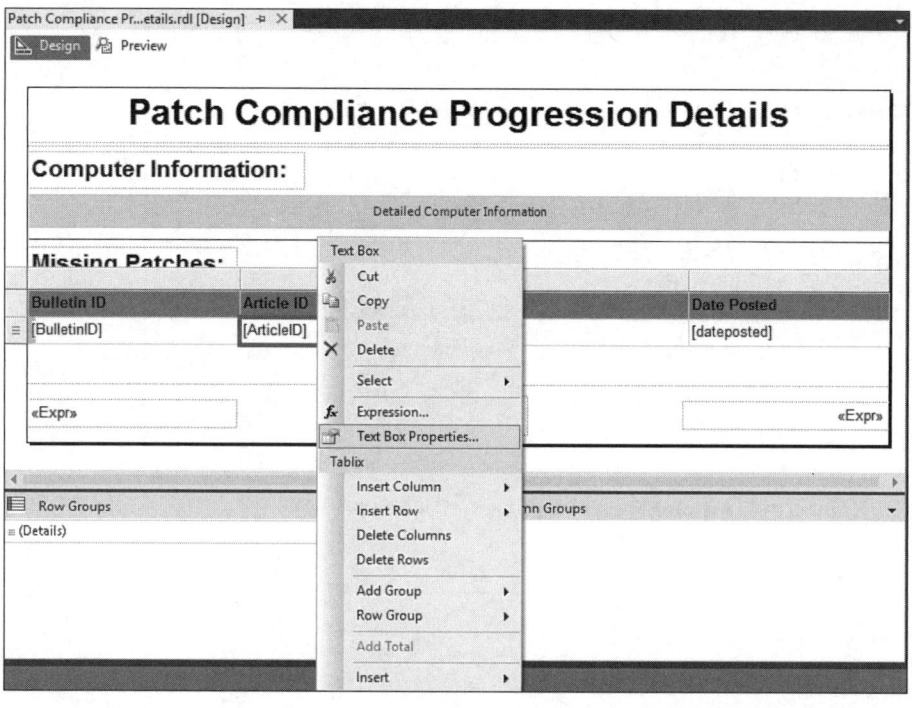

FIGURE 8.17   Right-clicking the **[ArticleID]** cell and selecting **Text Box Properties**.

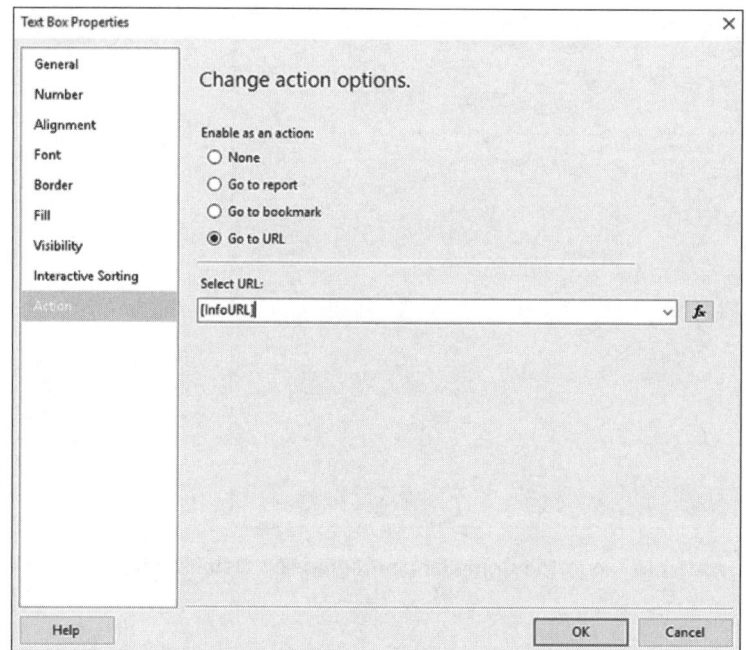

FIGURE 8.18   Completing the Action tab for the **[ArticleID]** cell.

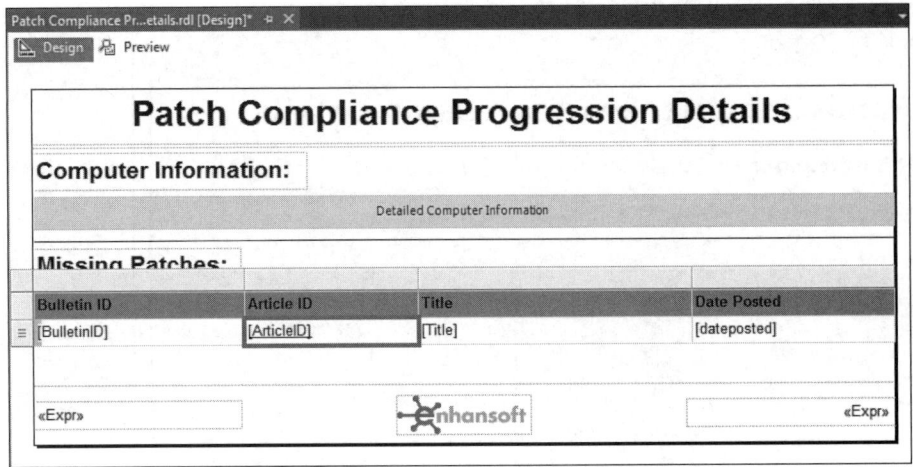

FIGURE 8.19   Setting the **[ArticleID]** cell font style to Underline.

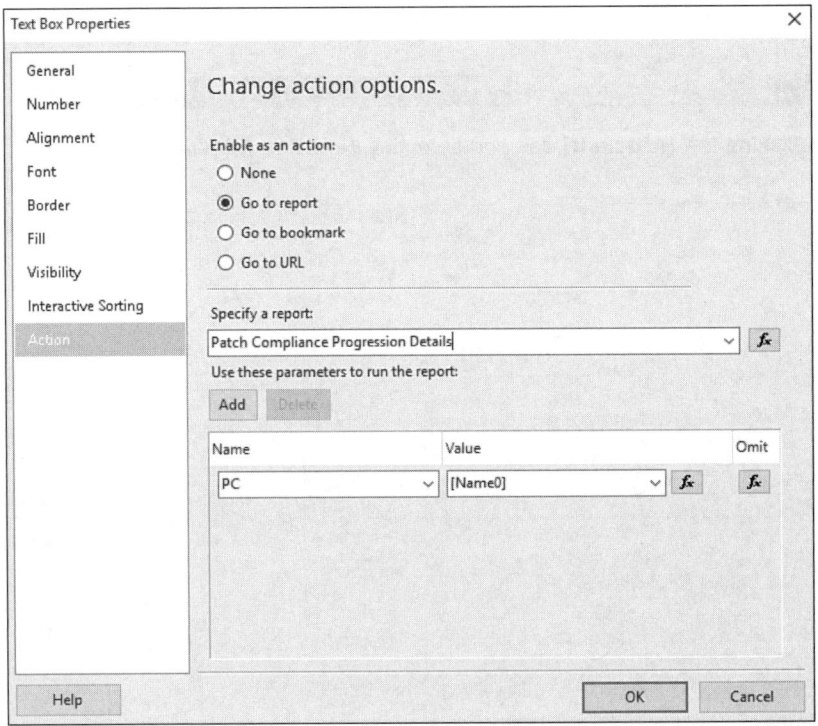

FIGURE 8.20   Changing the action to the Patch Compliance Progression Details report.

15. In the Patch Compliance Progression report, change the action on the [Name0] cell to go to the Patch Compliance Progression Details report. To do this, right-click the [Name0] cell and select **Text Box Properties**. Select the **Action** tab and change the Specify a report field to **Patch Compliance Progression Details**. Leave the parameters section set to **PC** as the Name, and [Name0] as the Value. Click **OK** when the Text Box Properties dialog is complete, as shown in Figure 8.20, and then save the report.

16. Preview the Patch Compliance Progression report. At the prompt, select a collection and click **View Report**. Once the report is displayed, click a PC Name from the table.

The Patch Compliance Progression Details report is now displayed, as shown in Figure 8.21. The PC Name value you clicked was passed to the report without requiring further information. Notice that the subreport item is populated with the Detailed

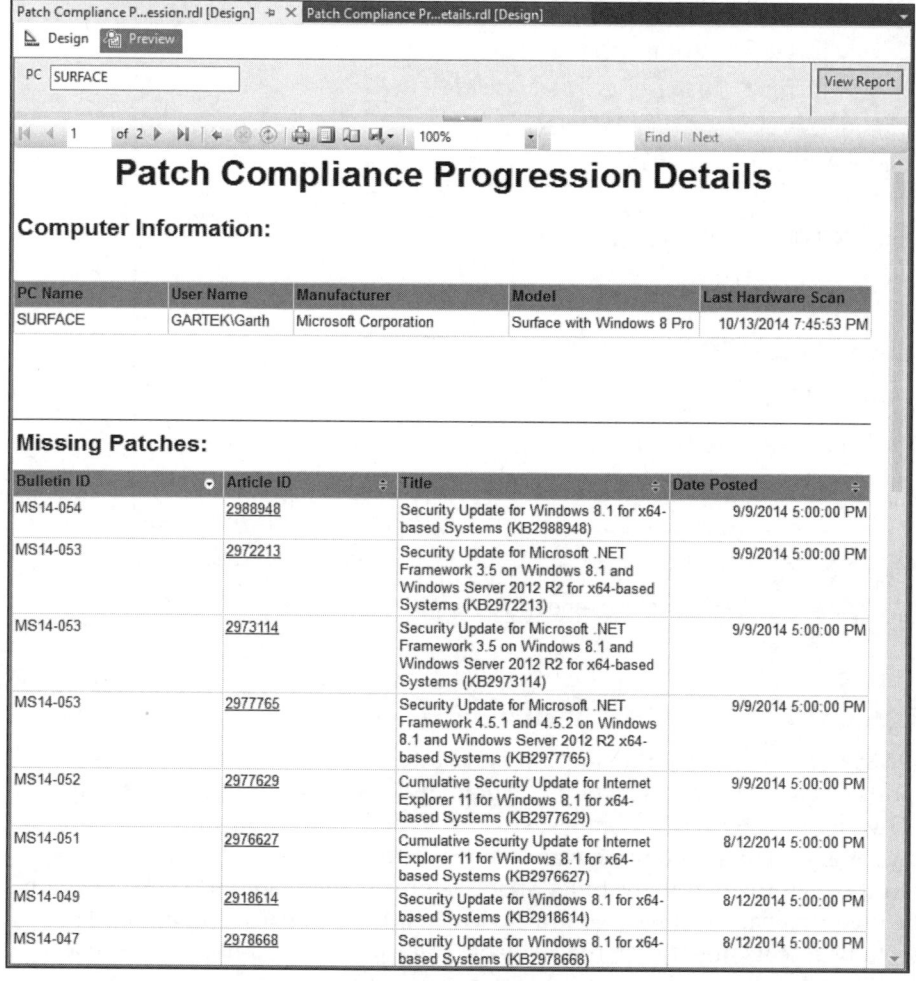

FIGURE 8.21   Drillthrough to Patch Compliance Progression Details report.

Computer Information report for the PC Name selected, and a list of all missing patches for the PC are provided in the table item, below the Missing Patches label. In the table of missing patches, an action was added to the **[ArticleID]** cell. Clicking one of the listed article IDs opens the Microsoft Knowledge Base article for that patch. For example, clicking the article ID **2988948** for Bulletin **MS14-054** opens its support page (see Figure 8.22).

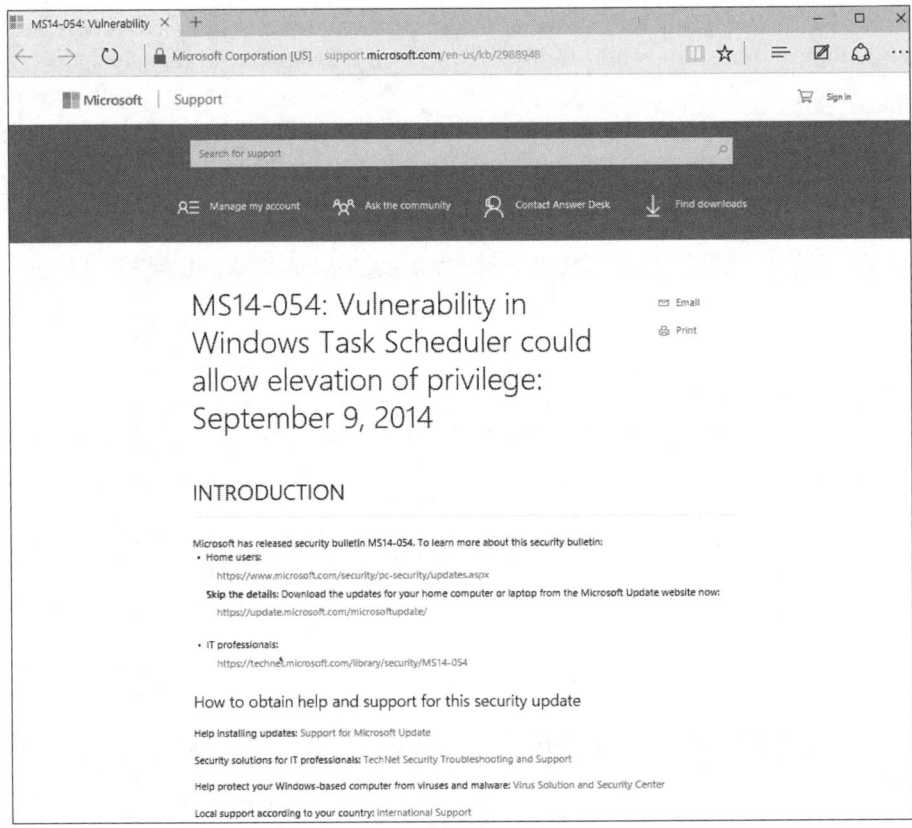

FIGURE 8.22   Knowledge Base article opened from a report hyperlink.

Creating Custom Color Palettes

As you create SSRS reports, the authors recommend integrating company branding into the reports to give the readers a familiar, company-specific feel to the data being presented. This can be achieved in many ways, such as adding the company's letterhead, color scheme, or logo. The selection of available out-of-the-box color palettes is very limited when it comes to chart items in reports. Customizing and adding a custom color palette to be used for charts can help you further match the company's branding. The following sections discuss how to use the available color palettes and how to create a custom color palette and group result values to specific colors.

Available Out-of-the-Box Color Palettes

Before discussing how to create custom color palettes for your report, let's look at the out-of-the-box palettes available. Although there are not many options to choose from, the palettes for chart items can easily be changed via the Properties section in SSDT-BI. Follow these steps to select one of the predefined palettes:

1. Using the Patch Compliance Progression Chart.rdl report as a basis, select the chart item in the body of the report.

2. In the Properties section at the bottom right, ensure that the focus is set to **Chart**, as shown in Figure 8.23.

3. In the Properties section, click the dropdown list next to the Palette value, shown in Figure 8.24, to select from the list of available color palettes.

4. Select a different palette to immediately update the chart in Design mode (see Figure 8.25), so you can view your selection without having to preview the entire report.

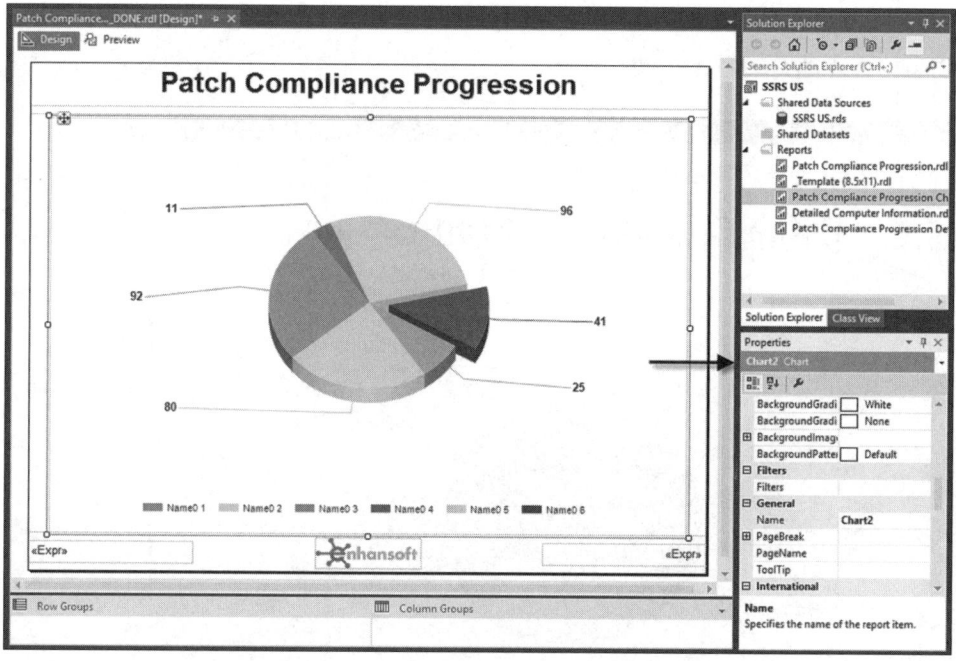

FIGURE 8.23   In the Properties section, ensuring that the focus is set to Chart.

Setting Custom Color Codes

You can use custom color codes to provide a color scheme for a report. You can define color schemes in different ways, either by providing a list of colors to cycle through or by grouping a color to a specific value. You can use both the color name and the color's hex

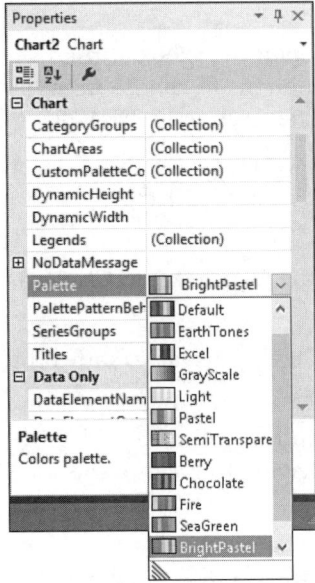

FIGURE 8.24   Available palette values.

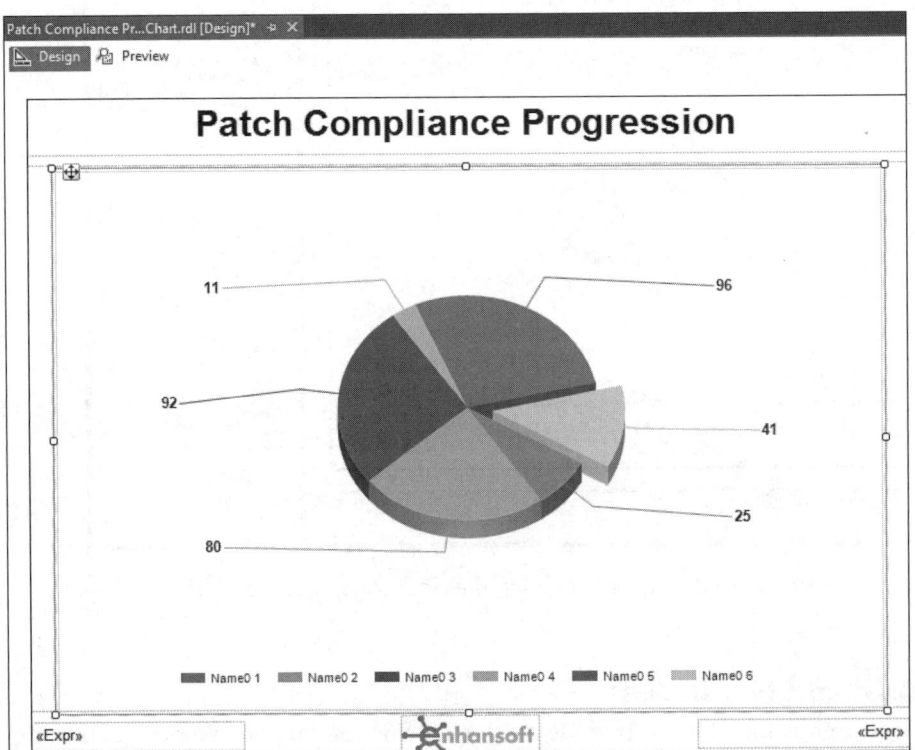

FIGURE 8.25   Updated chart palette in Design mode.

value when specifying color codes for reports. To set a color palette that cycles through the provided colors, using custom codes, follow these steps:

1. Open the Patch Compliance Progression Chart.rdl report.

2. From the SSDT-BI toolbar menu, select **Report -> Report Properties**, as shown in Figure 8.26.

3. In the Report Properties dialog, select the **Code** tab. On the Code tab, under the Custom Code field, enter the expression shown in Listing 8.4. When the Report Properties dialog is complete, as shown in Figure 8.27, click **OK** to apply the changes and close the dialog.

LISTING 8.4   Custom Color Code Expression

```
Private colorPalette As String() =
    {"#0000FF", "Red", "Green", "#FFFF00", "Orange", "#800080"}

Private count As Integer = 0
Private mapping As New System.Collections.Hashtable()

Public Function GetColor(ByVal groupingValue As String) As String
    If mapping.ContainsKey(groupingValue) Then
        Return mapping(groupingValue)
    End If
    Dim c As String = colorPalette(count Mod colorPalette.Length)
    count = count + 1
    mapping.Add(groupingValue, c)
    Return c
End Function
```

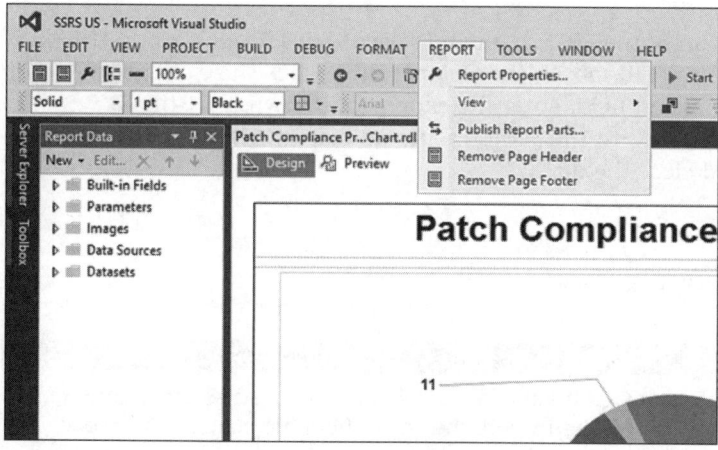

FIGURE 8.26   Selecting **Report -> Report Properties**.

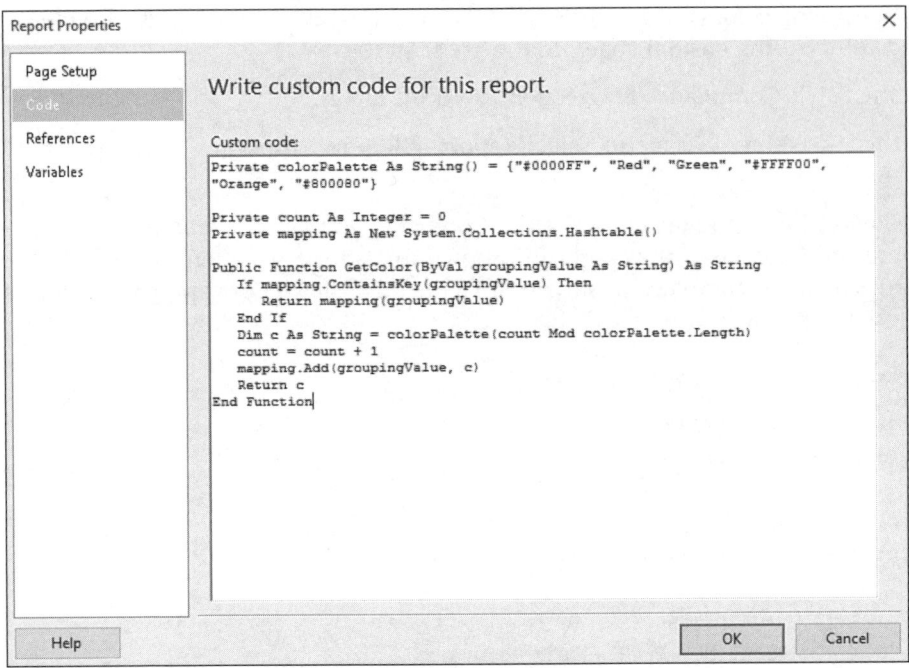

FIGURE 8.27   Entering the custom code expression.

TIP: USING COLOR CODES

The colors that will be used are defined on the first line between the curly brackets. Include your own colors by specifying color names or color hex codes.

The expression identified in Listing 8.4 is set to cycle through the colors in the order in which they appear between the curly brackets on the first line. If the expression has cycled through all available colors, it restarts the cycle with the first color.

4. Right-click the pie section of the chart item and select **Series Properties**. In the Properties dialog, select the **Fill** tab. In the Color section, click the expression button (**fx**). In the Expression field, enter the expression shown in Listing 8.5 (see Figure 8.28) and click **OK**. In the Series Properties dialog, click **OK** again to apply your changes and close the dialog.

LISTING 8.5   Color Expression

```
=Code.GetColor(Fields!Name0.Value)
```

TIP: COLOR EXPRESSION

The Name0 field in Listing 8.5 indicates the dataset column that is used as the chart's Category field. This is the field of the chart where the colors from the custom color code will be applied.

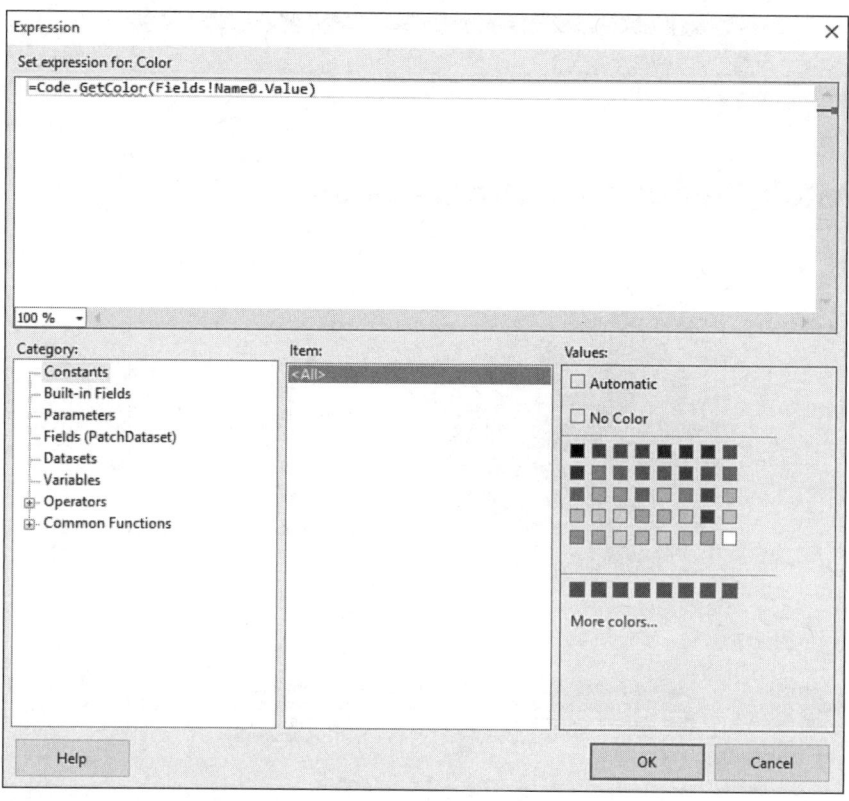

FIGURE 8.28   Completed Expression dialog.

5. Notice when using color expressions that the chart item's colors are not updated based on the color codes; the previously selected palette is still shown in Design mode. To confirm that the custom color codes are functioning as expected, preview the report, and you get a view like that shown in Figure 8.29.

TIP: MULTIPLE SAME COLORED WEDGES

In Figure 8.29 there is more than one wedge of the same color (blue) in the pie chart. This occurs when a chart item contains more categories than the number of colors defined in your custom color palette. In this scenario, the colors repeat through the palette's cycle. To avoid having multiple wedges of the same color, define more color codes than you have expected values.

Setting Custom Color Codes by Values

Another method of using custom color codes is to set colors based on specific values returned in a report. This section uses a new Software Update Compliance report to demonstrate associating colors with specific values. This report is provided as an extra to the book, available for download. (For information on obtaining these extras,

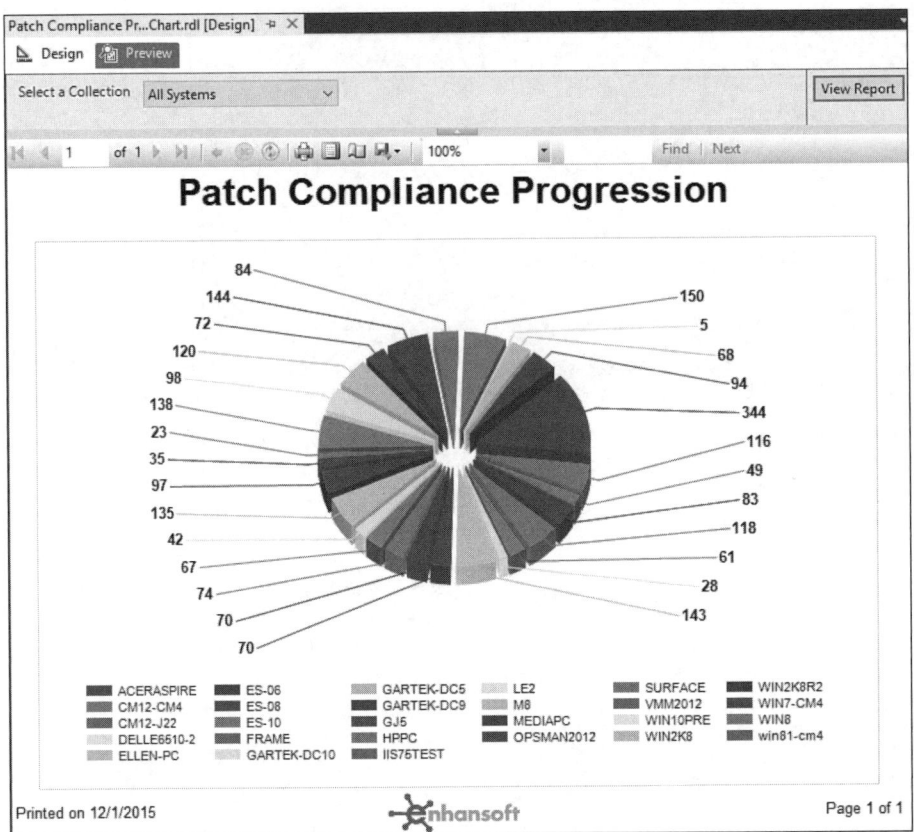

FIGURE 8.29   Previewing the report to see the new color palette used by the chart item.

see Appendix C, "Available Online.") The Software Update Compliance report is similar to the Configuration Manager (ConfigMgr) out-of-the-box report named Compliance 1 - Overall compliance. The new report returns a count of systems in a compliance state (compliant, noncompliant, or unknown), based on a specified collection and update list from your ConfigMgr environment. It includes a pie chart as well as a table to illustrate system compliance. To create a custom color palette based on values, follow these steps:

1. From the SSDT-BI toolbar menu, select **Report -> Report Properties**.

2. In the Report Properties dialog, select the **Code** tab. On the Code tab, in the Custom code field, enter the expression shown in Listing 8.6. Click **OK** when this is complete, as shown in Figure 8.30, to apply the changes and close the dialog box.

LISTING 8.6   Custom Color Code by Value Expression

```
Public Function GetColor(ByVal groupingValue As String) As String
   Dim c As String
    If groupingValue = "Compliant" Then
        c = "Green"
    elseif groupingValue = "Non-compliant" Then
        c = "Red"
    elseif groupingValue = "Compliance state unknown" Then
        c = "Orange"
    End if
    Return c
End Function
```

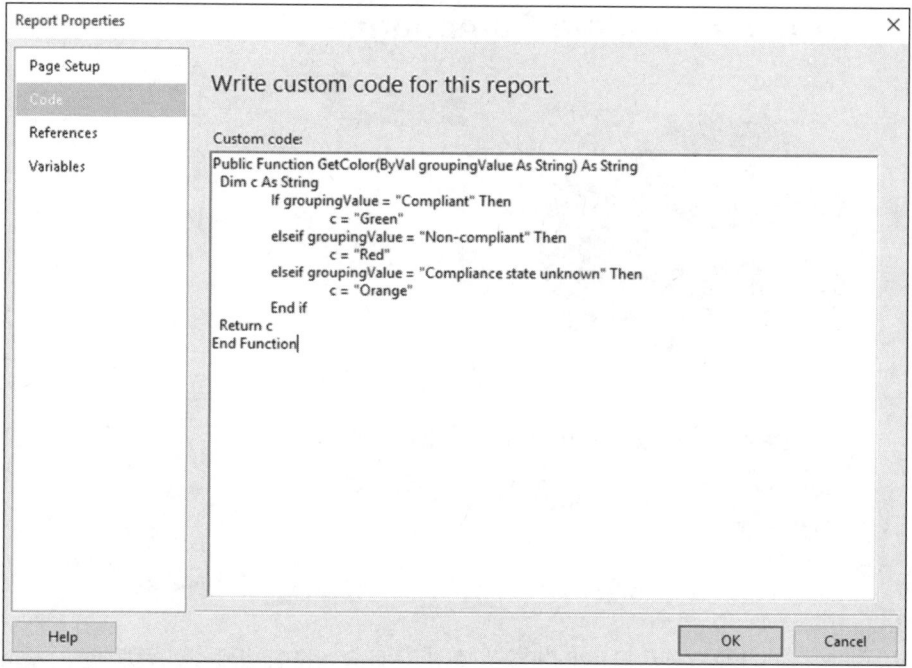

FIGURE 8.30   Entering the custom code expression.

TIP: COLOR CODE BY VALUE

The GetColor function shown in Listing 8.6 associates a color based on the defined groupingValue variables. As shown, the compliant state will be displayed in green, the noncompliant state in red, and the unknown state in orange. To add more values, simply add another elseif statement with a different value and color.

3. Right-click the pie section of the chart item and select **Series Properties**. In the dialog, select the **Fill** tab. Under the **Color** section, click the expression button (**fx**). In the expression field, enter the expression shown in Listing 8.7 and click **OK** to apply your changes and close the Series Properties dialog.

LISTING 8.7   Color Expression Based on Status Values

```
=Code.GetColor(Fields!Status.Value)
```

4. Much as with the custom color code example in the "Setting Custom Color Codes" section of this chapter, the chart item is not updated based on the color codes in Design mode. To confirm that the custom color codes are functioning as expected, preview the report to see a result like the example shown in Figure 8.31.

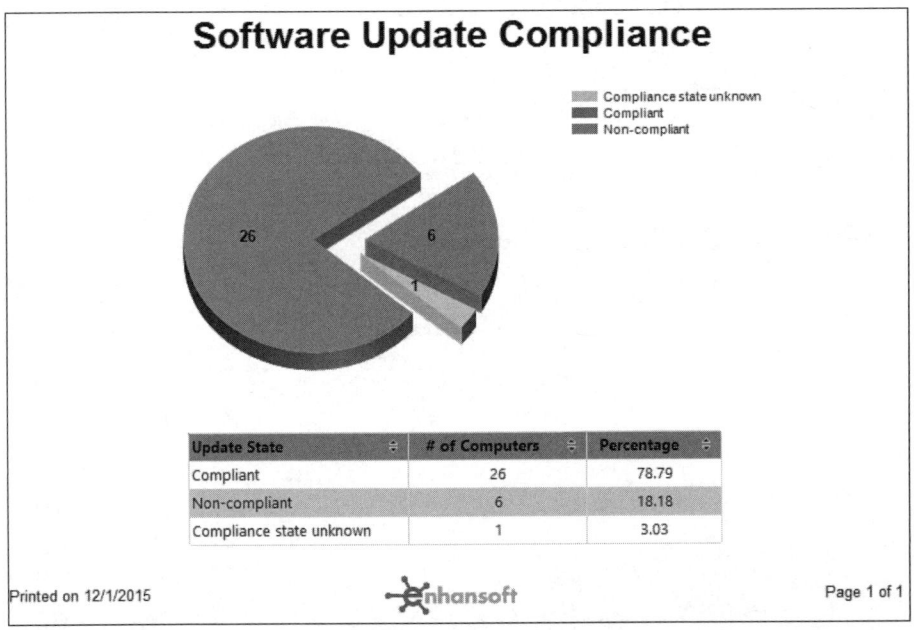

FIGURE 8.31   Previewing the report to see the colors chosen based on the Status value.

Much as when applying a custom color code on a chart item, you can apply the color value expression in Listing 8.7 to any chart item that displays information based on the Status value. Follow these steps to set a color value expression on a table item's background color:

1. Select the data value row of a table item. In the Properties section at the bottom-right, under the Fill section, set the BackgroundColor property value to the expression shown in Listing 8.7 (see Figure 8.32) by selecting **Expression** from the dropdown list.

2. Preview the report, as shown in Figure 8.33. Notice that the table's background color is set based on the Status value for the row.

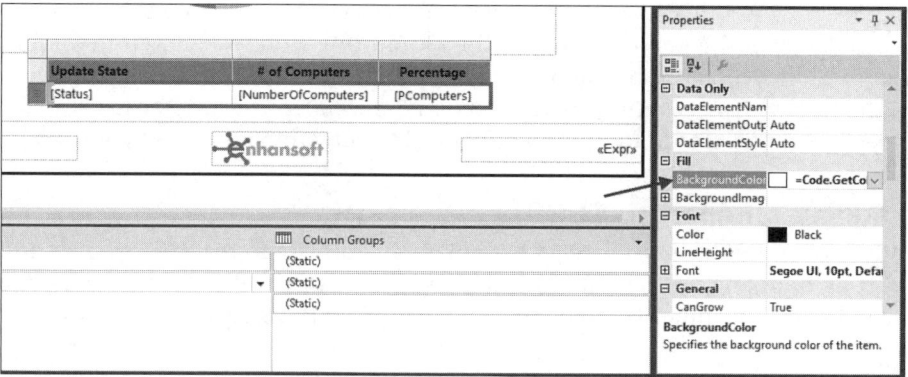

FIGURE 8.32   Setting the color expressing from Listing 8.7 as the BackgroundColor value.

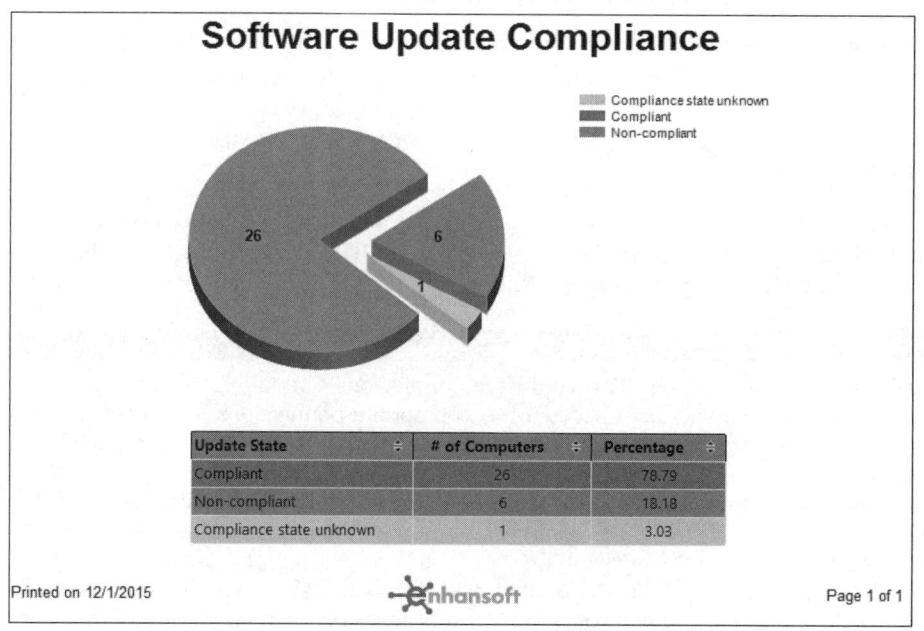

FIGURE 8.33   Previewing the report to see the updated background color for the table rows.

Adding Reports to SSRS

This book has discussed multiple aspects of report writing, from creating SQL queries in SQL Server Management Studio to creating SSRS reports in SSDT-BI. However, these reports are not yet available or published to the ConfigMgr reporting services point or SSRS website. The following sections describe different methods of adding or publishing completed reports to the SSRS website for users to run. They also detail how to configure subscriptions for users to automatically email or save a report.

Once reports are added to the SSRS website, they also become available from the ConfigMgr console under the Reports folder in the Monitoring workspace. Even though all reports can be launched and run from the console, the authors recommend running reports from the SSRS website, as this provides better performance and also means you do not have to deploy the console to users who only need to run and view report data.

Manually Adding a Report to SSRS

A simple method of adding a report to SSRS is to manually browse to the SSRS website and upload a report by browsing for the .rdl file. The downside of this method is that only one report can be uploaded at a time. To manually add a report to the SSRS website, follow these steps:

1. Open a web browser and browse to the SSRS report website. For this example, the SSRS website address is **http://CM16/Reports**, as configured in Chapter 1, "Installing SQL Server Reporting Services," and Chapter 2, "Installing and Configuring Configuration Manager Reporting" (see Figure 8.34).

2. From the SQL Server Reporting Services home page, click the **ConfigMgr_CM6** folder, which you specified during the ConfigMgr reporting services point installation in Chapter 2. A list of ConfigMgr folders is displayed; these folders are created during the installation of the reporting services point in ConfigMgr and contain out-of-the-box reports.

3. Create a new folder to store your custom reports by clicking **New Folder**, as shown in Figure 8.35, and specifying a Name for the new folder, as shown in Figure 8.36. You can also add a description for the folder, although it is not required. Click **OK**.

TIP: PERMISSION ERROR

If you receive an error saying that you do not have permissions to add a folder or upload a report, you need to grant your user account the appropriate permissions. Only accounts with the system administrator permission can create new folders and upload reports. To grant this access, launch your browser by specifying **Run As a different user** and entering an account with administrator privileges to the SSRS server. From the browser, navigate to the SSRS home page (http://<SSRS *servername*>/reports) and select **Site Settings** in the top-right corner. Click the **Security** tab on the left to view current permissions. Either add your user account to one of the groups that already has the system administrator role or click New Role Assignment to add your user account to the system administrator role.

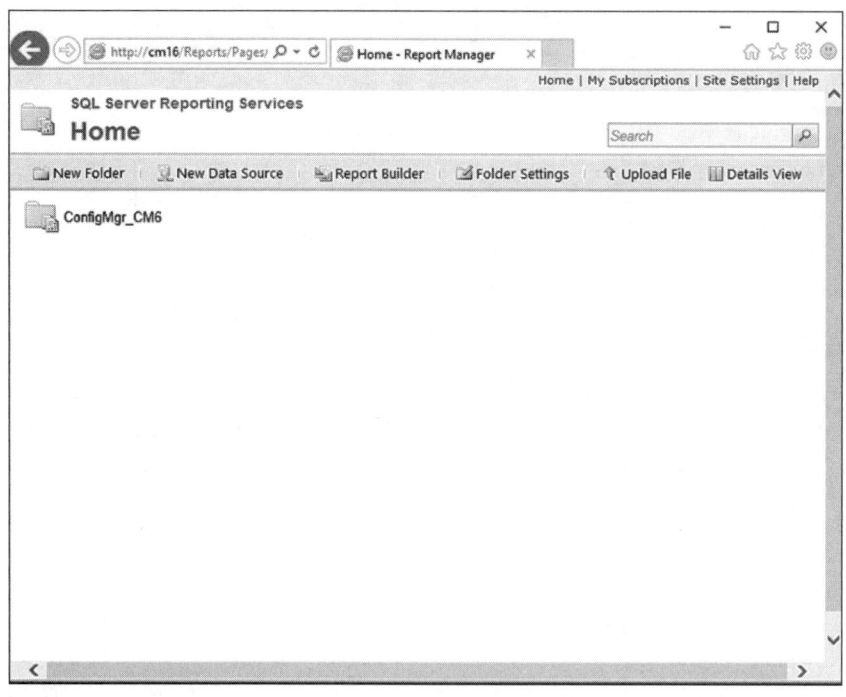

FIGURE 8.34   Browsing to the SSRS home page.

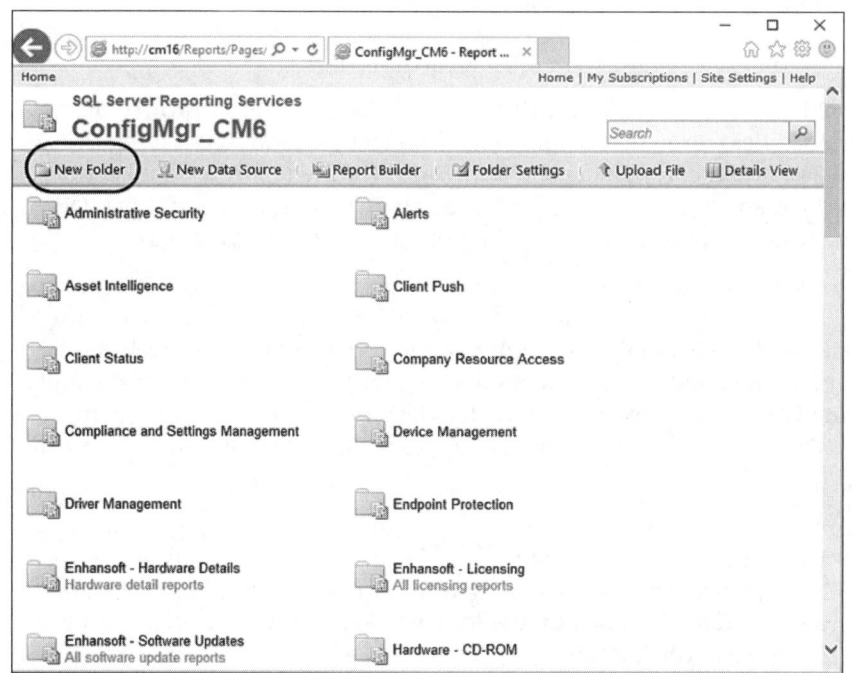

FIGURE 8.35   Clicking **New Folder**.

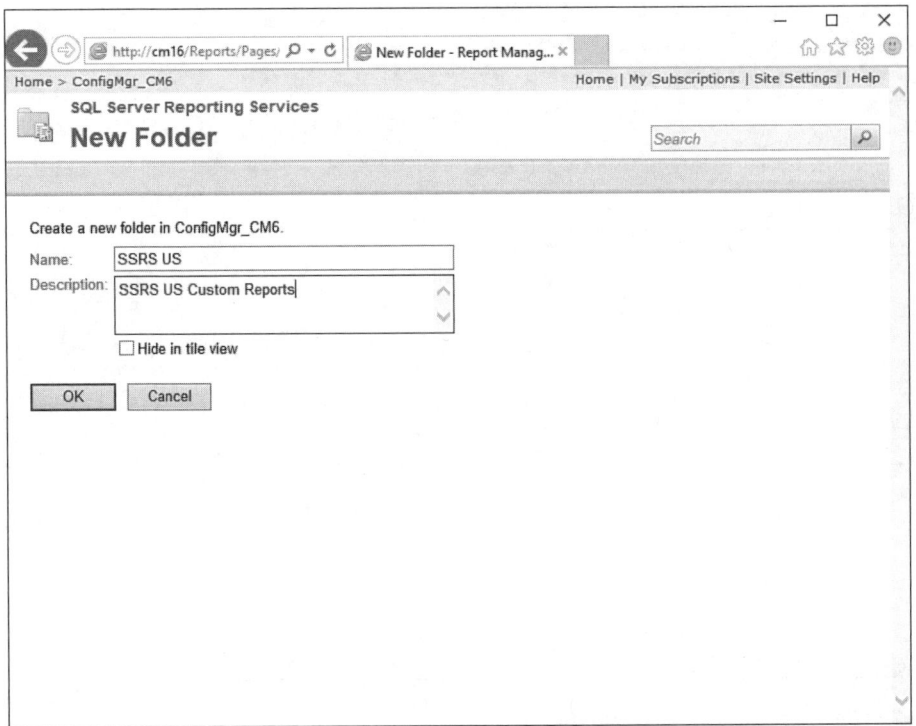

FIGURE 8.36   Entering a name for the new folder.

4. From the list of folders, click the folder just created in step 3.

5. In the new folder, click **Upload File**. At the Upload File page, select **Browse** next to the File to upload field. Browse to your SSDT-BI project location, select a report RDL file to upload, and then click **Open**. The Name field for the report is populated by default with the name of the RDL file, and you can change it if desired. Click **OK** when you are ready to upload the selected report, as shown in Figure 8.37.

6. When you are redirected to the folder view where the report was uploaded, click the newly added report to execute it. You receive the error shown in Figure 8.38, which indicates that the shared data source is not valid for use from the SSRS website. To fix the error, you must update the report's data source in the properties of the report on the website. To do so, go back to the folder view, hover your cursor over the report name, click the downward arrow that appears, and select **Manage**, as shown in Figure 8.39.

7. From the report's properties page, select the **Data Sources** tab in the left pane. Click **Browse** next to the Select a shared data source option. Under the location field, expand the ConfigMgr folder, scroll to the bottom of the list, and select the data source item (the last item identified by the long unique ID between curly brackets), as shown in Figure 8.40. Click **OK**.

8. Back at the Data Sources page shown in Figure 8.41, click **Apply** at the bottom of the page to save the changes.

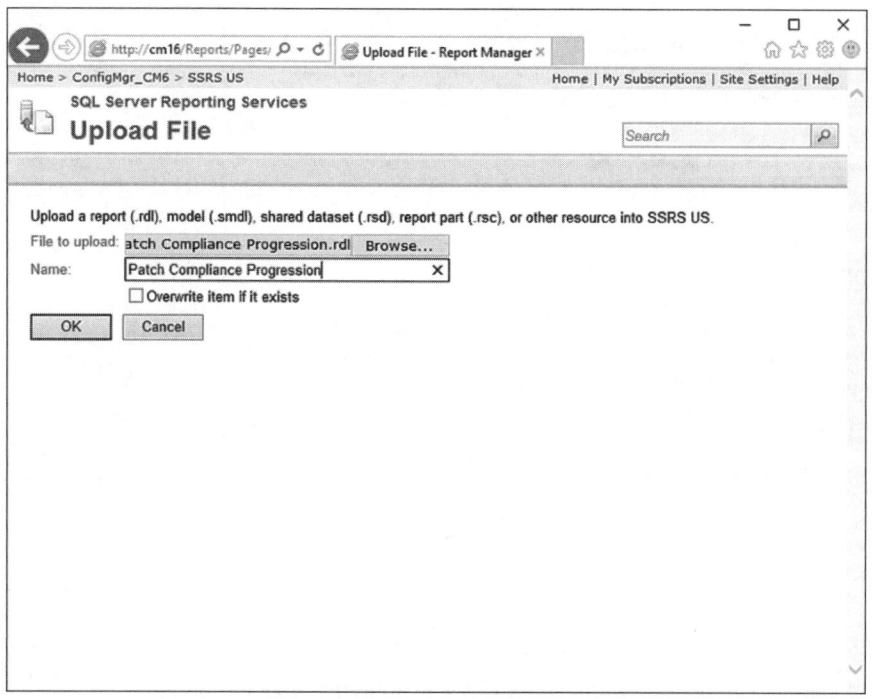

FIGURE 8.37   Specifying the report to upload to the SSRS website.

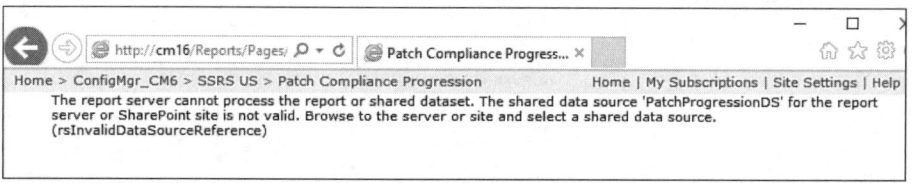

FIGURE 8.38   SSRS Invalid source error.

9. To test the changes and run the report, click the report name at the top of the page or go back to the folder view and click the report. Confirm that the report now runs without errors and displays properly, as shown in Figure 8.42.

10. To add additional reports now that a folder has been created, repeat steps 5 through 9.

TIP: PRINTING AND EXPORTING FROM SSRS

SSRS allows you to export reports to the same file formats as described for SSDT-BI by clicking the diskette icon in the bar above the report title shown in Figure 8.42. SSRS also allows you to print reports on paper by using the printer icon. Also available from SSRS reports is the Find field, to the left of Export, which looks up specified text across all pages of a report.

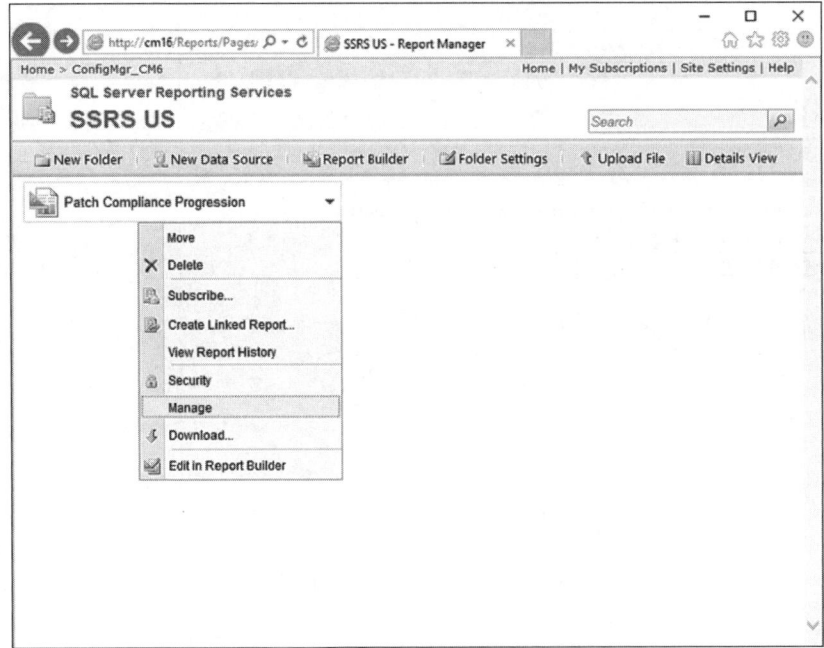

FIGURE 8.39   Editing the properties of the report by selecting the **Manage** option.

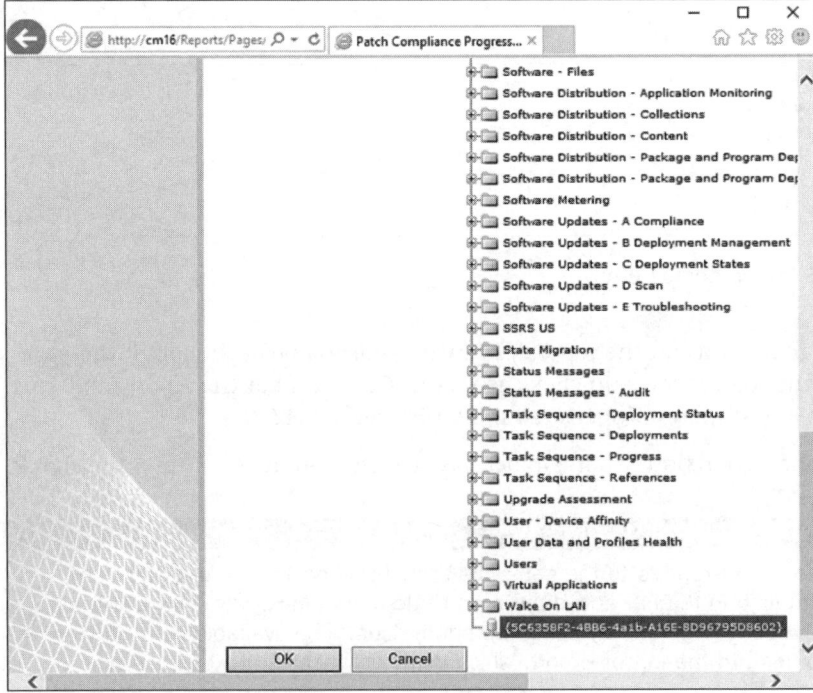

FIGURE 8.40   Selecting the data source item from the list.

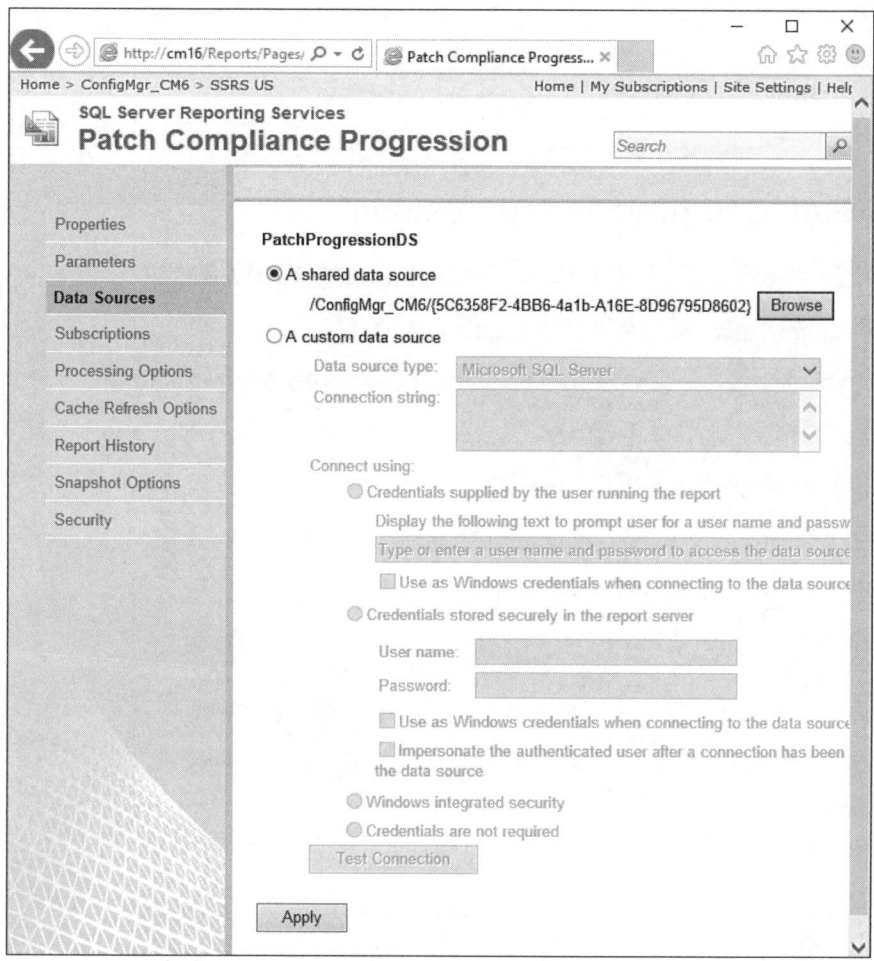

FIGURE 8.41   Clicking **Apply** to save the changes to the report.

Publishing Reports from SSDT-BI to the SSRS Website

Manually adding each individual report to the SSRS website may be acceptable for several reports; however, this can be very time-consuming if you have dozens of custom-created reports. SSDT-BI provides an option to *deploy* reports directly to the SSRS website. Perform the following steps to configure the required deployment options and publish reports from SSDT-BI without having to manually upload each one:

1. In SSDT-BI, open the SSRS project that contains your custom reports.

2. From the SSDT-BI menu at the top, select **Project** and click **Properties**, as shown in Figure 8.43.

3. Click **Configuration Manager** from the top-right of the Project Properties page.

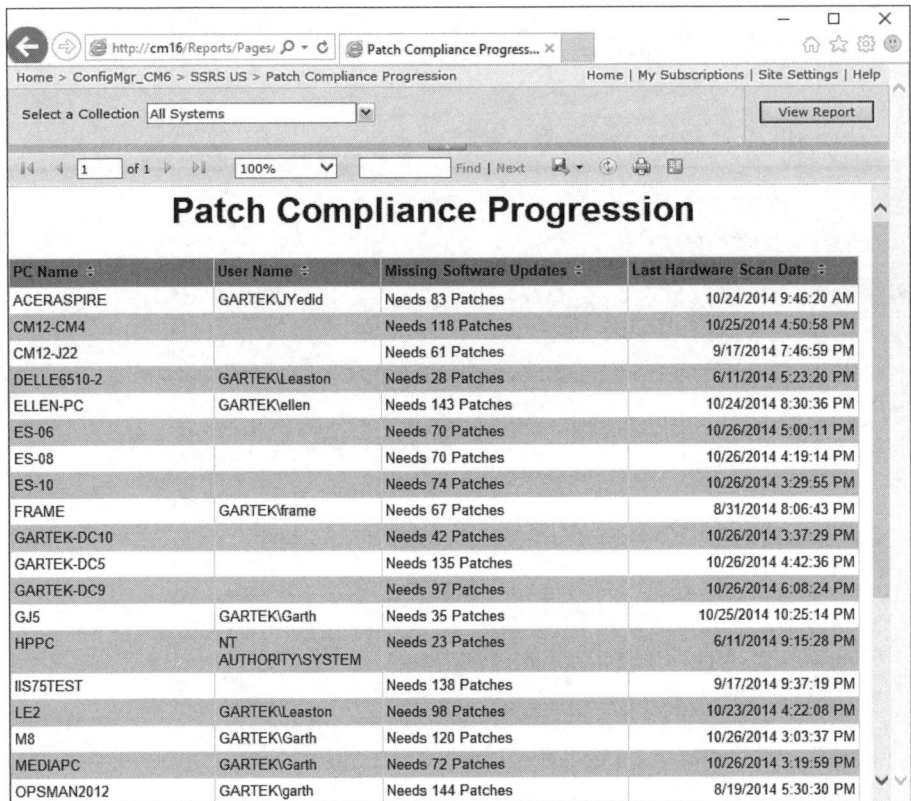

FIGURE 8.42   Running a report in SSRS and confirming that it runs without errors.

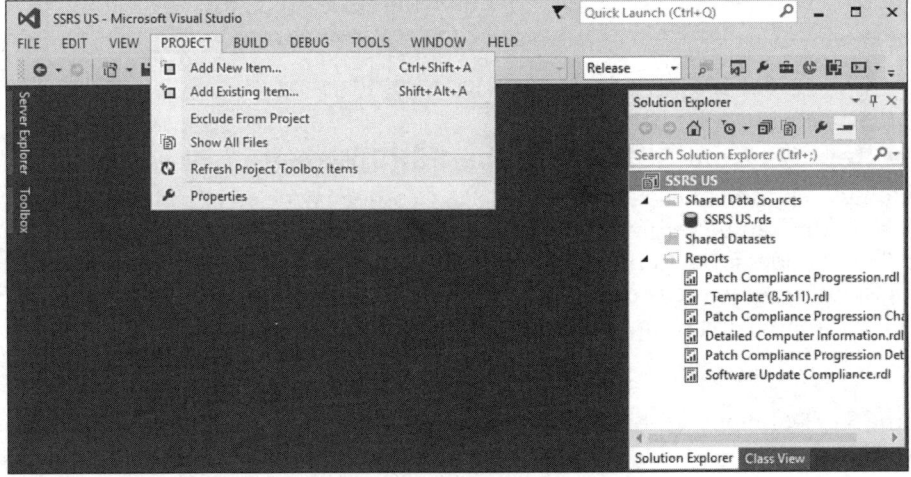

FIGURE 8.43   Selecting **Project -> Properties**.

4. In the Configuration Manager page, in the Configuration column of the project row, use the dropdown list to change the value to **Release**, as shown in Figure 8.44. Ensure that the Build and Deploy column values are checked and then click **Close**.

5. On the Properties page, under the Deployment section, enter the SSRS virtual directory URL under the TargetServerURL value. For this example, the value is **http://cm16/ReportServer**. Optionally, to set the folder in SSRS to store your reports, set the folder path as the TargetReportFolder value. The value is set to **ConfigMgr_CM6/SSRS US** to store the reports under the same folder created in the "Manually Adding a Report to SSRS" section of this chapter. Click **OK** when the Properties page is finished, as shown in Figure 8.45, to apply the changes.

TIP: TARGETSERVERURL VALUE

To get the correct TargetServerURL value, find the web service URL in the Reporting Services configuration on the SSRS server (described in Chapter 1). By default, this path is http://<SSRS servername>/ReportServer.

---

6. Before a report can be published to SSRS, you must first publish the shared data source created in SSDT-BI. To publish the data source, expand the Shared Data Source folder in the Solution Explorer, right-click the .rds object, and select **Deploy**, as shown in Figure 8.46.

7. Once the shared data source is deployed to SSRS, right-click a report in the Solution Explorer and click **Deploy**.

8. To confirm that the report is deployed, use a web browser to navigate to the SSRS website and browse to the folder identified in the TargetReportFolder value from step 5. Verify that the report is listed in the folder and runs successfully without errors.

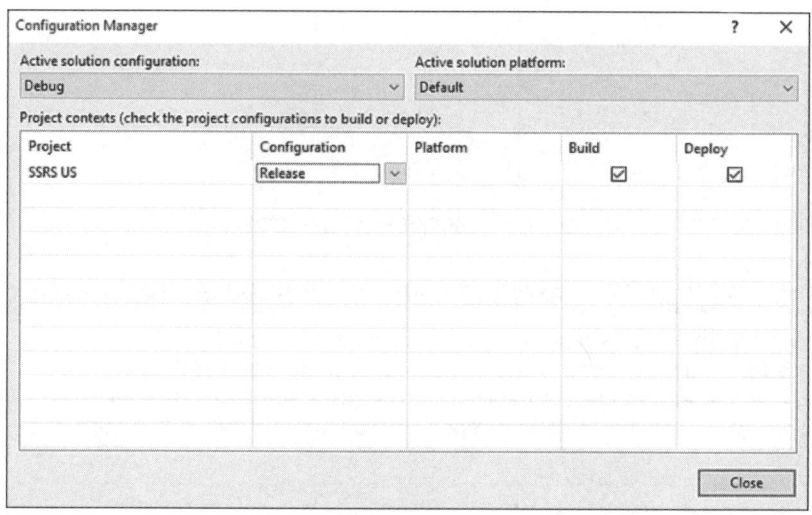

FIGURE 8.44   Setting the project configuration to **Release**.

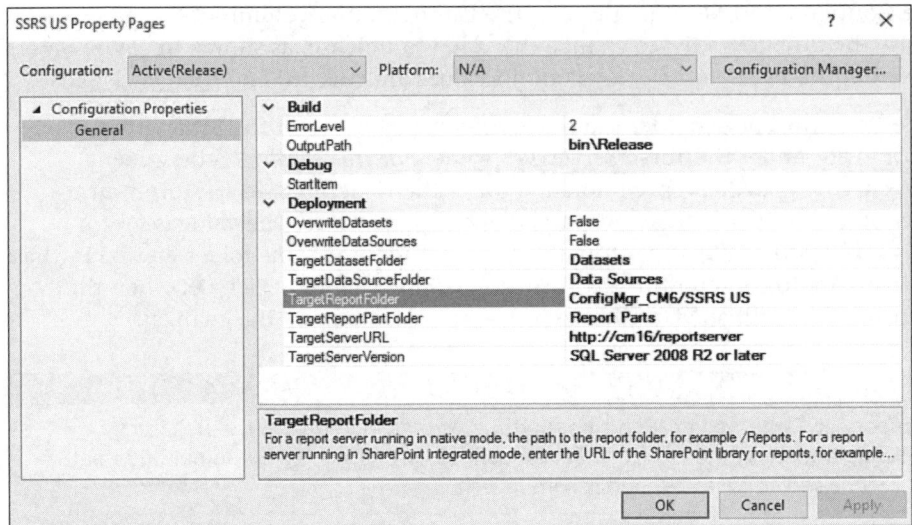

FIGURE 8.45   Completed Properties page for deploying reports.

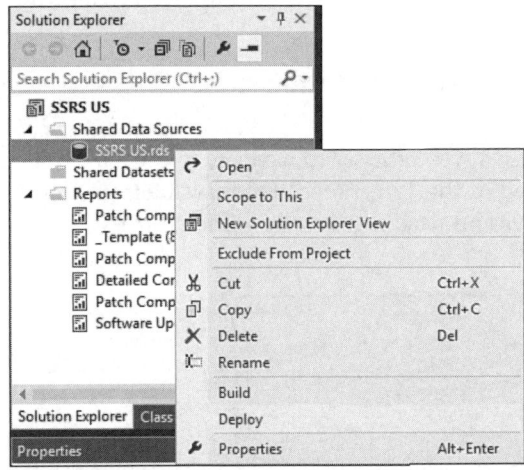

FIGURE 8.46   Right-clicking the shared data source and selecting **Deploy**.

TIP: DEPLOYING AN ENTIRE PROJECT

Rather than deploying one report at a time, you can deploy an entire project to SSRS by right-clicking the project name under the Solution Explorer and selecting **Deploy**. All shared data sources and all reports are published to SSRS. Once all reports are deployed, any actions set on objects to go to a report will function as they did in the SSDT-BI Preview mode.

Creating Report Subscriptions

Report subscriptions in SSRS allow for reports to be run on a schedule and either exported to a file share or emailed directly to users. This feature is often used for compliance reports emailed to users on a weekly or monthly basis as a reminder to verify the status of specific compliance data or keep an audit record of the specific results for that environment. Report subscriptions are set on individual reports and can specify parameters for the report to run, if applicable. To create a report subscription, follow these steps:

1. Open a web browser and browse to the SSRS report website (**http://CM16/Reports**).

2. From the SQL Server Reporting Services home page, browse to the folder that contains the report where you want to add a subscription.

3. Hover your cursor over the report name. Click the downward arrow that appears to the right of the report and select **Manage**, as shown in Figure 8.39, earlier in this chapter.

4. Click the **Subscriptions** tab on the left side and click **New Subscription** at the top of the page, as shown in Figure 8.47.

TIP: SUBSCRIPTION ERROR

When you click **New Subscription**, you could receive an error stating that the subscription cannot be created because of the credentials used. This typically occurs because the shared data source used for the report is set to use Windows integrated security. The authors recommend always changing the data source of reports once they have been added to the ConfigMgr reporting services point or SSRS website to use the default Microsoft-created data source, described in the "Manually Adding a Report to SSRS" section of this chapter. While this might add an extra step to publishing reports, it ensures that all reports are consistent and support the creation of subscriptions, as it uses the service account specified during the configuration of the ConfigMgr reporting services point when running reports.

From the New Subscription page, there are two subscription types available for reports:

▶ Windows File Share

▶ Email

These methods are described in the following sections.

Windows File Share Subscriptions

You can configure a Windows File Share subscription to export the selected report to the specified file type and store it at the share path identified. Follow these steps to configure a Windows File Share subscription:

1. From the Delivered dropdown, select **Windows File Share**. The subscription detail fields changes based on the selected delivery format. Figure 8.48 shows the options for Windows File Share delivery.

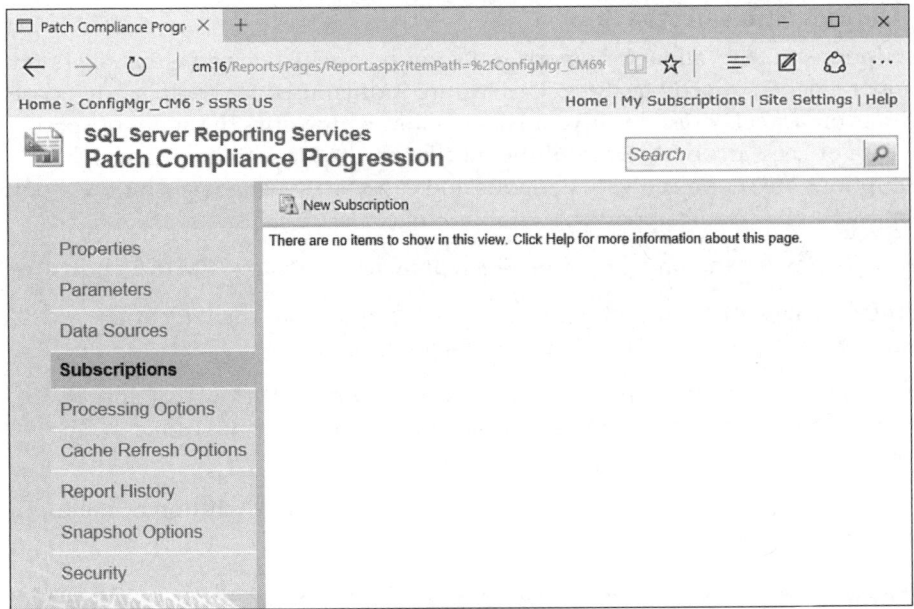

FIGURE 8.47   Clicking **New Subscription**.

2. For the Path field, enter the share path where the report export file should be stored.

3. From the Render Format dropdown, identify the file type for the report export, as shown in Figure 8.49.

4. For the Credentials used to access the file share field, specify the username and password of an account that has access to save the report to the share.

5. For the Overwrite options field, select the behavior that should occur if the exported report already exists on the share. Select to either overwrite the existing file, not overwrite the file (it will not be exported), or increment the file names as newer versions are added (which is the ideal option if you need to keep track of reports over weeks, months, years, and such).

6. In the Subscription Processing Options section, specify a schedule for the report to run by clicking **Select Schedule**.

7. If the report contains any parameters, the Report Parameter Values section appears. The parameter prompts here look similar to when you're running the report: simple textbox, dropdown list, or multi-value select. Specify the parameter used to run the report for the subscription.

8. Click **OK** to create the subscription.

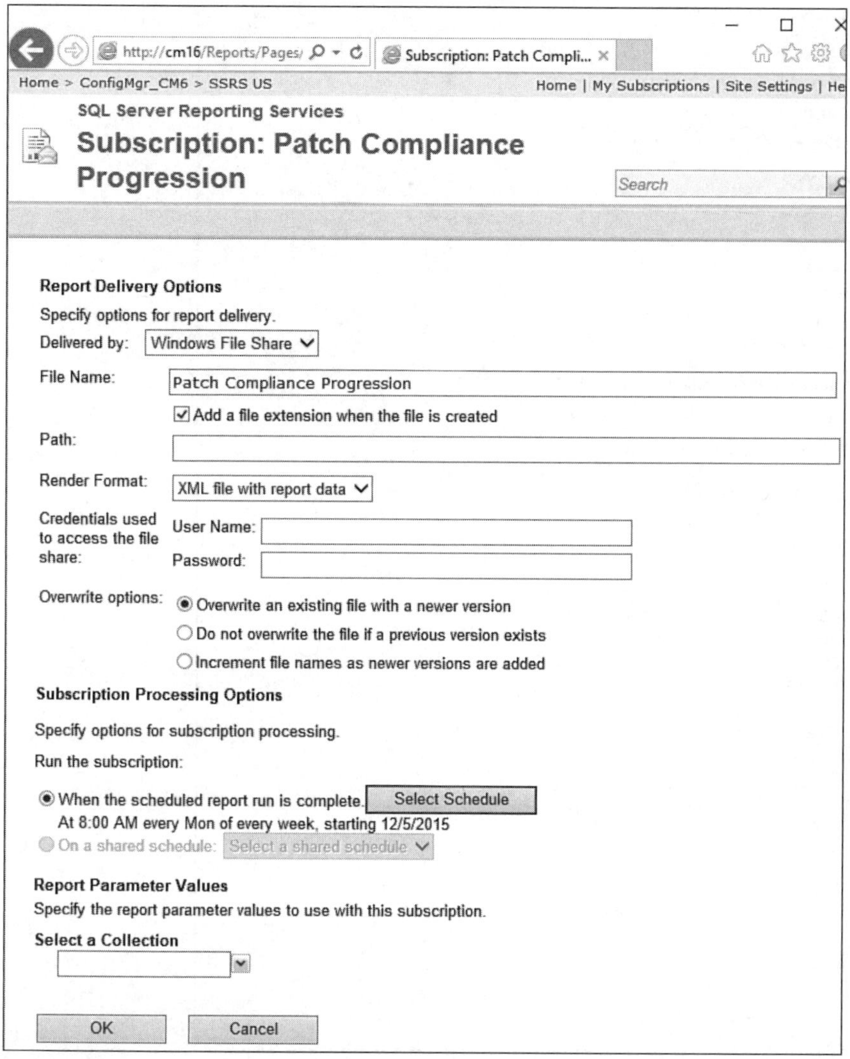

FIGURE 8.48   Windows File Share subscription fields.

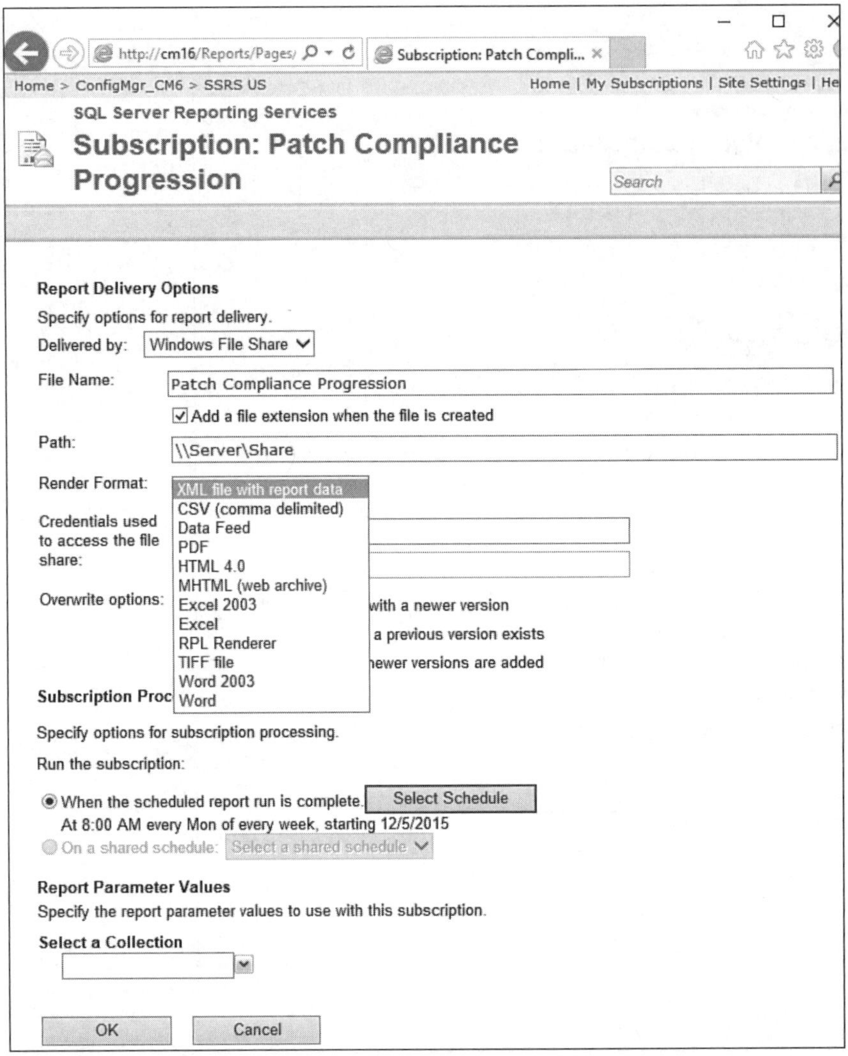

FIGURE 8.49   Available render formats for subscriptions.

Email Subscriptions

An email subscription sends an email to specified addresses and attaches the export of the selected report. To configure an email subscription, follow these steps:

1. At the Delivered by field, select **E-Mail** from the dropdown. The subscription detail fields change based on the selected delivery format. Figure 8.50 shows the options for email delivery.

2. In the To, CC, and BCC fields, specify the email addresses for the recipients of the report.

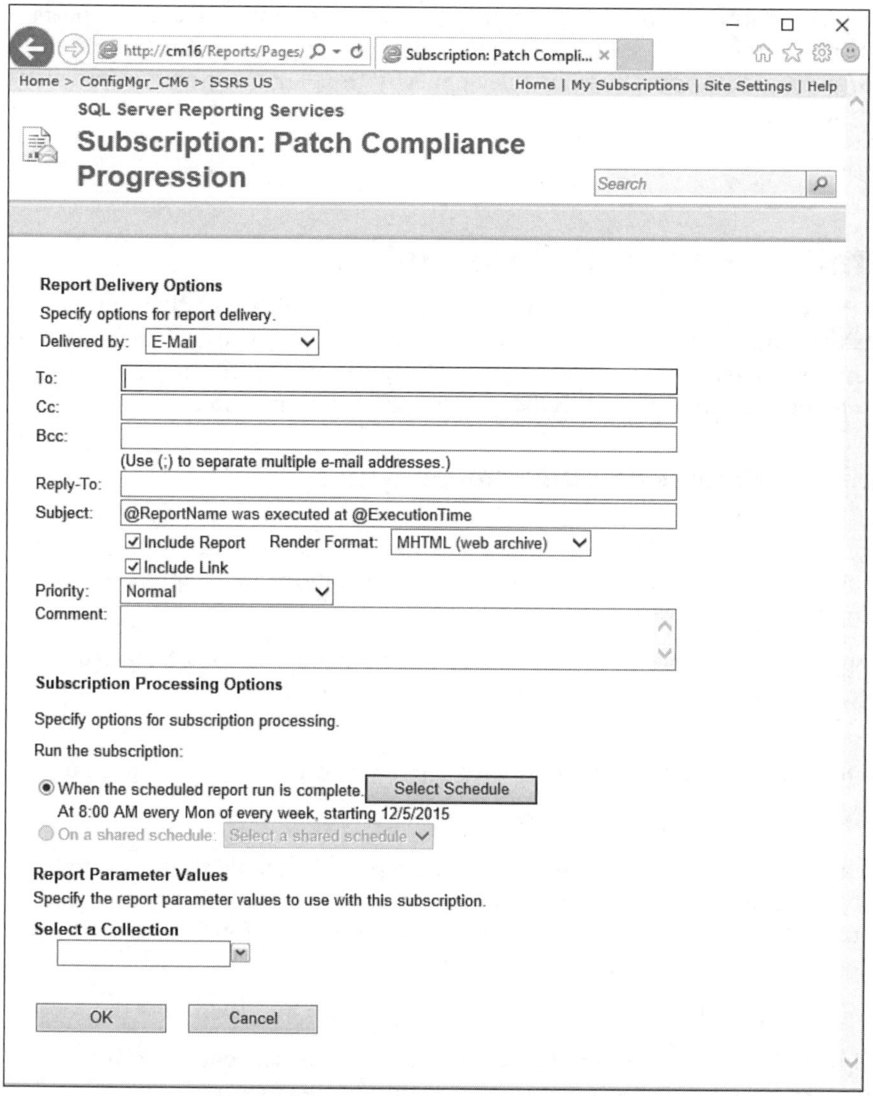

FIGURE 8.50   Email subscription fields.

3. Optionally specify an email address in the Reply-To field that will appear when a recipient replies to the automatic subscription email.

4. Use the Subject field to specify the email's subject.

5. Select from the Render Format dropdown to identify the file type for the report export.

6. Under the Subscription Processing Options section, click **Select Schedule** and specify a schedule for the report to run.

7. If the report contains any parameters, the Report Parameter Values section appears. The parameter prompts look similar to when you're running the report: simple textbox, dropdown list, or multi-value select. Specify the parameter used to run the report for the subscription.

8. Click **OK** to create the subscription.

Demonstrating Report Drillthroughs

The purpose of this demonstration is for you to become familiar with the different ways to create reports that allow users to drillthrough to detailed reports. You will create reports that contain many of the features discussed in the "Using Report Drillthroughs" section, including Go to report actions, Go to URL (hyperlinks), and subreport items.

Patch Compliance Progression Drillthrough Series

Follow the procedure in the "Using Report Drillthroughs" section of this chapter to create the following items and features. You will be creating new reports and modifying existing ones. Ensure that you have completed the previous demonstrations in Chapters 6 and 7 before proceeding with the following actions:

▶ Make a copy of the _Template (8.5x11).rdl report and name the copy **Detailed Computer Information**. Do the following for the Detailed Computer Information report:

   ▶ Create a data source for the report with reference to your shared data source.

   ▶ Create a dataset using the query from Listing 8.1.

   ▶ Add a table item to the body section of the report. The table should contain all five columns from the dataset, proper labels for the column headers, and interactive sorting. The header row should be set to bold font style with a red background color, and the table should span the width of the page.

   ▶ Preview the report to ensure that it displays properly and then save the report.

▶ Make a copy of the _Template (8.5x11).rdl report and name the copy **Patch Compliance Progression Details**. Do the following for this report:

   ▶ Create a data source for the report with reference to your shared data source.

   ▶ Create a dataset using the query from Listing 8.2.

   ▶ Add a horizontal line in the middle of the body section to split the body in two.

   ▶ In the top half of the body section, add a text box that contains the text **Computer Information**. Add a subreport item below the text box with reference to the Detailed Computer Information report, as detailed in the "Adding a Subreport Item" section of this chapter.

   ▶ In the bottom half of the body section, add a text box that contains the text **Missing Patches**. Add a table item below the text box. In the table item, add the BulletinID, ArticleID, Title, and DatePosted columns from the dataset. Set the header row font to bold and the background color to red. Ensure that the table spans the width of the page. Enable interactive sorting on each column header.

▶ Set an action on the [ArticleID] cell to go to the URL specified in the [InfoURL] column of the dataset.

▶ Set a hyperlink on the image item of the footer to go to a specific website address.

▶ Save the report.

▶ Modify the Patch Compliance Progression report to add an action on the [Name0] cell to go to the Patch Compliance Progression Details report. Save the report.

▶ Preview the Patch Compliance Progression report and test the drillthrough functionality set on the PC Name values of the table.

When clicking on a PC Name value, ensure that the Patch Compliance Progression Details report is displayed and the PC Name value is passed to the report's parameter without a prompt. Confirm that the subreport item is also displayed with information for the selected PC. Verify that the ArticleID values contain a link that opens the specific Microsoft Knowledge Base article in your browser and that clicking the image in the footer opens the URL that was specified.

Computer Hardware Information Drillthrough Series

For this part of the demonstration, you will create a drillthrough series of reports based on the Computer Hardware Information report. You will need to create a new report from the Computer Hardware Information Chart as well as modify the Computer Hardware Information Prompt report. The information to create this drillthrough series follows:

▶ Make a copy of the Computer Hardware Information Chart.rdl report and name the copy **Hardware Model Chart.rdl**. Modify this new report as follows:

  ▶ Modify the Dataset query to add the WHERE statement shown in Listing 8.3.

  ▶ Set the Chart Data Value section to **Count(Model0)** and the Category Group section to **Model0**.

  ▶ Enable Show Data Values on the pie chart.

  ▶ Remove all actions from the pie chart.

  ▶ Save the report.

LISTING 8.3   WHERE Statement for the Hardware Model Chart Report

```
WHERE
    CS.Manufacturer0 LIKE @Make
```

▶ Open and modify the Computer Hardware Information Prompt.rdl report as follows:

    ▶ Add a subreport item in the body of the report, above the existing table item.

    ▶ Set the subreport item's size to 3×3in.

    ▶ Set the subreport value to the **Hardware Model Chart**. Add to the subreport a parameter with the Name field set to **Make** and the Value field set to an expression for the Parameter value Manu.

    ▶ Save the Computer Hardware Information Prompt.rdl report.

▶ Open and Preview the Computer Hardware Information Chart.rdl report. From the pie chart, click on a manufacturer's pie wedge.

Clicking a pie wedge displays the Computer Hardware Information Prompt report. The subreport item should be populated with a chart of all computer models for that specific manufacturer, and the table item should provide a list of every system from that manufacturer. Ensure that the reports are working as detailed before proceeding.

Demonstrating Custom Color Palettes

The purpose of this demonstration is to practice creating custom color palettes and applying the colors both in a cycle and for specific values. For these demonstrations, you will update both the previously created Patch Compliance Progression Chart and Computer Hardware Information Chart reports. Ensure that these reports are up to date from previous demonstrations and are working as intended before continuing.

Applying a Custom Color Palette to Cycle Through Color Codes

For this demonstration, using the Patch Compliance Progression Chart.rdl report, add a custom color palette with color codes of your choice. This color palette should cycle through all specified colors. Set the pie chart's color value to the newly created color palette.

Remember to preview the report to ensure that the color palette is properly applied to the chart item, as you will not see any indication while in Design mode. Specify enough unique colors to reduce the number of times the same colors are repeated in the chart.

Applying a Custom Color Palette Based on Values

Modify the previously created Computer Hardware Information Chart.rdl report by adding a custom color palette. The color code function should display a specific unique color for each manufacturer name value in the chart.

Run the report and take note of all manufacturers returned in the report. Then create your color code function, associating each manufacturer with a unique color. Set the pie chart's color value to the newly created color palette, using an expression, as demonstrated in the "Setting Custom Color Codes by Value" section of this chapter.

When you are finished, preview the report to validate that the colors specified for each manufacturer are displayed correctly.

Demonstrating Adding Reports to SSRS

The purpose of this demonstration is to add the reports created throughout the book to your SSRS website. This will help you become familiar with the different methods of manually adding reports, publishing reports, and setting subscriptions in SSRS for your environment. At the end of this demonstration, you should have a good understanding of the benefits and effort involved with each method and should be able to determine the best approach for your environment.

Manually Adding Reports to the SSRS Website

For this section of the demonstration, manually add the reports listed below to your SSRS website. Begin by creating a new folder under the ConfigMgr_<*SiteCode*> folder in SSRS. Set a name for this folder. Manually add the following reports to the folder by using the Upload File button in SSRS:

- ▶ Patch Compliance Progression.rdl

- ▶ Patch Compliance Progression Chart.rdl

- ▶ Patch Compliance Progression Details.rdl

- ▶ Detailed Computer Information.rdl

Run each report to ensure that there are no errors and to ensure that the reports display properly. Remember that you need to modify the data sources value of each report once it is added to SSRS for it to run without errors. When running the report, try clicking the actions on items within the report to ensure that they function as expected; for example, click a system name in the Patch Compliance Progression report to verify that the Patch Compliance Progression Details report is displayed without further prompts.

Publishing Reports to SSRS

For this demonstration, you will update the SSDT-BI project properties to allow publishing of reports directly to SSRS. Begin by opening the project properties page. Set the report configuration to **Release** (by clicking the Configuration Manager icon). On the properties page, set the TargetServerURL value to your SSRS Web Service URL and the TargetReportFolder value to the folder path of the new folder created in the previous demonstration (see "Manually Adding Reports to the SSRS Website"). Before publishing reports to SSRS, publish the shared data source. Then publish the following reports to SSRS:

- ▶ Computer Hardware Information.rdl

- ▶ Computer Hardware Information Prompt.rdl

- ▶ Computer Hardware Information Chart.rdl

- ▶ Hardware Model Chart.rdl

8

Open the SSRS website and run each report to ensure that there are no errors and to ensure that each report displays properly. When running a report, try clicking the actions on items within the report to ensure that they function as expected; for example, click a pie wedge in the Computer Hardware Information Chart report to verify that the Computer Hardware Information Prompt report is displayed and the Subreport item is populated without errors or further prompts.

Creating a Subscription

For this part of the demonstration, add a subscription to one of the newly added reports of your choice at the SSRS website. To add the subscription, hover over a report title from the folder view, click the downward arrow that appears beside the name, and select **Manage**. On the **Subscriptions** tab, create a new Windows File Share subscription. Have the subscription create a PDF format of the report and store it on a share. (If you do not have a share available, create one on your ConfigMgr server for test purposes.) Enter the user name and password for an account that has read and write access to the share. Set the subscription schedule to run once and enter a start time a few minutes ahead of your current time. Remember, if you are using a published report instead of a manually added report, you must modify the data source on the report before creating the subscription.

Summary

This chapter has discussed many advanced features available in SSRS reports to help you create a more complete and enhanced reader experience. You have learned how to enable readers to view high-level reports and then seamlessly drillthrough to more detailed and specific reports by adding actions on report items. With SSRS reports you can also link software updates to Microsoft Knowledge Base articles. In this chapter you have also learned how to create custom color palettes for reports and apply them to items such as charts. In addition, you have learned how to define custom colors for specific values and how to apply custom colors to any report item, such as table rows.

You have already created many reports throughout the book. This chapter has explained and demonstrated how to make these reports available from an SSRS website. The chapter has discussed different methods for this, and the demonstrations at the end of the chapter have provided opportunities to both manually add reports to the SSRS website individually and publish reports from the SSDT-BI tool directly to SSRS. Once reports are added to SSRS, you can create subscriptions to allow users to automatically receive reports either by email or by retrieving them from a network share.

Role-Based Administration and Reporting

Role-based administration (RBA), first introduced with Configuration Manager (ConfigMgr) 2012, enables you to restrict who can administer specific features and who can access, view, or deploy to a collection. Restricted access to collections means that a ConfigMgr administrator might only be allowed to see a particular set of computers or users. Starting with ConfigMgr 2012 R2, reports also have the ability to leverage RBA.

You used RBA in Chapter 2, "Installing and Configuring Configuration Manager Reporting," to create a security role for a software updates report. You also used RBA with two collections (All Workstations and All Servers) to restrict users in Active Directory (AD) security groups (CM16 Report Reader - Software Updates - Server and CM16 Report Reader - Software Updates - Workstation) to see only their respective devices. You accomplished this by creating a security role to view software updates and then restricting that role to see only members of the All Workstations collection. In Chapter 2 you also learned about creating a second ConfigMgr security group to view members of the All Servers collection with an AD security group. RBA can be a powerful tool for limiting access in ConfigMgr.

In order to leverage RBA within your reports, you need to make several changes to your query, report prompts, and the report itself. This chapter steps through the details of converting a query to be RBA compliant and adjusting report prompts and reports to ensure that RBA is used. It also includes tips on how to avoid the most common mistakes for both SQL Server Data Tools 2014 Business Intelligence (SSDT-BI) for Visual Studio 2013 and the SQL Server Reporting Services (SSRS) website, and it discusses performance of RBA queries, best practices, and tips to improve performance.

How Role-Based Administration and Reporting Work

Before converting a SQL query so that it leverages RBA, let's discuss how SSRS reporting and RBA work together. Here's what the process looks like:

1. As with non-RBA reports, a user browses to the SSRS site http://<*SSRS servername*>/ Reports, which automatically forwards to http://<*SSRS servername*>/Reports/Pages/ Folder.aspx.

2. The user is presented with folders to which he has access (as shown in Figure 9.1). What the user doesn't see at this point is that in the background he is automatically logging onto the SSRS server.

> **TIP: AUTOMATIC LOGON TO SSRS**
>
> The automatic logon to the SSRS site is controlled by a security setting in the browser. If you are forced to logon each time you visit the SSRS site, you can adjust this setting. For more details on this and other settings, see the "RBA Tips and Troubleshooting" section, later in this chapter.

3. Once the user selects a report, two hidden cascading prompts execute before showing the user any additional prompts:

   ▶ The first prompt, UserTokenSIDs, gathers the report user's name and domain and passes these details to a ConfigMgr report server DLL, SrsResources.dll, which in turn converts the information into a list of security identifiers (SIDs).

   ▶ The second prompt, UserSIDs, compares the list of SIDs to the list of security groups and users with access to ConfigMgr. This information is used to limit a user's access within SSRS.

4. Once the UserSIDs details are collected, this information is used by each query to limit access to what that user can see in SSRS reporting. The only information returned as part of the query is what the user has access to in the console.

5. From this point on, SSRS runs much like any other report without ConfigMgr RBA.

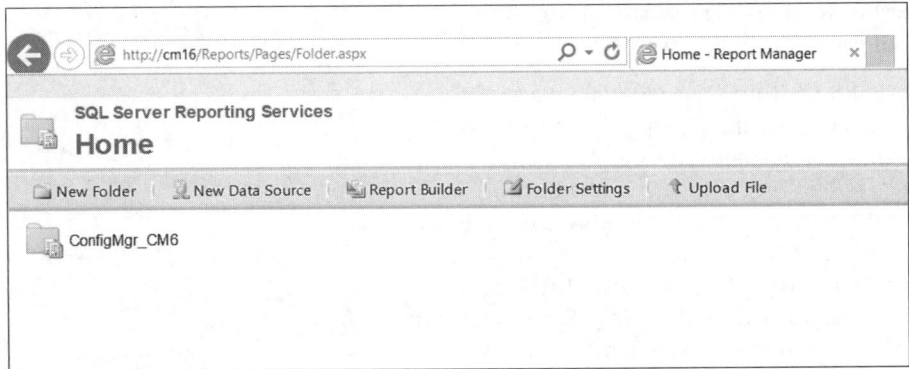

FIGURE 9.1   A sample SSRS home page.

Using SQL Queries with RBA

The following sections break down the discussion of SQL queries into two areas: converting a SQL query to a ConfigMgr RBA SQL query and testing a ConfigMgr RBA SQL query.

Converting a SQL Query to a ConfigMgr RBA SQL Query

As discussed in Chapter 4, "Transact-SQL Primer," and Chapter 7, "Intermediate Reporting Concepts," you should always start with a query and build on it to create the report you want. You need to follow this guideline when creating RBA queries.

Chapter 3, "Understanding Configuration Manager Data," discussed the SQL views used to create ConfigMgr queries. Since SQL views have no automatic method of filtering data based on parameters, ConfigMgr creates parallel table-value functions for each of the SQL views that can be using in ConfigMgr reporting. This means the user security identifier (SID) information can be used to limit what information a user can see based on his or her SIDs. This is also exactly the same data that the user would see in the ConfigMgr console.

The RBA functions all have names related to the SQL view, with the v_ in the SQL view being replaced with fn_rbac_, and (@UserSIDs) appended to the end of a SQL view name. For example, to convert v_R_System to its RBA function name, first remove the v_ and replace it with fn_rbac_ and then append (@UserSIDs), to come up with fn_rbac_R_System(@UserSIDs).

Table 9.1 through Table 9.8 repeat the view information from tables in Chapter 3 but now convert those views to their RBA counterparts. Please see the descriptions in Chapter 3 for what each SQL view and corresponding RBA function does.

To convert a standard query to RBA, you need only change the FROM section. For example, Listing 9.1 shows Listing 3.5 in Chapter 3 modified to an RBA query. Note the use of RBA functions instead of SQL views.

TABLE 9.1   Discovery Data Views

SQL View	RBA Function
v_R_System	fn_rbac_R_System(@UserSIDs)
v_R_User	fn_rbac_R_User(@UserSIDs)
v_R_System_Valid	fn_rbac_R_System_Valid(@UserSIDs)

TABLE 9.2   Current Hardware Data Views

SQL View	RBA Function
v_GS_COMPUTER_SYSTEM	fn_rbac_GS_COMPUTER_SYSTEM(@UserSIDs)
v_GS_DISK	fn_rbac_GS_DISK(@UserSIDs)
v_GS_ADD_REMOVE_PROGRAMS	fn_rbac_GS_ADD_REMOVE_PROGRAMS(@UserSIDs)
v_GS_ADD_REMOVE_PROGRAMS_64	fn_rbac_GS_ADD_REMOVE_PROGRAMS_64(@UserSIDs)

9

TABLE 9.3   History Hardware Data Views

SQL View	RBA Function
v_HS_COMPUTER_SYSTEM	fn_rbac_HS_COMPUTER_SYSTEM(@UserSIDs)
v_HS_DISK	fn_rbac_HS_DISK(@UserSIDs)
v_HS_ADD_REMOVE_PROGRAMS	fn_rbac_HS_ADD_REMOVE_PROGRAMS(@UserSIDs)
v_HS_ADD_REMOVE_PROGRAMS_64	fn_rbac_HS_ADD_REMOVE_PROGRAMS_64(@UserSIDs)

TABLE 9.4   Current Software Data Views

SQL View	RBA Function
v_GS_LastSoftwareScan	fn_rbac_GS_LastSoftwareScan(@UserSIDs)
v_GS_SoftwareFile	fn_rbac_GS_SoftwareFile(@UserSIDs)

TABLE 9.5   Software Update Data Views

SQL View	RBA Function
v_UpdateComplianceStatus	fn_rbac_UpdateComplianceStatus(@UserSIDs)
v_CategoryInfo	fn_rbac_CategoryInfo(@lcid, @UserSIDs) (Notice that language ID has been added to the function.)

TABLE 9.6   Software Metering Data Views

SQL View	RBA Function
v_MeterData	n/a - Use v_MeterData joined with fn_rbac_R_System_Valid(@UserSIDs)
v_MeteredProductRule	fn_rbac_MeteredProductRule(@UserSIDs)

TABLE 9.7   Status Message Data Views

SQL View	RBA Function
v_StatusMessage	fn_rbac_StatusMessage(@UserSIDs)
v_StatMsgAttributes	fn_rbac_StatMsgAttributes(@UserSIDs)
v_StatMsgInsStrings	fn_rbac_StatMsgInsStrings(@UserSIDs)

TABLE 9.8   Collection Data Views

SQL View	RBA Function
v_Collection	fn_rbac_Collection(@UserSIDs)
v_FullCollectionMembership	fn_rbac_FullCollectionMembership(@UserSIDs)

LISTING 9.1   Converted Software Update Sample Query

```
SELECT distinct
   CS.Name0,
   CS.UserName0,
   CASE
    when (sum(case when UCS.status=2 then 1 else 0 end))>0
     then ('Needs '+(cast(sum(case when UCS.status=2 then 1 else 0 end)
     as varchar(10))+ ' Patches'))
    else 'Good Client'
   end as 'Status',
   WS.lasthwscan as 'Last HW scan'
   FROM
   fn_rbac_UpdateComplianceStatus(@UserSIDs) as UCS
   LEFT OUTER JOIN fn_rbac_GS_COMPUTER_SYSTEM(@UserSIDs) as CS
    on CS.ResourceID = UCS.ResourceID
   JOIN fn_rbac_CICategories_All(@UserSIDs) as catall2
    on catall2.CI_ID = UCS.CI_ID
   JOIN fn_rbac_CategoryInfo(1033,@UserSIDs) as catinfo2
    on catall2.CategoryInstance_UniqueID = catinfo2.CategoryInstance_UniqueID
    and catinfo2.CategoryTypeName = 'UpdateClassification'
   LEFT JOIN fn_rbac_GS_WORKSTATION_STATUS(@UserSIDs) as WS
    on ws.resourceid = CS.ResourceID
   LEFT JOIN fn_rbac_FullCollectionMembership(@UserSIDs) as FCM
    on FCM.ResourceID = CS.ResourceID
   WHERE
   UCS.Status = '2'
   and FCM.CollectionID = 'SMS00001'
   GROUP BY
   CS.Name0,
   CS.UserName0,
   WS.lasthwscan,
   FCM.CollectionID
   ORDER BY
   CS.Name0,
   CS.UserName0
```

NOTE: HARDCODING THE LANGUAGE CODE

As previously identified in Table 9.5, the `fn_rbac_CategoryInfo(@lcid, @UserSIDs)` function takes an additional field for language code. This can be hardcoded to English by typing 1033, as shown in Listing 9.1.

Testing a ConfigMgr RBA SQL Query

After you convert a query to be RBA compliant, the authors recommend that you test it in SQL Server Management Studio before importing it into SSDT-BI. This allows you to ensure that the query results and the performance of the query are working in a manner acceptable to you. In addition, it is easier to troubleshoot the query in SQL Server Management Studio than in SSDT-BI. However, if RBA queries use UserSID details, how do you determine what UserSIDs to use to test those queries? To help answer this question, the authors provide a report you can utilize that displays this information. Follow these steps to use the report:

1. Download www.enhansoft.com/downloads/cm12/siddetails.zip from the Enhansoft website.

2. Upload the SIDDetails RDL from the zip file to your ConfigMgr SSRS site. Chapter 8, "SSRS Reporting Features," provides information on how to do this.

3. Using the user account with which you want to test your RBA query, browse to your SSRS site and view the SID Details report. Figure 9.2 shows an example of this report.

4. Copy the CM12 user SIDs text from the report.

5. Using the RBA query in Listing 9.1, add and define the @UserSIDs as a varchar(max) variable to the query. The final result should look similar to Listing 9.2.

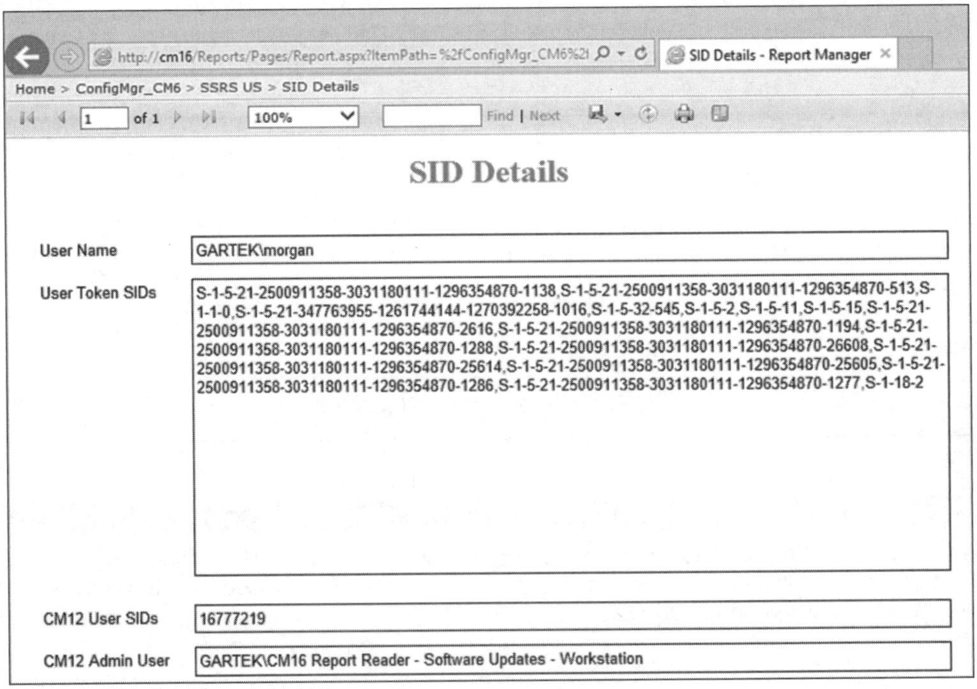

FIGURE 9.2   ConfigMgr SID details for test user account.

TIP: COLLECTIONID AND SMS00001

Generally, when you create an RBA security role, you apply that security role to a group or user and limit the group's or user's access to a particular collection of computers or users. In Listing 9.2, SMS00001 is the CollectionID for the All Systems collection, and CM600016 is a custom-created collection used to enable a user to view only computers with that particular collection. If a user does not have access to a collection such as All Systems, as in Listing 9.1, he does not see any results, so you should change to the CollectionID to a collection to which that user has access—for example, CM600016 in Listing 9.2—or, better yet, turn this hardcoded CollectionID into an RBA prompt.

LISTING 9.2   RBA Software Update Sample Query

```
Declare @UserSIDs as varchar(Max) =
'16777219'

SELECT distinct
 CS.Name0,
 CS.UserName0,
 CASE
  when (sum(case when UCS.status=2 then 1 else 0 end))>0
   then ('Needs '+(cast(sum(case when UCS.status=2 then 1 else 0 end)
   as varchar(10))+ ' Patches'))
  else 'Good Client'
 end as 'Status',
 WS.lasthwscan as 'Last HW scan'
FROM
 fn_rbac_UpdateComplianceStatus(@UserSIDs) as UCS
 LEFT OUTER JOIN fn_rbac_GS_COMPUTER_SYSTEM(@UserSIDs) as CS
  on CS.ResourceID = UCS.ResourceID
 JOIN fn_rbac_CICategories_All(@UserSIDs) as catall2
  on catall2.CI_ID = UCS.CI_ID
 JOIN fn_rbac_CategoryInfo(1033,@UserSIDs) as catinfo2
  on catall2.CategoryInstance_UniqueID = catinfo2.CategoryInstance_UniqueID
  and catinfo2.CategoryTypeName = 'UpdateClassification'
 LEFT JOIN fn_rbac_GS_WORKSTATION_STATUS(@UserSIDs) as WS
  on ws.resourceid = CS.ResourceID
 LEFT JOIN fn_rbac_FullCollectionMembership(@UserSIDs) as FCM
  on FCM.ResourceID = CS.ResourceID
WHERE
 UCS.Status = '2'
 and FCM.CollectionID = 'CM600016'
GROUP BY
 CS.Name0,
 CS.UserName0,
 WS.lasthwscan,
 FCM.CollectionID
```

9

LISTING 9.2   RBA Software Update Sample Query

```
ORDER BY
  CS.Name0,
  CS.UserName0
```

When you execute this query in SQL Server Management Studio, you see all the computers to which this user and his security group have access. Figure 9.3 shows sample results.

> **TIP: CHANGING @USERSIDS TO DISABLED**
>
> To confirm that a query works correctly regardless of which user executes it or has object access, change the @UserSIDs variable to 'Disabled'. This tells RBA queries to return all information and not to filter on what the user should see in the results.
>
> ```
> Declare @UserSIDs as varchar(Max) = 'Disabled'
> ```

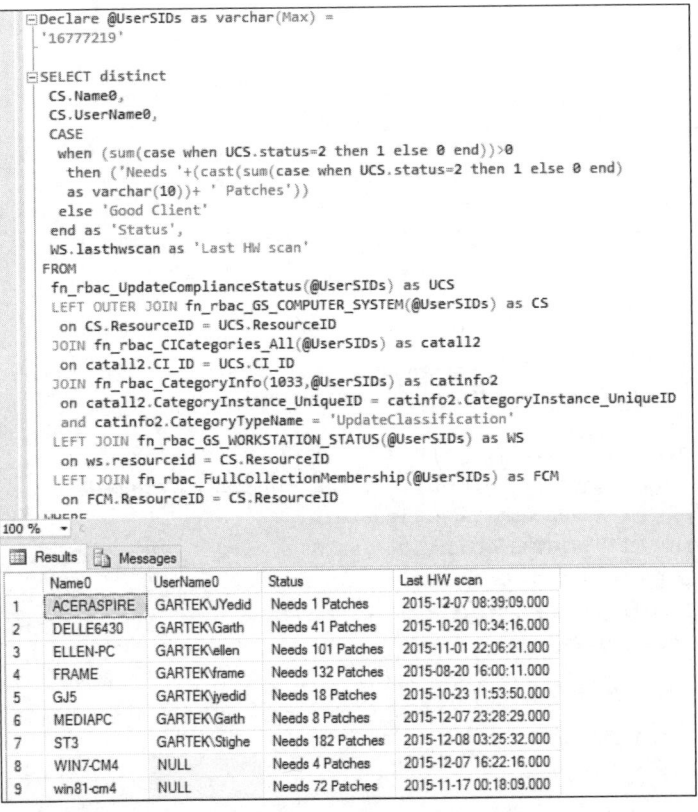

FIGURE 9.3   Results from an RBA query.

Using Reports and RBA

So far in this chapter you have learned how to convert a standard query to a ConfigMgr RBA query. This section completes the process, showing you how to update the Patch Compliance Progression report from Chapter 6 to be a RBA report. Once the RBA report is complete, you can use the ConfigMgr security roles created in Chapter 2 to limit the computers about which the report will provide information.

Updating SSDT-BI for RBA

Earlier, the "How Role-Based Administration and Reporting Work" section of this chapter discussed how the user name is gathered by a built-in SSRS function as part of the report execution. The user name is then passed to a ConfigMgr DLL called SrsResources.dll. In order to make use of this DLL in SSDT-BI, you first need to copy it to a workstation that has SSDT-BI installed. Based on the version of SSDT-BI or SQL Server Business Intelligence Development Studio (BIDS) being used, the DLL must be copied to the correct location in order for SSDT-BI or BIDS to leverage it for report previews.

The SrsResources.dll file is located at the root of your ConfigMgr reporting point folder. The default location is *%ProgramFiles%\SMS_SRSRP*.

After locating the SrsResources.dll, copy the DLL to the appropriate folder location. Table 9.9 provides details.

TABLE 9.9   PrivateAssemblies Location for Each Version of SSDT-BI and BIDS

SSDT-BI and BIDS Versions	Report Builder
SSDT-BI 2014 for Visual Studio 2013	*%ProgramFiles(x86)%*\Microsoft Visual Studio 12.0\Common7\IDE\PrivateAssemblies
SSDT-BI 2012 for Visual Studio 2012	*%ProgramFiles(x86)%*\Microsoft Visual Studio 11.0\Common7\IDE\PrivateAssemblies
BIDS 2008 R2	*%ProgramFiles(x86)%*\Microsoft Visual Studio 10.0\Common7\IDE\PrivateAssemblies
BIDS 2008	*%ProgramFiles(x86)%*\Microsoft Visual Studio 9.0\Common7\IDE\PrivateAssemblies
BIDS 2005	*%ProgramFiles(x86)%*\Microsoft Visual Studio 8\Common7\IDE\PrivateAssemblies

Now edit RSPreviewPolicy.config within the PrivateAssemblies folder and add a `CodeGroup` block (provided in Listing 9.3 and available as online content as CodeGroup.txt; see Appendix C, "Available Online") at the top of the `CodeGroup` section, as shown in Figure 9.4.

LISTING 9.3   `CodeGroup` Entry for RSPreviewPolicy.Config

```
<CodeGroup
  class="UnionCodeGroup"
  version="1"
  PermissionSetName="FullTrust"
```

LISTING 9.3   `CodeGroup` Entry for RSPreviewPolicy.Config

```
Name="Microsoft ConfigMgr Reporting Code Assembly"
Description=
    "Grants the ConfigMgr Reporting Code assembly full trust permission.">
    <IMembershipCondition class="AllMembershipCondition" version="1" />
</CodeGroup>
```

TIP: ACCESSING A PROTECTED FOLDER

Since the PrivateAssemblies folder is under the Program Files (x86) folder, and Program Files (x86) and all subfolders are considered protected folders, you must run Windows Notepad or your favorite text editor in elevated mode. When you do this, you can save the RSPreviewPolicy.Config file in the PrivateAssemblies folder.

This is a one-time set of tasks for each computer using SSDT-BI; you will not need to perform these tasks again.

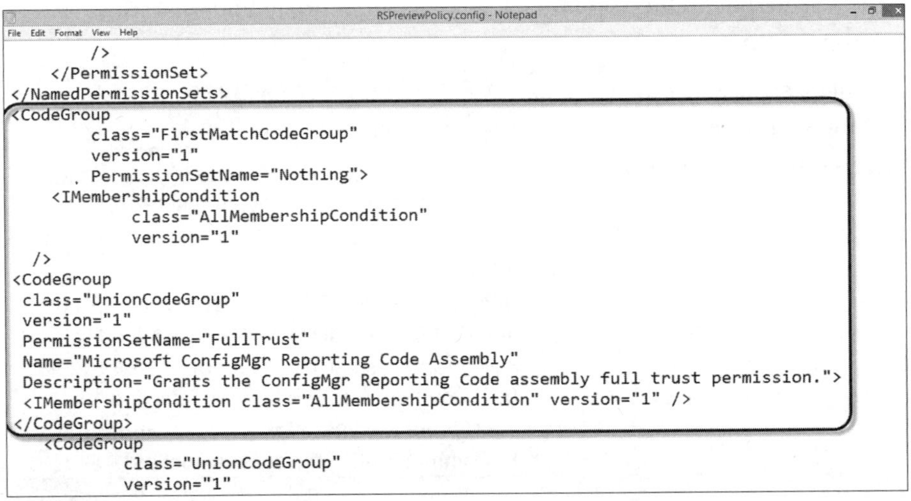

FIGURE 9.4   `CodeGroup` block added to the `CodeGroup` section in RSPreviewPolicy.Config.

Adding the DLL to a Report

After you add the SrsResources.dll file to SSDT-BI and "tie" it to a report, SSDT-BI can leverage it. Perform the following steps to reference the SrsResources.dll file within an existing report in an existing SSDT-BI project:

1. In SSDT-BI, select **Report -> Report Properties**, as shown in Figure 9.5.

2. In the Report Properties dialog, select the **References** node, as shown in Figure 9.6.

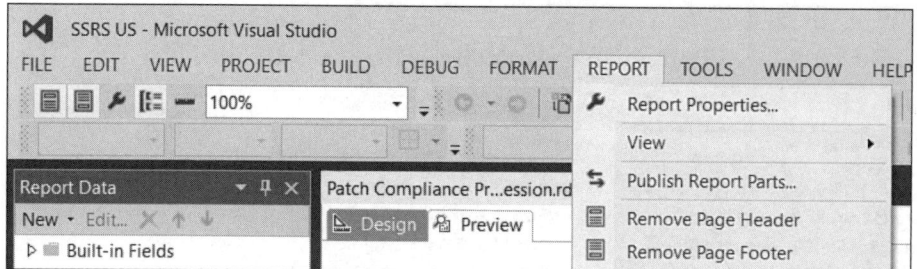

FIGURE 9.5   Selecting the **Report Properties** menu item.

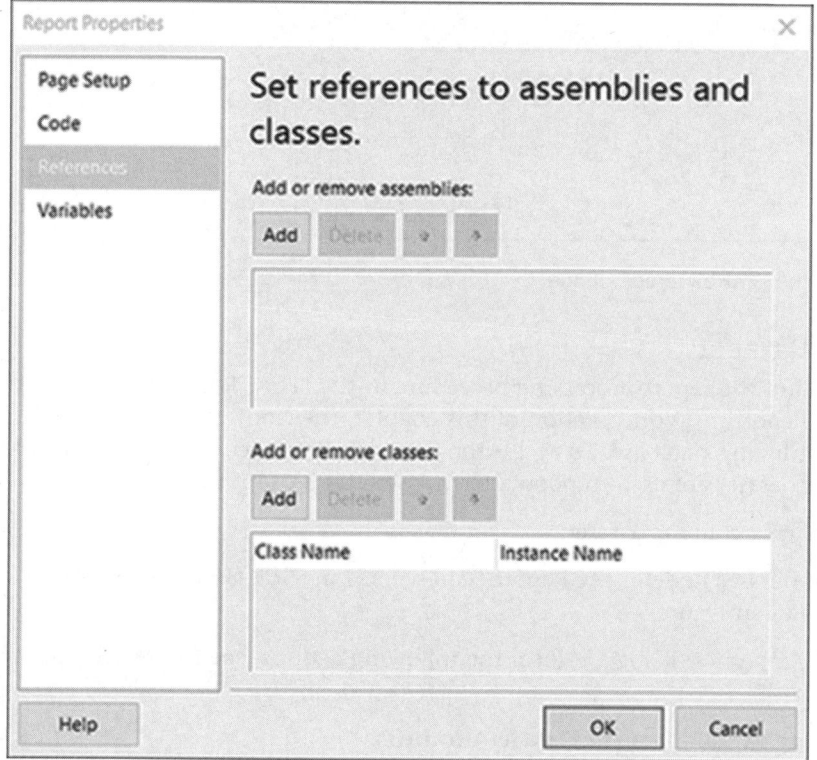

FIGURE 9.6   References node in the Report Properties dialog.

3. Click **Add** in the Add or remove assemblies section.

4. Click the ... **button**.

5. In the Add Reference dialog, click **Browse** and locate the SrsResources.dll file, as shown in Figure 9.7. Click **OK** twice to return to Report Designer.

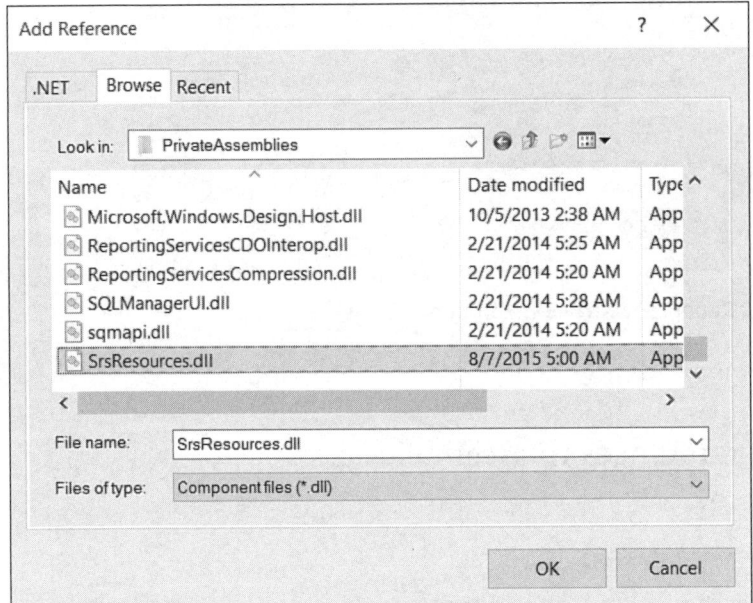

FIGURE 9.7   Adding the SrsResources.dll file.

Adding an RBA Dataset

As indicated in step 3 of the report-processing procedure in the "How Role-Based Administration and Reporting Work" section of this chapter, the ConfigMgr UserSID is queried from the ConfigMgr database. To access the database, you need to create a dataset. The results from this dataset are used to populate the UserSIDs prompt variable.

Follow these steps to create a new dataset:

1. Right-click the Dataset node in the Report Data section in SSDT-BI and select **Add Dataset**, as shown in Figure 9.8.

2. In the Dataset Properties dialog, perform the following actions (see Figure 9.9) and then click **OK**:

   ▶ Change the dataset name to **DataSetAdminID**.

   ▶ Select **Use a dataset embedded in my report**.

   ▶ Select the existing data source from the dropdown menu.

   ▶ Paste the text from Listing 9.4 into the Query section.

LISTING 9.4   Query to determine ConfigMgr UserSIDs

```
SELECT dbo.fn_rbac_GetAdminIDsfromUserSIDs(@UserTokenSIDs)
        as UserSIDs
```

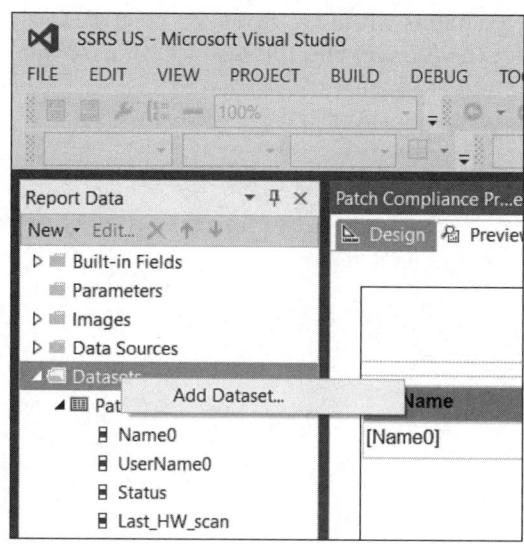

FIGURE 9.8   Adding a dataset.

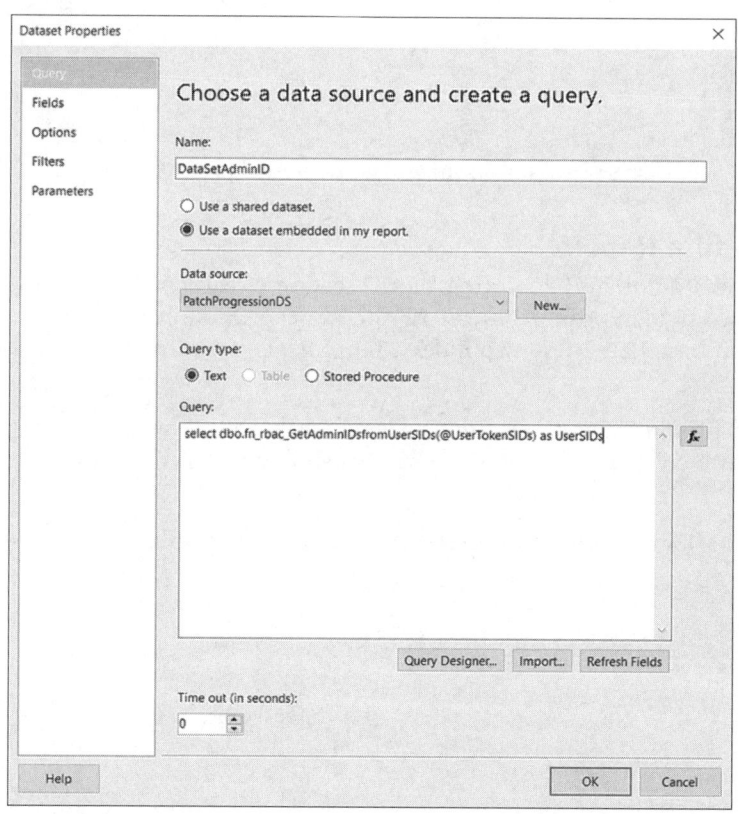

FIGURE 9.9   Specifying dataset properties for DataSetAdminID.

With these steps complete, there should be two datasets within your report. Your dataset should look similar to Figure 9.10—one for your main query and the second to query the UserSIDs details.

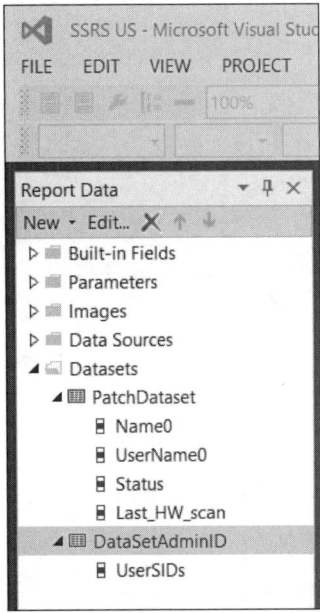

FIGURE 9.10 Two datasets with DataSetAdminID included.

Adding RBA Prompts to a Report

The "How Role-Based Administration and Reporting Work" section of this chapter mentioned that there are two hidden prompts in the RBA report execution process. This section discusses how to add or update these two hidden prompts. Perform the following steps:

1. In the Report Data section in SSDT-BI, expand the Parameters node. The DataSetAdminID dataset created in the previous section should be listed, as shown in Figure 9.11.

2. Right-click **UserTokenSIDs** and select **Parameter Properties**, as shown in Figure 9.12.

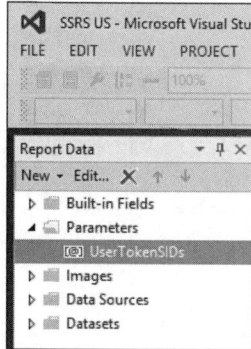

FIGURE 9.11   UserTokenSIDs parameter.

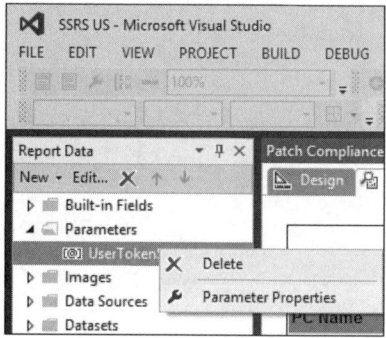

FIGURE 9.12   Setting the UserTokenSIDs parameters properties.

3. In the General tab of the Report Parameter Properties dialog, change the Select parameter visibility to **Internal**, as shown in Figure 9.13.

4. Select the **Default Values** node, select the **Specify values** radio button, click **Add**, and paste the following text into the Value area (as shown in Figure 9.14):

```
=SrsResources.UserIdentity.GetUserSIDs(User!UserID)
```

Click **OK.**

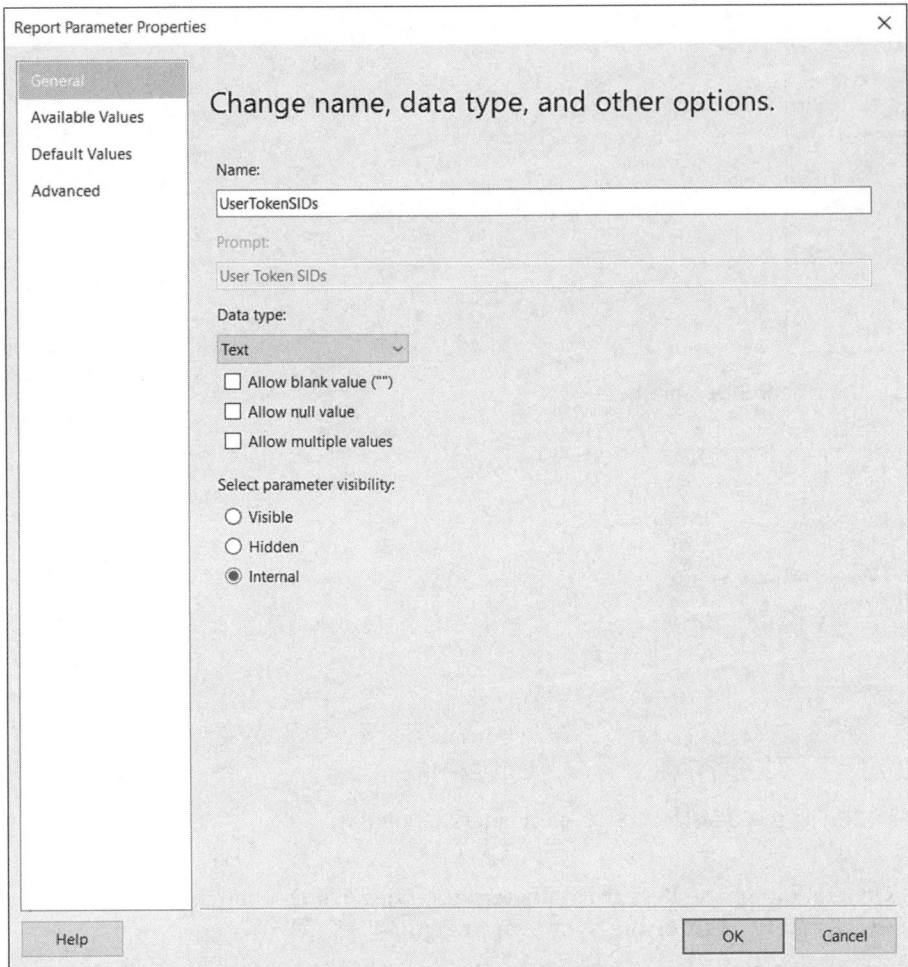

FIGURE 9.13   Configuring the internal prompt setting.

5. With the first prompt now updated, create a second prompt as described in Chapter 7. As you create this new prompt, do the following:

   ▶ Name the prompt **UserSIDs**.

   ▶ Set the visibility to **Internal**.

   ▶ On the Default values node, select **Get values from a query**.

   ▶ Select **DataSetAdminID** for the dataset.

   ▶ Select **UserSIDs** for the Value field.

The Default node should look like the one in Figure 9.15.

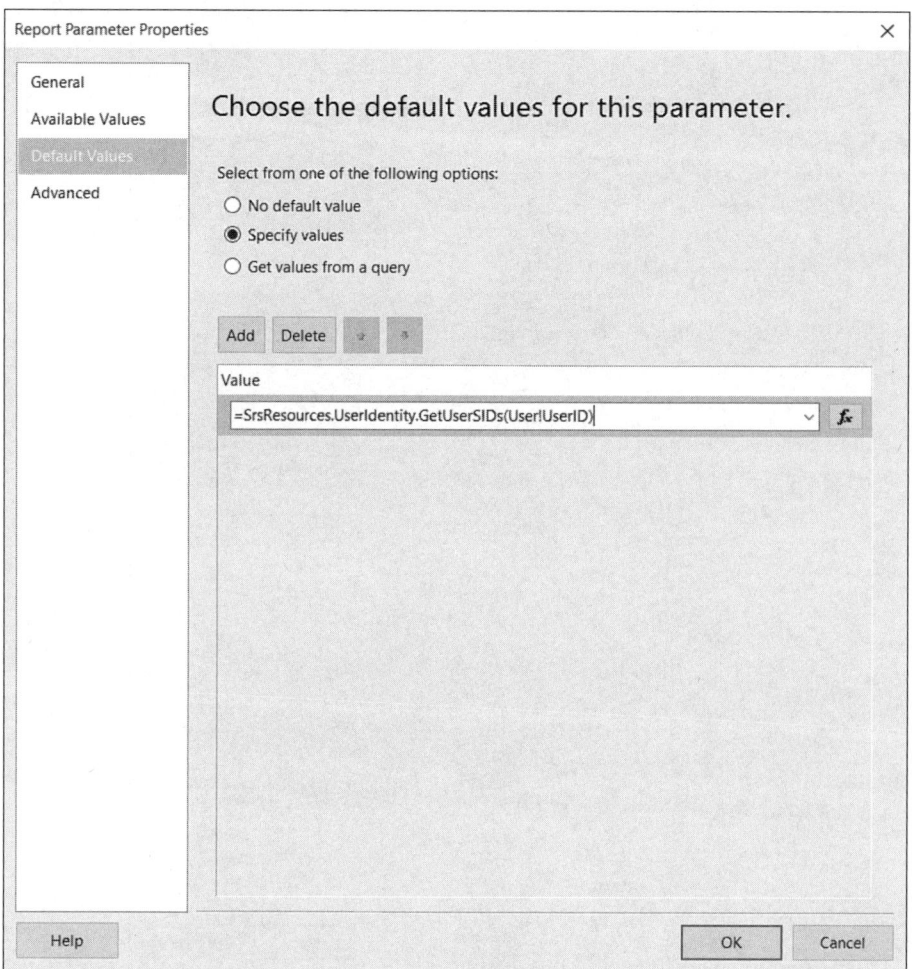

FIGURE 9.14   Viewing the Default Values node.

Now that you have created an RBA report, you can preview it in SSDT-BI, as shown in Figure 9.16.

TIP: CREATING RBA TEMPLATES

Use this RBA report to create three RBA templates (8.5×11, 11×8.5, and 14×8.5). This will save you time and effort later, as you will not have to perform these tasks on new reports.

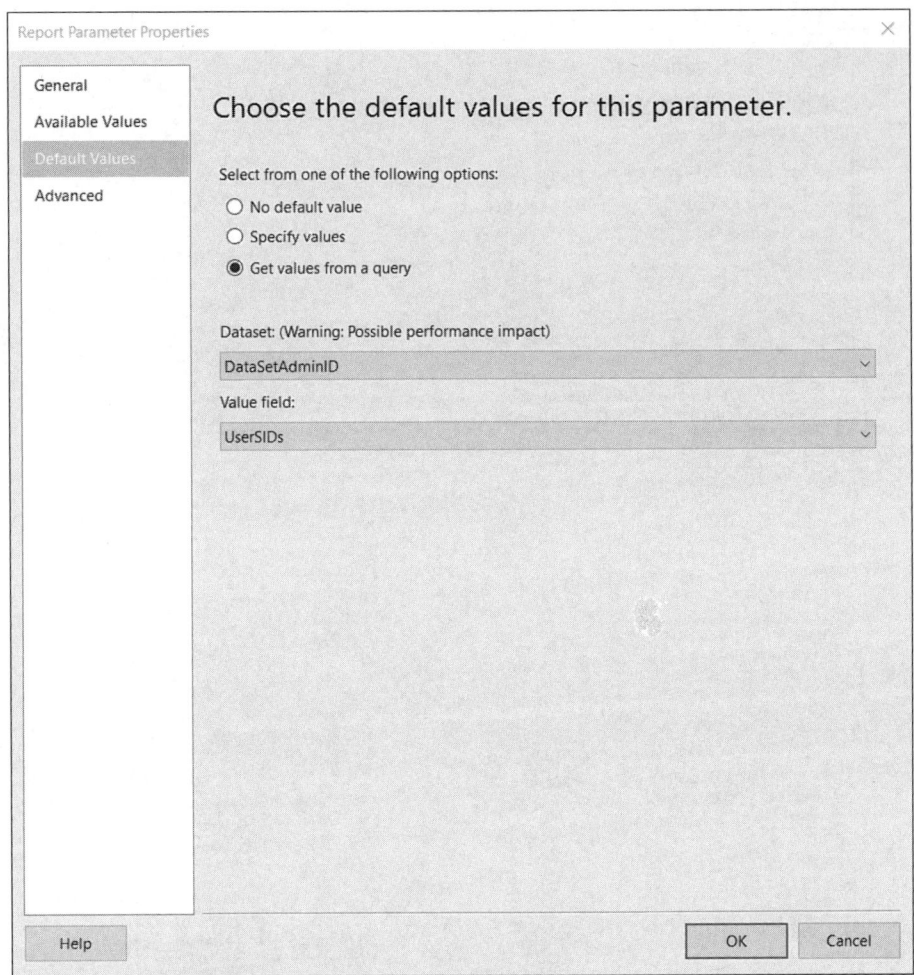

FIGURE 9.15   Viewing the UserSIDs Default Values node.

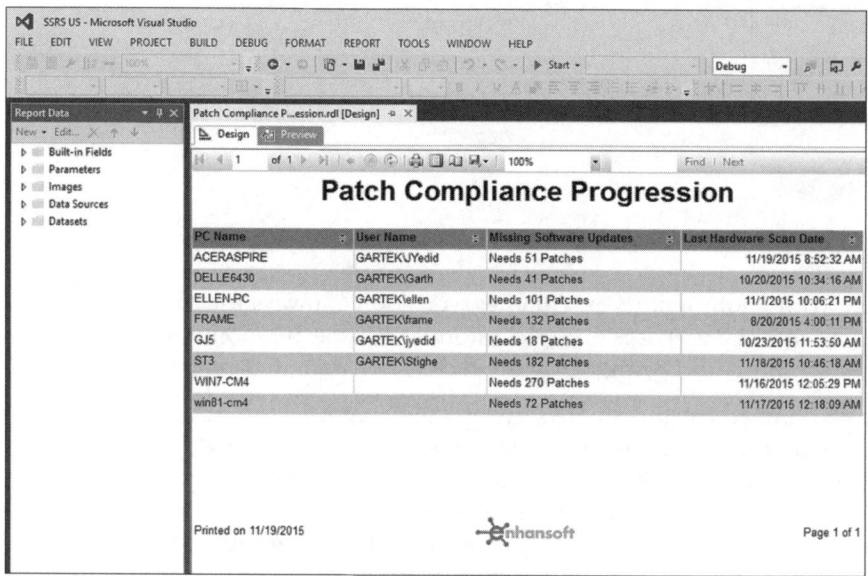

FIGURE 9.16   RBA report previewed in SSDT-BI.

RBA Tips and Troubleshooting

As with many other topics, the authors have tips and troubleshooting information for RBA. RBA reporting can be broken down into several sections: RBA role configuration within the ConfigMgr console, SQL queries, and SSRS reports. This book is not primarily about RBA role configurations, although Chapter 2 discussed creating a ConfigMgr RBA role to limit access to software update reports for the All Workstations collection. The following sections discuss RBA SQL query performance tips and troubleshooting, followed by SSRS report tips and troubleshooting.

RBA SQL Query Performance

Because RBA queries use table-value functions in their execution, there is additional overhead when running these queries against your ConfigMgr database. In many cases, this overhead is not very noticeable when the query is executed; however, particularly with software update queries, the overhead can be considerable. Notice in Figure 9.17 the execution times of 2 seconds (right arrow) for a non-RBA query and 32 seconds (left arrow) for the second query, which is an RBA query. The larger the environment, the longer both of these queries will take to run. This is one of the reasons you should test your queries in SQL Server Management Studio prior to creating a report. There are other reasons for executing your query in SQL Server Management Studio as well:

▶ You can check for syntax errors.

▶ You can confirm that the query produces the expected results.

▶ SQL Server Management Studio is easier to use for query design than SSDT-BI.

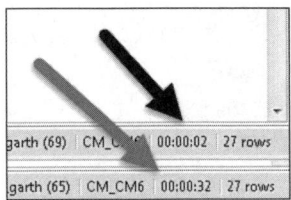

FIGURE 9.17   Non-RBA versus RBA query execution times.

Recall that when writing RBA reports and queries, you should always use the RBA functions to ensure that the user sees only the information that he should see—whether that be computer inventory or ConfigMgr items such as software update groups.

Chapter 2 discussed how to create a single security role to allow access to all software update information and how to apply that role to two ConfigMgr collections: All Workstations and All Servers. Review Listing 9.2 and notice that all SQL views have been changed to their corresponding RBA functions. You may also notice that there are a number of RBA functions that redundantly filter RBA results. For example, the following list of RBA functions controls what computers a user can see:

▶ fn_rbac_UpdateComplianceStatus(@UserSIDs)

▶ fn_rbac_GS_COMPUTER_SYSTEM(@UserSIDs)

▶ fn_rbac_GS_WORKSTATION_STATUS(@UserSIDs)

▶ fn_rbac_FullCollectionMembership(@UserSIDs)

Say that you mixed both RBA functions and SQL views to reduce this overhead by allowing only one RBA function per ConfigMgr object type—in this case, computer and software updates, as per Listing 9.5. Figure 9.18 shows that the execution time drops to 12 seconds (left arrow) when using Listing 9.5 but does not follow the guidelines listed earlier in this section for writing RBA queries.

LISTING 9.5   Mixed RBA Software Update Sample Query

```
SELECT distinct
  CS.Name0,
  CS.UserName0,
  CASE
   when (sum(case when UCS.status=2 then 1 else 0 end))>0
    then ('Needs '+(cast(sum(case when UCS.status=2 then 1 else 0 end)
    as varchar(10))+ ' Patches'))
    else 'Good Client'
   end as 'Status',
  WS.lasthwscan as 'Last HW scan'
FROM
  fn_rbac_UpdateComplianceStatus(@UserSIDs) as UCS
```

LISTING 9.5   Mixed RBA Software Update Sample Query

```
  LEFT OUTER JOIN v_GS_COMPUTER_SYSTEM as CS
    on CS.ResourceID = UCS.ResourceID
  JOIN fn_rbac_CICategories_All(@UserSIDs) as catall2
    on catall2.CI_ID = UCS.CI_ID
  JOIN v_CategoryInfo as catinfo2
    on catall2.CategoryInstance_UniqueID = catinfo2.CategoryInstance_UniqueID
    and catinfo2.CategoryTypeName = 'UpdateClassification'
  LEFT JOIN v_GS_WORKSTATION_STATUS as WS
    on ws.resourceid = CS.ResourceID
  LEFT JOIN v_FullCollectionMembership as FCM
    on FCM.ResourceID = CS.ResourceID
WHERE
  UCS.Status = '2'
  and FCM.CollectionID = 'CM600016'
GROUP BY
  CS.Name0,
  CS.UserName0,
  WS.lasthwscan,
  FCM.CollectionID
ORDER BY
  CS.Name0,
  CS.UserName0
```

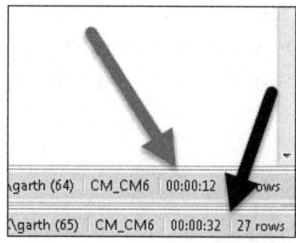

garth (64) | CM_CM6 | 00:00:12 | ows
garth (65) | CM_CM6 | 00:00:32 | 27 rows

FIGURE 9.18   Mixed RBA and non-RBA versus RBA query execution time.

Because RBA groups and users are limited to collections, consider whether a collection parameter was added to the report to allow a CollectionID to be selected from a prompt. The collection prompt shown in Listing 9.6 does not contain the necessary RBA functions. However, Listing 9.7 has been converted to an RBA query, removing the need for RBA limiting on computer devices in the main query.

Refer to Chapter 7 for more details on how to add a prompt to the query. Listing 9.6 provides an alphabetical list of all collection names and their collection IDs, regardless of the user's RBA scoping.

LISTING 9.6   Query for All Collection Names and IDs

```
SELECT
  Col.Name,
  Col.CollectionID
FROM
  v_Collection Col
ORDER BY
  Col.Name
```

Listing 9.7 provides a sorted list of all collection names and their collection IDs, limiting the returned collections based on the user's RBA scoping.

LISTING 9.7   RBA Query for Collection Names and IDs

```
SELECT
  Col.Name,
  Col.CollectionID
FROM
    fn_rbac_Collection(@UserSIDs) Col
ORDER BY
  Col.Name
```

Given that it is extremely rare to scope the software updates a user can see, if scoping what software updates a user can see is not necessary, you could remove the RBA on those ConfigMgr items as well. Ultimately, this would bring you back to Listing 3.5 from Chapter 3 with a prompt to enter a collection; the updated version of this is shown in Listing 9.8. This prompt limits the collections the user could see using RBA, and it changes the execution time in that query from 32 seconds to 2 seconds.

LISTING 9.8   Software Update Sample Query

```
SELECT DISTINCT
 CS.Name0,
 CS.UserName0,
 case
  when (sum(case when UCS.status=2 then 1 else 0 end))>0
   then ('Needs '+(cast(sum(case when UCS.status=2 then 1 else 0 end)
   as varchar(10))+ ' Patches'))
  else 'Good Client'
 end as 'Status',
 ws.lasthwscan as 'Last HW scan'
FROM
 dbo.v_UpdateComplianceStatus as UCS
 LEFT OUTER JOIN dbo.v_GS_COMPUTER_SYSTEM  as CS
  on CS.ResourceID = UCS.ResourceID
 INNER JOIN v_CICategories_All as catall2
```

LISTING 9.8   Software Update Sample Query

```
  on catall2.CI_ID = UCS.CI_ID
 INNER JOIN v_CategoryInfo as catinfo2
  on catall2.CategoryInstance_UniqueID = catinfo2.CategoryInstance_UniqueID
  and catinfo2.CategoryTypeName = 'UpdateClassification'
 LEFT OUTER JOIN v_gs_workstation_status as ws
  on ws.resourceid = CS.ResourceID
 LEFT OUTER JOIN dbo.v_FullCollectionMembership as FCM
  on FCM.ResourceID = CS.ResourceID
WHERE
 UCS.Status = '2'
 and FCM.CollectionID = @Coll
GROUP BY
 CS.Name0,
 CS.UserName0,
 ws.lasthwscan,
 FCM.CollectionID
ORDER BY
 CS.Name0,
  CS.UserName0
```

With the RBA query moved to the collection prompt, what is the effect on the execution time of the non-RBA collection prompt (Listing 9.6) versus using an RBA collection prompt (Listing 9.7)? This is one of those cases where the overhead would be unnoticed, as shown in Figure 9.19. In both cases, the query is so fast in SQL Server Management Studio that the results indicate that it took 0 seconds to complete!

By testing your RBA queries within SQL Server Management Studio and understanding how RBA functions, you can adjust your queries to be efficient without sacrificing or limiting how RBA was intended to work.

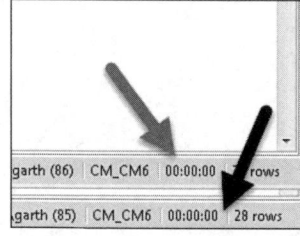

FIGURE 9.19   Execution times for Listings 9.6 and 9.7.

Troubleshooting and Errors

One of the most common issues you will see when viewing reports in SSRS is being prompted for a user name and password every time you access the ConfigMgr reporting site (see Figure 9.20). The steps to correct this issue vary from browser to browser; use the instructions in the section appropriate for your browser.

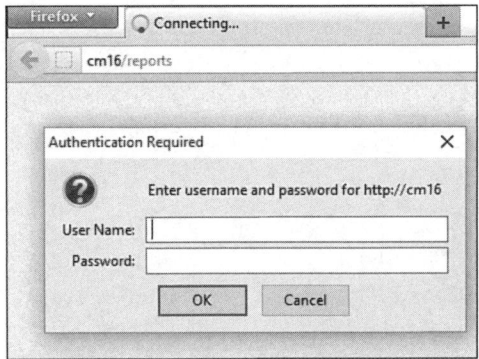

FIGURE 9.20   Prompt to access the SSRS website every time.

Automatically Logging In to SSRS in Internet Explorer
To automatically log in to SSRS using Internet Explorer, perform the following steps on each computer that accesses the SSRS website:

1. Open Internet Explorer and access **Tools -> Internet Options**.

2. Under Internet Options, select the Security tab.

3. Select **Local intranet -> Custom Level**.

4. Locate **User Authentication -> Logon** and select **Automatic logon only in Intranet zone** (see Figure 9.21). Click **OK** twice to return to Internet Explorer, accepting any warning message that arise.

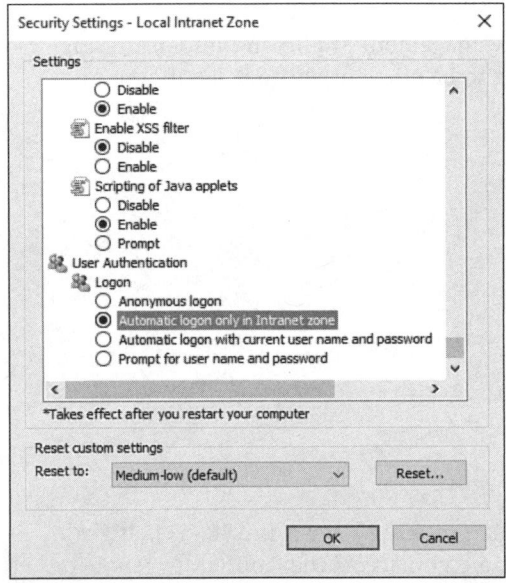

FIGURE 9.21   Security Settings - Local Intranet Zone for Internet Explorer.

Automatically Logging In to SSRS in Firefox

To automatically log in to SSRS using the Firefox browser, perform the following steps on each computer that accesses the SSRS website:

1. Open Firefox, type **about:config** in the address bar, and press Enter.

2. Enter **network.automatic-ntlm-auth.trusted-uri** in the search dialog.

3. Double-click the **network.automatic-ntlm-auth.trusted-uris** preference name.

4. In the Enter string value dialog, enter both the NetBIOS and FQDN URLs for your SSRS server, as a comma-separated list (see Figure 9.22).

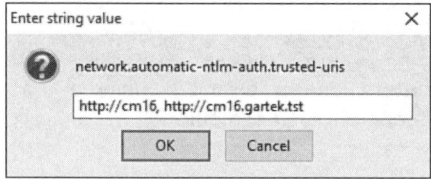

FIGURE 9.22   NetBIOS and FQDN URLs for Firefox trusted sites.

Automatically Logging In to SSRS in Chrome and Yandex

To automatically log in to SSRS using Chrome and Yandex browsers, the steps are the same. Perform the following steps on each computer that accesses the SSRS website using one of these browsers:

1. Open the browser and select the menu icon then **Settings**. Then, do one of the following, depending on the browser:

    ▶ Click the **Show advanced settings** link (in Chrome).

    ▶ Select the **Show advanced settings** check box (in Yandex).

2. Locate the Network section and click the **Change proxy settings** button.

3. On the Internet Properties page, selected the **Security** tab.

> **NOTE: ABOUT CHANGING INTERNET PROPERTIES**
>
> Note that the Internet Properties page is actually part of Internet Explorer settings, and therefore any changes you make within the Internet Properties page will affect Chrome, Opera, Yandex, and Internet Explorer.

4. Select the **Local intranet** zone and then click **Custom Level**.

5. Locate **User Authentication -> Logon** and select **Automatic logon only in Intranet zone**. Click **OK** twice to return to your browser, accepting any warning message that arise.

Automatically Logging In to SSRS in Opera

Opera browsers use Internet Explorer settings for automated logon settings. Perform the following steps on each computer that accesses the SSRS website using the Opera browser:

1. Open **Opera**, select the Opera menu, and then select **Settings**.

2. Locate the Network section and click **Change proxy settings**.

3. On the Internet Properties page, select the **Security** tab.

4. Select the **Local intranet** zone and then click **Custom Level**.

5. Locate **User Authentication** -> **Logon** and select **Automatic logon only in Intranet zone**. Click **OK** twice to return to Opera, accepting any warning message that arises.

REAL WORLD: USING GROUP POLICY OBJECTS

For many of the browsers discussed, you can set the automatic logon setting by using a Group Policy Object (GPO) instead of performing these steps on each computer.

Resolving the Error `Request for the permission of type 'System.Security.Permissions.SecurityPermission`

If you receive an error message similar to this, it likely means that you have not added `CodeGroup` to the RSPreviewPolicy.config found within in the PrivateAssemblies folder:

```
An error occurred during local report processing. The DefaultValue expression for
the report 'UserTokenSIDs' contains an error: Request for the permission of type
'System.Security.Premissions.SecurityPermission, mscorlib, Version=4.0.0.0,
Culture=neutral, PublicKeyToken=b77a5c561934e089' failed.
```

See the "Updating SSDT-BI for RBA" section of this chapter for more details.

Resolving the Error `'SrsResources' is not declared`

When you receive an error message similar to this one, it means that you have not added SRSResource.dll to the report:

```
An error occurred during the local report processing.
The definition of the report '/Patch Compliance Progression' is invalid.
The Value expression for the report parameter 'UserTokenSIDs' contains an error:
[BC30451] 'SrsResources' is not declared. It may be inaccessible due to its
protection level.
```

To resolve this error, see the "Adding the DLL to a Report" section of this chapter.

Resolving the Error `The system cannot find the file specified`

The following error message means that the SRSResouce.dll file is missing from the computer that is running the report:

```
An error occurred during the local report processing.
The definition of the report '/Patch Compliance Progression' is invalid.
```

```
Error while loading code module: 'SrsResources, Version=5.0.0.0, Culture=neutral,
PublicKeyToken=31bf3856ad364e35'. Details: Could not load file or assembly
'SrsResources, Version=5.0.0.0, Culture=neutral,
 PublicKeyToken=31bf3856ad364e35' or one of its dependencies.
The system cannot find the file specified.
```

To resolve this error, see the "Updating SSDT-BI for RBA" section of this chapter.

Getting a Blank SSRS Report

With SQL Server 2012 and earlier versions of SQL Server, you may receive a blank page, as shown in Figure 9.23, when using a browser like Chrome. If this happens to you, after executing the report, perform the following steps to resolve this issue:

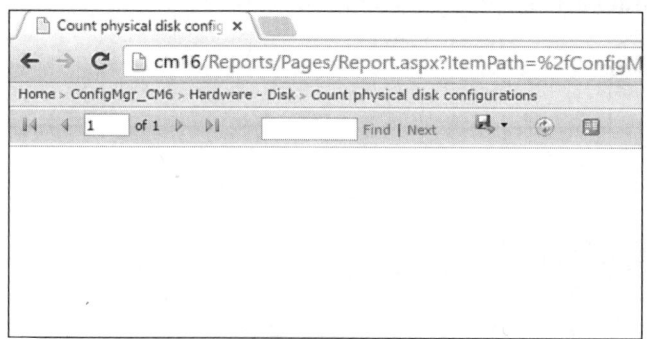

FIGURE 9.23   Blank SSRS report with Chrome.

1. Locate ReportingServices.js. This is generally found under *%Program Files%*\Microsoft SQL Server\MSRS11.MSSQLSERVER\Reporting Services\ReportManager\js\.

2. Back up ReportingServices.js.

3. Run Windows Notepad or your favorite text editor in elevated mode. Based on your version of SQL, append the appropriate function to the ReportServices.js file. Listings 9.9, 9.10, and 9.11 show the fixes for SQL 2012, 2008 R2, and 2008, respectively.

4. Restart the SSRS service to reload the updated ReportingServices.js file.

Use the SQL 2012 `pageLoad` function (see Listing 9.9) to correct a blank page being displayed on browsers such as Chrome.

LISTING 9.9   `pageLoad` Function for SQL 2012

```
Function pageLoad() {
var element = document.getElementById("ctl32_ctl09");
if (element)
{
    element.style.overflow = "visible";
} }
```

The `pageLoad` function for SQL 2008 R2 (see Listing 9.10) is used to correct a blank page being displayed on browsers such as Chrome.

LISTING 9.10   `pageLoad` Function for SQL 2008 R2

```
Function pageLoad() {
var element = document.getElementById("ctl31_ctl09");
if (element)
{
    element.style.overflow = "visible";
} }
```

To correct the blank page issue with browser such as Chrome, using SQL 2008 SSRS, use the `pageLoad` function shown in Listing 9.11.

LISTING 9.11   `pageLoad` Function for SQL 2008

```
Function pageLoad() {
var element = document.getElementById("ctl31_ctl10");
if (element)
{
    element.style.overflow = "visible";
} }
```

Once the `pageLoad` function is added to ReportingServices.js, the SSRS report displays normally in Chrome and other browsers, as shown in Figure 9.24.

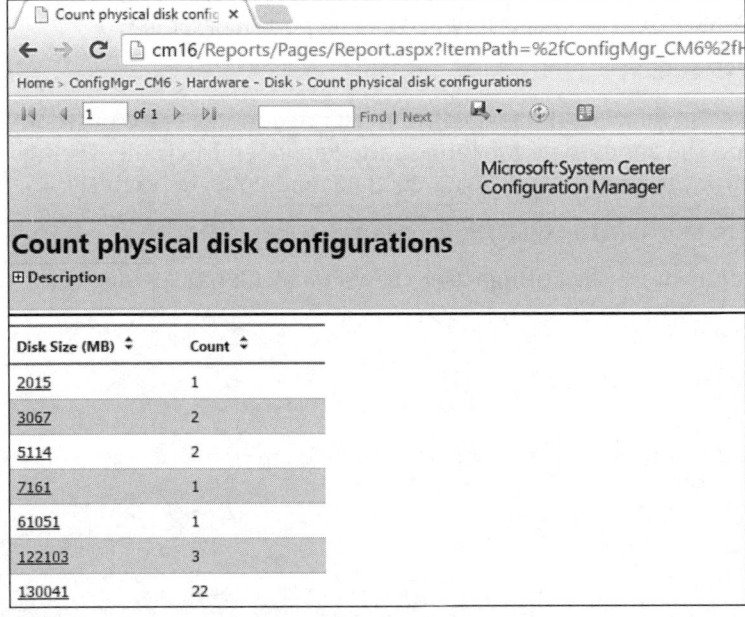

FIGURE 9.24   Normal SSRS report.

Demonstrating Creating an RBA Report

The purpose of this demonstration is to become familiar with converting a SQL query to RBA table-value functions and testing it in SQL Server Management Studio. You will also learn how to update the query and RDL within an existing report using SSDT-BI.

Converting the Patch Compliance Progression Query to an RBA Query and Testing It

Following the information in the "Converting a SQL Query to a ConfigMgr RBA SQL Query" section of this chapter, make the required modifications to the Patch Compliance Progression query. As part of this process, you should do the following:

▶ Within SQL Server Management Studio, add a Declare and Set @UserSIDs variable.

▶ Modify the query to change the SQL views to RBA table-value functions.

Execute the query and save it for the next step.

> **TIP:** DECLARE **AND** SET **STATEMENTS**
>
> Remember that the DECLARE and SET statements are used in SQL Server Management Studio only to test a query. They are not needed in the dataset query. If left within that query, incorrect results will be returned to RBA users.

Converting the Patch Compliance Progression Report to an RBA Report

Following the instructions in the "Using Reports and RBA" section of this chapter, make the required modifications to SSDT-BI and the Patch Compliance Progression report. As part of this process, you should do the following:

▶ Update SSDT-BI to include the SrsResources.dll file.

▶ Add the CodeGroup entry to RSPreviewPolicy.Config.

▶ Make a copy of the Patch Compliance Progression report and name it Patch Compliance Progression RBA.rdl.

▶ Add the assembly reference to the RDL.

▶ Using the converted query, update the main dataset.

▶ Add a dataset for DataSetAdminID.

▶ Update and add prompts used by RBA.

When you have finished these steps, preview the report and confirm that all settings and features are functioning properly, as described in this section.

Converting the Computer Hardware Information Query to an RBA Query and Testing It

Extract the SQL query from the Computer Hardware Information Chart.rdl created in Chapter 7 and update the SQL view to the RBA table-value functions. As part of this process, you should do the following:

▶ In SQL Server Management Studio, add a Declare and Set @UserSIDs variable.

▶ Modify the query to change the SQL views to RBA table-value functions.

Execute the query and save it for the next demonstration.

Adding a Chart to the Computer Hardware Information Report

Make a copy of the Computer Hardware Information report, created in Chapter 6, and name this copy Computer Hardware Information RBA.rdl. Modify the new RBA report as follows:

▶ Add the assembly reference to the RDL.

▶ Using the converted query from the previous demonstration, update the main dataset.

▶ Add a dataset for DataSetAdminID.

▶ Update and add prompts used by RBA.

When you have finished these steps, preview the report and confirm that all settings and features are functioning properly, as described in this section.

Summary

This chapter has presented an overview of how ConfigMgr RBA reporting works. It has examined a normal SQL query and reports covered in previous chapters and shown you how to enhance the reports so they can be used with the RBA feature of ConfigMgr and SSRS. This chapter has also described the steps and naming conventions necessary for converting a standard SQL query to RBA table-value functions.

The chapter has also discussed the one-time configuration of SSDT-BI to add the SRSResource.dll and `CodeGroup` block. If these steps are not performed on a computer with SSDT-BI, an RBA report cannot be previewed on that system.

The last part of the chapter has described advanced RBA tips and troubleshooting techniques, including RBA query performance tips to show how an understanding of RBA can reduce the execution time for an RBA query. This allows you to make an RBA query as efficient as possible without removing RBA. This chapter has also discussed some common errors and how to resolve them. In addition, you have updated the demonstration reports to allow the RBA feature to limit the user's ability to see information.

PART IV

Appendixes

IN THIS PART

APPENDIX A
Glossary

This appendix contains a glossary of terms and acronyms used with System Center Configuration Manager and SQL Server Reporting Services. An acronym is typically an abbreviated term formed from the first letter (or first few letters) of several words. Many acronyms are used in Microsoft technologies and System Center, and new ones appear constantly. Often someone unfamiliar with the acronym does not even know the technology area to which it refers.

Glossary of Terms

AD: Active Directory

AI: Configuration Manager Asset Intelligence

Applications: ConfigMgr applications are similar to ConfigMgr 2007 packages; however, applications allow for user-centric deployments with a smart installation for each device type (PC, mobile, and so on.)

APP-V: Microsoft Application Virtualization

BIDS: SQL Server Business Intelligence Development Studio

BITS: Background Intelligent Transfer Service

CAS: central administration site

CCM: Change and Configuration Management

CI: configuration item

CM: System Center Configuration Manager

CM12: System Center 2012 Configuration Manager

CM12R: System Center 2012 R2 Configuration Manager

ConfigMgr: System Center Configuration Manager

DCM: desired configuration management

DP: distribution point

FQDN: fully qualified domain name

FSP: fallback status point

GPO: Group Policy Object

LAN: local area network

MAN: metropolitan area network

MP: management point

MSI: Microsoft Installer

OU: organizational unit

Package: A traditional application deployment method

RB: Report Builder

RBA: role-based administration

RBAC: role-based access control, sometimes referred to as role-based security

RDL: Report Definition Language

RP: Configuration Manager reporting services point

SCCM: System Center Configuration Manager

SCEP: System Center Endpoint Protection

SID: security identifier

SMS: Systems Management Server

SQL: Structured Query Language

SSDT: SQL Server Data Tools, which is the SQL Server development environment. Earlier versions of SSDT included the business intelligence tools.

SSDT-BI: SQL Server Data Tools 2014 Business Intelligence for Visual Studio 2013

SSMS: SQL Server Management Studio

SSRS: SQL Server Reporting Services

SUP: Configuration Manager software update point

SWM: software metering

WAN: wide area network

WMI: Windows Management Instrumentation

WOL: Wake on LAN

WQL: WMI Query Language

WSUS: Windows Server Update Services

For additional information on acronyms and terms not described in this appendix, see http://social.technet.microsoft.com/wiki/contents/articles/20580.wiki-glossary-of-technology-acronyms.aspx.

A

Demonstration Outcomes

This appendix provides the expected outcomes for all the end-of-chapter demonstrations throughout the book. Refer to the specific chapters for information on each demonstration.

Chapter 2 Demonstration Outcomes

Chapter 2, "Installing and Configuring Configuration Manager Reporting," discussed creating a reporting services point, using Configuration Manager (ConfigMgr) security roles, and accessing ConfigMgr SQL Server Reporting Services (SSRS) reports. The demonstrations from this chapter were designed to expose you to ConfigMgr role-based administration (RBA) and show you how to create RBA roles to leverage your ConfigMgr environment.

Working with the Report Reader Security Role

This demonstration was designed to familiarize you with creating an RBA security role that allows users in the ConfigMgr Report Reader Active Directory (AD) group to access ConfigMgr SSRS reports without using the ConfigMgr console. This demonstration was also used as an example in Chapter 2. Any user assigned to the AD user group would be able to see all reports and folders, as shown in Figure B.1.

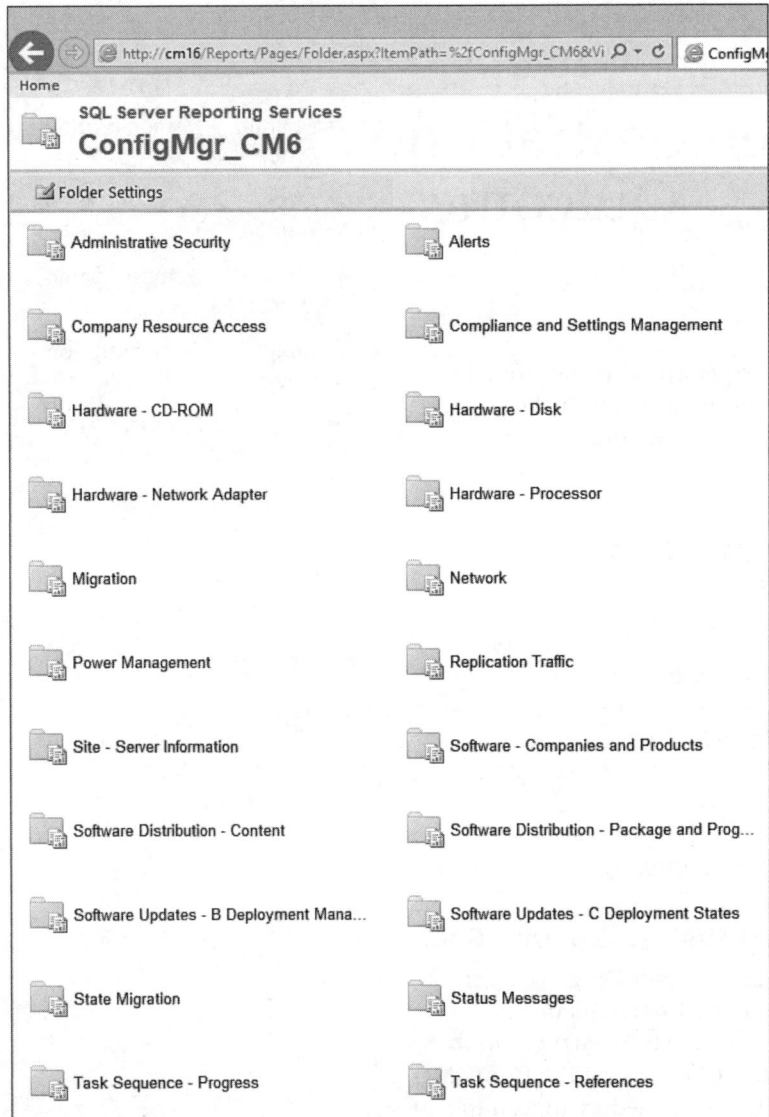

FIGURE B.1   Report Reader Security Role SSRS folder access.

Working with the Software Updates Report Reader Security Role

This demonstration was designed to show you how easy it is to import a security role from one ConfigMgr environment to another ConfigMgr environment. As such, see Chapter 2 for the steps necessary to import a ConfigMgr security role and assign it to an AD security group. Remember with this demonstration that users are limited to what collections they see, and therefore there is a limit on the computers for which they can view results. Figure B.2 shows the resulting folders that a user with this ConfigMgr security role can view.

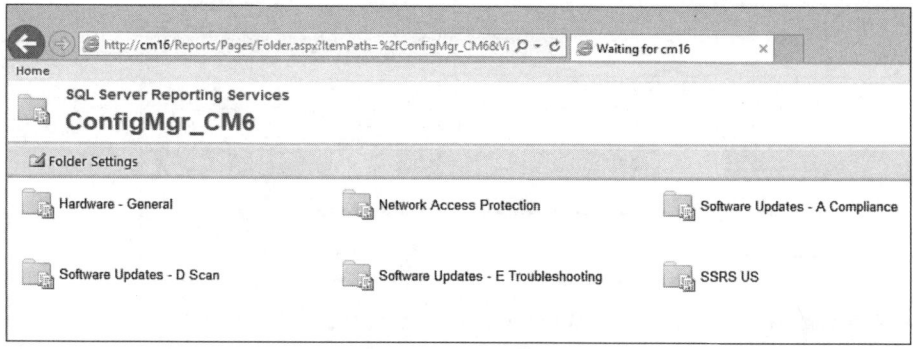

FIGURE B.2   SSRS folder access with Software Update Report Reader security role.

Working with the Inventory Report Reader Security Role

The demonstration for the Inventory Report Reader role grants access to users assigned with the ConfigMgr Inventory Report Reader AD security group to view inventory reports accessing the ConfigMgr console. The properties of your Inventory Report Reader security role should look similar to Figure B.3.

In addition, your test user account in the ConfigMgr Inventory Report Reader AD security group will only be able to access the folders and report as shown in Figure B.4. The export for the Inventory Report Readers security role can be found in the online file Inventory Report Readers.xml. See Appendix C for further information regarding this file.

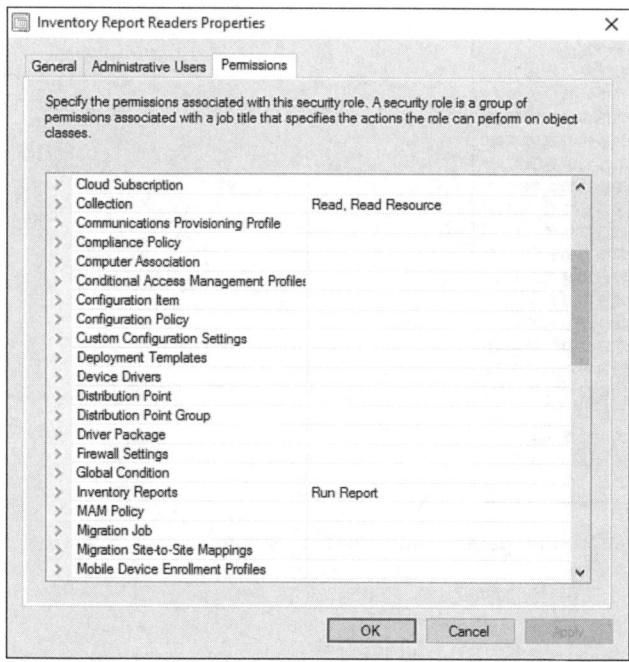

FIGURE B.3   Inventory Report Reader security role properties.

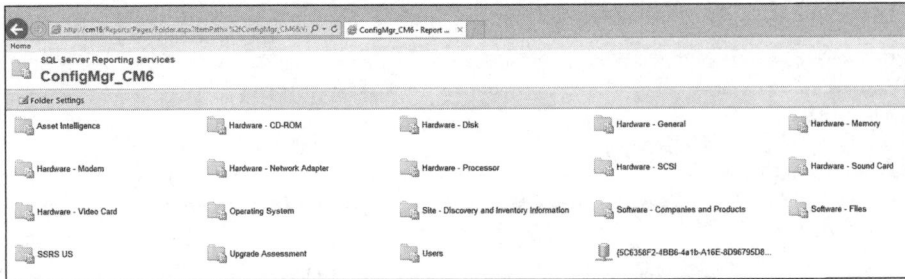

FIGURE B.4   Inventory Report Reader SSRS folder and report access.

Chapter 3 Demonstration Outcomes

As discussed in Chapter 3, "Understanding Configuration Manager Data," ConfigMgr gathers and stores in its database a large amount of data across many different views. Chapter 3 introduced the most common and important SQL data views. The demonstrations from this chapter were designed to expose you to this data and help you understand how to access it using SQL Server Management Studio.

Creating and Executing a Query

This demonstration was designed to help you become familiar with SQL Server Management Studio and executing a saved query. The results for this demonstration should look similar to Figure B.5.

	Name0	UserName0	Status	Last HW scan
1	AZUREAD	NULL	Needs 47 Patches	2015-11-13 21:58:38.000
2	CM12R2-CM6	NULL	Needs 45 Patches	2015-11-16 17:30:19.000
3	DELLE6430	GARTEK\Garth	Needs 41 Patches	2015-10-20 10:34:16.000
4	ELLEN-PC	GARTEK\ellen	Needs 101 Patches	2015-11-01 22:06:21.000
5	ES-06	NULL	Needs 2 Patches	2015-12-04 11:25:42.000
6	ES-08	NULL	Needs 1 Patches	2015-12-05 12:09:51.000
7	ES-10	NULL	Needs 58 Patches	2015-11-18 18:16:24.000
8	ES-20	NULL	Needs 64 Patches	2015-12-04 19:24:48.000
9	FRAME	GARTEK\frame	Needs 132 Patches	2015-08-20 16:00:11.000
10	GARTEK-DC10	NULL	Needs 9 Patches	2015-12-04 20:28:47.000
11	GARTEK-DC21	NULL	Needs 48 Patches	2015-12-03 12:35:33.000
12	GARTEK-DC5	NULL	Needs 36 Patches	2015-12-03 19:35:13.000
13	GARTEK-DC9	NULL	Needs 1 Patches	2015-12-03 03:23:49.000
14	GJ5	GARTEK\jyedid	Needs 18 Patches	2015-10-23 11:53:50.000
15	M8	NULL	Needs 181 Patches	2015-09-18 12:21:30.000
16	MEDIAPC	GARTEK\Garth	Needs 7 Patches	2015-11-27 00:40:44.000
17	OPSMAN2012	NULL	Needs 9 Patches	2015-12-05 06:46:50.000
18	SM12	NULL	Needs 1 Patches	2015-12-05 12:42:57.000
19	SM12-DW	GARTEK\jyedid	Needs 1 Patches	2015-12-04 16:26:47.000

FIGURE B.5   Results for the demonstration on creating and executing a query.

Looking at Views

The `v_R_System` SQL view is one of the most common ConfigMgr SQL views and contains a lot of information. For example, computer name, virtual machine status, and logged-on user details are available in this SQL view. The results for this demonstration should look similar to Figure B.6.

`v_GS_Computer_System` is another common view that provides details about a computer, such as manufacturer, model, and role within a domain. The results for this demonstration should look similar to Figure B.7.

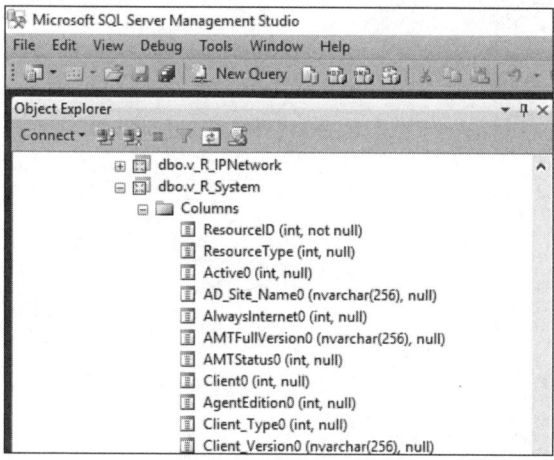

FIGURE B.6   List of columns for the `v_R_System` SQL view.

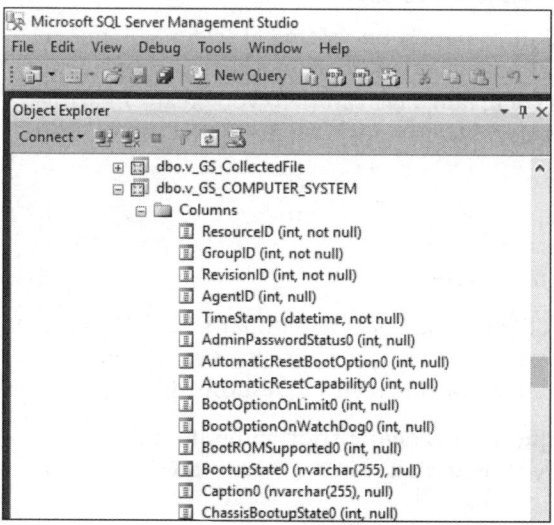

FIGURE B.7   List of columns for the `v_GS_Computer_System` SQL view.

The v_Add_Remove_Programs SQL view is used to determine what software is installed on a computer. This view provides exactly the same column information as v_GS_ADD_REMOVE_PROGRAMS and v_GS_ADD_REMOVE_PROGRAMS_64, with the data of both views combined. This demonstration was designed to acquaint you with the columns available; your v_Add_Remove_Programs SQL view should look similar to Figure B.8.

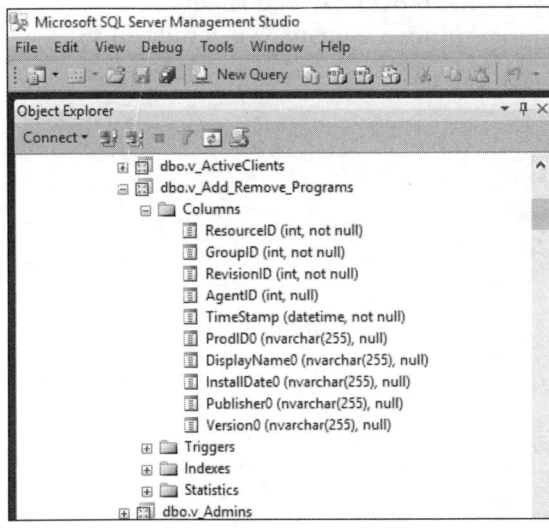

FIGURE B.8   List of columns for the v_Add_Remove_Programs SQL view.

Chapter 4 Demonstration Outcomes

Chapter 4, "Transact-SQL Primer," provided information on writing efficient SQL queries, which are used to create the foundation of effective and efficient Configuration Manager reports. Having a good understanding of the SQL language can help you create amazing reports. The Chapter 4 demonstrations provided examples of both an ineffective query and an efficient query.

Demonstrating SQL Operators

Several exercises were included with this demonstration:

▶ You were provided with a sample SQL file to help become familiar with SQL Server Management Studio by executing an existing query. Since no two ConfigMgr environments are exactly alike, your results for this review question will vary.

▶ You were also asked to edit a sample query. This demonstration built on the previous demonstration, and the query should look similar to Listing B.1, available as online content. See Appendix C for details.

LISTING B.1   Editing the Sample Query

```
SELECT DISTINCT
 ARP.Publisher0 as 'Publisher',
 ARP.DisplayName0 as 'Display Name',
 ARP.Version0 as 'Version'
FROM
 dbo.v_Add_Remove_Programs ARP
WHERE
 ARP.Publisher0 in (
  'Dell',
  'Microsoft Corporation',
  'Adobe Systems Incorporated')
ORDER BY
 ARP.Publisher0,
 ARP.DisplayName0,
 ARP.Version0
```

Once the query is executed, your results should look similar to those shown in Figure B.9.

▶ For the review questions, your answers will be unique, except for the part where you were asked to order the results. As shown in Figure B.9, the results should be sorted alphabetically by publisher, display name, and finally version.

	Publisher	Display Name	Version
1	Adobe Systems Incorporated	Acrobat.com	2.0.0
2	Adobe Systems Incorporated	Acrobat.com	2.0.0.0
3	Adobe Systems Incorporated	Adobe Acrobat Reader DC	15.009.20069
4	Adobe Systems Incorporated	Adobe Acrobat Reader DC	15.009.20079
5	Adobe Systems Incorporated	Adobe AIR	2.6.0.19140
6	Adobe Systems Incorporated	Adobe AIR	3.7.0.1530
7	Adobe Systems Incorporated	Adobe Download Assistant	1.2.6
8	Adobe Systems Incorporated	Adobe Flash Player 11 ActiveX	11.1.102.55
9	Adobe Systems Incorporated	Adobe Flash Player 18 ActiveX	18.0.0.232
10	Adobe Systems Incorporated	Adobe Flash Player 18 NPAPI	18.0.0.232
11	Adobe Systems Incorporated	Adobe Flash Player 19 ActiveX	19.0.0.226
12	Adobe Systems Incorporated	Adobe Flash Player 20 ActiveX	20.0.0.228
13	Adobe Systems Incorporated	Adobe Reader X MUI	10.0.0
14	Adobe Systems Incorporated	Adobe Reader XI (11.0.03)	11.0.03
15	Adobe Systems Incorporated	Adobe Reader XI (11.0.13)	11.0.13
16	Adobe Systems Incorporated	Adobe Refresh Manager	1.8.0
17	Dell	Dell OpenManage Client Instrumentation	8.2.0.154
18	Dell	Dell OpenManage Inventory Agent (for Dell Servers)	1.3.2
19	Dell	Dell OpenManage Server Administrator	6.2.0
20	Microsoft Corporation	NULL	10.2.4000.0
21	Microsoft Corporation	NULL	10.2.4064.0
22	Microsoft Corporation	NULL	10.50.1617.0
23	Microsoft Corporation	NULL	11.0.2218.0
24	Microsoft Corporation	NULL	11.1.3000.0
25	Microsoft Corporation	NULL	11.1.3128.0
26	Microsoft Corporation	NULL	11.1.3153.0
27	Microsoft Corporation	NULL	11.1.3156.0
28	Microsoft Corporation	SQL_PRODUCT_SHORT_NAME Data Tools - ...	12.0.2430.0
29	Microsoft Corporation	SQL_PRODUCT_SHORT_NAME SSIS 64Bit Fo...	12.0.2430.0

FIGURE B.9   Editing the sample query results.

▶ You were asked to create a SQL query, using aliases. This query was to retrieve a list of computer names (PC), user names (User), application names (Application), and versions (Version) of systems with Adobe Reader installed. Your query should look similar to Listing B.2, available as online content. See Appendix C for details.

LISTING B.2   Creating a Query with Aliases Sample Query

```
SELECT
 RV.Netbios_Name0 as 'PC',
 RV.User_Name0 as 'User',
 ARP.DisplayName0 as 'Application',
 ARP.Version0 as 'Version'
FROM
 dbo.v_R_System_Valid RV
 join dbo.v_Add_Remove_Programs ARP
  on RV.ResourceID = ARP.ResourceID
WHERE
 ARP.DisplayName0 like '%Adobe Reader%'
ORDER BY
  RV.Netbios_Name0
```

The results of executing this query should look similar to those shown in Figure B.10.

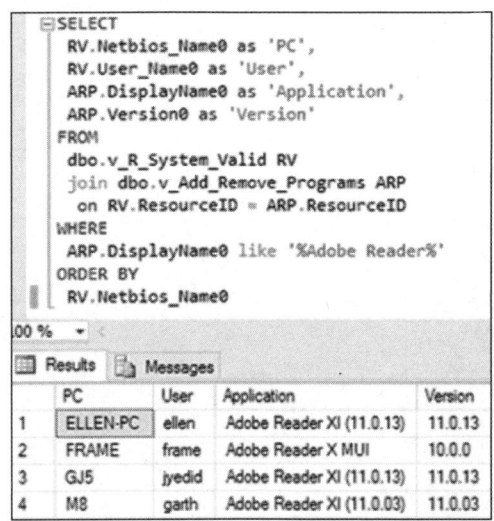

FIGURE B.10   Sample results of the query with aliases.

Working with Aggregate Functions

This demonstration included two exercises:

▶ You were asked to create a query that finds the minimum, average, and maximum hard disk sizes for system roles. Your query should look similar to Listing B.3, and the results of your query execution should be similar to those shown in Figure B.11, available as online content. See Appendix C for details.

LISTING B.3   Aggregate Functions: Creating a New Query Sample Query

```
SELECT
 S.SystemRole0 as 'System Role',
 MIN (HD.Size0) as 'Min HD for a System Role',
 AVG (HD.Size0) as 'Avg HD for a System Role',
 MAX (HD.Size0) as 'Max HD for a System Role'
FROM
 dbo.v_GS_DISK as HD
 JOIN dbo.v_GS_SYSTEM as S on S.ResourceID = HD.ResourceID
GROUP BY
 S.SystemRole0
```

	System Role	Min HD for a System Role	Avg HD for a System Role	Max HD for a System Role
1	Server	3067	1385949	15261177
2	Workstation	2015	295234	1907726

FIGURE B.11   Result of using aggregate functions to create a new query.

▶ The second exercise asked you to create a query to show the COUNT of each installed application (DisplayName0). Your query should look similar to Listing B.4, available as online content (see Appendix C for details), and the results of executing your query should be similar to Figure B.12.

For the review question, each answer will vary.

LISTING B.4   COUNT Function Sample Query

```
SELECT
    v_Add_Remove_Programs.Publisher0,
    v_Add_Remove_Programs.DisplayName0,
    v_Add_Remove_Programs.Version0,
    COUNT(v_Add_Remove_Programs.DisplayName0) as 'Total'
FROM
    dbo.v_Add_Remove_Programs
GROUP BY
    v_Add_Remove_Programs.Publisher0,
    v_Add_Remove_Programs.DisplayName0,
    v_Add_Remove_Programs.Version0
```

	Publisher	Application	Version	Total
1	NULL	AMD VISION Engine Control Center	1.00.0000	1
2	NULL	CanoScan Toolbox Ver4.9	NULL	3
3	NULL	Enhanced Web Reporting	NULL	3
4	NULL	Fiddler Syntax-Highlighting Addons	NULL	1
5	NULL	HighPoint RAID Management Software	NULL	2
6	NULL	HighPoint Web RAID Management Service	NULL	3
7	NULL	IIS Express Application Compatibility Database for x64	NULL	3
8	NULL	IIS Express Application Compatibility Database for x86	NULL	3
9	NULL	Magic ISO Maker v5.5 (build 0281)	NULL	2
10	NULL	MagicDisc 2.7.106	NULL	5
11	NULL	Matrox Graphics Software (remove only)	NULL	1
12	NULL	Microsoft SQL Server 2012	NULL	2
13	NULL	Microsoft SQL Server 2012 (64-bit)	NULL	9
14	NULL	Microsoft SQL Server 2014	NULL	3
15	NULL	Microsoft SQL Server 2014 (64-bit)	NULL	8
16	NULL	Monitor Asset Manager	NULL	1
17	NULL	Software Update for ConfigMgr 2007 SP2 (KB977384)	NULL	2
18	Acer Incorporated	Live Updater	2.00.3010	1
19	Adersoft	Vbsedit	5.8.4.0	1
20	Adersoft	Vbsedit	6.7.4.0	1
21	Adersoft	Vbsedit	7.99.0.0	1
22	Adersoft	Vbsedit 32-bit	5.8.4.0	1
23	Adersoft	Vbsedit 32-bit	6.7.4.0	1
24	Adersoft	Vbsedit 32-bit	7.99.0.0	1
25	Adobe Systems	Adobe Acrobat XI Pro	11.0.00	1
26	Adobe Systems ...	Adobe AIR	1.5.3.91...	2
27	Adobe Systems ...	Adobe AIR	2.5.1.17...	2
28	Adobe Systems ...	Acrobat.com	2.0.0	1
29	Adobe Systems ...	Acrobat.com	2.0.0.0	1
30	Adobe Systems ...	Adobe Acrobat Reader DC	15.009....	1
31	Adobe Systems ...	Adobe Acrobat Reader DC	15.009....	3
32	Adobe Systems ...	Adobe AIR	2.6.0.19...	2

FIGURE B.12   COUNT function sample query results.

Working with Date and Time Functions

The purpose of this demonstration was to help you become familiar with the different date and time functions. Your query should find the following information from all systems in your environment:

▶ The current date

▶ The date of the last hardware inventory scan

▶ The number of minutes since the last hardware inventory scan occurred

▶ The day of the month on which the last hardware inventory scan occurred

Your query should look similar to Listing B.5, available as online content (see Appendix C for details), and the results of your query execution should be similar to those shown in Figure B.13.

LISTING B.5   Date and Time Functions Sample Query

```
SELECT
R.Netbios_Name0 as 'PC',
GETDATE () as 'Today Date',
WS.LastHWScan as 'Last Hardware Inventory Scan',
DATEDIFF (MINUTE, WS.LastHWScan, getdate())
  as 'Minutes since the last hardware inventory scan',
DATEPART (dd, WS.LastHWScan)
  as 'Day of month last hardware inventory scan'
FROM
v_R_System as R
JOIN dbo.v_GS_WORKSTATION_STATUS as WS
  on R.ResourceID = WS.ResourceID
ORDER BY
R.Netbios_Name0
```

	PC	Today Date	Last Hardware Inventory Scan	Minutes since the last hardware inventory scan	Month last hardware inventory scan
1	ACERASPIRE	2015-12-17 20:32:05.770	2015-12-16 16:37:19.000	1675	16
2	AZUREAD	2015-12-17 20:32:05.770	2015-11-13 21:58:38.000	48874	13
3	CM12R2-CM6	2015-12-17 20:32:05.770	2015-12-17 17:52:16.000	160	17
4	CM16	2015-12-17 20:32:05.770	2015-12-17 05:50:39.000	882	17
5	DELLE6430	2015-12-17 20:32:05.770	2015-12-09 14:34:50.000	11878	9
6	ELLEN-PC	2015-12-17 20:32:05.770	2015-11-01 22:06:21.000	66146	1
7	ES-06	2015-12-17 20:32:05.770	2015-12-17 10:42:51.000	590	17
8	ES-08	2015-12-17 20:32:05.770	2015-12-17 14:26:56.000	366	17
9	ES-10	2015-12-17 20:32:05.770	2015-12-17 02:34:42.000	1078	17
10	ES-20	2015-12-17 20:32:05.770	2015-12-17 17:15:29.000	197	17
11	FRAME	2015-12-17 20:32:05.770	2015-08-20 16:00:11.000	171632	20
12	GARTEK-DC10	2015-12-17 20:32:05.770	2015-12-16 18:23:05.000	1569	16
13	GARTEK-DC21	2015-12-17 20:32:05.770	2015-12-17 11:15:49.000	557	17
14	GARTEK-DC5	2015-12-17 20:32:05.770	2015-12-17 18:11:23.000	141	17
15	GARTEK-DC9	2015-12-17 20:32:05.770	2015-12-14 13:51:22.000	4721	14
16	garth_Android_7/29/2015_6:16 PM	2015-12-17 20:32:05.770	2015-09-01 08:00:32.000	154832	1
17	Garth's iPhone	2015-12-17 20:32:05.770	2015-12-16 19:50:46.000	1482	16
18	GJ5	2015-12-17 20:32:05.770	2015-10-23 11:53:50.000	79719	23
19	M6	2015-12-17 20:32:05.770	2015-12-17 10:48:48.000	584	17

FIGURE B.13   Date and time functions sample query results.

Working with Data Transforms

This demonstration included a number of exercises to help you become familiar with the SQL functions CASE, CAST, COVERT, and ISNULL:

▶ To use the CASE function, you were asked to create a query displaying all computer names and system enclosure chassis types and to convert the chassis type numeric codes to their actual meanings. Your query should look similar to Listing B.6, available as online content (see Appendix C for details), and the results of your query execution should be similar to those shown in Figure B.14.

LISTING B.6   CASE Function Sample Query

```
SELECT
 R.Netbios_Name0 as 'PC',
 CASE SE.ChassisTypes0
  WHEN'1' THEN 'Other'
  WHEN'2' THEN 'Unknown'
  WHEN'3' THEN 'Desktop'
  WHEN'4' THEN 'Low-profile desktop'
  WHEN'5' THEN 'Pizza box'
  WHEN'6' THEN 'Mini tower'
  WHEN'7' THEN 'Tower'
  WHEN'8' THEN 'Portable'
  WHEN'9' THEN 'Laptop'
  WHEN'10' THEN 'Notebook'
  WHEN'11' THEN 'Handheld'
  WHEN'12' THEN 'Docking station'
  WHEN'13' THEN 'All-in-one'
  WHEN'14' THEN 'Sub-notebook'
  WHEN'15' THEN 'Space-saving'
  WHEN'16' THEN 'Lunch box'
  WHEN'17' THEN 'Main system chassis'
  WHEN'18' THEN 'Expansion chassis'
  WHEN'19' THEN 'Subchassis'
  WHEN'20' THEN 'Bus expansion chassis'
  WHEN'21' THEN 'Peripheral chassis'
  WHEN'22' THEN 'Storage chassis'
  WHEN'23' THEN 'Rack mount chassis'
  WHEN'24' THEN 'Sealed-case PC'
END as 'Chassis Type'
FROM
 v_R_System as R
 JOIN dbo.v_GS_SYSTEM_ENCLOSURE as SE
  on R.ResourceID = SE.ResourceID
ORDER BY
 R.Netbios_Name0
```

▶ To become familiar with the CAST and CONVERT functions, you were asked to create a query to get all system names and the last hardware scan date and convert the last hardware scan date to ANSI date format YYYY.MM.DD. Your query should look similar to Listing B.7, available as online content (see Appendix C for details), and the query results should be similar to those shown in Figure B.15.

	PC	Chassis Type
1	ACERASPIRE	Notebook
2	CM12-CM4	Desktop
3	CM12-J22	Desktop
4	DELLE6510	Laptop
5	DELLE6510-2	Laptop
6	ELLEN-PC	Sub-notebook
7	ES-06	Rack mount chassis
8	ES-08	Rack mount chassis
9	ES-10	Main system chassis
10	FRAME	All-in-one
11	GARTEK-DC10	Desktop
12	GARTEK-DC5	Desktop
13	GARTEK-DC9	Desktop
14	GJ5	Laptop
15	HPPC	Notebook
16	IIS75TEST	Desktop
17	LE2	Laptop
18	M8	Laptop
19	MEDIAPC	Desktop

FIGURE B.14   CASE function sample query results.

LISTING B.7   CAST and CONVERT Functions Sample Query

```
SELECT
 R.Netbios_Name0 as 'PC',
 WS.LastHWScan as 'Last Hardware Inventory Scan',
 CONVERT(nvarchar(30),WS.LastHWScan, 102) as 'Last Hardware Inventory Scan'
FROM
 v_R_System as R
 JOIN dbo.v_GS_WORKSTATION_STATUS as WS
  on R.ResourceID = WS.ResourceID
ORDER BY
 R.Netbios_Name0
```

	PC	Last Hardware Inventory Scan	Last Hardware Inventory Scan
1	ACERASPIRE	2015-12-16 16:37:19.000	2015.12.16
2	AZUREAD	2015-11-13 21:58:38.000	2015.11.13
3	CM12R2-CM6	2015-12-17 17:52:16.000	2015.12.17
4	CM16	2015-12-17 05:50:39.000	2015.12.17
5	DELLE6430	2015-12-09 14:34:50.000	2015.12.09
6	ELLEN-PC	2015-11-01 22:06:21.000	2015.11.01
7	ES-06	2015-12-17 10:42:51.000	2015.12.17
8	ES-08	2015-12-17 14:26:56.000	2015.12.17
9	ES-10	2015-12-17 02:34:42.000	2015.12.17
10	ES-20	2015-12-17 17:15:29.000	2015.12.17
11	FRAME	2015-08-20 16:00:11.000	2015.08.20
12	GARTEK-DC10	2015-12-16 18:23:05.000	2015.12.16
13	GARTEK-DC21	2015-12-17 11:15:49.000	2015.12.17
14	GARTEK-DC5	2015-12-17 18:11:23.000	2015.12.17
15	GARTEK-DC9	2015-12-14 13:51:22.000	2015.12.14
16	garth_Android_7/29/2015_6:16 PM	2015-09-01 08:00:32.000	2015.09.01
17	Garth's iPhone	2015-12-16 19:50:46.000	2015.12.16
18	GJ5	2015-10-23 11:53:50.000	2015.10.23
19	M6	2015-12-17 10:48:48.000	2015.12.17

FIGURE B.15   CAST and CONVERT functions sample query results.

▶ The next exercise used the ISNULL function. You were asked to create a query to return all system names and user names (User_Name0) from v_R_System_Valid and have the query replace any NULL values in the v_R_System_Valid User_Name0 column with the value n/a. Your query should look similar to Listing B.8, available as online content (see Appendix C for details), and the results of executing the query should be similar to those shown in Figure B.16.

LISTING B.8   ISNULL Function Sample Query

```
SELECT
 RV.Netbios_Name0 as 'PC',
 ISNULL(RV.User_Name0,'n/a') as 'User'
FROM
 dbo.v_R_System_Valid RV
ORDER BY
 RV.Netbios_Name0
```

	PC	User
1	ACERASPIRE	JYedid
2	AZUREAD	jyedid
3	CM12R2-CM6	n/a
4	CM16	n/a
5	DELLE6430	jyedid
6	ELLEN-PC	ellen
7	ES-06	garth
8	ES-08	Garth
9	ES-10	n/a
10	ES-20	Garth
11	FRAME	frame
12	GARTEK-DC10	n/a
13	GARTEK-DC21	n/a
14	GARTEK-DC5	jyedid
15	GARTEK-DC9	n/a
16	garth_Android_7/29/2015_6:16 PM	n/a
17	Garth's iPhone	n/a
18	GJ5	jyedid
19	M6	garth

FIGURE B.16   ISNULL function sample query results.

Executing an Inefficient Query

The results of the demonstration on executing an inefficient query should look similar to those shown in Figure B.17. Notice the execution time of 4:16 minutes and 990,176 rows.

Writing an Efficient Query

Your SQL query for this demonstration should look similar to Listing B.9, and when executed, the results should be similar to those shown in Figure B.18. Notice that the execution time is 1 second and the number of rows is 5,086. Comparing this to the inefficient query helps demonstrate the need for proper SQL joins.

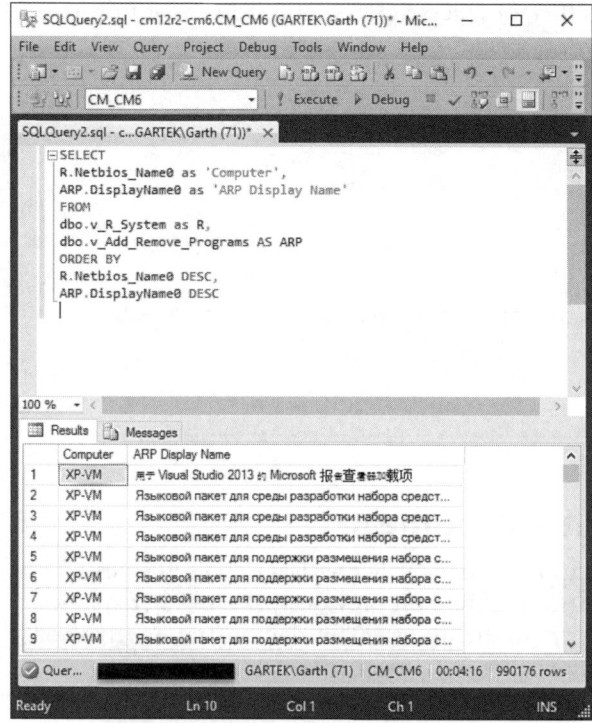

FIGURE B.17 Results for the demonstration on executing an inefficient query.

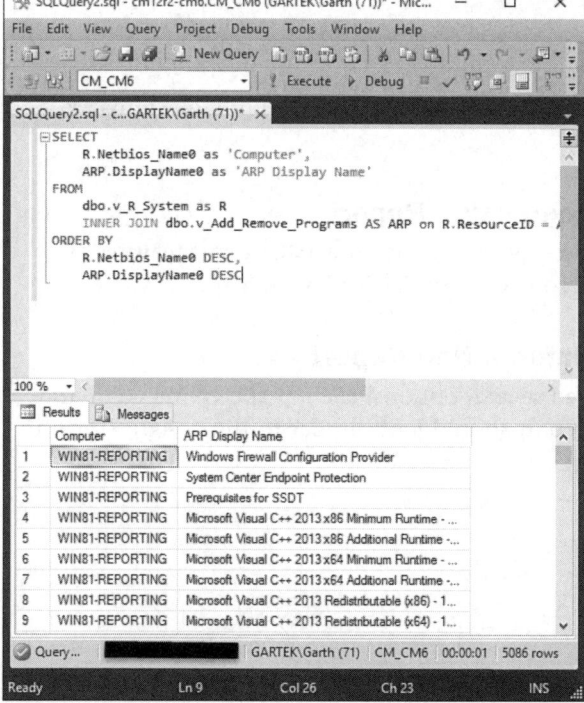

FIGURE B.18 Results of the demonstration on executing an efficient query.

Listing B.9 is available in the online file Efficient Query.sql. See Appendix C for further information.

LISTING B.9   INNER JOIN Sample Query

```
SELECT
  R.Netbios_Name0 as 'Computer',
  ARP.DisplayName0 as 'ARP Display Name'
FROM
  dbo.v_R_System as R
  INNER JOIN dbo.v_Add_Remove_Programs AS ARP on R.ResourceID = ARP.ResourceID
ORDER BY
  R.Netbios_Name0 DESC,
ARP.DisplayName0 DESC
```

Chapter 6 Demonstration Outcomes

Chapter 6, "Building a Basic Report," discussed using SQL Server Data Tools Business Intelligence (SSDT-BI) for Visual Studio 2013. Building on previously created SQL queries, you were to create a project and add a report to the project. This demonstration involved creating several reports and leveraging an existing SQL query to create a SSRS report with the core features. The first demonstration provides involved creating the Patch Compliance Progression report, and the second demonstration involved creating the Computer Hardware Information report.

Creating a New Project

After creating a project and shared data source, your end results should look similar to those in Figure B.19.

Creating a Patch Compliance Progression Report

Creating a Patch Compliance Progression report using the core SSRS report features as described in Chapter 6 should produce an outcome similar to Figure B.20.

Creating a Computer Hardware Information Report

The demonstration for this report provided several options, such as specifying color and logo. However, the basic design of your report should look similar to the design shown in Figure B.21.

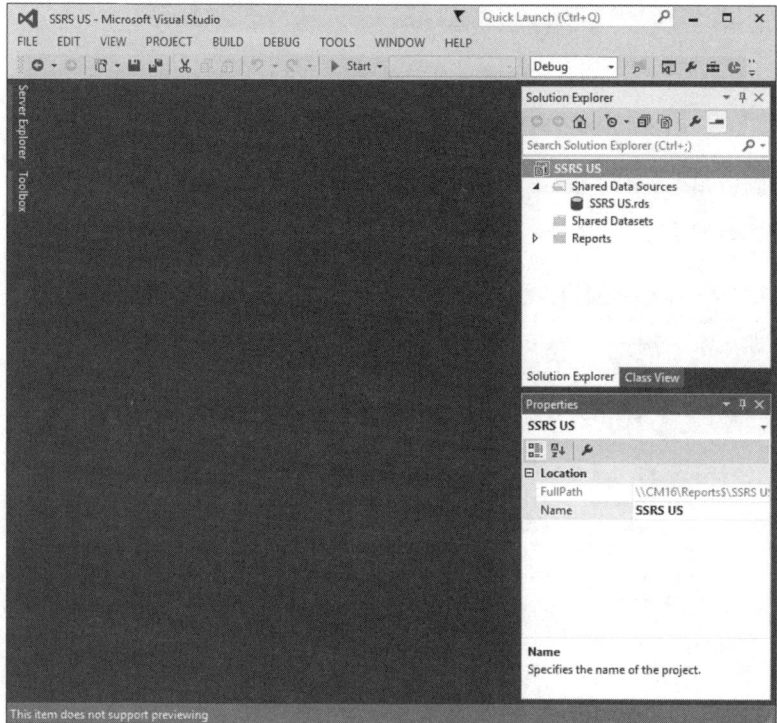

FIGURE B.19
Creating a new
project.

Patch Compliance Progression

PC Name	User Name	Missing Software Updates	Last Hardware Scan Date
ACERASPIRE	GARTEK\JYedid	Needs 83 Patches	10/24/2014 9:46:20 AM
CM12-CM4		Needs 118 Patches	10/25/2014 4:50:58 PM
CM12-J22		Needs 61 Patches	9/17/2014 7:46:59 PM
DELLE6510-2	GARTEK\Leaston	Needs 28 Patches	6/11/2014 5:23:20 PM
ELLEN-PC	GARTEK\ellen	Needs 143 Patches	10/24/2014 8:30:36 PM
ES-06		Needs 70 Patches	10/26/2014 5:00:11 PM
ES-08		Needs 70 Patches	10/26/2014 4:19:14 PM
ES-10		Needs 74 Patches	10/26/2014 3:29:55 PM
FRAME	GARTEK\frame	Needs 67 Patches	8/31/2014 8:06:43 PM
GARTEK-DC10		Needs 42 Patches	10/26/2014 3:37:29 PM
GARTEK-DC5		Needs 135 Patches	10/26/2014 4:42:36 PM
GARTEK-DC9		Needs 97 Patches	10/26/2014 6:08:24 PM
GJ5	GARTEK\Garth	Needs 35 Patches	10/25/2014 10:25:14 PM
HPPC	NT AUTHORITY\SYSTEM	Needs 23 Patches	6/11/2014 9:15:28 PM
IIS75TEST		Needs 138 Patches	9/17/2014 9:37:19 PM

Printed on 12/6/2015   enhansoft   Page 1 of 1

FIGURE B.20
Results of
creating the
Patch Compliance
Progression report.

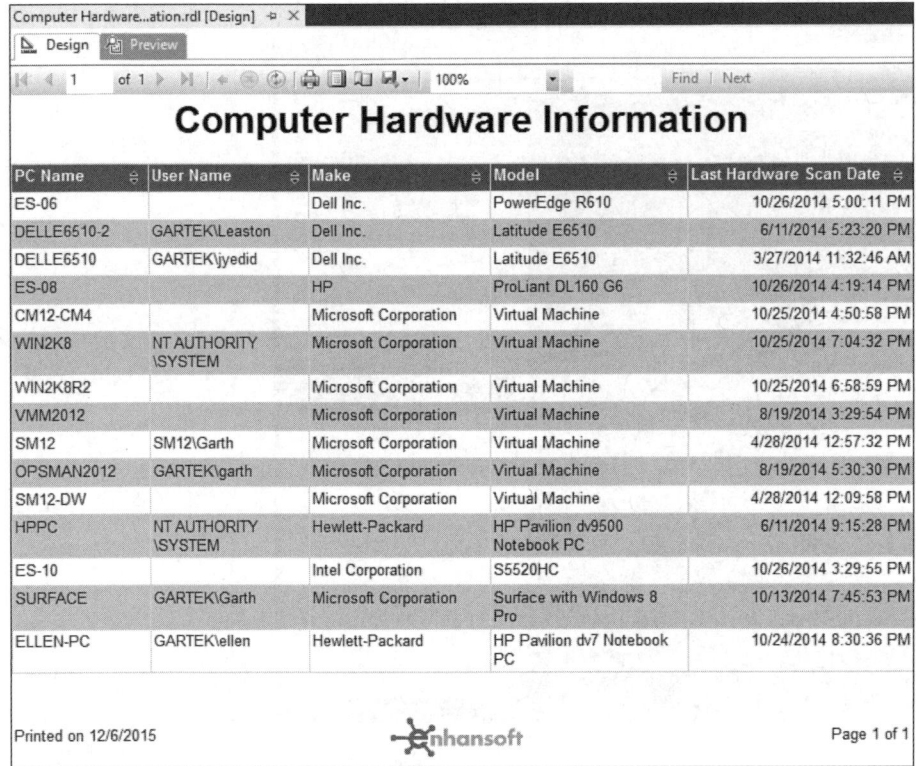

FIGURE B.21 Results of creating the Computer Hardware Information report.

Chapter 7 Demonstration Outcomes

Chapter 7, "Intermediate Reporting Concepts," built on Chapter 6 by having you add prompts and chart to existing reports. Such items add tremendous value for report users, allowing them to visualize results and allowing them to select the exact value they need for a prompt.

Creating Template Reports

The results of the Creating Template Reports demonstrations should look similar to those in Figure B.22. Only the 14×8.5 template is shown in Figure B.22.

Modifying Page Sizes for Existing Reports

After configuring the Computer Hardware Information report with the landscape page size, your output should appear similar to Figure B.23.

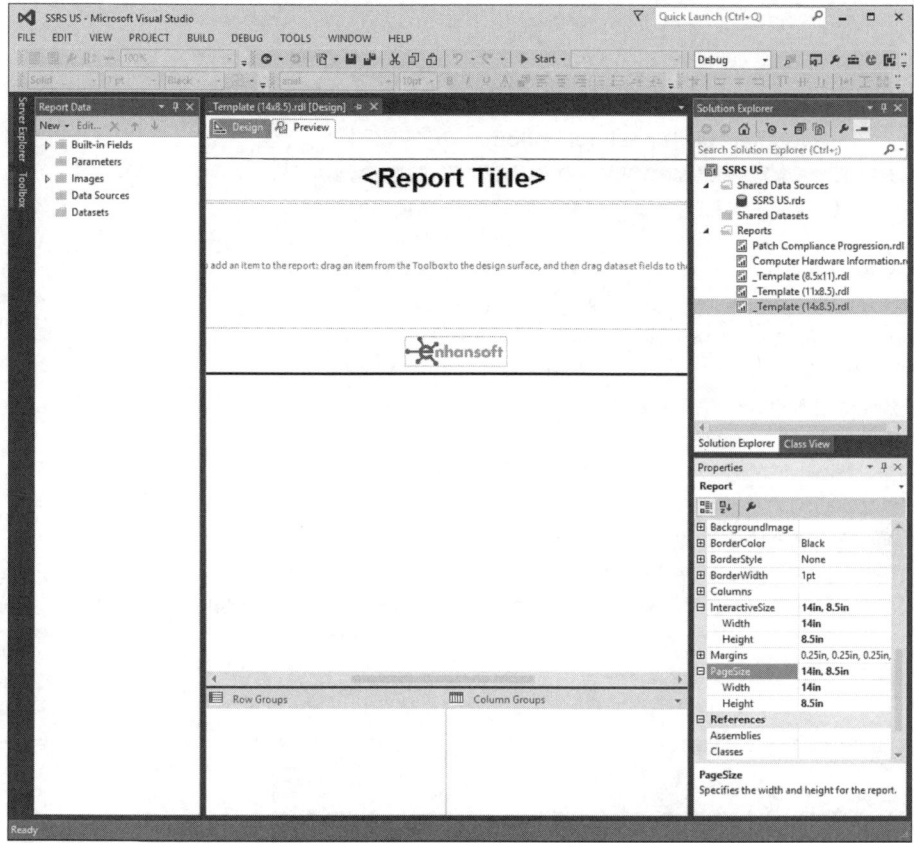

FIGURE B.22   Results of the creating template reports demonstration for the 14×8.5 template.

Updating the Patch Compliance Progression Report

Because the prompt for the Patch Compliance Progression report was the example used in Chapter 7, the output is not provided in this appendix. However, the RDL is available in the online files for Chapter 7. See Appendix C for further information.

Updating the Computer Hardware Information Report

The prompt added to the Computer Hardware Information report provides results similar to those shown in Figure B.24.

Adding a Chart to the Patch Compliance Progression Report

The output of the Patch Compliance Progression report was an example provided within the chapter. The RDL file for this example is available in the online files for Chapter 7. See Appendix C for further information.

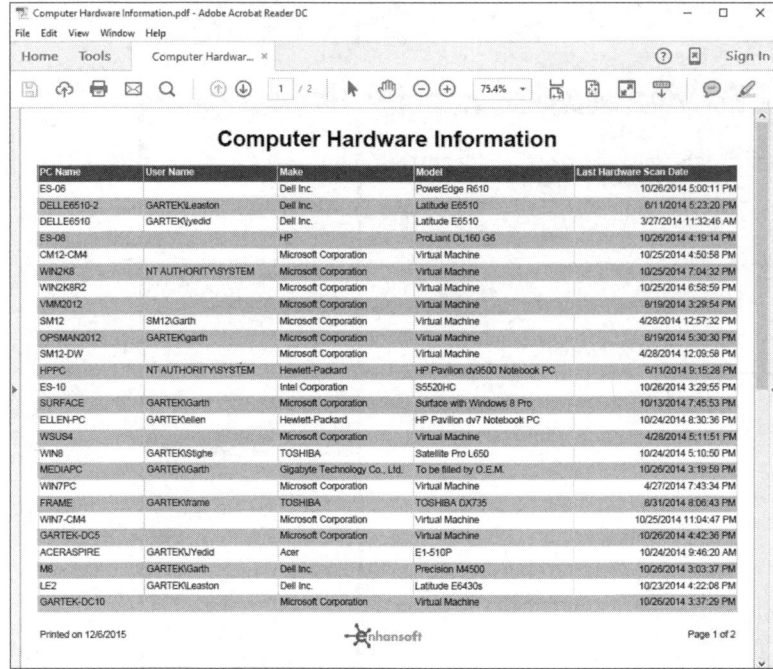

FIGURE B.23   PDF results for the Computer Hardware Information report.

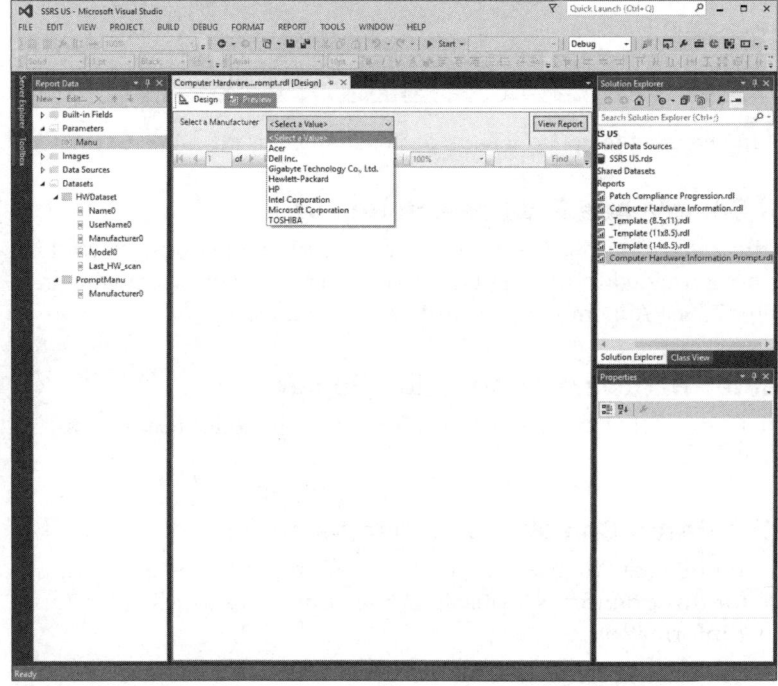

FIGURE B.24   Adding a prompt to the Computer Hardware Information report.

Adding a Chart to the Computer Hardware Information Report

Charts are an important part of SSRS reporting. Your demonstration on creating a
Computer Hardware Information report output should look similar to that in Figure B.25.

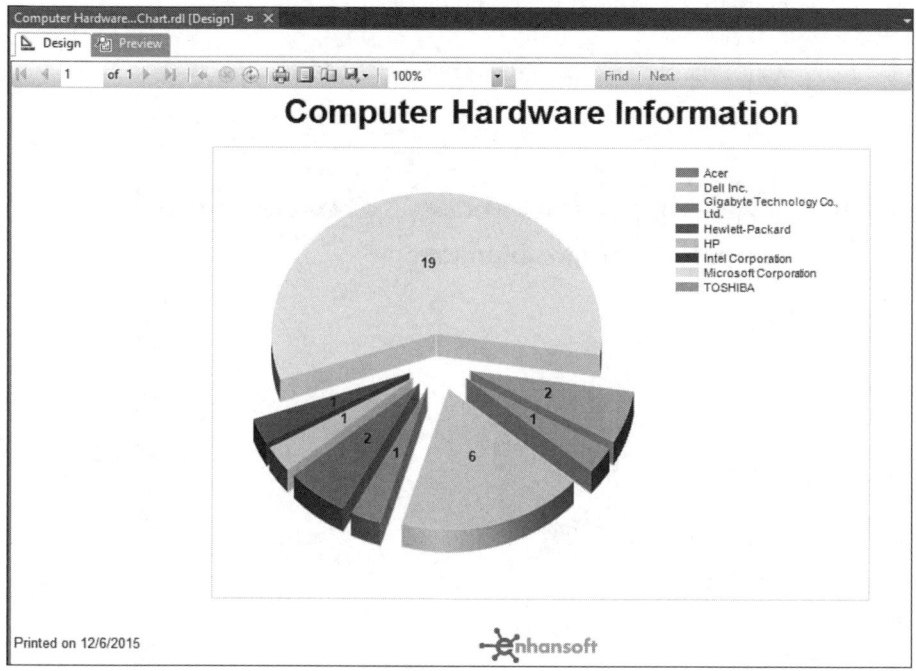

FIGURE B.25   Results of adding a chart to the Computer Hardware Information report.

Chapter 8 Demonstration Outcomes

Chapter 8, "SSRS Reporting Features," discussed some of the advanced features of SSRS
reports. The chapter discussed how to use report actions, which give you the ability to create
drillthroughs to other reports as well as add URLs to objects. The chapter also discussed
custom color palettes, which allow you to set your own color palettes for report items such as
charts, either as a cycle of colors or associated to specific values. Finally, Chapter 8 described
how to add your completed reports to the SSRS website and how to add a subscription.

Adding a Patch Compliance Progression Drillthrough Series

This demonstration asked you to create two new reports, a Patch Compliance Progression
Details report and a subreport item for the Detailed Computer Information report. You
modified the Patch Compliance Progression report, previously created in Chapter 6, by
adding a Go To Report action on the [Name0] cell of its table item to drill through to the
newly created Patch Compliance Progression Details report. To do this, you passed along
the [Name0] value that was selected. The new report populates a list of missing patches in
a table item and adds an action to the article ID values, linking to a URL for the specific
Microsoft Knowledge Base article.

In addition to creating the reports, you needed to run the Patch Compliance Progression Details report and click on a value in the PC Name column. Figure B.26 shows the resulting Patch Compliance Progression Details report when the Surface PC Name is clicked. Don't forget to click an article ID value from this report to view the Knowledge Base article for the patch, which opens in your web browser.

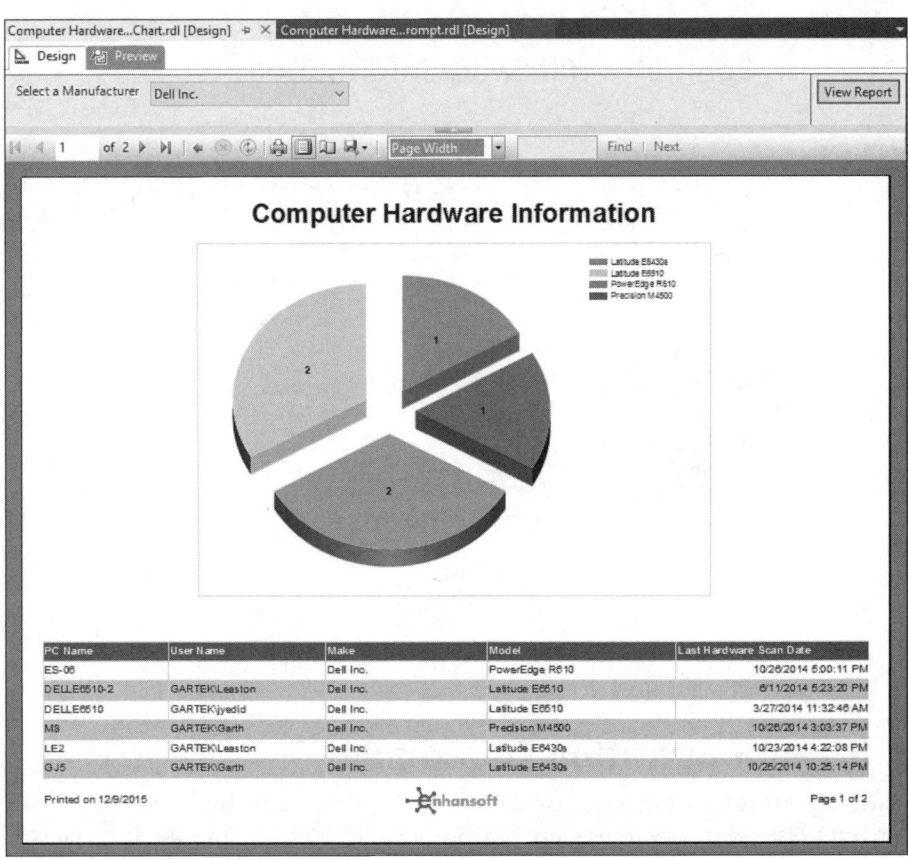

FIGURE B.26   Results of the Patch Compliance Progression Details report.

Adding a Computer Hardware Information Drillthrough Series

The demonstrations in Chapter 8 created a second drillthrough series, based on the Computer Hardware Information reports. Once completed, the Computer Hardware Information Chart report was previewed. Selecting a pie wedge in the chart opened the Computer Hardware Information Prompt report, which was modified in the demonstration to display a subreport of a newly created Hardware Model Chart report as well as a table of all models of computers belonging to the selected manufacturer.

Figure B.27 shows the resulting Computer Hardware Information Prompt report created by clicking the Dell Inc. pie wedge.

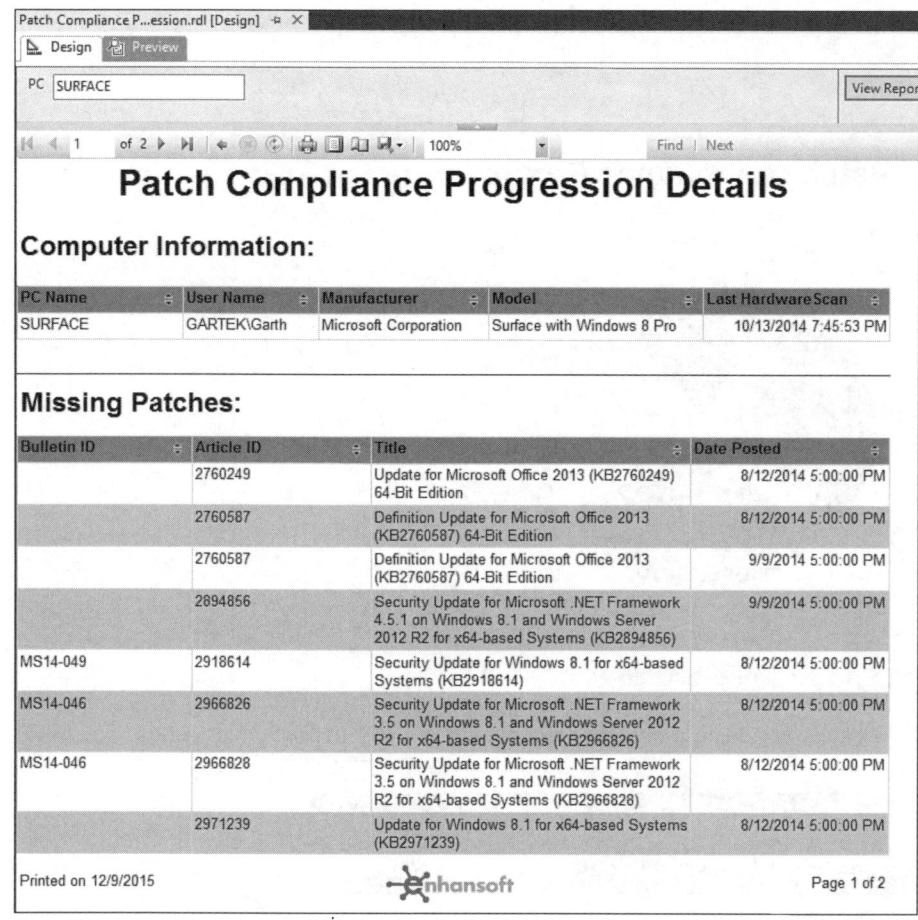

FIGURE B.27   Results of the updated Computer Hardware Information Prompt report.

Applying a Custom Color Palette to Cycle Through Color Codes

This demonstration asked you to add to the Patching Compliance Progression Chart report a custom color palette to cycle through color codes of your choice. Once completed, the report preview results should look similar to those shown in Figure B.28.

Applying a Custom Color Palette Based on Values

The demonstration asked you to add a custom color palette to the Computer Hardware Information Chart report to define a specific color value for each manufacturer value. Once assigned to the Chart item, the results should look similar to Figure B.29.

Manually Adding Reports to the SSRS Website

Once your custom reports are created with various features and items available in SSDT-BI, you will want to add them to the SSRS website to allow readers to run and view them.

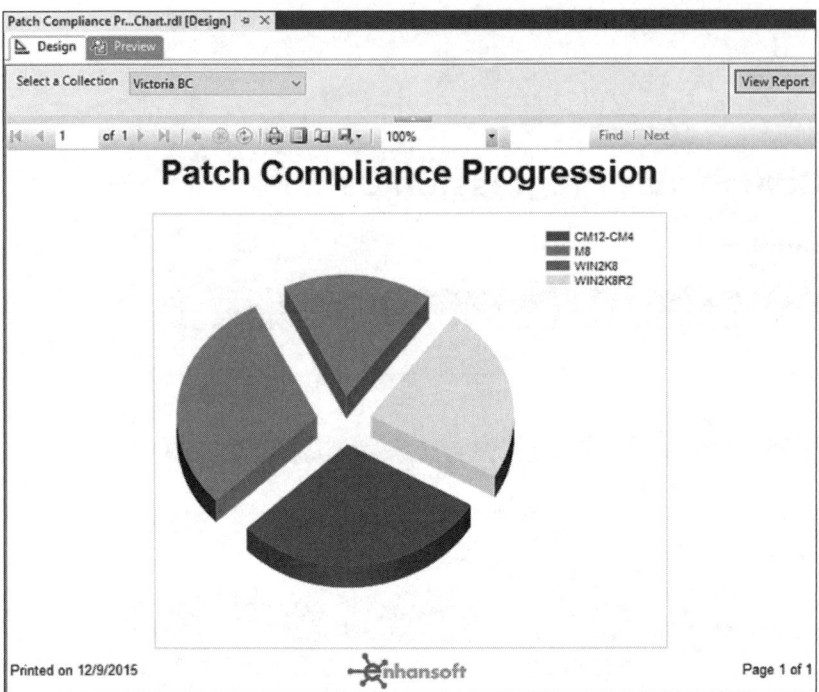

FIGURE B.28   Results of adding a custom color palette to cycle through color codes.

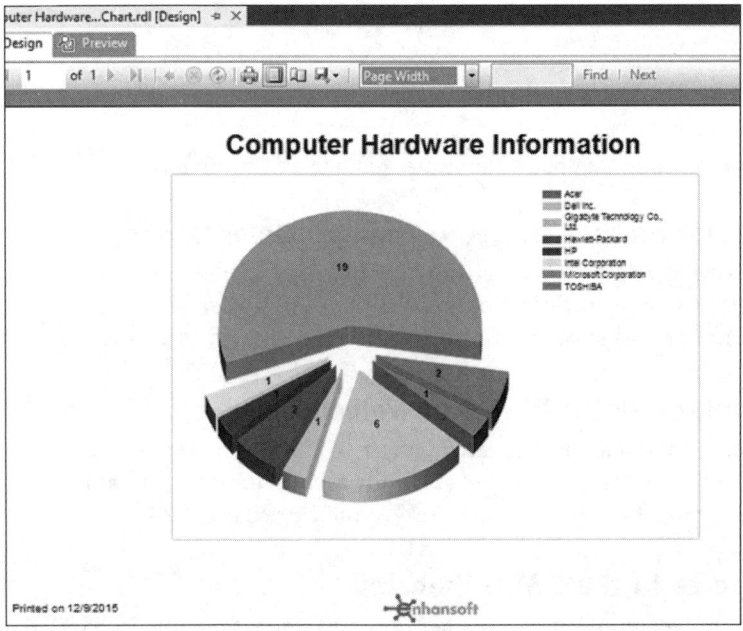

FIGURE B.29   Results of adding a custom color palette based on values.

This demonstration asked you to manually add the identified reports to a new folder created at the SSRS website. When complete, the listing of reports should be similar to that shown in Figure B.30. Be sure to run each report to ensure that it displays properly, without errors. Remember to change the report's data source to the default created data source for SSRS.

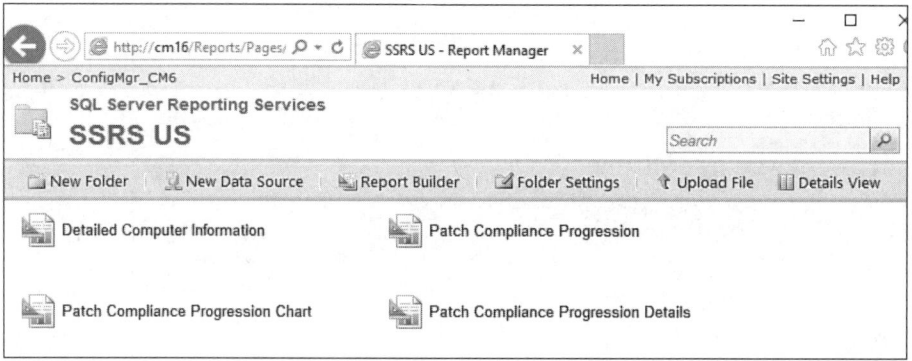

FIGURE B.30   Results of manually adding reports to SSRS.

Publishing Reports to SSRS

Another method of adding reports to the SSRS website is to publish them from SSDT-BI. To do so, configure the Deploy settings in SSDT-BI and then right-click a report from the Solution Explorer and select **Deploy**. Your reports are automatically added to the website, as shown in the example in Figure B.31.

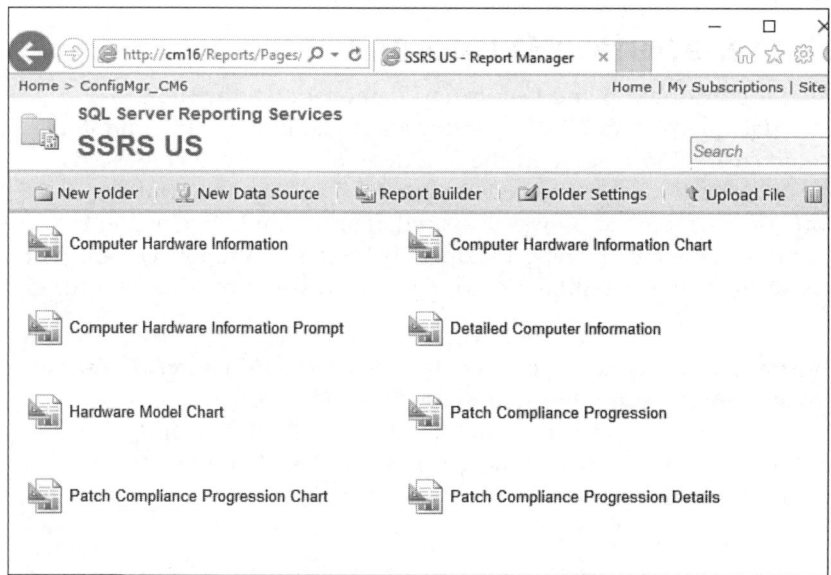

FIGURE B.31   Results of publishing reports from SSDT-BI to the SSRS website.

Creating a Subscription

Once you added reports to the SSRS website, you were asked to create a subscription for a report of your choice to export the report to a PDF file on a Windows file share. After creating and executing the subscription, you were to validate that it ran successfully by looking at the report's subscription tab, shown in Figure B.32, and verifying that the PDF file exists on the specified share.

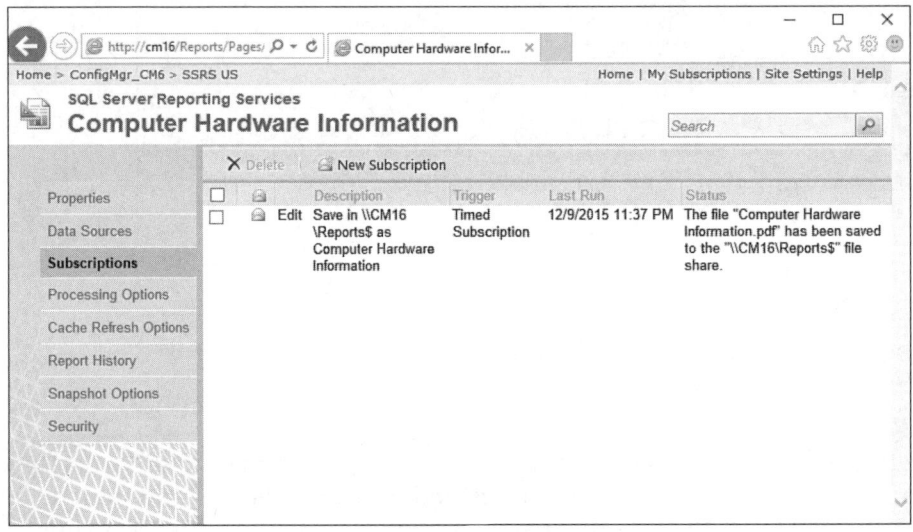

FIGURE B.32   Results of a subscription.

Chapter 9 Demonstration Outcomes

Chapter 9, "Role-Based Administration and Reporting," demonstrated the steps necessary to convert a SQL query to an RBA SQL query and included the one-time steps to ensure SSDT-BI could create RBA reports. In the first demonstration you converted the Patch Compliance Progression report created in Chapter 7 and updated it to be an RBA-complaint report. This demonstration was also used as an example in Chapter 9; you can follow along with the chapter as the report is upgraded to an RBA report version. The RDL for this report is available in the online files for Chapter 9; see Appendix C for further information.

In the second demonstration in Chapter 9 you were to convert the Computer Hardware Information query to an RBA query and test that query. The RBA query results for prompting for the manufacturer should look similar to Listing B.10. This listing is available in the online file RBA Prompt for Manufacturer.sql for Chapter 9; see Appendix C for further information.

LISTING B.10   RBA Prompt for Manufacturer

```
SELECT DISTINCT
  cs.Manufacturer0
FROM
  fn_rbac_GS_COMPUTER_SYSTEM(@UserSIDs) CS
ORDER BY
  cs.Manufacturer0
```

The primary query for the Computer Hardware Information report would look similar to Listing B.11. This listing is available in the online file Computer Hardware Information RBA Query.sql for Chapter 9. See Appendix C for further information.

LISTING B.11   Computer Hardware Information RBA Query

```
SELECT
  CS.Name0,
  CS.UserName0,
  CS.Manufacturer0,
  CS.Model0,
  WS.lasthwscan as 'Last HW scan'
FROM
  fn_rbac_GS_COMPUTER_SYSTEM(@UserSIDs) CS
  LEFT OUTER JOIN fn_rbac_GS_WORKSTATION_STATUS(@UserSIDs) WS
    on WS.resourceid = CS.resourceid
WHERE
  CS.Manufacturer0 = @Manu
```

APPENDIX C

Available Online

Online content is available to provide added value to readers of *System Center Configuration Manager Reporting Unleashed*. This material, organized by chapter, can be downloaded from http://www.informit.com/store/product .aspx?isbn=0672337789. This content is not available elsewhere. Note that the authors and publisher do not guarantee or provide technical support for the material.

Creating and Assigning ConfigMgr Security Roles

Chapter 2, "Installing and Configuring Configuration Manager Reporting," discussed how to install the Configuration Manager (ConfigMgr) reporting services point. It also discussed the importance of security and how to leverage ConfigMgr security roles and Active Directory (AD) groups to adhere to the principle of least privilege required. Three XML files are provided as online content:

▶ **Report Reader.xml:** This file includes the exported results of creating the Report Reader security role. This security role allows users to view all SQL Server Reporting Services (SSRS) reports within ConfigMgr; however, users are limited to seeing the computers and users within the collections to which they are assigned. You can import this file into your own ConfigMgr environment to avoid going to the effort of creating it on your own.

▶ **Software Updates Report Reader.xml:** This file includes the exported results of creating the Software Updates Report Reader security role. This security role allows users to view the software update reports within ConfigMgr; however, users are limited to seeing the computers and users within the collections to which they are assigned.

▶ **Inventory Report Readers.xml:** This file includes the outcome of the Inventory Report Readers security role demonstration. The security role allows users to view the inventory reports within ConfigMgr; users are limited to seeing the computers and users within the collections to which they are assigned.

Understanding Configuration Manager Data

Chapter 3, "Understanding Configuration Manager Data," discusses where ConfigMgr stores its inventory data and how to find that information. It also includes listings of sample SQL queries for several ConfigMgr views. These queries, available online for download, can be opened and executed against your ConfigMgr database using the SQL Server Management Studio tool. The following files are provided to accompany Chapter 3:

▶ **03list01_DiscoveryDataSampleQuery.sql:** This discovery data query lists all computers in the ConfigMgr environment, the last logged-on user name, and the last discovery time for heartbeat discovery.

▶ **03list02_HardwareInventorySampleQuery.sql:** This hardware inventory sample query lists computers with the Warranty Information Reporting v3 software product installed.

▶ **03list03_HardwareInventoryHistorySampleQuery.sql:** This hardware inventory history view query lists computers where the hard drive size has changed since a previous inventory cycle. This query provides an example of using the history views and current hardware views together for comparison purposes.

▶ **03list04_SoftwareInventorySampleQuery.sql:** This query uses software inventory information to provide a count of versions of Internet Explorer.

▶ **03list05_SoftwareUpdateSampleQuery.sql:** This software update query provides a count of all missing software updates for each computer in ConfigMgr.

▶ **03list06_SoftwareMeteringSampleQuery.sql:** This software metering sample query displays the start and stop times for all software metering data since February 16, 2013.

▶ **03list07_StatusMessageSampleQuery.sql:** This status message sample query returns the date and time of the last ConfigMgr backup for each site server.

▶ **03list08_StateMessageSampleQuery.sql:** This software update state message query returns the last enforcement message for each software update scanned on the computer named GJ5.

▶ **03list09_CollectionDataSampleQuery.sql:** This collection data sample query lists all computer names within the ConfigMgr All Systems collection.

▶ **PatchReport.txt:** This is a sample query used in the creating and executing a query demonstration in Chapter 3. When executed in SQL Server Management Studio, it lists all computers in ConfigMgr, the last logged-on user name for each system, the number of required updates to install, and date of the system's last hardware inventory scan.

Transact-SQL Primer

Chapter 4, "Transact-SQL Primer," discusses the basics of SQL queries to help you successfully write your own queries. The following .SQL query files, available online, provide the different queries discussed throughout this chapter. The file names beginning with xB_list are the outcomes of the demonstrations in Chapter 4:

▶ **04list01_PatchReportSample.sql:** This sample query is provided as Listing 4.1 and is used throughout the chapter to analyze sections of SQL code. When executed, this query provides a list of computer names, the last logged-on user name of each computer, the number of missing software updates for the computer, and date of the last hardware scan.

▶ **04list10_AggregateFunctionsQuery.sql:** This sample query is provided as Listing 4.10 and returns a list of system roles in the ConfigMgr environment. Along with each system role, the query provides a count of computers belonging to the role and the minimum, average, maximum, and sum of the RAM for all systems within each system role.

▶ **04list11_DateAndTimeSampleQuery.sql:** This date and time sample query, provided as Listing 4.11, demonstrates the GETDATE, DATEDIFF, and DATEPART functions.

▶ **04list13_CASESampleQuery.sql:** This CASE function sample query, provided as Listing 4.13, translates the month value of the last hardware scan date, using a CASE function.

▶ **04list14_CONVERTandCASTSampleQuery.sql:** This sample query, provided as Listing 4.14, demonstrates the use of the CAST and CONVERT functions and illustrates the differences between the two.

▶ **04list15_ISNULLSampleQuery.sql:** This sample query, provided as Listing 4.15, demonstrates the ISNULL function by replacing NULL values from the |Last_Logon_Timestamp with the date 1980-04-05. The query returns computer names, with the Last_Logon_Timestamp column shown next to the ISNULL function column for comparison.

▶ **04list16_SampleInefficientQuerywithoutJOINStatement.sql:** This is an example of an inefficient query, provided as Listing 4.16. Caution should be taken if this query is executed within your ConfigMgr environment.

> **CAUTION: RUNNING THE INEFFICIENT SAMPLE QUERY IS NOT RECOMMENDED**
>
> The authors do not recommend running 04list16_SampleInefficientQuerywithoutJOINstatement.sql in your environment; it is provided only for reference. The query will take a long time to execute, will produce a large number of results, and may have a negative performance impact on your ConfigMgr database. (Other than the performance impact, however, no negative or lasting effects will occur.)

▶ **04list17_SampleQueryUsingJOIN.sql:** This is a similar query to Listing 4.16; however, it uses a JOIN statement. This query (from Listing 4.17) is much more efficient and takes very little time to execute.

▶ **04list18_SampleINNERJOINStatement.sql:** This sample query uses an INNER JOIN statement to list all common values between multiple SQL views.

▶ **04list19_SampleLEFTOUTERJOINStatement.sql:** This sample query uses a LEFT OUTER JOIN statement. This query displays all values on the left side of the JOIN equation (v_R_System_Valid) and joins any common data from the right side of the equation (dbo.v_R_User).

▶ **04list20_SampleRIGHTOUTERJOINStatement.sql:** This sample query uses a RIGHT OUTER JOIN statement. This query is the opposite of the LEFT OUTER JOIN; it displays all data on the right-side of the equation (dbo.v_R_User) and joins any common data from the left side (dbo.v_R_System_Valid).

▶ **04list21_SampleFULLJOINStatement.sql:** This sample query uses a FULL JOIN statement to list all data on both sides of the equation.

▶ **04list22_DemonstratingAnInefficientQuery.sql:** This query is used in the JOIN demonstration in Chapter 4 to show the impacts and effects of an inefficient query.

▶ **Chapter4Demo.sql:** This is a sample query used in demonstrations from Chapter 4.

▶ **xB_list01_DemonstratingSQLOperators.sql:** This query shows the result of the SQL operators demonstration in Chapter 4, illustrated in Appendix B, "Demonstration Outcomes."

▶ **xB_list02_CreatingAQueryWithAliases.sql:** This query shows the demonstration outcome, listed in Appendix B, from Chapter 4, where a new query was written using aliases to list computer names, user names, application names, and versions of systems with Adobe Reader installed.

▶ **xB_list03_AggregateFunctions.sql:** This query is the aggregate function demonstration outcome listed in Appendix B from Chapter 4. The query returns the minimum, average, and maximum hard disk size for system roles in ConfigMgr.

▶ **xB_list04_COUNTFunction.sql:** This query is the demonstration outcome, listed in Appendix B, for the COUNT function in Chapter 4. This query is based from the Chapter4Demo.sql file and adds the function to show the number of installs for each application.

▶ **xB_list05_DateAndTimeFunctions.sql:** This query is the demonstration outcome, listed in Appendix B, of the date and time functions in Chapter 4. This query is based on the 04list11_DateAndTimeSampleQuery.sql file, previously described in this section, and has been updated to include the current date, last hardware inventory scan, number of minutes since last scan, and day of the month of the last scan.

▶ **xB_list06_CASEFunction.sql:** This query is the demonstration outcome, listed in Appendix B, for the CASE function in Chapter 4. This query uses the function to convert the system enclosure chassis type numeric codes to actual names.

▶ **xB_list07_CONVERTFunction.sql:** This query is the demonstration outcome, listed in Appendix B, for the CONVERT function in Chapter 4. This query uses that function on the last hardware scan date to change the data to ANSI date format (YYYY.MM.DD).

- ▶ **xB_list08_ISNULLFunction.sql:** This query is the demonstration outcome, listed in Appendix B, for the ISNULL function in Chapter 4. This query uses that function on the User_Name0 column to replace any NULL values with n/a.

- ▶ **xB_list09_JOINStatement.sql:** This query is the demonstration outcome listed in Appendix B of the JOIN statement in Chapter 4. This query updates the inefficient query provided (04list22_DemonstratingAnInefficientQuery.sql) to use JOIN statements.

Basic Report Design

Chapter 5, "Basic Report Design," discusses important concepts related to designing a report. It explains the different types of reports in a series and basic design rules, such as having a consistent look and feel across all reports, using standard page sizes, and using templates. A sample report request form that can be used in your environment, Requesting a Report.docx, is provided as online content for this chapter. This is the request form that is discussed and analyzed throughout Chapter 5 to help demonstrate how to gather important report information before beginning to write a report. You can tailor this document to gather specific report details for your environment.

Building a Basic Report

Chapter 6, "Building a Basic Report," introduces creating reports with SQL Server Data Tools 2014 Business Intelligence (SSDT-BI) for Visual Studio 2013. This tool is used to create reports that can be added to your ConfigMgr SSRS website. The following SQL query (.sql) and report (.rdl) files, available online, can be opened with SQL Server Management Studio and SSDT-BI, respectively:

- ▶ **06list01_PatchProgressionQuery.sql:** This is the query used for the PatchDataset of the Patch Compliance Progression report created in Chapter 6.

- ▶ **Chap6_Patch Compliance Progression.rdl:** This report is the finished outcome, shown in Appendix B, of the Patch Compliance Progression report in Chapter 6.

- ▶ **Chap6_Computer Hardware Information query.sql:** This is the query outcome for the Computer Hardware Information report in Chapter 6.

- ▶ **Chap6_Computer Hardware Information.rdl:** This report is the finished outcome, shown in Appendix B, for the Computer Hardware Information report in Chapter 6.

To successfully preview the files with data from your ConfigMgr database, simply add them to an already created SSDT-BI project, as explained in Chapter 6, and modify the data source of the report to use the shared data source in your environment.

Intermediate Reporting Concepts

Chapter 7, "Intermediate Reporting Concepts," illustrates how to create and use report templates as a starting point when creating new reports. The chapter described how to use parameters to create fewer and more generic reports that prompt readers for the details to filter and tailors the results to their specific requirements. The chapter also explained and demonstrated chart items, which you can use to make report data more visual. The following SQL query (.sql) and report (.rdl) files are available as online content to provide you with the different reports demonstrated throughout this chapter.

▶ **07list03_AllCollectionNamesAndIDs.sql:** This query returns all collection names and their collection IDs from the ConfigMgr environment. This is used in Chapter 7 to populate the Collection Prompt parameter with available values.

▶ **Chap7_Template (8.5x11).rdl:** This report is the letter portrait (8.5×11in) template outcome from the demonstration in Chapter 7.

▶ **Chap7_Template (11x8.5).rdl:** This report is the letter landscape (11×8.5in) template outcome from the demonstration in Chapter 7.

▶ **Chap7_Template (14x8.5).rdl:** This report is the legal landscape (14×8.5in) template outcome from the demonstration in Chapter 7, shown in Appendix B.

▶ **Chap7_Patch Compliance Progression(Modified Page Size).rdl:** This is the report outcome from modifying the page size of the Patch Compliance Progression report to fit on a paper size of 8.5×11in, created as part of the demonstrations in Chapter 7.

▶ **Chap7_Computer Hardware Information(Modified Page Size).rdl:** This is the report outcome from modifying the page size of the Computer Hardware Information report to fit on a paper size of 11×8.5in, created as part of the demonstrations in Chapter 7 shown in Appendix B.

▶ **Chap7_Patch Compliance Progression (Prompt).rdl:** This is the report outcome of modifying the Patch Compliance Progression report to add a multi-value prompt for ConfigMgr collection names, created as part of the demonstrations in Chapter 7.

▶ **Chap7_Computer Hardware Information Prompt.rdl:** This is the report outcome for the Computer Hardware Information Prompt report, part of the Chapter 7 demonstrations shown in Appendix B. The report contains a dropdown list prompt of manufacturer names from the computers in your ConfigMgr environment.

▶ **Chap7_Patch Compliance Progression Chart.rdl:** This is the report outcome for the Patch Compliance Progression Chart report, part of the Chapter 7 demonstrations. This report includes a 3D exploded pie chart to illustrate the number of missing patches for systems in your ConfigMgr environment. The report also includes an action on the pie chart's wedges that go to the Patch Compliance Progression report, passing along the CollectionID value to the prompt.

▶ **Chap7_Computer Hardware Information Chart.rdl:** This is the report outcome for the Computer Hardware Information Chart report, part of the Chapter 7 demonstrations shown in Appendix B. This report includes a 3D exploded pie chart to illustrate the count of computers by manufacturer in your ConfigMgr environment. The report also includes an action on the pie chart's wedges to go to the Computer Hardware Information Prompt report, passing along the Manufacturer value that was selected.

As discussed in the previous "Building a Basic Report" section, these reports must be added to an existing SSDT-BI project and have their data source updated for your environment; for the report actions to function properly, it is also required to download and add all reports (.rdl) listed in this chapter to the same SSDT-BI project.

SSRS Reporting Features

Chapter 8, "SSRS Reporting Features," demonstrates advanced report features available in reports. These features include drillthroughs, custom color palettes for report objects, and different methods of adding completed reports to the SSRS website. The following files, discussed throughout the chapter, are provided for your reference:

▶ **08list01_DetailedComputerQuery.sql:** This query is used to create the dataset for the Detailed Computer Information report, discussed in Chapter 8.

▶ **08list02_DetailedPatchComplianceQuery.sql:** This query is used to create the dataset for the Patch Compliance Progression Details report, discussed in Chapter 8.

▶ **Software Update Compliance.rdl:** This is the report used to illustrate custom color codes based on specific values, discussed in Chapter 8.

▶ **Chap8_Detailed Computer Information (Drillthrough).rdl:** This is the report outcome for the Detailed Computer Information report, part of the Chapter 8 demonstrations. This report lists the computer name, user name, hardware make and model, and last hardware scan date for a computer specified by the user in a parameter.

▶ **Chap8_Patch Compliance Progression Details (Drillthrough).rdl:** This is the report outcome for the Patch Compliance Progression Details report, part of the Chapter 8 demonstrations, shown in Appendix B. This report contains a subreport item, referencing the Detailed Computer Information report, and a table with a detailed list of missing patches for a specific computer. An action is added on the [ArticleID] value of the table that goes to a URL using the value of the [InfoURL] column from the dataset.

▶ **Chap8_Patch Compliance Progression (Drillthrough).rdl:** This is the modified report named Patch Compliance Progression that was created in Chapter 7. The report is modified during the demonstrations in Chapter 8 to add an action on the [Name0] cell to go to the Patch Compliance Progression Details report, passing along the PC Name value to the report parameter.

▶ **Chap8_Hardware Model Chart (Drillthrough).rdl:** This is the report outcome for the Hardware Model Chart report, part of the Chapter 8 demonstrations. This report contains a chart showing the count of models for a specific manufacturer.

▶ **Chap8_Computer Hardware Information Prompt (Drillthrough).rdl:** This is the modified report named Computer Hardware Information Prompt, created in Chapter 7 and shown in Appendix B. The report is modified as part of the Chapter 8 demonstrations to add a subreport item referencing the Hardware Model Chart report.

▶ **Chap8_Patch Compliance Progression Chart (Custom Color Palette - Cycle).rdl:** This is the report outcome of the custom color palette created to cycle through color codes, part of the Chapter 8 demonstrations and shown in Appendix B. The custom color palette is applied to the chart item in the Patch Compliance Progression Chart report, created in Chapter 7.

▶ **Chap8_Computer Hardware Information Chart (Custom Color Palette - Values). rdl:** This is the report outcome of the custom color palette created to apply specific color codes based on dataset values, part of the Chapter 8 demonstrations and shown in Appendix B. The custom color palette is applied to the chart item in the Computer Hardware Information Chart report, created in Chapter 7. Colors are applied based on the hardware manufacturer values.

Role-Based Administration and Reporting

Chapter 9, "Role-Based Administration and Reporting," illustrated how ConfigMgr RBA reporting works. The chapter examined a normal SQL query and reports covered in earlier chapters and showed how to enhance the reports so they can be used with the role-based administration (RBA) feature of ConfigMgr and SSRS. The following files are provided for your reference:

▶ **09list01_RBA_PatchReportSample.sql:** This sample query provides a list of computer names, the last logged-on user name, the number of missing software updates for the computer, and the date of the last hardware scan.

▶ **09list02_RBA Software Update Sample Query.sql:** This query is an updated version of Listing 9.1. It returns a list of computer names, the last logged-on user name, the number of missing software updates for the computer, and the date of the last hardware scan for a given user (defined by the @UserSIDs variable).

▶ **09list04_Query to determine ConfigMgr UserSIDs.sql:** This query is used to query ConfigMgr for the UserSIDs. It returns a list of UserSIDs for a particular @UserTokenSIDs, The UserSIDs information is used to limit the information a user can see within SSRS reporting.

▶ **09list05_Mixed RBA Software Update Sample Query.sql:** This sample query is an updated version of Listing 9.1 and provides a list of computer names, the last logged-on user name, the number of missing software updates for the computer, and the date of the last hardware scan for a given user. However, it does not follow best practices of always using RBA functions, which actually decreases the execution time for the query. This mixed query's execution time is faster than that of the full RBA listing, 09list01_RBA_PatchReportSample.sql.

▶ **09list06_Query for all collection names and IDs.sql:** This sample query is the non-RBA version of 09list07_RBA query for collection names and IDs.sql and provides a list of collection names and collection IDs.

▶ **09list07_RBA query for collection names and IDs.sql:** This sample RBA query returns a list of collection names and collection IDs.

▶ **09list08_Software Update Sample Query.sql:** This query is a non-RBA version of 09list01_RBA_PatchReportSample.sql and returns a list of computer names, the last logged-on user name, the number of missing software updates for the computer, and the date of the last hardware scan.

▶ **CodeGroup.txt:** This text file includes edits to RSPreviewPolicy.config within the PrivateAssemblies folder and adds a `CodeGroup` block to grant the ConfigMgr reporting code assembly full trust permission, allowing RBA reports to be previewed in SSDT-BI.

▶ **Computer Hardware Information RBA Query.sql:** This sample RBA query returns a list of computer names, the last logged-on user name, manufacturer, computer model, and date of the last hardware scan.

▶ **pageLoad function for SQL 2008.txt:** This text file includes the edits to ReportingServices.js for SQL 2008. Implementing this edit allows web browsers such as Chrome to view ConfigMgr reports.

▶ **pageLoad function for SQL 2008 R2.txt:** This text file includes the edit to ReportingServices.js for SQL 2008 R2. Implementing this edit allows web browsers such as Chrome to view ConfigMgr reports.

▶ **pageLoad function for SQL 2012.txt:** This text file includes the edit to ReportingServices.js for SQL 2012. Implementing this edit allows browsers such as Chrome to view ConfigMgr reports.

▶ **Patch Compliance Progression.rdl:** This report is the finished outcome, as shown in Appendix B, of the Patch Compliance Progression report in Chapter 9.

▶ **RBA Prompt for Manufacturer.sql:** This RBA query returns a list of computer manufacturers.

▶ **Chap9_RBA_Computer Hardware Information Prompt.rdl:** This report is the finished outcome, shown in Appendix B, of the Computer Hardware Information report in Chapter 9.

Index

Symbols

+ (addition) operator, 105

/ (division) operator, 105

= (equals) operator, 105

> (greater than) operator, 105

< (less than) operator, 105

* (multiplication) operator, 105

"" (quotation marks), SQL operators, 106

– (subtraction) operator, 105

% (wildcard) operator, 105

3D effects (charts), 226

A

accessing

    collections, 293

    protected folders, 296

    report items, 175-177

    reports, 71-72

Access Required to ConfigMgr Collection field (report request form Security section), 152

accounts

    AD security user, creating, 44

    network service, configuring, 16

    RP user, selecting, 46, 48

    Windows user account credentials (RPs), 49

G

H

online content, 352

software

cycle, changing, 55

Internet Explorer versions query, 87

online content, 352

overview, 86

RBA functions with SQL views, 290

SQL views, listing of, 86

software metering

overview, 89

RBA functions with SQL views, 290

rules, creating, 90

SQL views, listing of, 89

start/stop times query, 89-90

software update

missing software updates query, 88-89

overview, 87

permissions, 57

point (SUP), 320

RBA functions with SQL views, 290

SQL views, listing of, 88

Inventory Report Reader security role, applying, 76, 325-326

ISNULL function, 114

online content, 353, 355

replacing NULL values from v_R_System_Valid view, 130, 336

resources, 114

sample query, 114

syntax, 114

J-K

joins

defined, 116

demonstrating, 130-131

full

defined, 123

online content, 354

query results, 124-125

query sample, 123

inner, 119, 354

left outer, 120-121, 354

online content, 353-354, 355

ResourceID column, 116

right outer, 121-123, 354

sample query, 117

user *versus* computer real world example, 117

v_R_System_Valid view, 117-118

Justification field (report request form Report Customizations section), 153

L

label fields (reports), 209

labels (charts)

customizing, 228

displaying outside charts, 229-231

spacing between, 230, 232

LAN (local area network), 320

layout consistency (reports), 142-144

LEFT OUTER JOIN statement, 120-121, 354

Legal Landscape template, 143

legal-size paper reports, 144

Legend Properties dialog, 226

legends (charts), moving, 226, 228

less than (<) operator, 105

Letter Landscape template, 143

letter paper sizes, 138

letter portrait (8.5x11in) report template, creating, 142, 200-204, 340-341

licensing (SQL client tools), 32, 33

LIKE operator, 105

line charts, 220

line items (reports), 176

M

P

T

V

W

UNLEASHED

Unleashed takes you beyond the basics, providing an exhaustive, technically sophisticated reference for professionals who need to exploit a technology to its fullest potential. It's the best resource for practical advice from the experts and the most in-depth coverage of the latest technologies.

informit.com/unleashed

Universal Windows Apps with XAML and #C Unleashed
ISBN-13: 9780672337260

OTHER UNLEASHED TITLES

C# 5.0 Unleashed
ISBN-13: 9780672336904

Microsoft SQL Server 2014 Unleashed
ISBN-13: 9780672337291

Microsoft System Center 2012 Unleashed
ISBN-13: 9780672336126

System Center 2012 Configuration Manager (SCCM) Unleashed
ISBN-13: 9780672334375

Windows Server 2012 Unleashed
ISBN-13: 9780672336225

Microsoft Exchange Server 2013 Unleashed
ISBN-13: 9780672336119

System Center 2012 Service Manager Unleashed
ISBN-13: 9780672337079

System Center 2012 Operations Manager Unleashed
ISBN-13: 9780672335914

Microsoft Dynamics CRM 2013 Unleashed
ISBN-13: 9780672337031

Microsoft Lync Server 2013 Unleashed
ISBN-13: 9780672336157

SharePoint 2013 Unleashed
ISBN-13: 9780672337338

WPF 4.5 Unleashed
ISBN-13: 9780672336973

Visual Basic 2015 Unleashed
ISBN-13: 9780672334504

XAML Unleashed
ISBN-13: 978067233722

SAMS

informit.com/sams

REGISTER YOUR PRODUCT at informit.com/register
Access Additional Benefits and SAVE 35% on Your Next Purchase

- Download available product updates.

- Access bonus material when applicable.

- Receive exclusive offers on new editions and related products.
  (Just check the box to hear from us when setting up your account.)

- Get a coupon for 35% for your next purchase, valid for 30 days. Your code will
  be available in your InformIT cart. (You will also find it in the Manage Codes
  section of your account page.)

Registration benefits vary by product. Benefits will be listed on your account page
under Registered Products.

InformIT.com—The Trusted Technology Learning Source
InformIT is the online home of information technology brands at Pearson, the world's foremost
education company. At InformIT.com you can

- Shop our books, eBooks, software, and video training.
- Take advantage of our special offers and promotions (informit.com/promotions).
- Sign up for special offers and content newsletters (informit.com/newsletters).
- Read free articles and blogs by information technology experts.
- Access thousands of free chapters and video lessons.

Connect with InformIT—Visit informit.com/community
Learn about InformIT community events and programs.

the trusted technology learning source

Addison-Wesley · Cisco Press · IBM Press · Microsoft Press · Pearson IT Certification · Prentice Hall · Que · Sams · VMware Press